THIS IS YOUR **PASSBOOK®** FOR ...

MILLER ANALOGIES TEST

NATIONAL LEARNING CORPORATION®
passbooks.com

COPYRIGHT NOTICE

Copyright © 2020 by

NLC®

National Learning Corporation

212 Michael Drive, Syosset, NY 11791
(516) 921-8888 • www.passbooks.com
E-mail: info@passbooks.com

PUBLISHED IN THE UNITED STATES OF AMERICA

PASSBOOK® SERIES

THE *PASSBOOK® SERIES* has been created to prepare applicants and candidates for the ultimate academic battlefield – the examination room.

At some time in our lives, each and every one of us may be required to take an examination – for validation, matriculation, admission, qualification, registration, certification, or licensure.

Based on the assumption that every applicant or candidate has met the basic formal educational standards, has taken the required number of courses, and read the necessary texts, the *PASSBOOK® SERIES* furnishes the one special preparation which may assure passing with confidence, instead of failing with insecurity. Examination questions – together with answers – are furnished as the basic vehicle for study so that the mysteries of the examination and its compounding difficulties may be eliminated or diminished by a sure method.

This book is meant to help you pass your examination provided that you qualify and are serious in your objective.

The entire field is reviewed through the huge store of content information which is succinctly presented through a provocative and challenging approach – the question-and-answer method.

A climate of success is established by furnishing the correct answers at the end of each test.

You soon learn to recognize types of questions, forms of questions, and patterns of questioning. You may even begin to anticipate expected outcomes.

You perceive that many questions are repeated or adapted so that you can gain acute insights, which may enable you to score many sure points.

You learn how to confront new questions, or types of questions, and to attack them confidently and work out the correct answers.

You note objectives and emphases, and recognize pitfalls and dangers, so that you may make positive educational adjustments.

Moreover, you are kept fully informed in relation to new concepts, methods, practices, and directions in the field.

You discover that you arre actually taking the examination all the time: you are preparing for the examination by "taking" an examination, not by reading extraneous and/or supererogatory textbooks.

In short, this PASSBOOK®, used directedly, should be an important factor in helping you to pass your test.

The *Miller Analogies Test*

The *Miller Analogies Test* (MAT) is a high-level test of analytical ability that requires the solution of problems stated as analogies. The MAT consists of 120 partial analogies that are to be completed in 60 minutes. The test measures your ability to recognize relationships between ideas, your fluency in the English language, and your general knowledge of the humanities, natural sciences, mathematics, and social sciences.

The Structure of MAT Analogies

An analogy is a statement that suggests two terms are related to each other in the same way that two other terms are related to each other. The MAT analogy items are written as equations in the form "A : B :: C : D." This can be read as either "A is related to B in the same way that C is related to D" or as "A is related to C in the same way as B is related to D."

In each MAT analogy item, one term is missing and you must choose which of the four answer options correctly completes the analogy. For example:

Plane : Air :: Car : (*a.* motorcycle, *b.* engine, *c.* land, *d.* atmosphere)

The first step in solving a MAT analogy is to decide which two of the three given terms form a complete pair. In the example, this could either be "Plane is related to Air" (the first term is related to the second term) or "Plane is related to Car" (the first term is related to the third term).

On the MAT, **the first term is never related to the fourth term**. Therefore, this example could **NOT** be read as "Plane is related to (*a.* motorcycle, *b.* engine, *c.* land, *d.* atmosphere)."

The solution to a MAT analogy item requires that you select the option that forms a second pair of terms that are in the same relationship to each other as the terms in the complete pair. In this example, none of the available options form a second pair of terms if the analogy is seen as a relationship between two vehicles—Air is definitely not a vehicle. However, when the complete pair is seen as "Plane travels on Air," the second pair, and the correct answer, becomes obvious as "Car travels on *c.* land":

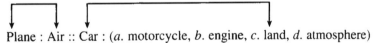

Plane : Air :: Car : (*a.* motorcycle, *b.* engine, *c.* land, *d.* atmosphere)

The missing term in a MAT analogy—the term represented by the four answer options—could be in any one of the four positions. All of the possible formats for MAT analogies are represented in the following examples:

> Salt : Hypertension :: Sugar : (*a.* cholesterol, *b.* carbohydrates, *c.* hyperthyroidism, *d.* diabetes)
> **Solution**—The answer is "*d.* diabetes"; salt contributes to or aggravates the symptoms of hypertension, and sugar does the same for diabetes.

> Seek : Find :: (*a.* locate, *b.* book, *c.* retrieve, *d.* listen) : Hear
> **Solution**—The answer is "*d.* listen"; one seeks something in order to find it, and one listens to something in order to hear it.

> Induction : (*a.* confirmation, *b.* graduation, *c.* ordination, *d.* resistance) :: Soldier : Priest
> **Solution**—The answer is "*c.* ordination"; induction is the ceremony for becoming a soldier, and ordination is the ceremony for becoming a priest.

₃ (*a.* cure, *b.* epidemic, *c.* immunity, *d.* patient) : Shade :: Inoculation : Parasol
Solution—The answer is "*c.* immunity"; a parasol produces shade, and an inoculation produces immunity.

Regardless of how the terms in a MAT analogy are presented, there is only one valid and logical relationship that exists between each pair of terms.

Solving MAT Analogies

There are four basic steps in solving a MAT analogy:

1. Read the three given terms in the analogy carefully.

2. Determine the relationships between the two possible pairs among the three given terms.

3. Without looking at the answer options, think of a fourth term that would complete an analogy along with the three given terms. You may be able to identify more than one possible analogy that would include the three given terms.

4. Examine the answer options, and select the option that most closely resembles your idea of a term that would complete the analogy.

If none of the answer options seems to form an analogy, rethink the relationship you identified in the given terms. You may need to repeat the steps to arrive at an acceptable answer.

For example, consider the following:

Pint : (*a.* cup, *b.* quart, *c.* liter, *d.* gallon) :: 1 : 2

Reading the three given terms in this analogy may not initially seem to provide obvious clues as to which option will complete it, until you consider the relationship of 1 to 2, a likely candidate for a complete pair. These two numerals can be seen as either a sequence of numbers or as one representing twice the value of the other.

If the relationship is seen as a sequence, then none of the answer options seems to form a similar relationship with "Pint," the third given term. However, if the relationship is seen as 2 being twice the value of 1, then the correct answer would be a measure that is twice the volume of a pint.

This solution seems to work, because answer choice "*b.* quart" represents a volume that is twice that of a pint. While the other options are related to *pint* in the sense that each one is a measure of volume, none is related in the same way that 1 is to 2.

Types of Relationships in MAT Analogies

There are many ways in which a pair of words can be related. Sometimes the relationship is obvious as soon as you read the terms. Sometimes, however, you have to formulate a statement before the relationship becomes apparent. Although there are many possible types of relationships, within a particular item only one or two types will be present.

The relationships found in MAT items can be grouped into four broad categories: semantic, classification, association, and logical/mathematical. Each of these groups contains several sub-classifications.

When you take the MAT, you do not need to classify each item. Nevertheless, reviewing these types of relationships may help you see the relationships between pairs of words that form MAT analogy items.

Semantic

This type of analogy can be thought of as involving definitions of the terms. Relationships of this type have to do with what a word stands for and how that word is linguistically connected to others. The words may be any part of speech.

1. **Synonym or Definition**—The terms have the same or similar meaning.

Teach : Instruct	Both words mean "to impart knowledge."
Edge : Border	Both words refer to a boundary.
Empty : Vacuous	Both words mean "lacking in substance."
Eire : Ireland	Both words are accepted names for the same country.

2. **Antonym or Contrast**—The terms have opposite meanings or are used to express unlike concepts.

Rarely : Frequently	The word *rarely* means "not often" or "infrequently."
Order : Chaos	Chaos is a state of total disorder, the opposite of order.
Legalize : Outlaw	To outlaw something is not to legalize it but to make it illegal.

3. **Intensity**—One term expresses a greater size or degree of something than the other. This category can be difficult if you misinterpret the analogy as a simple synonym or antonym.

Joyful : Ecstatic	To be ecstatic is to be wildly and intensely joyful.
Slam : Close	To slam is to close forcefully and loudly.
Stream : Torrent	A torrent is a swift-flowing stream.

4. **Word Part/Meaning**—One term explains what the other term means.

–ism : Practice	One meaning of the suffix *–ism* is the practice of something; for example, criticism is the act or practice of criticizing.
Not : Un–	The prefix *un–* means "not"; for example, something unalterable cannot be changed.
Penta– : Five	The prefix *penta–* means five; for example, a pentagon is a five-sided polygon.

Classification

The classification type of analogy concerns the hierarchy of words and concepts. For example, when you outline a topic, you list main headings, subtitles, and so on. In a classification analogy, one word could be a heading for the other word, or both words might fall under the same heading.

1. **Category**—One term is a subordinate or superordinate class of the other. In other words, one term is a type or example of the other one.

Species : Genus	A species is a subdivision of a genus.
Emotion : Love	Love is one type of emotion.
Measles : Disease	Measles is an example of a disease.

2. **Membership**—Both terms are parts of the same thing or members of a larger category.

Wheel : Fender	Both are parts of a car.
Fingers : Thumbs	Both are digits of the hand.
Love : Fear	Both are examples of emotions.

3. **Whole/Part**—One term is a part of another term.

Wheel : Car	A wheel is part of a car.
Galaxy : Star	A galaxy is made up of stars.
Year : Century	A century consists of one hundred years.

Association

The association type of analogy represents the largest group. This type deals with relationships between two distinct but related ideas. The terms are often nouns but may be any part of speech.

1. **Object/Characteristic**—One term is a characteristic, source, or location of another term.

   One term is an attribute, characteristic, or description of the other:

Parrot : Beak	A parrot has a beak as its jaws.
Monster : Ferocious	A monster usually has a ferocious disposition.
Imaginary : Fable	A fable is a story about imaginary characters.

   One term is an attribute that the other term lacks:

Hair : Bald	A person who has no hair is bald.
Inept : Skill	An inept person is lacking in skill.
Deliberate : Haste	A deliberate action does not involve haste.

One term is the source of the other or the material out of which the other is composed:

Book : Paper	A book is printed on paper.
Flour : Bread	Bread is made from flour.
Cable : Wire	A cable is composed of wires.

One term gives the location or setting of the other:

India : Rupee	A rupee is a denomination of the currency used in India.
Stomata : Leaf	Stomata are tiny pores in a leaf.
Parthenon : Athens	The Parthenon temple is in Athens, Greece.

2. **Order**—The terms are in a sequential or reciprocal relationship to one another.

The terms have a time or other sequential relationship, but one does not cause the other:

Dawn : Sunrise	The dawn occurs just before a sunrise.
7 : 11	These are consecutive prime numbers.
Alpha : Omega	These are the first and last letters of the Greek alphabet.

The terms have a reciprocal relationship so that one concept cannot exist without the other:

Aunt : Niece	A niece is related to an aunt through the same person; the niece's parent is the aunt's sibling.
Weight : Mass	On earth, anything with mass also has weight, due to the force of gravity acting upon it.
Object : Transitive	In a sentence, a transitive verb must have a direct object that it links to the subject.

One word is a grammatical transformation of the other:

Bring : Brought	The verb changes from present to past tense.
My : Mine	The possessive form changes from adjective to pronoun.
Datum : Data	The noun changes from singular to plural.

3. **Agent/Object**—There are many possibilities within this group, all of which involve one term that causes, creates, provides, requires, uses, or in some other way relies on the other term. Some of the most common types of agent/object analogies include the following examples.

Cause/Effect—One term causes the other:

Rain : Flood	Excessive rain can cause a flood.
Hunger : Fasting	Fasting from food results in hunger.
Crime : Punishment	Punishment is a consequence of crime.

Creator/Creation—One term creates the other:

Robin : Nest	A robin builds a nest.
Suit : Tailor	A tailor makes a suit.
Homer : Iliad	Homer wrote the epic poem the *Iliad*.

One term provides the other or makes it possible:

Education : Teacher	A teacher provides education.
Food : Nutrition	Food provides the body with nutrition.
Postage : Mail	Postage covers the cost and enables mail to be delivered.

One term represents the function or purpose of the other:

Knife : Cut	A knife is used to cut something.
Sound : Audiometer	The purpose of an audiometer is to measure sound.
Salute : Respect	A salute shows respect.

One term is a tool or object used by the other:

Plumber : Wrench	A plumber uses a wrench to work on a pipe.
Seamstress : Needle	A seamstress uses a needle to pull thread through cloth.
Violinist : Bow	A violinist uses a bow to play a violin.

Logical/Mathematical

A few MAT items may include logical or mathematical equations, numerical fractions, multiples, negation, or letter and sound patterns.

1. **One term is a fraction or multiple of another:**

   11 : 121   121 is the square of 11.

   Annual : Biennial   A biennial time period (two years) is twice as long as an annual time period (one year).

   $$\frac{1}{2} : \frac{1}{20} \qquad \frac{1}{2} \text{ is ten times as much as } \frac{1}{20}.$$

2. **The terms are related through some non-semantic similarity or change, such as rhyming, homophones, letter reversal, or other wordplay.** There are not many such word puzzles on the MAT, but you should be prepared for the few that you may encounter.

   Emit : Time   The two words are spelled with the same letters in reverse order.

   Bough : Bow   Two of the meanings of the word *bow* ("the front of a ship" and "to bend downward") are pronounced the same as the word *bough*.

   Sprung : Run   The word *run* is contained within the word *sprung*.

The Content of MAT Analogies

The terms in most of the MAT analogy items are words, but in some cases they may be numbers, symbols, or word parts. A number of items are drawn from areas of everyday experience, such as food, clothing, tools, transportation, education, and common expressions. Other analogy items rely upon your knowledge of the various academic disciplines or subjects that are typically studied by American undergraduate students.

When the terms in an analogy are taken from a specific academic area, the two pairs of terms that form the analogy come from that same subject matter.

Washington : Adams :: Bush : Clinton

In this analogy, all four of the terms involve some knowledge of American history; the analogy here is that John Adams followed George Washington into the presidency, just as Bill Clinton followed George H. W. Bush.

However, sometimes the terms in the two pairs that form the analogy come from different subject matter.

Steinbeck : Gershwin :: Literature : Music

An analogy such as this involves pairs of terms from different subject areas. Nevertheless, it is the relationship between terms that is crucial here: both John Steinbeck and George Gershwin were creative artists in their respective areas—literature and music.

While there is no specific body of information that can be studied or memorized to improve your MAT score, you may find it useful to be aware of the subject areas represented on the MAT.

Language and Vocabulary

These analogy items include aspects of English grammar and usage to test your understanding of word meanings and your ability to recognize the relationships between those meanings.

Language analogy items most often use one of three relationships: synonym (words with similar meanings), antonym (words with opposite meanings), or intensity (words with the same general meaning but with a difference in degree).

> Naive : (*a.* cosmopolitan, *b.* credulous, *c.* experienced, *d.* pretentious) ::
> Sophisticated : Worldly

This analogy requires the recognition that *sophisticated* and *worldly* have similar meanings and form a complete pair. The correct answer will then be a synonym for *naive*. Thus, the correct answer is *credulous*. This item can also be interpreted as an antonym analogy by interchanging the middle terms: *naive* is an antonym for *sophisticated*, *worldly* is an antonym for *credulous*.

> Annoy : Enrage :: Enlarge : (*a.* increase, *b.* exaggerate, *c.* augment, *d.* reduce)

This analogy involves degrees of meaning: to enrage is to annoy to a greater degree. The correct answer should then be the word that means to enlarge, but to a greater degree. Thus, the correct answer is "*b.* exaggerate." This is an example of an item that requires you to distinguish fine shades of meaning between terms. If you incorrectly consider *annoy* and *enrage* to be synonyms, then you would have to choose between "*a.* increase," "*b.* exaggerate," or "*c.* augment" for an answer, all of which are generally related to *enlarge*. However, to choose between these three options, you need to see that the difference between them is the same as the difference between *annoy* and *enrage*—a difference in degree.

Humanities

MAT analogy items involving content from the humanities include subject matter from literature, philosophy, and the fine arts. Literature items may test your knowledge of authors, their works, literary genres, or literary devices. Philosophy items are concerned with philosophers, their works, and their beliefs or schools of thought. Fine arts analogy items cover the entire spectrum of the fine arts: the performing arts of music, drama, and dance; the visual arts of painting and sculpting; and other arts such as filmmaking and sound recording. These items use a variety of relationships. Two common ones are creator/creation and whole/part.

> Frost : Poetry :: Miller : (*a.* grain, *b.* drama, *c.* literature, *d.* bard)

Looking at the three given terms in this literary analogy there is a creator/creation relationship between *Frost* and *poetry*: Robert Frost is best known for his poetry. For this reason, the correct answer should be the type of literature that the American playwright Arthur Miller is best known for creating—"*b.* drama."

> Poem : (*a.* line, *b.* rhyme, *c.* stanza, *d.* sonnet) :: Book : Chapter

In this analogy, the last two of the three given terms have a whole/part relationship to each other. A section of a book is a chapter. The missing term, then, should be a section of a poem.

The correct answer is "*c.* stanza." Even though a line (option *a*) is also part of a poem, it is not a complete section in the same way that a chapter is a complete section of a book.

Social Sciences

MAT analogy items with content from the social sciences include subject matter from history, geography, political science, economics, sociology, and psychology. Analogy items with content from the social sciences may use many different types of relationships. For example, a historical event may be paired with the year it occurred, a key person associated with the event, the country in which it occurred, a piece of legislation associated with the event, or a cause or result of the event.

Independence : 1776 :: Emancipation : (*a.* 1783, *b.* 1863, *c.* 1876, *d.* 1920)

In this analogy, the relationship between the first two given terms is event/date. You need to supply implied words in order for the relationship to become obvious. The Declaration of Independence was issued in 1776, whereby the American colonies declared their independence from Great Britain. The missing term should then be the year that the Emancipation Proclamation was issued in the United States, whereby slaves were declared free in the states still at war with the federal government. The correct answer is "*b.* 1863."

Strike : (*a.* customer, *b.* employer, *c.* picket, *d.* union) :: Boycott : Merchant

The agent/object relationship between the terms may not be immediately obvious until the given terms are considered in an economic sense. Then it is seen that a boycott is a protest action taken against a merchant in the form of abstaining from buying or using. Similarly, a strike is a protest in the form of work stoppage directed against an employer (option *b*).

Natural Sciences

Both the biological and physical sciences provide subject matter for MAT analogy items. Some commonly used relationships in such items include agent/object (such as Flower : Bloom) and category (such as Hydrogen : Element).

Carnivore : Herbivore :: Tiger : (*a.* antelope, *b.* lion, *c.* predator, *d.* vegetation)

A tiger is an example of a carnivore—a meat-eating animal. The missing term should be an example of an herbivore—an animal that eats only plants. Thus, the correct answer is "*a.* antelope."

Limestone : (*a.* cement, *b.* metamorphic, *c.* sedimentary, *d.* volcano) :: Granite : Igneous

The last two given terms have a member/group relationship. Granite is an example of igneous rock. Limestone is an example of sedimentary (option *c*) rock.

Mathematics

Mathematics analogies may include concepts from number theory, arithmetic, algebra, or geometry. Mathematics analogy items may use numbers, words, symbols, or combinations of these. Mathematics items often employ transformation, order, or object/characteristic relationships.

In solving mathematics analogies, you must recognize the conceptual relationship between two of the three given terms. For some of these items, you may also have to use computation to determine the value of the missing term.

(*a.* radius, *b.* diameter, *c.* area, *d.* circumference) : Perimeter :: Circle : Square

Examining the three given terms, you may recognize that a perimeter is the distance around a square. You can then also recognize that the distance around a circle is "*d.* circumference."

$$4 : 64 :: 5 : (a.\ 8,\ b.\ 25,\ c.\ 32,\ d.\ 125)$$

You might suppose that a possible relationship between the first two given numbers is that an implied 16 multiplied by 4 equals 64. However, this cannot be the relationship, because 16 multiplied by 5 equals 80, which is not one of the answer choices. The relationship here is that 4 cubed equals 64. Because 5 cubed equals 125, the correct answer is *d.*

Test-Taking Strategies for the MAT

Read All the Answer Options Carefully

Avoid selecting the first answer that seems to make sense. One choice may seem to fit, but a better answer choice may also be listed. Remember that you are looking for the best answer among options that may all seem plausible. Many of the incorrect answer options on the MAT have some relationship to the term that you are trying to match it with. However, you will correctly solve the analogy only when you determine which answer option most accurately reflects the same relationship as the two given terms that form a complete pair.

Consider Alternative Meanings of Words

If at first an analogy does not seem to make sense, you may need to think of one or more of the terms in a different way. For instance, consider the following analogy:

Napoleon : Pergola :: (*a.* baker, *b.* general, *c.* lumber, *d.* trellis) : Carpenter

This analogy makes no sense if you think of Napoleon as the French general and emperor. However, a napoleon is also a pastry. Therefore, a napoleon (the pastry) is made by a baker (option *a*), just as a wooden pergola (a trelliswork arbor or patio covering) is built by a carpenter.

Reorder the Analogy

Sometimes you can clarify the relationship in an analogy by changing the order of the terms, because the location of the terms of a valid analogy can be changed without affecting the meaning. In other words, the analogy "A is to B as C is to D" will remain valid even if it is rearranged to "A is to C as B is to D." For example, consider the following analogy:

French : Roman :: Russian : Cyrillic

The relationship here is that the French language uses the Roman alphabet, and the Russian language uses the Cyrillic alphabet, and the analogy remains valid even when it is reordered to read "French : Russian :: Roman : Cyrillic." In this second arrangement, the relevant relationships remain the same: the French language uses the Roman alphabet in the same way that the Russian language uses the Cyrillic alphabet.

Check the Part of Speech

The answer you choose should be the same part of speech as the corresponding term in the complete pair.

For example, consider the following analogy:

Food : Ate :: Ball : (*a.* red, *b.* slow, *c.* game, *d.* threw)

The correct answer in this analogy would have to be the verb *threw* (*d*), corresponding to the verb *ate* in the complete pair. However, it is not always this obvious. For instance, consider this analogy:

Table : Bill :: (*a.* chair, *b.* direct, *c.* gesture, *d.* shelve) : Motion

In this analogy, two options are nouns and two options are verbs, requiring a solution that involves a further distinction. If your first reaction is to think of the words *table*, *bill*, and *motion* as nouns, then none of the options seems to make complete sense. However, once you think of the word *table* as a verb, it becomes clear that to delay consideration of a legislative bill is to table it and, similarly, to delay consideration of a motion (a formal proposal) is to shelve it (option d). Thus, it is necessary to recognize both the part of speech and the relevant meaning of the terms in order to solve an analogy like this one.

Reduce the Number of Choices

If you are uncertain about the answer to an analogy, try to eliminate the answer options that do not seem to fit and then guess from among the remaining options. The more options you can eliminate the more likely you are to select the correct answer.

If an analogy completely baffles you, look for clues. For instance, you may at first be uncertain about the following analogy:

Sinanthropus : Pithecanthropus :: (*a.* Peking, *b.* Hong Kong, *c.* Cairo, *d.* Kabul) : Java

However, the root *anthropus* in the first and second terms suggests that this analogy has to do with human beings. From there you may well make the connection between the first two terms and the common names for two famous early anthropological finds—Peking man and Java man—and arrive at the correct answer of "*a.* Peking." Another way that you might reason through this analogy is that because the first two terms share the same root (*anthropus*), it must be the prefixes that distinguish them. If you know that *Sino*– means "Chinese," you can reasonably narrow the choices to either "*a.* Peking" (currently called Beijing) or "*b.* Hong Kong," both of which are cities in China.

Postpone Difficult Items

The MAT is a timed test. Because you have 60 minutes to answer 120 questions, you have an average of 30 seconds to solve each analogy and to indicate your answer. Because each item counts the same, you may not want to spend too much time on an analogy if the relationship is not apparent to you. Your time would be more wisely used by moving on to analogies that are clear to you. Try to use the last 10 minutes or so of the testing period to go back to items that were unclear.

When you return to an analogy, you may understand it more clearly than you did the first time you looked at it. One explanation for this new clarity may be that the more analogies you complete the more skilled at solving them you become. Another reason may be that you have unconsciously been thinking about the analogies you skipped. If the answer does not come to you quickly on your second try, make your best guess and move on.

Answer Every Question

Your scores are based on the number of items you answer correctly. Points are not deducted for incorrect responses. If you are not sure which answer choice is correct for an item, eliminate as many incorrect options as you can first. If you have doubts about an answer to an item, change your answer only if you have a valid reason.

Indicate Your Answers Carefully

When taking the computer-based MAT, the answer you select is shown on the screen. You will not be able to select more than one answer per item on the screen display, but it is up to you to confirm that the answer you intend is the one that is displayed on the screen before you move to the next item. You will have the opportunity to review your answer choices at the end of the test if time permits.

Sample Analogies

One of the best ways to prepare for the MAT is to become familiar with analogies through practice in solving them. Like the Practice Tests available on the MAT website (see "Online Practice Tests"), these sample analogies will give you a sense of what to expect when you take the MAT.

In the "Annotated Answers" section, the sample analogies are complete with the correct answer and explanation provided for each one.

One effective way to improve your performance on the actual MAT will be to look for patterns in your incorrect answers to the sample analogies or the items on the online Practice Tests. If you notice that your errors are caused by misinterpreting the relationships between terms, then you may need more practice with the analogy format. If you notice that your errors result from not knowing the meanings of words or from unfamiliarity with certain facts, then you may need more background in vocabulary or specific content areas.

If you would like to time yourself, allow 5 minutes to complete the 10 items, which is an amount of time proportional to the 60 minutes allowed to complete the 120 items on the actual MAT.

1. Spring : Ring :: Coil : (*a.* rope, *b.* loop, *c.* cowl, *d.* stretch)

2. 97° : 45° :: (*a.* obtuse, *b.* equilateral, *c.* angle, *d.* cosine) : Acute

3. Mollusk : (*a.* fish, *b.* cell, *c.* plant, *d.* mammal) :: Pearl : Ambergris

4. (*a.* epistemology, *b.* axiology, *c.* teleology, *d.* pedagogy) : Ontology :: Knowledge : Being

5. Elbow : Nerve :: Hinge : (*a.* lever, *b.* electricity, *c.* fulcrum, *d.* wire)

6. Individual : Municipality :: Loan : (*a.* county, *b.* bond, *c.* stock, *d.* certificate)

7. Homophone : (*a.* paradigm, *b.* antonym, *c.* synonym, *d.* acronym) :: Sound : Meaning

8. (*a.* Rembrandt, *b.* Dalí, *c.* Cassatt, *d.* Matisse) : Monet :: Whistler : Cézanne

9. –ive : –ion :: Adjective : (*a.* verb, *b.* noun, *c.* conjunction, *d.* adverb)

10. Constitution : Magna Carta :: United States : (*a.* Pilgrims, *b.* Virginia, *c.* England, *d.* Rome)

Annotated Answers

1. Spring : Ring :: Coil : (*b.* loop)

    A spring forms or has the shape of a coil, and a ring forms a loop.

2. 97° : 45° :: (*a.* obtuse) : Acute

    An acute angle is any angle less than 90°, so a 45° angle is acute. An obtuse angle is any angle between 90° and 180°, so a 97° angle is obtuse. Thus, 97° is to 45° as *obtuse* is to *acute*.

3. Mollusk : (*d.* mammal) :: Pearl : Ambergris

    Pearls are found in oysters, a type of mollusk; ambergris is found in sperm whales, a type of mammal.

4. (*a.* epistemology) : Ontology :: Knowledge : Being

    In the discipline of philosophy, ontology is the branch that deals with the nature of being or existence, and epistemology is the branch that deals with the nature of knowledge.

5. Elbow : Nerve :: Hinge : (*d.* wire)

    The elbow of an arm and a hinge on a door or gate function similarly; a nerve (a cordlike bundle of fibers) functions in the nervous system similar to the way a wire functions in an electrical system.

6. Individual : Municipality :: Loan : (*b.* bond)

    An individual borrows money by obtaining a loan; a municipality borrows money by issuing a bond.

7. Homophone : (*c.* synonym) :: Sound : Meaning

    Words that have the same sound are called homophones; words that have the same meaning are called synonyms.

8. (*c.* Cassatt) : Monet :: Whistler : Cézanne

    Claude Monet and Paul Cézanne were two French painters, and Mary Cassatt and James Whistler were two American painters, all of whom were born in the nineteenth century and lived into the early twentieth century.

9. –ive : –ion :: Adjective : (*b.* noun)

    The suffix *–ive* is used to form an adjective denoting action; the suffix *–ion* is used to form a noun denoting the result of an action or a state or condition.

10. Constitution : Magna Carta :: United States : (*c.* England)

    The Constitution is the defining political and legal document of the United States; the Magna Carta was a political charter granted by the King of England in which basic rights were delineated.

HOW TO TAKE A TEST

You have studied long, hard and conscientiously.

With your official admission card in hand, and your heart pounding, you have been admitted to the examination room.

You note that there are several hundred other applicants in the examination room waiting to take the same test.

They all appear to be equally well prepared.

You know that nothing but your best effort will suffice. The "moment of truth" is at hand: you now have to demonstrate objectively, in writing, your knowledge of content and your understanding of subject matter.

You are fighting the most important battle of your life—to pass and/or score high on an examination which will determine your career and provide the economic basis for your livelihood.

What extra, special things should you know and should you do in taking the examination?

I. YOU MUST PASS AN EXAMINATION

A. *WHAT EVERY CANDIDATE SHOULD KNOW*
Examination applicants often ask us for help in preparing for the written test. What can I study in advance? What kinds of questions will be asked? How will the test be given? How will the papers be graded?

B. *HOW ARE EXAMS DEVELOPED?*
Examinations are carefully written by trained technicians who are specialists in the field known as "psychological measurement," in consultation with recognized authorities in the field of work that the test will cover. These experts recommend the subject matter areas or skills to be tested; only those knowledges or skills important to your success on the job are included. The most reliable books and source materials available are used as references. Together, the experts and technicians judge the difficulty level of the questions.

Test technicians know how to phrase questions so that the problem is clearly stated. Their ethics do not permit "trick" or "catch" questions. Questions may have been tried out on sample groups, or subjected to statistical analysis, to determine their usefulness.

Written tests are often used in combination with performance tests, ratings of training and experience, and oral interviews. All of these measures combine to form the best-known means of finding the right person for the right job.

II. HOW TO PASS THE WRITTEN TEST

A. BASIC STEPS

1) Study the announcement

How, then, can you know what subjects to study? Our best answer is: "Learn as much as possible about the class of positions for which you've applied." The exam will test the knowledge, skills and abilities needed to do the work.

Your most valuable source of information about the position you want is the official exam announcement. This announcement lists the training and experience qualifications. Check these standards and apply only if you come reasonably close to meeting them. Many jurisdictions preview the written test in the exam announcement by including a section called "Knowledge and Abilities Required," "Scope of the Examination," or some similar heading. Here you will find out specifically what fields will be tested.

2) Choose appropriate study materials

If the position for which you are applying is technical or advanced, you will read more advanced, specialized material. If you are already familiar with the basic principles of your field, elementary textbooks would waste your time. Concentrate on advanced textbooks and technical periodicals. Think through the concepts and review difficult problems in your field.

These are all general sources. You can get more ideas on your own initiative, following these leads. For example, training manuals and publications of the government agency which employs workers in your field can be useful, particularly for technical and professional positions. A letter or visit to the government department involved may result in more specific study suggestions, and certainly will provide you with a more definite idea of the exact nature of the position you are seeking.

3) Study this book!

III. KINDS OF TESTS

Tests are used for purposes other than measuring knowledge and ability to perform specified duties. For some positions, it is equally important to test ability to make adjustments to new situations or to profit from training. In others, basic mental abilities not dependent on information are essential. Questions which test these things may not appear as pertinent to the duties of the position as those which test for knowledge and information. Yet they are often highly important parts of a fair examination. For very general questions, it is almost impossible to help you direct your study efforts. What we can do is to point out some of the more common of these general abilities needed in public service positions and describe some typical questions.

1) General information

Broad, general information has been found useful for predicting job success in some kinds of work. This is tested in a variety of ways, from vocabulary lists to questions about current events. Basic background in some field of work, such as sociology or economics, may be sampled in a group of questions. Often these are principles which have become familiar to most persons through exposure rather than through formal training. It is difficult to advise you how to study for these questions; being alert to the world around you is our best suggestion.

2) Verbal ability

An example of an ability needed in many positions is verbal or language ability. Verbal ability is, in brief, the ability to use and understand words. Vocabulary and grammar tests are typical measures of this ability. Reading comprehension or paragraph interpretation questions are common in many kinds of civil service tests. You are given a paragraph of written material and asked to find its central meaning.

IV. KINDS OF QUESTIONS

1. Multiple-choice Questions

Most popular of the short-answer questions is the "multiple choice" or "best answer" question. It can be used, for example, to test for factual knowledge, ability to solve problems or judgment in meeting situations found at work.

A multiple-choice question is normally one of three types:
- It can begin with an incomplete statement followed by several possible endings. You are to find the one ending which *best* completes the statement, although some of the others may not be entirely wrong.
- It can also be a complete statement in the form of a question which is answered by choosing one of the statements listed.
- It can be in the form of a problem – again you select the best answer.

Here is an example of a multiple-choice question with a discussion which should give you some clues as to the method for choosing the right answer:

When an employee has a complaint about his assignment, the action which will *best* help him overcome his difficulty is to
A. discuss his difficulty with his coworkers
B. take the problem to the head of the organization
C. take the problem to the person who gave him the assignment
D. say nothing to anyone about his complaint

In answering this question, you should study each of the choices to find which is best. Consider choice "A" – Certainly an employee may discuss his complaint with fellow employees, but no change or improvement can result, and the complaint remains unresolved. Choice "B" is a poor choice since the head of the organization probably does not know what assignment you have been given, and taking your problem to him is known as "going over the head" of the supervisor. The supervisor, or person who made the assignment, is the person who can clarify it or correct any injustice. Choice "C" is, therefore, correct. To say nothing, as in choice "D," is unwise. Supervisors have and interest in knowing the problems employees are facing, and the employee is seeking a solution to his problem.

2. True/False

3. Matching Questions
   Matching an answer from a column of choices within another column.

V. RECORDING YOUR ANSWERS

Computer terminals are used more and more today for many different kinds of exams.

For an examination with very few applicants, you may be told to record your answers in the test booklet itself. Separate answer sheets are much more common. If this separate answer sheet is to be scored by machine – and this is often the case – it is highly important that you mark your answers correctly in order to get credit.

VI. BEFORE THE TEST

YOUR PHYSICAL CONDITION IS IMPORTANT
   If you are not well, you can't do your best work on tests. If you are half asleep, you can't do your best either. Here are some tips:

1) Get about the same amount of sleep you usually get. Don't stay up all night before the test, either partying or worrying—DON'T DO IT!
2) If you wear glasses, be sure to wear them when you go to take the test. This goes for hearing aids, too.
3) If you have any physical problems that may keep you from doing your best, be sure to tell the person giving the test. If you are sick or in poor health, you relay cannot do your best on any test. You can always come back and take the test some other time.

Common sense will help you find procedures to follow to get ready for an examination. Too many of us, however, overlook these sensible measures. Indeed, nervousness and fatigue have been found to be the most serious reasons why applicants fail to do their best on civil service tests. Here is a list of reminders:

- Begin your preparation early – Don't wait until the last minute to go scurrying around for books and materials or to find out what the position is all about.
- Prepare continuously – An hour a night for a week is better than an all-night cram session. This has been definitely established. What is more, a night a week for a month will return better dividends than crowding your study into a shorter period of time.
- Locate the place of the exam – You have been sent a notice telling you when and where to report for the examination. If the location is in a different town or otherwise unfamiliar to you, it would be well to inquire the best route and learn something about the building.
- Relax the night before the test – Allow your mind to rest. Do not study at all that night. Plan some mild recreation or diversion; then go to bed early and get a good night's sleep.
- Get up early enough to make a leisurely trip to the place for the test – This way unforeseen events, traffic snarls, unfamiliar buildings, etc. will not upset you.

- Dress comfortably – A written test is not a fashion show. You will be known by number and not by name, so wear something comfortable.
- Leave excess paraphernalia at home – Shopping bags and odd bundles will get in your way. You need bring only the items mentioned in the official notice you received; usually everything you need is provided. Do not bring reference books to the exam. They will only confuse those last minutes and be taken away from you when in the test room.
- Arrive somewhat ahead of time – If because of transportation schedules you must get there very early, bring a newspaper or magazine to take your mind off yourself while waiting.
- Locate the examination room – When you have found the proper room, you will be directed to the seat or part of the room where you will sit. Sometimes you are given a sheet of instructions to read while you are waiting. Do not fill out any forms until you are told to do so; just read them and be prepared.
- Relax and prepare to listen to the instructions
- If you have any physical problem that may keep you from doing your best, be sure to tell the test administrator. If you are sick or in poor health, you really cannot do your best on the exam. You can come back and take the test some other time.

VII. AT THE TEST

The day of the test is here and you have the test booklet in your hand. The temptation to get going is very strong. Caution! There is more to success than knowing the right answers. You must know how to identify your papers and understand variations in the type of short-answer question used in this particular examination. Follow these suggestions for maximum results from your efforts:

1) Cooperate with the monitor
The test administrator has a duty to create a situation in which you can be as much at ease as possible. He will give instructions, tell you when to begin, check to see that you are marking your answer sheet correctly, and so on. He is not there to guard you, although he will see that your competitors do not take unfair advantage. He wants to help you do your best.

2) Listen to all instructions
Don't jump the gun! Wait until you understand all directions. In most civil service tests you get more time than you need to answer the questions. So don't be in a hurry. Read each word of instructions until you clearly understand the meaning. Study the examples, listen to all announcements and follow directions. Ask questions if you do not understand what to do.

3) Identify your papers
Civil service exams are usually identified by number only. You will be assigned a number; you must not put your name on your test papers. Be sure to copy your number correctly. Since more than one exam may be given, copy your exact examination title.

4) Plan your time
Unless you are told that a test is a "speed" or "rate of work" test, speed itself is usually not important. Time enough to answer all the questions will be provided, but this

does not mean that you have all day. An overall time limit has been set. Divide the total time (in minutes) by the number of questions to determine the approximate time you have for each question.

5) Do not linger over difficult questions

If you come across a difficult question, mark it with a paper clip (useful to have along) and come back to it when you have been through the booklet. One caution if you do this – be sure to skip a number on your answer sheet as well. Check often to be sure that you have not lost your place and that you are marking in the row numbered the same as the question you are answering.

6) Read the questions

Be sure you know what the question asks! Many capable people are unsuccessful because they failed to *read* the questions correctly.

7) Answer all questions

Unless you have been instructed that a penalty will be deducted for incorrect answers, it is better to guess than to omit a question.

8) Speed tests

It is often better NOT to guess on speed tests. It has been found that on timed tests people are tempted to spend the last few seconds before time is called in marking answers at random – without even reading them – in the hope of picking up a few extra points. To discourage this practice, the instructions may warn you that your score will be "corrected" for guessing. That is, a penalty will be applied. The incorrect answers will be deducted from the correct ones, or some other penalty formula will be used.

9) Review your answers

If you finish before time is called, go back to the questions you guessed or omitted to give them further thought. Review other answers if you have time.

10) Return your test materials

If you are ready to leave before others have finished or time is called, take ALL your materials to the monitor and leave quietly. Never take any test material with you. The monitor can discover whose papers are not complete, and taking a test booklet may be grounds for disqualification.

VIII. EXAMINATION TECHNIQUES

1) Read the general instructions carefully. These are usually printed on the first page of the exam booklet. As a rule, these instructions refer to the timing of the examination; the fact that you should not start work until the signal and must stop work at a signal, etc. If there are any *special* instructions, such as a choice of questions to be answered, make sure that you note this instruction carefully.

2) When you are ready to start work on the examination, that is as soon as the signal has been given, read the instructions to each question booklet, underline any key words or phrases, such as *least, best, outline, describe*

and the like. In this way you will tend to answer as requested rather than discover on reviewing your paper that you *listed without describing*, that you selected the *worst* choice rather than the *best* choice, etc.

3) If the examination is of the objective or multiple-choice type – that is, each question will also give a series of possible answers: A, B, C or D, and you are called upon to select the best answer and write the letter next to that answer on your answer paper – it is advisable to start answering each question in turn. There may be anywhere from 50 to 100 such questions in the three or four hours allotted and you can see how much time would be taken if you read through all the questions before beginning to answer any. Furthermore, if you come across a question or group of questions which you know would be difficult to answer, it would undoubtedly affect your handling of all the other questions.

4) If the examination is of the essay type and contains but a few questions, it is a moot point as to whether you should read all the questions before starting to answer any one. Of course, if you are given a choice – say five out of seven and the like – then it is essential to read all the questions so you can eliminate the two that are most difficult. If, however, you are asked to answer all the questions, there may be danger in trying to answer the easiest one first because you may find that you will spend too much time on it. The best technique is to answer the first question, then proceed to the second, etc.

5) Time your answers. Before the exam begins, write down the time it started, then add the time allowed for the examination and write down the time it must be completed, then divide the time available somewhat as follows:
   - If 3-1/2 hours are allowed, that would be 210 minutes. If you have 80 objective-type questions, that would be an average of 2-1/2 minutes per question. Allow yourself no more than 2 minutes per question, or a total of 160 minutes, which will permit about 50 minutes to review.
   - If for the time allotment of 210 minutes there are 7 essay questions to answer, that would average about 30 minutes a question. Give yourself only 25 minutes per question so that you have about 35 minutes to review.

6) The most important instruction is to *read each question* and make sure you know what is wanted. The second most important instruction is to *time yourself properly* so that you answer every question. The third most important instruction is to *answer every question*. Guess if you have to but include something for each question. Remember that you will receive no credit for a blank and will probably receive some credit if you write something in answer to an essay question. If you guess a letter – say "B" for a multiple-choice question – you may have guessed right. If you leave a blank as an answer to a multiple-choice question, the examiners may respect your feelings but it will not add a point to your score. Some exams may penalize you for wrong answers, so in such cases *only*, you may not want to guess unless you have some basis for your answer.

7) Suggestions
   a. Objective-type questions
      1. Examine the question booklet for proper sequence of pages and questions
      2. Read all instructions carefully
      3. Skip any question which seems too difficult; return to it after all other questions have been answered
      4. Apportion your time properly; do not spend too much time on any single question or group of questions
      5. Note and underline key words – *all, most, fewest, least, best, worst, same, opposite,* etc.
      6. Pay particular attention to negatives
      7. Note unusual option, e.g., unduly long, short, complex, different or similar in content to the body of the question
      8. Observe the use of "hedging" words – *probably, may, most likely,* etc.
      9. Make sure that your answer is put next to the same number as the question
      10. Do not second-guess unless you have good reason to believe the second answer is definitely more correct
      11. Cross out original answer if you decide another answer is more accurate; do not erase until you are ready to hand your paper in
      12. Answer all questions; guess unless instructed otherwise
      13. Leave time for review

   b. Essay questions
      1. Read each question carefully
      2. Determine exactly what is wanted. Underline key words or phrases.
      3. Decide on outline or paragraph answer
      4. Include many different points and elements unless asked to develop any one or two points or elements
      5. Show impartiality by giving pros and cons unless directed to select one side only
      6. Make and write down any assumptions you find necessary to answer the questions
      7. Watch your English, grammar, punctuation and choice of words
      8. Time your answers; don't crowd material

8) Answering the essay question

Most essay questions can be answered by framing the specific response around several key words or ideas. Here are a few such key words or ideas:

M's: manpower, materials, methods, money, management
P's: purpose, program, policy, plan, procedure, practice, problems, pitfalls, personnel, public relations
a. Six basic steps in handling problems:
   1. Preliminary plan and background development
   2. Collect information, data and facts
   3. Analyze and interpret information, data and facts
   4. Analyze and develop solutions as well as make recommendations

5. Prepare report and sell recommendations
6. Install recommendations and follow up effectiveness

b. Pitfalls to avoid
1. *Taking things for granted* – A statement of the situation does not necessarily imply that each of the elements is necessarily true; for example, a complaint may be invalid and biased so that all that can be taken for granted is that a complaint has been registered
2. *Considering only one side of a situation* – Wherever possible, indicate several alternatives and then point out the reasons you selected the best one
3. *Failing to indicate follow up* – Whenever your answer indicates action on your part, make certain that you will take proper follow-up action to see how successful your recommendations, procedures or actions turn out to be
4. *Taking too long in answering any single question* – Remember to time your answers properly

EXAMINATION SECTION

MILLER ANALOGIES TEST (MAT)
PREFACE

Today, this examination has become a required or suggested step for admission to leading graduate schools, for matriculation, qualification, or classification in a masters or doctoral program.

The Psychological Corporation, the administrators of the examination, officially describe the MAT as "a high-level mental abilities test which requires the solution of a series of intellectual problems stated in terms of verbal analogies" and as "a difficult test of information and verbal reasoning ability used in the admission of students to graduate school." For many years, graduate students and other applicants have had to take this elite examination without the channeled preparation to be derived from the use of express learning resource materials and, consequently, have faced this trial of mental ability with great insecurity.

This book should be of purposeful aid to graduate school applicants:

1. It is based on the most authoritative principle of learning, the functional way of "learning by doing."
    The candidate "takes" the actual examination as he grapples with the thousands of valid and authentic questions and problems in the book and, then, diagnostically checks himself.
2. It is sequential and systematic.
    The book follows the actual format and content of the test and provides programmed, step-by-step instruction together with intensive practice and drill.
3. The emphases are appropriate and balanced.
    Comprehensively adequate emphasis in appropriate detail has been given o each of the fields of learning touched upon in the examination. Thus, it is reasonable to expect that the largest part of the material would be devoted to the aspects of general vocabulary and general information. But the other fields—classics, history, literature, mathematics, science, and social science—have been treated with a proportional balance.
    Never before in academic history has material of this type been presented in a full-scale book. While verbal analogy questions in the fields of general vocabulary and general information are fairly standard in college-entrance, aptitude, and mental-ability testing, this question-type has never before been adapted for, or applied to, achievement testing, on a graduate level, in so many major academic fields. THE MATERIAL PRESENTED IN THIS BOOK ARE UNIQUE. They have been SPECIFICALLY created and developed for passing the MILLER ANALOGIES TEST.
    This book, too, is pointedly encyclopedic in content, going far beyond the essential needs of the candidate for the examination itself. The hundreds of questions presented in the various fields are not only varied in form and sampling in content, but are also progressive in conception and contemporary in reference, with a freshness and subtlety that make for interest and invite challenge. The aim has been to furnish a wealth of practice-drill materials so that this book may continue to be a source of learning for the student and a resource for the instructor.

4. <u>A climate of success is established for the candidate.</u>
   The correct answers which are furnished for all questions make self-testing and diagnosis feasible and practicable by educationally-sound placement at the end of each unit.

5. <u>The book is on a GRADUATE level.</u>
   The special, higher level nature of the MILLER ANALOGIES TEST has been recognized and respected. This is reflected by and extended in the professional plane of the scholarship and the academic quality of the included materials.

6. <u>The book fulfills the purpose intended.</u>
   Pointedly and precisely, ONLY materials that will specifically help prepare the candidate for the MILLER ANALOGIES TEST have been included in this book. Tangential and "filler" materials have been rigidly excluded.

TABLE OF CONTENTS

EXAMINATION SECTION

MILLER ANALOGIES TEST

1. WHAT IS THE MILLER ANALOGIES TEST (MAT)

Applicants seeking admission to leading graduate schools are required or advised to take the MILLER ANALOGIES TEST for admission to graduate study or for financial aid in graduate institutions. Government agencies, other institutions or organizations of a scientific, social, or educational nature, and certain business firms, require this test of applicants for employment or qualification.

The MAT is officially described as "a high-level mental ability test which requires the solution of a series of intellectual problems stated in terms of verbal analogies." Thus, couched in the form of verbal analogies, the Miller Test draws upon the fields of general vocabulary, general information, the classics, history, literature, mathematics, science, and social science.

The Miller is a multiple-choice (four-item), objective-type examination, which appears in several equivalent forms. Each form contains the same number of items (100), which, it is claimed, appear in order of difficulty on the examination.

The (analogy) questions (stems) themselves are all of the one-blank type, that is, only one word or term is to be supplied, and the items (answer-items) are all of the four-choice type, which are presented in a parenthetical form, instead of the usual progressive block form. In addition, on the Miller, the missing item (blank) may occur in any part (position) of the question-stem. That is, the usual traditional sequence of the one-blank verbal analogy question is violated in that the missing item (blank) may be in the first, second, or third part of the stem, instead of in the fixed fourth position. However, this has (and should have) little bearing on the nature, or the difficulty, of the verbal analogy question as presented.

It is interesting to note that the Miller Test is of the one-blank type rather than of the two-blank type; nor does it contain a mixture of both. Moreover, it is a four-choice type of test rather than a five-choice. These facts are important in assaying the difficulty level of the Miller: difficult is increased by the two-blank type of question and by the five-item choice. However, there is no guarantee that the format of the Miller will remain the same. We have, therefore, included in this book not only the two-blank type of question, but have also kept rigidly to the five-item presentation of answer-items.

Fifty minutes are allotted for answering the 100 analogies. (Answers are to be recorded on a separate Answer Sheet.) The analogies are claimed to occur in order of difficulty, and candidates are advised not to waste time on those that are troublesome but to come back to them after they have tried all of the analogies. There is evidently no deduction for wrong answers since the candidate is directed — pointedly — to guess if he is not sure of the answers. Therefore, it is to the candidate's interest to answer each and every question — even if this entails sheer guessing.

Because of its composition, in that it specifically lists subject areas in addition to the usual fields of general vocabulary and general information, the Miller must be considered both an aptitude and an achievement test at the same time. So far as the Miller samples the strength of ability of the candidate to see relationships, to analyze relationships, to make relationships, it may be considered an aptitude test, particularly in the areas of general vocabulary and general information. So far as it measures the ability of the candidate to rearrange learned materials and information, e.g., in the various academic fields, it must be considered an achievement test.

Thus, the MILLER ANALOGIES TEST becomes a fine instrument appropriate to the graduate level with which to probe and measure the mental ability of the graduate student.

The student or candidate who takes this examination must have reviewed and overlearned the basic knowledges and understandings contained in the various academic fields if he is to successfully readapt this content in the form of verbal analogies. The MAT implicitly presupposes a strong grounding in the essential content of the several academic disciplines with which it deals in the reorganized form of the verbal analogy. The conclusion is inevitable that this examination is much harder than it appears, and must be prepared for specifically.

2. WHEN IS THE MILLER ANALOGIES TEST GIVEN

This examination is given throughout the year by appointment at registered testing centers, a list of which is contained in the official Bulletin of Information, a copy of which appears hereafter.

The fee is payable at the time of testing, and includes the score report sent to the examinee, and up to three (3) transcripts of the results, sent to three (3) addresses of the examinee's choice provided that they are listed at the time of the examination. Reports are mailed the same day of the test.

Inquire of the graduate school(s) to which you are applying as to which of the administration dates would best meet their requirements.

3. HOW DOES THE CANDIDATE APPLY TO A GRADUATE SCHOOL

To apply to a graduate school, obtain directly from the school or schools in which you are interested their admissions application. You are then to complete the application, including all requirements and details therein outlined, and return this material directly to the school(s). One of the requirements on the application form of certain graduate schools is to apply for and to take the MILLER ANALOGIES TEST.

4. HOW DOES THE CANDIDATE APPLY FOR THE MILLER ANALOGIES TEST?

Visit the Pearson website (www.pearsonassessments.com) to search a directory of MAT Testing Centers. In this directory, locate the Center nearest and most convenient to you. Make an appointment with that Center for a testing date. Under special circumstances, such as excessive distance from a Center, or unavailability or inability on your part to keep the appointment, write to The Psychological Corporation, requesting a special examination and giving the reasons therefor. Arrangements for tests can be made not only in the United States, but in many foreign countries as well.

5. HOW ARE SCORES ON THE MILLER ANALOGIES TEST REPORTED

An Examinee's Report, self-addressed at the time of the examination, will be returned to you within a few days with your score on it; this will constitute your personal record. The institution(s) to which your scores are to be reported will also receive your score within a few days.

6. IS RETESTING PERMITTED

In general, retesting is permitted when a period of more than two years has elapsed. Sometimes, a retest may be required by an institution. But it is incumbent upon you to state this fact and your reasons for seeking a retest if you have previously taken the test. A space is provided on the Registration Card for this declaration.

Since all test scores are recorded at The Psychological Corporation, when an examinee retakes the test, both current and previous scores are reported. This constitutes a policy of full disclosure but does NOT mean that retaking the test is forbidden.

7. WHAT IS THE IMPORTANCE OF THE SCORES ON THE MILLER ANALOGIES TEST

7. WHAT IS THE IMPORTANCE OF THE SCORES ON THE MILLER ANALOGIES TEST

It can be said without equivocation that the scores on the MILLER ANALOGIES TEST are important for the candidate's acceptance. It can be equally firmly stated that this professional program places a high value on the scores achieved on this examination. This is for the reason that the MILLER ANALOGIES TEST is considered to be the <u>one common denominator</u> by which applicants from <u>all</u> institutions may be compared.

However, this does not mean that the results on the MILLER ANALOGIES TEST are of greater importance than, or exclude attention from, the other — more general and more usual — factors for selection, such as previous college and university records, letters of recommendation, reports of committees that have interviewed the applicant, the high school record, and similar data concerning the ability, character, and personality of the applicant. Stated in another way, the results of this graduate-level examination will never constitute the sole basis for considering the application for admission. However, it is an important factor to be considered with the others.

VERBAL ANALOGIES

The verbal-analogy type question is now a very popular component of scholastic aptitude tests, intelligence tests, and civil service examinations; this form is also used in achievement testing.

The verbal analogy is considered an excellent measure for evaluating the ability of the student to reason with and in words. It is not a test of vocabulary per se, for very rarely are the words that are used in this type of question difficult or abstruse in meaning (as they are, for example, in the same-opposite or sentence-completion type). Rather, they are everyday terms and phrases descriptive of materials and actions familiar to all of us.

The verbal analogy is a test of <u>word relationships</u> and <u>idea relationships</u>, involving a neat and algebraic-like arrangement in ratio (proportion) form not of numbers but of words. Some testers see in this type of question the development on the verbal (linguistic or qualitative) side of the same logical reasoning as occurs on the mathematical (numerical or quantitative) side in number problems. This type of question is ranked just after the reading-comprehension type in difficulty. However, it constitutes by far the most fascinating and challenging area in aptitude testing.

In general, three levels of ability are involved in answering the verbal analogy question: first, and easiest in this connection, is the ability to understand the meanings of the words used in the question (understanding); second, and more difficult, is the ability to comprehend the relationship between the subject, or question, pair of words (the process of logical reasoning); and third, and most difficult of all, is the ability to select from the five (pairs of) choices given, that choice which bears the same relationship to (within) itself as the subject words bear to one another. This involves analysis, comparison, and judgment (the process of evaluation).

In the verbal-analogy type of question, two important symbols are generally employed, which must be thoroughly understood. These are the colon (:), which is to be translated into words when reading the question in the same way as its mathematical equivalent, that is, "is to"; and the double colon(::), which is to be translated as "in the same way as." Thus, the analogy, THIEF : PRISON :: juvenile delinquent : reformatory, is to be read, <u>A thief is to a prison in the same way as a juvenile delinquent is to a reformatory.</u> Or, reading for meaning, we would say instead, "A thief is punished by being sent to a prison in the same way as a juvenile delinquent is punished by being sent to a reformatory."

Sample Questions and Explanations

DIRECTIONS: Each question in this part consists of a pair of words in capital letters, which have a certain relationship to each other, followed by either by a third word in capital letters and five lettered words in small letters (1 blank missing) OR by five lettered pairs of words in small letters (2 blanks missing). Choose either the letter of the word that is related to the third word in capital letters OR of the pair of words that are related to each other in the same way as the first two capitalized words are related to each other, and print the letter in the space at the right.

1. EROSION : ROCKS :: DISSIPATION : _____   1._____
    A. character   B. temperance   C. penance
    D. influence   E. sincerity

2. SKELETON : BODY :: LAW : _____   2._____
    A. criminal   B. jail   C. judge
    D. society   E. jury

3. TRAIN : WHISTLE :: _____ : _____   3._____
    A. air raid : siren   B. swimmer : raft   C. singer : song
    D. car : horn   E. airplane : propeller

4. ANARCHY : LAWLESSNESS :: _____ : _____   4._____
    A. autocracy : peace   B. disturbance : safety
    C. government : order   D. confusion : law
    E. democracy : dictatorship

5. UMBRELLA : RAIN :: _____ : _____   5._____
    A. roof : snow   B. screen : insects   C. sewer : water
    D. body : disease   E. gong : dinner

Explanation of Question 1
Item A., character, is correct.
   Erosion is a geological development that wears away rocks. This is an example of a
      cause-effect relationship – a concrete relationship.
   Dissipation wears away character (Item A) in the same way; however, this is an abstract
      relationship.
   But the comparison is apt and appropriate. This is a usual, general type of analogy whose
      difficulty is compounded by the fact that a concrete relationship is compared with an
      abstract one.
Item B., temperance (moderation), is merely one aspect of character.
Item C., penance (repentance), bears no relationship to dissipation in the sense of the subject
      words.
Item D., influence, and Item E., sincerity, may or may not be affected by dissipation.
This question is an example of a one-blank analogy, that is, only one word is to be supplied in
the answer (a subject pair with a third subject word being given in the question itself).

Explanation of Question 2

Item D., <u>society</u>, is correct.

    The <u>skeleton</u> is the structural element of the <u>body</u>. This is an example of a <u>part-whole relationship</u> – a concrete relationship.

    <u>Law</u> is the structural element of society – an abstract relationship.

Item A., <u>criminal</u>, Item B., <u>jail</u>, Item C., <u>judge</u>, and Item E., <u>jury</u> are not related in the same way to <u>law</u>.

Explanation of Question 3

Item D., <u>car : horn</u>, is correct.

    A <u>train</u> uses its <u>whistle</u> for warning purposes just as a <u>car</u> uses its <u>horn</u> for the same purpose. This is an example of an <u>object-method</u> relationship.

Item A., <u>air raid : siren</u> is incorrect because an air raid is an event and not an object or thing in the sense of a train or a car.

Item B., <u>swimmer : raft</u>, Item C., <u>singer : song</u>, and Item E., <u>airplane : propeller</u>, obviously do not bear the same relationship to the subject pair.

This is an example of a two-blank analogy, that is, a pair of words is to be supplied. This is the more difficult type of analogy, and the one most frequently encountered on the examination.

Explanation of Question 4

Item C., <u>government : order</u>, is correct.

    <u>Anarchy</u>, or no government, is characterized by <u>lawlessness</u> while a <u>government</u> is characterized by <u>order</u>. This is an example of an <u>object (situation) : characteristic</u> relationship.

Item A., <u>autocracy : peace</u>, is incorrect since very often autocracy (absolute monarchy or rule by an individual) is characterized by war.

Item B., <u>disturbance : safety</u>, is manifestly untrue.

Item D., <u>confusion : law</u>, is likewise untrue.

Item E., <u>democracy : dictatorship</u>, bears no relationship to the meaning conveyed by the subject pair.

Explanation of Question 5

Item B., <u>screen : insects</u>, is correct.

    By means of an <u>umbrella</u>, one keeps the <u>rain</u> off his person just as a <u>screen</u> keeps <u>insects</u> out of the house. This is an example of an <u>object : assists</u> relationship.

Item A., <u>roof : snow</u>, is not correct since a roof keeps out many other things as well, e.g., light, heat, rain, insects, etc.

Item C., <u>sewer : water</u>, is incorrect since a sewer keeps water <u>in</u> or water flows through and in a sewer.

Item D., <u>body : disease</u>, is incorrect since often disease enters and destroys the body.

Item E., <u>gong : dimmer</u>, is incorrect since the gong merely summons to dinner but does not keep anyone away.

    As can be discerned from the examples above, there are many possible relationships on which word analogies may be formed. Some of these will be listed and illustrated below. However, the important point is not to ponder over labels and attempt to peg the relationships thereby. This is unnecessary as well as time-consuming. The real object or the real method is to examine and to fully comprehend the relationship expressed in the subject pair and then to select as the correct answer that item which most <u>approximately</u> is in greatest consonance with all or most of the aspects of the given relationship.

Types of Analogies

Some or all of the following types of analogies or relationships are to be found on scholastic aptitude tests:

1. PART : WHOLE
   Example: LEG : BODY :: wheel : car

2. CAUSE : EFFECT
   Example: RAIN : FLOOD :: disease : epidemic

3. CONCRETE : ABSTRACT
   Example: ROAD : VEHICLE :: life : person

4. WORD : SYNONYM
   Example: VACUOUS : EMPTY :: seemly : fit

5. WORD : ANTONYM
   Example: SLAVE : FREEMAN :: desolate : joyous

6. OBJECT : MATERIAL
   Example: COAT : WOOL :: dress : cotton

7. OBJECT : DEFINITION
   Example: ASSEVERATE : AFFIRM :: segregate : separate

8. OBJECT : SEX
   Example: COLT : MARE :: buck : doe

9. TIME : TIME
   Example: DAY : NIGHT :: sunrise : sunset

10. DEGREE : DEGREE
    Example: HAPPY : ECSTATIC :: warm : hot

11. OBJECT : TOOL
    Example: STENCIL : TYPEWRITER :: thread : needle

12. USER : TOOL
    Example: FARMER : HOE :: dentist : drill

13. CREATOR : CREATION
    Example: ARTIST : PICTURE :: poet : poem

14. CATEGORY : TYPE
    Example: RODENT : SQUIRREL :: fish : flounder

15. PERSON (ANIMAL, ETC.) : CHARACTERISTIC
    Example: MONSTER : FEROCITY :: baby : helplessness

16. OBJECT : CHARACTERISTIC
    Example: PICKLE : SOUR :: sugar : sweet

17. PERSON : FUNCTION
    Example: TEACHER : EDUCATION :: doctor : health

18. INSTRUMENT : FUNCTION
    Example: CAMERA : PHOTOGRAPHY :: ruler : measurement

19. WORD : GRAMMATICAL FORM
    Example: WE : I :: they : he

20. SYMBOL : ATTITUDE
    Example: SALUTE : PATRIOTISM :: prayer : religion

21. REWARD : ACTION
    Example: MEDAL : BRAVERY :: trophy : championship

22. OBJECT : HINDERS
    Example: NOISE : STUDY :: rut : car

23. OBJECT : ASSISTS
    Example: WATER : THIRST :: food : hunger

24. PERSON : RELATIONSHIP
    Example: FATHER : SON :: uncle : nephew

25. OBJECT : LOCALE
    Example: SHIP : WATER :: airplane : air

26. OBJECT : METHOD
    Example: DOOR : KEY :: safe : combination

27. QUALITY : ABSENCE
    Example: FORTITUDE : COWARDICE :: carefully : casually

28. QUALITY : PROFUSION
    Example: WIND : TORNADO :: water : flood

29. SIZE : SIZE
    Example: BOAT : SHIP :: lake : sea

30. GENUS : SPECIES
    Example: RODENT : RAT :: canine : wolf

There are other relationships, but these will suffice to show some of those more frequently occurring.

SUGGESTIONS FOR ANSWERING THE VERBAL ANALOGY QUESTION (APTITUDE)

1.   Always keep in mind that a verbal analogy is a relationship of likeness between two things, consisting in the resemblances not, usually, of the things themselves but of two or more of their attributes, functions, circumstances, or effects. Therefore, in the one-blank or two-blank fill-ins, you are not looking so much for similarity in structure (although this may prove to be a factor, too), as you are for a relationship in the <u>functioning</u> of the subject words.

2.   How do we proceed to answer the verbal-analogy type question? First, discover for yourself in a meaningful way the exact relationship existing between the subject words. Whether you are able to label or tag this relationship is not so important (as we have said before) as to <u>understand</u> the relationship that exists. The logical second and final step is to examine the possible answers given and to ascertain which of these possibilities, on the basis of <u>meaning</u>, <u>order</u>, and <u>form</u>, best bears a similar relationship to the subject pair.

3.   For the analogy in question, the subject words (i.e., the question words given in the first part of the analogy) need not be of the same class, type, order, or species as the object words (i.e., the answer words or fill-ins). For example, in the analogy. BUCCANEER : SAILOR :: fungus : plant, the subject words in capital letters are types of people, the object words in small letters refer to types of things. However, the analogy that exists is on the basis of a descriptive relationship between these two different sets of words. (The first word in each pair constitutes the depredatory or despoiling form of the second, which is the general category name.) Thus, it is actually the <u>total</u> effect of the first pair on each other that is being compared with the <u>total</u> effect of the second pair on each other: this is what really counts, and not the individual components of each pair.

4.   The order of the object words must be in the same sequence as the order of the subject words. For example, the analogy, INAUGURATION : PRESIDENT :: ordination : priest, is correct. But, INAUGURATION : PRESIDENT :: priest : ordination, would be incorrect. Watch for the reversal of order in word sequence; it is a common source of entrapment for the uninitiated.

5.   Likewise, it is necessary to check to see that the parts of speech used in the analogy are the same, and occur in the same sequence. For example, if the subject pair contains a noun and an adjective in that order, the object pair <u>must</u> contain a noun and an adjective in that order. Thus, MOTHER : GOOD :: murderer : bad, is correct. But, MOTHER ; GOOD :: murderer : badly, is incorrect.

6.   The best way to answer this type of question — one-blank or two-blanks — is to study intensively the relationship contained in the given pair. Having fully comprehended this relationship and, perhaps, having "labeled" it, proceed to scan the possible answers, choosing the most likely one. This will save time, and avoid needless trial and error.

SUGGESTIONS FOR ANSWERING THE VERBAL ANALOGY QUESTION (ACHIEVEMENT)

1.   All of the suggestions for answering the verbal analogy question (aptitude) listed above are equally valid for answering the achievement-type of verbal analogy question. In addition, the various types of analogies or relationships, in one form or other, previously tabulated, may also be found in this second type of verbal analogy question.

2.   However, by virtue of the fact that this second type is testing achievement or acquired knowledge, by far the greatest number of these questions will stress content or fact. In other words, while it is entirely possible (and many such questions are provided in the various tests that follow) that abstract conceptual relationships may be used in connection with the achievement type, comparatively few will exclusively emphasize or deal with evaluator abstractions per se. Rather, facts in the form of events, authorship, locale, time, size, shape, color, rank, family, etc., will form the basis of the analogous relationships to be discerned and applied.

3.   But, this does not mean that the achievement-type of verbal analogy question will be easier to answer than the aptitude-type. On the contrary. By keen and analytical reasoning, the aptitude question can be successfully answered. Not so with the achievement question. Here, one must have knowledge — and positive grasp — of the material presented. Inductive or deductive thinking will still play a part in rendering a choice. But this factor will be a small one compared to the much larger concern of comprehending and identifying the information presented. Therefore, knowledge of subject matter is of paramount importance in this area, and the suggestions made in the Introduction for further study of the achievement areas, are of vital importance to the candidate.

4.   Let us illustrate by some concrete examples.
     (The following analogy questions are all of the 2-blank type.)
     <u>From the area of literature</u>
     (1)   CLYDE GRIFFITHS : THEODORE DREISER ::
           1.   Budd Schulberg : F. Scott Fitzgerald
           2.   Scarlett O'Hara : Harper Lee
           3.   Julien Sorel : John Galsworthy
           4.   Frederic Henry : Ernest Hemingway
           5.   Becket : Henry II
     It becomes readily apparent that this analogy is based upon the relationship of a character in a book to the author of that book. In the aptitude-type, the pith of the challenge would reside in <u>seeing this relationship of character to author</u> (with the question, of course, expressed in a less specific form). This insight alone would probably suffice to achieve an answer or would be the answer itself. However, this is where the achievement verbal analogy question begins. Having perceived the relationship (the easiest part of the task), one must now grapple with the facts. What other item in the answer-stem reflects a similar relationship in fact (not in concept alone)? The answer here is Item 4.

(2) WILLIAM TYNDALE : BIBLE ::
1. Dante : <u>Divina Commedia</u>
2. George Chapman : <u>Iliad</u>
3. Christopher Marlowe : <u>Tamburlaine the Great</u>
4. Alexander Pope : <u>The Dunciad</u>
5. Thomas Gray : <u>Elegy Written in a Country Churchyard</u>

The relationship here is one of author to his work in a particular form — a translation of the work. This fact of scholarship content must be known to enable the candidate to go beyond the relationship, that is, to find the correct factual answer. The correct answer is 2.

(3) CHRISTINA ROSSETTI : DANTE GABRIEL ROSSETTI
1. Rose Macaulay : Thomas Babington Macaulay
2. Mary Shelley : Percy Bysshe Shelley
3. Elizabeth Barrett : Robert Browning
4. Edith Sitwell : Sacheverell Sitwell
5. Emily Dickinson : Elinor Wylie

The relationship is evidently one of sister to brother, both of whom were distinguished authors. More important is knowledge of the fact that there is only one pair among the answer-items which fulfills the special blood relationship as well as the general author relationship. This cannot come from mere deduction. It must be based upon acquired information, learned and overlearned. The correct answer is 4.

Enough has been said and hinted at up to this point to clinch the thesis that has been proposed, namely, that the achievement-type question begins where the aptitude-type leaves off; that the MILLER TEST becomes a graduate vehicle in the sense, and in the directions, that it calls upon the faculties of content and learning; that the degree of mastery entailed in answering the aptitude-type is exceeded by the demands of the achievement-type; and that, finally, specific preparation in the form of review of content — preferably in the form of area summaries — must be attempted for effective preparation.

———————

There follow Tests in the various areas of the MILLER examination which should serve to achieve for the candidate the most thorough-going, functional, directed preparation ever developed for this test. More than 2,000 questions — both of the 1-blank and 2-blank-types — ae comprised in these Tests, the most overwhelming array of such questions ever assembled in any one vehicle of study. It is now up to the candidate to essay as many of these questions as possible, without failing at least to <u>sample</u> all of the fields. A complete, page-by-page, question-by-question, application should be the desideratum.

TESTS IN VERBAL ANALOGIES – 1 BLANK
— GENERAL INFORMATION
— GENERAL VOCABULARY

DIRECTIONS: Each question in this part consists of two capitalized words which have a certain relationship to each other, and a third capitalized word which is followed by five lettered words in small letters. Choose the letter of the word which is related in the SAME way to the third capitalized word as the first two capitalized words are related to each other. *PRINT THE LETTER OF THE CORRECT ANSWER IN THE SPACE AT THE RIGHT.*

TEST 1

1. VIAREGGIO AND SANTANDER : SEASIDE RESORTS :: CARNAVALET AND   1.____
   UFFIZI : _____
   A. military academies   B. opera houses   C. museums
   D. banks   E. theaters

2. REBOZO AND HUARACHE : ARTICLES OF CLOTHING :: FANDANGO AND   2.____
   SEVILLANA : _____
   A. gymnastic exercises   B. orchestral compositions
   C. dances   D. games
   E. priest's vestments

3. ZUM BEI-SPIEL : FOR EXAMPLE :: AMOUR PROPRE : _____   3.____
   A. love   B. propriety
   C. one's possessions   D. self-esteem
   E. kindness

4. CIRCA : ABOUT :: QUID PRO QUO : _____   4.____
   A. something of value   B. the same thing
   C. nothing for nothing   D an equivalent
   E. ubiquitous

5. LAS RAMBLAS AND VITTORIO VENETO : BOULEVARDS :: LYONS AND   5.____
   AVIGNON : _____
   A. railroads   B. wine   C. silk
   D. oil refineries   E. airports

6. ENCHILADAS AND POLENTA : FOODS :: SORBONNE AND SALERNO : _____   6.____
   A. stadiums   B. universities   C. monasteries
   D. towns   E. schools

7. CARPE DIEM : ENJOY THE DAY :: DEUS EX MACHINA : _____   7.____
   A. Superman   B. feat of skill   C. unmotivated device
   D. Deuteronomy   E. oracle

8. SIC : THUS :: IBID : _____   8.____
    A. ipse dixit   B. tantamount   C. as before
    D. in the same chapter E. ibis

9. WILTON : RUG :: "THE ABRAHAM LINCOLN OF MEXICO" : _____   9.____
    A. Hidalgo   B. Cardenas   C. Camacho
    D. Villa   E. Juarez

10. THE INVALIDES : PARIS :: SANTA CROCE : _____   10.____
    A. Florence   B. Naples   C. Rome
    D. Milan   E. Venice

11. MODELING: CHASING:: PLANISHING : _____   11.____
    A. repousse   B. filigree   C. piercing
    D. sawing   E. peening

12. SPRIGGING : CERAMICS :: WEDGING : _____   12.____
    A. impasto   B. intaglio   C. sgraffito
    D. gouging   E. phenolics

13. SOFTWOOD : CEDAR :: HARDWOOD : _____   13.____
    A. pine   B. fir   C. redwood
    D. larch   E. walnut

14. DISTORTION AND ELONGATION IN PAINTING : EL GRECO ::   14.____
    DISTORTION AND ELONGATION IN SCULPTURE : _____
    A. Maillol   B. Rodin   C. Saint-Gaudens
    D. Da Vinci   E. Lehmbruck

15. GARDEN CITY : RADIAL CITY PLAN :: PARIS : _____   15.____
    A. Rome   B. San Francisco   C. Washington, D.C.
    D. London   E. St. Louis

16. SURPRISE SYMPHONY : HAYDN :: JUPITER SYMPHONY : _____   16.____
    A. Handel   B. Mendelssohn   C. Tchaikovsky
    D. Mozart   E. Berlioz

17. THE ITALIAN SYMPHONY : MENDELSSOHN :: NEW WORLD SYMPHONY :   17.____
    _____
    A. Dvorak   B. Liszt   C. Scheimann
    D. Bach   E. Williams

18. MARCH OF THE LITTLE LEAD SOLDIERS : PIERNET :: MARCH OF THE   18.____
    TIN SOLDIERS : _____
    A. von Weber   B. de Koven   C. Wagner
    D. Herbert   E. Tchaikovsky

19. FAUST SYMPHONY : LISZT :: FAUST OVERTURE _____   19.____
    A. Bach   B. Beethoven   C. Brahms
    D. Wagner   E. Verdi

20. AIDA : VERDI :: FAUST : _____   20.____
    A. Rossini   B. Puccini   C. Bizet
    D. Gounod   E. Delibes

21. PINKERTON : CHO-CHO-SAN :: FIGARO : _____   21.____
    A. Susanna   B. Louise   C. Lucia
    D. Santuzza   E. Gilda

22. DESDEMONA : OTELLO :: AIDA : _____   22.____
    A. Rudolph   B. Rhadames   C. Boris
    D. Don Jose   E. Don Giovanni

23. CEZANNE : APPLES :: BONHEUR : _____   23.____
    A. trees   B. landscapes   C. marines
    D. animals   E. peasants

24. MONET : IMPRESSIONISM :: PICASSO : _____   24.____
    A. pointillism   B. nocturnes   C. cubism
    D. surrealism   E. etchings

25. CLOISTERS : MEDIEVAL ART :: WHITNEY MUSEUM : _____   25.____
    A. Romanesque and Gothic sculpture
    B. Textiles and applied art
    C. Rembrandt collection
    D. American art
    E. Contemporary America

_____

KEY (CORRECT ANSWERS)

1	C	6.	B	11.	E	16.	D	21.	A
2.	C	7.	C	12.	C	17.	A	22.	B
3.	D	8.	D	13.	E	18.	E	23.	D
4.	D	9.	E	14.	E	19.	D	24.	C
5.	C	10.	A	15.	C	20.	D	25.	D

_____

TEST 2

1. SYSTOLE : DIASTOLE :: TRUNCATION : _____   1.____
   - A. shortening
   - B. shrinkage
   - C. elongation
   - D. mutilation
   - E. dicacity

2. BLANCHED : PALLOR :: TELIC : _____   2.____
   - A. ecbasis
   - B. summary
   - C. intuitior
   - D. beginning
   - E. end

3. PLETHORIC : SUPERFLUOUS :: SUBLIMINAL : _____   3.____
   - A. subterranean
   - B. subconscious
   - C. superb
   - D. fantastic
   - E. Freudian

4. PARIAH : OUTCAST :: MULLAH : _____   4.____
   - A. teacher
   - B. judge
   - C. martinet
   - D. constable
   - E. priest

5. KEYNOTE : TONICITY :: DIAPASON: _____   5.____
   - A. gamut
   - B. clef
   - C. chord
   - D. organ
   - E. harmony

6. JABBER : GIBBERISH :: QUIDNUNC : _____   6.____
   - A. quisling
   - B. factotum
   - C. theorist
   - D. testator
   - E. executor

7. FIREPROOF : FLAMMABLE :: HALCYON : _____   7.____
   - A. calm
   - B. heavenly
   - C. stormy
   - D. ancient
   - E. pandemic

8. FINIAL : PINNACLE :: PEDIMENT : _____   8.____
   - A. basement
   - B. footing
   - C. gable
   - D. obstruction
   - E. sediment

9. DEBIT : CREDIT :: DENOUEMENT : _____   9.____
   - A. climax
   - B. untying
   - C. complication
   - D. outcome
   - E. demission

10. CINCTURE: WAIST :: SPHINCTER : _____   10.____
    - A. didoes
    - B. bone splint
    - C. blood clot
    - D. orifice
    - E. spirene

11. CATAMARAN : RAFT :: TERMAGANT : _____   11.____
    - A. spinster
    - B. benedict
    - C. grisette
    - D. osprey
    - E. virago

12. CATALYST : CHANGE :: ACCELERATOR : _____   12.____
    - A. cylinder
    - B. inertia
    - C. motion
    - D. orology
    - E. actinism

13. CAPE : PROMONTORY :: WADI : _____

    A. river   B. fen   C. meadow

    D. waterfall   E. savanna

13.____

14. BRASS : COPPER :: PEWTER : _____

    A. lead   B. zinc   C. silver

    D. bronze   E. tin

14.____

15. ACOLYTE : ALTAR :: CAMPANOLOGIST : _____

    A. tours   B. bells   C. harebells

    D. fields   E. campaigns

15.____

16. SAUTEEING : COOKERY :: FAGOTING : _____

    A. juggling   B. forestry   C. embroidery

    D. burning   E. faience

16.____

17. PROLOGUE : EPILOGUE :: PROTASIS : _____

    A. synecdoche   B. epigenesis   C. apódosis

    D. apogee   E. apotheosis

17.____

18. PHILIPPIC : DENUNCIATION :: EUREKA : _____

    A. approbation   B. confirmation   C. Archimedes

    D. Demothenes   E. discovery

18.____

19. LOGGIA : GALLERY :: JALOUSIE : _____

    A. jamb   B. dowel   C. lintel

    D. balcony   E. louver

19.____

20. EUPEPTIC : DIGESTION :: EUPHEMISTIC : _____

    A. speech   B. race   C. sound

    D. drug   E. manner

20.____

21. ETYMOLOGY : WORDS :: HAGIOLOGY : _____

    A. saints   B. senility   C. selling

    D. haplosis   E. idolatry

21.____

22. DOWSER : ROD :: GEOMANCER : _____

    A. plants   B. maps   C. pebbles

    D. configurations E. dice

22.____

23. ANNULAR : RING :: NUMMULAR : _____

    A. shell   B. mummy   C. limb

    D. stamps   E. coin

23.____

24. NOMARCHY : PROVINCE :: ENTROPY : _____

    A. hypothec   B. enzyme   C. noil

    D. satrapy   E. energy

24.____

25. ASPIC : GARNISH :: FILATURE : _____   25.____
    A. filiation   B. fillisters   C. silk
    D. graupel   E. weaving

KEY (CORRECT ANSWERS)

1	E	6.	B	11.	E	16.	C	21.	A
2.	E	7.	C	12.	C	17.	C	22.	D
3.	B	8.	C	13.	A	18.	E	23.	E
4.	A	9.	C	14.	A	19.	E	24.	E
5.	A	10.	D	15.	B	20.	A	25.	C

TEST 3

1. FAN : AIR :: NEWSPAPER : _____   1.____
    A. literature   B. reporter   C. information
    D. subscription   E. reader

2. AQUARIUM : FISH :: APIARY : _____   2.____
    A. bees   B. eagles   C. flowers
    D. monkeys   E.. cattle

3. WALL : MORTAR :: NATION : _____   3.____
    A. family   B. people   C. patriotism
    D. geography   E. boundaries

4. DISPARAGE : DESPISE :: PRAISE : _____   4.____
    A. dislike   B. adore   C. acclaim
    D. advocate   E. compliment

5. POUR : SPILL :: LIE : _____   5.____
    A. deception   B. misstatement   C. falsehood
    D. perjury   E. fraud

6. SAPPHIRE : EMERALD :: SKY : _____   6.____
    A. storm   B. world   C. star
    D. grass   E. purity

7. APPLE : POTATO :: CHERRY : _____   7.____
    A. plum   B. blueberry   C. tomato
    D. squash   E. radish

8. PRODIGY : ABILITY :: OCEAN : _____   8.____
    A. water   B. waves   C. ships
    D. icebergs   E. current

9. CHIMNEY : SMOKE :: GUIDE : _____   9.____
    A. snare   B. compass   C. hunter
    D. firewood   E. wild game

10. WING : AIRPLANE :: HAND : _____   10.____
    A. finger   B. applause   C. dish
    D. clock   E. work

11. TAXES : OBLIGATION :: VOTING : _____   11.____
    A. election   B. campaign   C. tally
    D. restriction   E. privilege

12. LAWYER : COURT :: SOLDIER : _____   12.____
    A. battle   B. victory   C. training
    D. rifle   E. discipline

13. SYNONYM : MEANING :: HOMONYM : _____
    A. purport   B. position   C. pronunciation
    D. relationship   E. sameness

    13.____

14. SENILE : INFANTILE :: SUPPER : _____
    A. snack   B. breakfast   C. dinner
    D. daytime   E. evening

    14.____

15. FURNITURE : PERIOD :: WINE : _____
    A. vintage   B. aroma   C. bouquet
    D. proof   E. mellowness

    15.____

16. OBSTRUCT : IMPEDE :: IMPENETRABLE : _____
    A. forebearing   B. hidden   C. impervious
    D. merciful   E. open

    16.____

17. FELICITY : BLISS :: CONGENIAL : _____
    A. clever   B. compatible   C. fierce
    D. unfriendly   E. witty

    17.____

18. CAUTIOUS : CIRCUMSPECT :: PRECIPITOUS : _____
    A. deep   B. flat   C. high
    D prophetic   E. steep

    18.____

19. INQUISITIVE : INCURIOUS :: MANIFEST : _____
    A. latent   B. many-sided   C. obvious
    D. proclamation   E. unique

    19.____

20. FETISH : TALISMAN :: FEALTY : _____
    A. allegiance   B. faithlessness   C. payment
    D. real estate   E. sensitivity

    20.____

21. PERSPICACIOUS : DULL :: PACIFIC : _____
    A. arctic   B. bellicose   C. giddy
    D. quiet   E. restrained

    21.____

22. SHOE : CALF :: PILLOW : _____
    A. duck   B. curtain   C. sleep
    D. goose   E. soft

    22.____

23. ROCK : GRAVEL :: WHEAT : _____
    A. oats   B. mill   C. loaf
    D. flour   E. mill

    23.____

24. GINGHAM : SATIN :: LEAD : _____
    A. silk   B. copper   C. pewter
    D. smooth   E. platinum

    24.____

25. BLOW : DODGE :: GLARE : _____   25.____
     A. wink   B. squint   C. myopia
     D. myosis   E. leer

KEY (CORRECT ANSWERS)

1	C	6.	D	11.	E	16.	C	21.	B
2.	A	7.	E	12.	A	17.	B	22.	D
3.	C	8.	A	13.	C	18.	E	23.	D
4.	B	9.	C	14.	B	19.	A	24.	E
5.	B	10.	D	15.	A	20.	A	25.	B

TEST 4

1. WAR : SORROW :: PEACE : _____   1.____
   A. happiness   B. remorse   C. battle
   D. fright   E. Europe

2. UNKNOWN : KNOWN :: FUTURE : _____   2.____
   A. famous   B. past   C. present
   D. expensive   E. now

3. COSTLY : CHEAP :: SCARCE : _____   3.____
   A. expense   B. abundant   C. nasty
   D. bargain   E. buy

4. LEAD : CORK :: SINK : _____   4.____
   A. float   B. water   C. heavy
   Dl light   E. drop

5. GULF : OCEAN :: PENINSULA : _____   5.____
   A. cape   B. water   C. river
   D. lake   E. land

6. FALSIFICATION : FORGERY :: RECOLLECTION : _____   6.____
   A. negation   B. gross   C. cruelty
   D. memory   E. selfishness

7. DULL : BLUNT :: KEENNESS : _____   7.____
   A. file   B. knife   C. acuity
   D. tool   E. flint

8. GLOOM : MELANCHOLIC :: SIGN : _____   8.____
   A. symbolic   B. pariah   C. conic
   D. light   E. choleric

9. TIME : CLOCK :: TEMPERATURE : _____   9.____
   A. thermometer   B. warm   C. mercury
   D. degrees   E. cold

10. EXPLAIN : INTERPRET :: DOMETICATE : _____   10.____
    A. reveal   B. question   C. acclimatize
    D. acclaim   E. converse

11. IRRADIATION : EFFULGENCE :: CONCLUSION : _____   11.____
    A. doubt   B. proof   C. dissent
    D. decisive   E. casuistry

12. SCARCE : ABUNDANT :: COSTLY : _____   12.____
    A. luminous   B. fair   C. expense
    D. cheap   E. money

13. OCEAN : BAY :: CONTINENT : _____

    A. lake   B. beats   C. peninsula

    D. pay   E. shore

13.____

14. DESPONDENCY : DEJECTION :: SHARP : _____

    A. prayer   B. piquant   C. desire

    D. election   E. projection

14.____

15. MISSIONARY : CONVERT :: MENTOR : _____

    A. disciple   B. expedition   C. choleric

    D. Protestant   E. Catholic

15.____

16. HAPPINESS : PEACE :: SORROW : _____

    A. trouble   B. war   C. fright

    D. death   E. bellicose

16.____

17. DELEGATE : REPRESENTATIVE :: RENEWAL : _____

    A. resignation   B. alive   C. relapse

    D. resurrection   E. end

17.____

18. CAUTIOUS : TRUSTFUL :: SUSPICIOUS : _____

    A. sordid   B. fearful   C. meticulous

    D. confiding   E. domineering

18.____

19. VIGILANT : CARELESS :: CONSERVATIVE : _____

    A. liberal   B. discriminative   C. reserve

    D. guarded   E. free

19.____

20. ELECTRICITY : DYNAMO :: HONEY : _____

    A. bee   B. wire   C. lightning

    D. tool   E. light

20.____

21. PRAISE : DEFAME :: ADMIRE : _____

    A. rile   B. despise   C. hate

    D. oppose   E. vile

21.____

22. CHASTE : SENSUOUS :: GOOD : _____

    A. deviltry   B. revel   C. candid

    D. evil   E. bad

22.____

23. PENURY : POVERTY :: LUXURY : _____

    A. waste   B. dread   C. wealth

    D. misery   E. dollars

23.____

24. INDUCT : INITIATE :: INDICT : _____

    A. deduct   B. indulge   C. charge

    D. prolong   E. instinct

24.____

25. JOY : AFFECTION :: MISERY : _____   25.____
    A. sympathy   B. deprivation   C. pity
    D. reverence   E. contempt

KEY (CORRECT ANSWERS)

1	A	6.	D	11.	D	16.	B	21.	B
2.	C	7.	C	12.	D	17.	D	22.	D
3.	B	8.	A	13.	C	18.	D	23.	C
4.	A	9.	A	14.	B	19.	A	24.	C
5.	E	10.	C	15.	A	20.	A	25.	E

TEST 5

1. ROOM : MAID :: CHURCH : _____
   A. sexton   B. library   C. servant
   D. madame   E. child

   1.____

2. SAGACIOUS : PROFOUND :: PROFUSE : _____
   A. copious   B. copy   C. erudite
   D. lack   E. paucity

   2.____

3. OBEDIENCE : SEDITION :: UNION : _____
   A. rendition   B. door   C. partition
   D. snare   E. dissociation

   3.____

4. ODOR : EFFLUVIUM :: DICTIONARY : _____
   A. effect   B. mucous   C. mouth
   D. encyclopedia E. effervescence

   4.____

5. RANCOR : HOSTILITY :: ABETTOR : _____
   A. amity   B. accessory   C. gratification
   D. diversion   E. enemy

   5.____

6. AVERSION : ATTRACTION :: LAW : _____
   A. theory   B. hypothesis   C. abstraction
   D. element   E. declaration

   6.____

7. WEEK : MONTH :: DAY : _____
   A. century   B. minute   C. year
   D. hour   E. week

   7.____

8. UNCLE : NIECE :: FATHER : _____
   A. cousin   B. son   C. daughter
   D. nephew   E. aunt

   8.____

9. HOTEL : LOBBY :: BOOK : _____
   A. elevator   B. page   C. preface
   D. author   E. porter

   9.____

10. DESIRABLE : ACCEPTABLE :: RESOLVED : _____
    A. deleterious B. determined   C. demure
    D. capricious   E. absolved

    10.____

11. JAIL : PRISON :: GUERDON : _____
    A. recompense   B. rabid   C. bars
    D. look   E. staid

    11.____

12. ADMISSION : RECEPTION :: ADJUST : _____
    A. discharge   B. omission   C. emission
    D. settle   E. session

    12.____

13. TREACHERY : TRAITOR :: PLANS : _____   13.____
    A. architect   B. builder   C. profession
    D. designer   E. destruction

14. REVEAL : CONCEAL :: DESCEND : _____   14.____
    A. convey   B. ascend   C. maintain
    D. exhibit   E. desolate

15. HIDE : LEATHER :: FLING : _____   15.____
    A. shoe   B. bird   C. fluid
    D. tannery   E. fire

16. RECURRENCE : PERIODIC :: DETERMINATION : _____   16.____
    A. secular   B. perish   C. rhetoric
    D. period   E. perseverance

17. CHEMISTRY : DISTILL :: GRAMMAR : _____   17.____
    A. differentiation   B. psychology   C. water
    D. conjugate   E. linguistic

18. LIBRARY : LIBRARIAN :: SCHOOL : _____   18.____
    A. porter   B. teacher   C. books
    D. catalogue   E. reference

19. MAGNITUDE : SMALLNESS :: ABSENT : _____   19.____
    A. present   B. largess   C. infinity
    D. universe   E. enormous

20. STEEL : BRIDGES :: WOOD : _____   20.____
    A. writing   B. library   C. paper
    D. news   E. papyrus

21. INVALIDATE : ABROGATE :: DELUSION : _____   21.____
    A. erosion   B. mirror   C. diffusion
    D. illusion   E. all

22. NEUROTIC : NORMAL :: HARMFUL : _____   22.____
    A. neurosis   B. neuter   C. harmless
    D. nervous   E. courageous

23. ERRONEOUS : EMENDATION :: NEBULOUS : _____   23.____
    A. failure   B. explanatory   C. hostility
    D. obscurity   E. clarification

24. BREACH : ACCORD :: DISSOCIATION : _____   24.____
    A. gap   B. cord   C. brake
    D. break   E. connection

25. CREATION : BEGINNING :: CATACLYSM : _____   25.____
    A. consumption   B. demolition   C. devastation
    D. development   E. destruction

KEY (CORRECT ANSWERS)

1	A	6.	B	11.	A	16.	E	21.	D
2.	A	7.	E	12.	D	17.	D	22.	C
3.	E	8.	C	13.	A	18.	B	23.	E
4.	D	9.	C	14.	B	19.	A	24.	E
5.	B	10.	B	15.	E	20.	C	25.	E

TEST 6

1. RIVER : DITCH :: NATURAL : _____   1._____
   A. synthetic   B. compound   C. swampland
   D. drainage   E. chemist

2. LITTLE : LESS :: LOW : _____   2._____
   A. least   B. big   C. small
   D. tiny   E. lower

3. FLOWER : PETAL :: ALL : _____   3._____
   A. garden   B. part   C. plant
   D. rose   E. blossom

4. HORSE : OAK :: ANIMAL : _____   4._____
   A. plant   B. cow   C. farm
   D. milk   E. cat

5. LIFE: LIGHT :: PEACE : _____   5._____
   A. dove   B. hope   C. bird
   D. fly   E. money

6. FACE : NOSE :: ALL : _____   6._____
   A. body   B. part   C. head
   D. man   E. people

7. MEND : REND :: SEND : _____   7._____
   A. beg   B. receive   C. fix
   D. sew   E. amend

8. MOVEMENT : FALLING :: SWIM : _____   8._____
   A. floating   B. rising   C. walking
   D. flying   E. dive

9. TAKE : BUT :: ACCEPT : _____   9._____
   A. except   B. bring   C. thus
   D. for   E. keep

10. KNIFE : CUT :: GUN : _____   10._____
    A. shoot   B. run   C. sharp
    D. bird   E. hat

11. NEPHEW : UNCLE :: NIECE : _____   11._____
    A. mother   B. cousin   C. sister
    D. brother   E. aunt

12. SPYGLASS : SEE :: TELEPHONE : _____   12._____
    A. lens   B. distance   C. telegraph
    D. hear   E. shout

13. HAT : HEAD :: ROOF : _____   13._____
    A. warm   B. attic   C. straw
    D. house   E. shoe

14. LAUGHTER : JOY :: TEAR : _____   14._____
    A. grief   B. sob   C. girls
    D. grin   E. sorrow

15. SEED : PLANT :: EGG : _____   15._____
    A. bird   B. feathers   C. root
    D. shell   E. leaf

16. HEAT : STEAM :: COLD : _____   16._____
    A. dry   B. ice   C. wet
    D. cold   E. stars

17. ROSE : PLANT : LION : _____   17._____
    A. red   B. animal   C. small
    D. bird   E. thorn

18. BOTTOM : TOP :: BELOW : _____   18._____
    A. above   B. down   C. slide
    D. surface   E. spin

19. GASOLINE : AUTOMOBILE :: COAL : _____   19._____
    A. locomotive   B. burns   C. wheels
    D. smoke   E. motorcycle

20. OCEAN : BAY :: CONTINENT : _____   20._____
    A. Massachusetts B. pay   C. boats
    D. peninsula   E. send

21. FOOD : BODY :: FUEL : _____   21._____
    A. wheels   B. fire   C. engine
    D. smoke   E. pump

22. HONEY : BEE :: BOOKS : _____   22._____
    A. novels   B. sting   C. writer
    D. hive   E. wasp

23. LATE : BEHIND :: EARLY : _____   23._____
    A. alone   B. dinner   C. before
    D. soon   E. after

24. SECOND : FIRST :: ADAMS : _____   24._____
    A. president   B. Washington   C. contrast
    D. best   E. last

25. PEACE : WAR :: ORDER : _____   25.____
    A. disorder   B. explosion   C. guns
    D. battle   E. army

KEY (CORRECT ANSWERS)

1	A	6.	B	11.	E	16.	B	21.	C
2.	E	7.	B	12.	D	17.	B	22.	C
3.	B	8.	E	13.	D	18.	A	23.	C
4.	A	9.	A	14.	E	19.	A	24.	B
5.	A	10.	A	15.	A	20.	D	25.	A

TEST 7

1. EXTOL : PRAISE :: RELINQUISH : _____
    A. repay   B. inquire   C. resign
    D. emigrate   E. send

    1.____

2. BOOK : LIBRARY :: CANNON : _____
    A. artillery   B. powder   C. shell
    D. war   E. encyclopedia

    2.____

3. BIOCHEMISTRY : BIOLOGY :: PSYCHOPHYSICS : _____
    A. physiology   B. physics   C. chemistry
    D. psychology   E. psychiatry

    3.____

4. SHEEP : FLOCK :: STAR : _____
    A. planet   B. Mars   C. moon
    D. astronomy   E. constellation

    4.____

5. PEARL : WHITE :: AMBER : _____
    A. gem   B. yellow   C. color
    D. purity   E. genuine

    5.____

6. WATER : DELUGE :: LAVA : _____
    A. fire   B. eruption   C. Mt. Etna
    D. volcano   E. mountain

    6.____

7. TOOTH : GUM :: EYE : _____
    A. glasses   B. eyebrow   C. eyelash
    D. socket   E. color

    7.____

8. RAIN : MUD :: DROUGHT : _____
    A. desert   B. land   C. dust
    D. hurricane   E. water

    8.____

9. PAPER : WHITE :: CLOTH : _____
    A. dress   B. gown   C. material
    D. style   E. sew

    9.____

10. WHEN : TIME :: HOW : _____
    A. place   B. manner   C. reason
    D. why   E. where

    10.____

11. STALACTITE : HANGING :: STALAGMITE : _____
    A. cavern   B. interior   C. falling
    D. rising   E. pit

    11.____

12. THIS : THOSE :: THAT : _____
    A. these   B. those   C. they
    D. them   E. this

    12.____

13. WITH : WITHOUT :: POSSESS : _____
    A. acquire   B. buy   C. possession
    D. without   E. lack

    13.____

14. WAR : PEACE :: TEMPEST : _____
    A. temper   B. rain   C. calm
    D. storm   E. wind

    14.____

15. FLOWERS : WREATH :: BEADS : _____
    A. diamonds   B. rhinestones   C. neck
    D. necklace   E. throat

    15.____

16. COFFEE : CAFFEINE :: TOBACCO : _____
    A. cigar   B. filter   C. nicotine
    D. cigarette   E. liquor

    16.____

17. BROAD : NARROW :: DELIGHTFUL : _____
    A. hospitable   B. disagreeable   C. placid
    D. friendly   E. pleasant

    17.____

18. ARM : ELBOW :: LEG : _____
    A. knee   B. stocking   C. toe
    D. ankle   E. shoe

    18.____

19. BUTTERFLY : AIR :: WORM : _____
    A. fish   B. earth   C. insect
    D. fly   E. crawl

    19.____

20. PALACE : RICH :: HUT : _____
    A. mud   B. unhappy   C. native
    D. wealth   E. poor

    20.____

21. LAUGHTER : JOY :: WEEPING : _____
    A. sorrow   B. happiness   C. tears
    D. eyes   E. cry

    21.____

22. BLIND : SEE :: PARALYZED : _____
    A. limbs   B. cane   C. walk
    D. hear   E. crutch

    22.____

23. CHALK : BLACKBOARD :: PENCIL : _____
    A. paper   B. eraser   C. ink
    D. desk   E. write

    23.____

24. SUMMER : HEAT :: WINTER : _____
    A. warmth   B. snow   C. ice
    D. cold   E. weather

    24.____

25. RELIGION : CHURCH :: EDUCATION : _____   25.____
     A. read`   B. pupil   C. teacher
     D. book   E. school

KEY (CORRECT ANSWERS)

1	C	6.	B	11.	D	16.	C	21.	A
2.	A	7.	D	12.	A	17.	B	22.	C
3.	D	8.	C	13.	E	18.	A	23.	A
4.	E	9.	E	14.	C	19.	B	24.	D
5.	B	10.	B	15.	D	20.	E	25.	E

TEST 8

1. OUR : WE :: YOUR : _____
    A. they   B. you   C. yours
    D. us   E. their
    1._____

2. PROTECT : PROTECTIVE :: ABHOR : _____
    A. abhorred   B. abhorative   C. abhorring
    D. abhorrent   E. abhor
    2._____

3. ITINERANT : ITINERANCY :: FEUDAL : _____
    A. feudalism   B. feud   C. feudancy
    D. feudally   E. feudalness
    3._____

4. OUR : I :: YOUR : _____
    A. mine   B. my   C. he
    D. me   E. you
    4._____

5. SIN : SINFULLY :: FRIVOLITY : _____
    A. frivolfully   B. frivolious   C. frivolous
    D. frivolessness E. frivolously
    5._____

6. MELODIOUS : MELODIOUSLY :: FLABBY : _____
    A. flabbly   B. flabbious   C. flabbily
    D. flabbiously   E. flabbously
    6._____

7. GLOBULE : GLOBULAR :: IRRADIATION : _____
    A. irradiating   B. irrediated   C. irradiant
    D. irradiated   E. irradiator
    7._____

8. NEBULA : NEBULAE :: MAN-OF-WAR : _____
    A. men-of-war   B. man-of-waries C. man-of-wars
    D. mens-of-war   E. men-of-wars
    8._____

9. STINKS : STANK :: SMITES : _____
    A. smitten   B. smote   C. smite
    D. smites   E. smate
    9._____

10. BOY : BOYISH :: INFANT : _____
    A. infantil   B. infant   C. childish
    D. infantile   E. infantlike
    10._____

11. ALTRUIST : ALTRUISTIC :: DISQUIETER : _____
    A. disquietistic B. disquietic   C. disquieting
    D. disquieted   E. disquietude
    11._____

12. VIRTUOUS : VIRTUE :: DEMENTED : _____
    A. demente   B. demented   C. dement
    D. demention   E. dementia
    12._____

13. MINIMAL : MINIMALLY :: INDISPENSABLE : _____   13.____
    A. indispense   B. indispensablly   C. indispensability
    D. indispensabily   E. indispensably

14. APE : APES :: ADDENDUM : _____   14.____
    A. addends   B. addendi   C. addendums
    D. addendae   E. addenda

15. CIRCULAR : CIRCLE :: DIAMETRIC : _____   15.____
    A. diameter   B. diametic   C. diametrical
    D. diameters   E. diametrist

16. INITIAL : INITIALLY :: MERCENARY : _____   16.____
    A. mercenarily   B. mercenal   C. mercenorially
    D. mercenially   E. mercenarilly

17. DISMAL : DISMALLY :: IMPLICIT : _____   17.____
    A. implicitally   B. implicity   C. implicadly
    D. implictally   E. implicitly

18. STEWARDSHIP : STEWARDESS :: TRAGEDY : _____   18.____
    A. tragedy   B. tragedies   C. tragedienne
    D. tragedian   E. tragic

19. RATABLE : RATABILITY :: IMPARTIAL : _____   19.____
    A. impartiality   B. impartiability   C. impartiallity
    D. impartially   E. impartialability

20. ALTRUIST : ALTRUISM :: TRUANT : _____   20.____
    A. truaney   B. truancy   C. truanism
    D. truants   E. tyranny

21. DERMA : DERMAL :: IDYL : _____   21.____
    A. idyll   B. idylly   C. idyial
    D. idyol   E. idyllic

22. COHESION : COHESIVE :: PERICRANIUM : _____   22.____
    A. pericrania   B. pericran   C. pericranisive
    D. pericranial   E. pericranive

23. SING : SONG :: WAGER : _____   23.____
    A. wager   B. wage   C. bet
    D. waged   E. wagered

24. PLAUSIBLE : PLAUSIBILITY :: WHEEZY : _____   24.____
    A. wheeziness   B. wheezable   C. wheezible
    D. wheezility   E. wheezibility

25. SANGUINE : SANGUINELY :: PERFUNCTORY : _____   25._____
    A. perfunctorily   B. perfuncate   C. perfunction
    D. perfunctorly   E. perfunct

KEY (CORRECT ANSWERS)

1	B	6.	C	11.	C	16.	A	21.	E
2.	D	7.	C	12.	E	17.	E	22.	D
3.	A	8.	A	13.	E	18.	C	23.	A
4.	E	9.	B	14.	E	19.	A	24.	A
5.	E	10.	D	15.	A	20.	B	25.	A

TEST 9

1. MURKY : DARK :: GYRATE : _____   1.____
    A. move sideways   B. jar
    C. spin   D. bob up and down
    E. move in a zigzag fashion

2. OCCULT : MYSTERIOUS :: BEVY : _____   2.____
    A. cart   B. trap   C. enclosure
    D. small group   E. carpenter's tool

3. COWL : HOOD :: IMPRUDENT : _____   3.____
    A. rash   B. poor   C. saucy
    D. boastful   E. unjustified

4. SUBLIME : EXALTED :: INCONTROVERTIBLE : _____   4.____
    A. immovable   B. indisputable   C. uncontrolled
    D. doubtful   E. uncomfortable

5. CONJECTURE : SURMISE :: ABNEGATION : _____   5.____
    A. persistence   B. downfall   C. retirement
    D. self-denial   E. arrogance

6. PASTORAL : RURAL :: WREAK : _____   6.____
    A. break up   B. wear out   C. delay
    D. inflict   E. waste

7. WINCH : MACHINE FOR HOISTING :: MIGNONETTE : _____   7.____
    A. flowering plant   B. graceful dance   C. young girl
    D. insecft   E. song

8. ANNALS : CHRONICLES :: FOP : _____   8.____
    A. swindler   B. drunkard   C. quarrel
    D. dandy   E. swine

9. ABROGATE : CANCEL :: FLAGRANT : _____   9.____
    A. cruel   B. glaring   C. wandering
    D. inevitable   E. patriotic

10. MALIGNANT : EVIL :: LASSITUDE : _____   10.____
    A. unwillingness   B. weariness   C. bravery
    D. generosity   E. wastefulness

11. DILATE : EXPAND :: COPSE : _____   11.____
    A. thicket   B. trench   C. body
    D. cloak   E. shadow

12. ALACRITY : EAGERNESS :: DIFFUSED : _____
    A. delayed   B. protected   C. lighted
    D. spread   E. mishandled
                                                  12. _____

13. HOSTLER : GROOM :: SCANTLING : _____
    A. young boy   B. piece of lumber   C. humorous remark
    D. thin sheet of paper   E. small bird
                                                  13. _____

14. AMENABLE : RESPONSIVE :: BRAN : (KIND OF) _____
    A. paper   B. plant   C. berry
    D. liquor   E. chaff
                                                  14. _____

15. CANTON : DISTRICT :: AFFLUENCE : _____
    A. conceit   B. friendliness   C. sickness
    D. wealth   E. honor
                                                  15. _____

16. DESULTORY : AIMLESS :: EMULATION : _____
    A. joy   B. stinginess   C. dislike
    D. regret   E. rivalry
                                                  16. _____

17. CABAL : PLOT :: ADVENTITIOUS : _____
    A. fraudulent   B. fortunate   C. accidental
    D. inherently evil   E. unnecessary
                                                  17. _____

18. SUPERFICIAL : SHALLOW :: EXPUNGE : _____
    A. enlarge   B. drown   C. blame
    D. despair   E. efface
                                                  18. _____

19. MANUMISSION : RELEASE FROM SLAVERY :: FILBERT : _____
    A. icing   B. hazelnut
    C. sweet fruit   D. ornamental metalwork
    E. songbird
                                                  19. _____

20. ROOK : (KIND OF) BIRD :: ORDNANCE : _____
    A. military police   B. food supplies   C. official orders
    D. military weapons   E. office equipment
                                                  20. _____

21. CAROL : SONG :: PARTITION : _____
    A. spasm   B. treatment   C. division
    D. bias   E. passageway
                                                  21. _____

22. TOXIN : POISON :: TOLERATE : _____
    A. allow   B. confess   C. disobey
    D. resent   E. suspect
                                                  22. _____

23. ALTERATION : CHANGE :: ANNUL : _____
    A. corrupt   B. revise   C. enforce
    D. approve   E. cancel
                                                  23. _____

24. COMPETITION : RIVALRY :: PREPOSTEROUS : _____   24.____
    A. disguised   B. noisy   C. heavy
    C. dignified   E. absurd

25. FLING : HURL :: RETARD : _____   25.____
    A. break   B. delay   C. resume
    D. blow   E. announce

_____

KEY (CORRECT ANSWERS)

1	C	6.	D	11.	A	16.	E	21.	C
2.	D	7.	A	12.	D	17.	C	22.	A
3.	A	8.	D	13.	B	18.	E	23.	E
4.	B	9.	B	14.	E	19.	B	24.	E
5.	D	10.	B	15.	D	20.	D	25.	B

_____

TEST 10

1. COW GRASS :: HEN : _____
   - A. egg
   - B. rooster
   - C. wheat
   - D. corn
   - E. coop

   1.____

2. HOUSE : CARPENTER :: DRESS : _____
   - A. material
   - B. color
   - C. style
   - D. suit
   - E. needlewoman

   2.____

3. DAY : NIGHT :: DAWN : _____
   - A. midnight
   - B. sunshine
   - C. afternoon
   - D. twilight
   - E. moon

   3.____

4. WE : THEY :: i : _____
   - A. them
   - B. me
   - C. him
   - D. my
   - E. he

   4.____

5. HEAT : EVAPORATION :: COLD : _____
   - A. ice
   - B. refrigeration
   - C. icy
   - D. condensation
   - E. winter

   5.____

6. BUSINESS : MARKET :: GOVERNMENT : _____
   - A. judge
   - B. lawyer
   - C. laws
   - D. decrees
   - E. parliament

   6.____

7. TRAIN : RAILS :: AUTOMOBILE : _____
   - A. distance
   - B. wheels
   - C. tires
   - D. highway
   - E. itinerary

   7.____

8. MIND : PSYCHOLOGY :: BODY : _____
   - A. arteries
   - B. physiology
   - C. medicine
   - D. psychiatry
   - E. diathermy

   8.____

9. EGGS : PROTEIN :: LIVER : _____
   - A. niacin
   - B. sugar
   - C. iron
   - D. oils
   - E. starch

   9.____

10. SAIL : CLOTH :: OAR : _____
    - A. wood
    - B. paddle
    - C. canoe
    - D. boat
    - E. row

    10.____

11. LITERATURE : FICTITIOUS :: COMPOSITION : _____
    - A. novel
    - B. essay
    - C. imaginative
    - D. historical
    - E. biography

    11.____

12. WEAK : FRAIL :: STRONG : _____
    - A. stalwart
    - B. brave
    - C. courageous
    - D. honesty
    - E. power

    12.____

13. BLACK : BLACKEN :: LARGE : _____   13.____
    A. lower   B. magnify   C. magnitude
    D. manufacture   E. gigantic

14. WARP : HORIZONTAL :: WOOF : _____   14.____
    A. horizontal   B. material   C. weave
    D. vertical   E. weft

15. ALTITUDE : ALTIMETER :: SOUND : _____   15.____
    A. condenser   B. phonograph   C. photometer
    D. telephone   E. audiometer

16. FOND : INFATUATION :: ENTHUSIASTIC : _____   16.____
    A. embrace   B. torpid   C. sentimentality
    D. fluency   E. fanaticism

17. WOLF : PROWL :: SWINDLER : _____   17.____
    A. build   B. ape   C. manipulate
    D. pursue   E. prey

18. STORY : MOTIVATION :: ACTION : _____   18.____
    A. incentive   B. plot   C. reward
    D. movement   E. interpose

19. ELLIPSE : CIRCLE :: OBLONG : _____   19.____
    A. radius   B. triangle   C. diamond
    D. area   E. square

20. ISLAND : OCEAN :: LAKE : _____   20.____
    A. water   B. city   C. cape
    D. continent   E. village

21. SEE : VISIBLE :: HEAR : _____   21.____
    A. audible   B. tone   C. drums
    D. tune   E. sound

22. TRIANGLE : HEXAGON :: BIPED : _____   22.____
    A. animal   B. human   C. quadruped
    D. male   E. female

23. BIOLOGY : SCIENCE :: SCULPTURE : _____   23.____
    A. art   B. fashion   C. clay
    D. bronze   E. wood

24. I : HE :: WE : _____   24.____
    A. them   B. their   C. they
    D. your   E. him

25. LOCOMOTIVE : TRANSPORTATION :: RADIO : _____   25.____
    A. television   B. communication   C. news
    D. telephone   E. musical

KEY (CORRECT ANSWERS)

1	D	6.	E	11.	C	16.	E	21.	A
2.	E	7.	D	12.	A	17.	E	22.	C
3.	D	8.	B	13.	B	18.	A	23.	A
4.	E	9.	C	14.	D	19.	E	24.	C
5.	D	10.	A	15.	E	20.	D	25.	B

TEST 11

1. TIGER : FELINE :: WOLF : _____
    A. leonine
    B. porcupine
    C. saline
    D. porcine
    E. canine
    1.____

2. HORTICULTURE : AGRICULTURE :: POULTRY RAISING : _____
    A. farming
    B. livestock
    C. tillage
    D. terrarium
    E. mining
    2.____

3. IDEALISM : PHILOSOPHY :: IMPRESSIONISM : _____
    A. diatetics
    B. pediatrics
    C. aesthetics
    D. existentialism
    E. realism
    3.____

4. GUN : HOLSTER :: SWORD : _____
    A. Zorro
    B. plowshare
    C. soldier
    D. relic
    E. scabbard
    4.____

5. HYDROGEN : GAS :: URANIUM : _____
    A. bomb
    B. mine
    C. metal
    D. geiger counter
    E. pericardium
    5.____

6. THIEF : PRISON :: SPEEDER : _____
    A. bail
    B. fine
    C. thrill
    D. policeman
    E. automobile
    6.____

7. RADAR : AIRPLANE :: SONAR : _____
    A. blimp
    B. jamming
    C. mine
    D. submarine
    E. the Atlas
    7.____

8. QUARANTINE : EPIDEMIC :: LEVEE : _____
    A. drought
    B. invasion
    C. flood
    D. rain
    E. revelry
    8.____

9. LAYOUT : ADVERTISEMENT :: BLUEPRINT : _____
    A. foundation
    B. house
    C. architect
    D. topography
    E. picture
    9.____

10. USURPATION : POWER :: COUP D'ETAT : _____
    A. government
    B. abdication
    C. succession
    D. absolutism
    E. revolution
    10.____

11. GOOD : FAIR :: PERFECT : _____
    A. excellent
    B. poor
    C. arrant
    D. flawless
    E. peerless
    11.____

12. FULL : OVERFLOWING :: ABUNDANCE : _____
    A. plethora
    B. scarcity
    C. capacity
    D. completion
    E. sundry
    12.____

13. LEAF : ROOT :: GABLE : _____   13._____
    A. floor   B. foundation   C. fable
    D. chimney   E. porch

14. INHIBITION : REMOVAL :: TUMOR : _____   14._____
    A. treatment   B. incision   C. therapy
    D. analysis   E. diagnosis

15. DEVOTEE : ADDICT :: ENTHUSIAST : _____   15._____
    A. follower   B. iconoclast   C. fanatic
    D. supporter   E. professional

16. BUTTER : DAFFODIL :: GOLD : _____   16._____
    A. yew   B. ivy   C. lemon
    D. cheese   E. silver

17. WHEEL : BRACELET :: RING : _____   17._____
    A. hoop   B. ellipse   C. pear
    D. arm   E. concave

18. GOPHER : HAMSTER :: SQUIRREL : _____   18._____
    A. wolf   B. panther   C. bear
    D. mink   E. python

19. DOE : VIXEN :: SOW : _____   19._____
    A. drake   B. buck   C. mare
    D. gander   E. capon

20. OIL : GREASE :: WAX : _____   20._____
    A. grit   B. bee   C. paraffin
    D. relish   E. sycophant

21. CHICKEN : EGG :: PLANT : _____   21._____
    A. tree   B. bush   C. nest
    D. seed   E. root

22. LEAVE : FAREWELL :: ARRIVE : _____   22._____
    A. leave   B. joy   C. au revoir
    D. meet   E. greeting

23. BETTER : GOOD :: WORSE : _____   23._____
    A. bad   B. better   C. as good
    D. poor   E. inferior

24. AUTHOR : LITERATURE :: TAILOR : _____   24._____
    A. design   B. material   C. clothes
    D. thread   E. color

25. CAR : BRAKES :: SHIP : _____   25.____
     A. anchor   B. engine   C. captain
     D. ocean   E. rudder

KEY (CORRECT ANSWERS)

1	E	6.	B	11.	A	16.	C	21.	D
2.	B	7.	D	12.	A	17.	A	22.	E
3.	C	8.	C	13.	B	18.	D	23.	A
4.	E	9.	B	14.	B	19.	C	24.	C
5.	C	10.	A	15.	C	20.	C	25.	A

TEST 12

1. CAPTURE : PRISONER :: ESCAPE : _____   1.____
   A. warden   B. jail   C. fugitive
   D. guard   E. prison

2. PLAY : TOYS :: WORK : _____   2.____
   A. profession   B. union   C. workers
   D. hands   E. tools

3. GREEN : EMERALD :: RED : _____   3.____
   A. gem   B. jewel   C. lips
   D. ruby   E. color

4. DRAW : PICTURE :: SING : _____   4.____
   A. music   B. song   C. orchestra
   D. vocalist   E. rhythm

5. FOOD : HUNGER :: WATER : _____   5.____
   A. rain   B. drought   C. weariness
   D. thirst   E. monsoon

6. MELANCHOLY : LUGUBRIOUS :: CHEERFULNESS : _____   6.____
   A. ludicrous   B. optimism   C. sad
   D. jovial   E. cruel

7. ENCOURAGE : DISHEARTEN :: ASSIST : _____   7.____
   A. help   B. encourage   C. cooperate
   D. obstacle   E. obstruct

8. WHAT : DEFINITION :: WHICH : _____   8.____
   A. place   B. who   C. condition
   D. selection   E. question

9. COURAGE : LION :: SPEED : _____   9.____
   A. airplane   B. flight   C. rate
   D. turtle   E. greyhound

10. LOUD : SOUND :: HOT : _____   10.____
    A. temperature   B. barometer   C. weather
    D. cool   E. frigid

11. GENUINE : ARTIFICIAL :: AUTHENTIC : _____   11.____
    A. autocratic   B. spurious   C. credible
    D. spontaneous   E. authoritative

12. ENOUGH : SUFFICIENCY :: IMPETUOUS : _____   12.____
    A. arrogance   B. arrogant   C. impertinence
    D. impulsive   E. impulse

13. LOQUACITY : VERBOSE :: POVERTY : _____   13.____
    A. wealth   B. hungry   C. craven
    D. lazy   E. indigent

14. STINGY : LAVISH :: SCARCE : _____   14.____
    A. copious   B. quantity   C. plethora
    D. rare   E. avaricious

15. ANTHROPOPHAGY : CANNIBALISTIC :: AUTOCHTHONY : _____   15.____
    A. indigenous   B. autopsy   C. indigent
    D. autocratic   E. anthropomorphic

16. IMPETUOUS : IMPETUOUSNESS :: CIRCUMSPECT : _____   16.____
    A. circumlocution B. prudence   C. cautious
    D. circumstance   E. circumscription

17. HYPER- : HYPO- :: EXCESSIVE : _____   17.____
    A. recessive   B. superfluous   C. excess
    D. insufficient   E hypothetical

18. HUNGER : INSATIABLE :: DISCOURSE : _____   18.____
    A. apt   B. arrogant   C. eloquent
    D. essential   E. garrulous

19. EXTRINSIC : EXTRANEOUS :: INTRINSIC : _____   19.____
    A. interior   B. intricate   C. inherent
    D. inner   E. intrepid

20. IRON : STEEL :: SAND : _____   20.____
    A. water   B. desert   C. wind
    D. glass   E. dust

21. BARBAROUS : CIVILIZATION :: AMORPHOUS : _____   21.____
    A. amortization   B. form   C. amorous
    D. morphology   E. conservation

22. DILEMMA : PARADOX :: ALTERNATIVE : _____   22.____
    A. atavism   B. antithesis   C. paroxysm
    D. anomaly   E. eczema

23. WHEN : TIME :: WHERE : _____   23.____
    A. how   B. who   C. locale
    D. manner   E. there

24. VEHICLE : AUTOMOBILE :: WEAPON : _____   24.____
    A. revolver   B. force   C. bullet
    D. trigger   E. battle

25. ANNIHILATE : EXTIRPATE :: CLANDESTINE : _____   25.____
    A. contemplative   B. occluded   C. surreptitious
    D. clamorous   E. subversive

_____

KEY (CORRECT ANSWERS)

1	C	6.	D	11.	B	16.	B	21.	B
2.	E	7.	E	12.	E	17.	D	22.	D
3.	D	8.	D	13.	E	18.	E	23.	B
4.	B	9.	E	14.	A	19.	C	24.	A
5.	D	10.	A	15.	A	20.	D	25.	C

_____

TEST 13

1. SKELETON : BODY :: LAW : _____
   A. prisoner   B. cell   C. sentence
   D. society   E. jury
      1.____

2. EDDY : CURRENT :: WHIM : _____
   A. refuge   B. haven   C. harbor
   D. river   E. purpose
      2.____

3. EROSION : ROCKS :: DISSIPATION : _____
   A. character   B. temperance   C. reparation
   D. atonement   E. moderation
      3.____

4. POINTER : PARTRIDGE :: CONSCIENCE : _____
   A. collection   B. picture   C. duty
   D. frame   E. artist
      4.____

5. MEGAPHONE : VOICE :: REFLECTOR : _____
   A. hose   B. radio   C. atomizer
   D. searchlight   E. electricity
      5.____

6. WIND : OCEAN :: ORATOR : _____
   A. asset   B. liability   C. mob
   D. parent   E. duty
      6.____

7. FERTILIZER : CROPS :: ADVERTISING : _____
   A. sales   B. paper   C. news
   D. magazine   E. ink
      7.____

8. BULLDOG : FOX :: TENACITY : _____
   A. frankness   B. slyness   C. freedom
   D. independence   E. sincerity
      8.____

9. FROST : FLOWERS :: JEALOUSY : _____
   A. love   B. tree   C. husband
   D. bride   E. bush
      9.____

10. PASSPORT : FOREIGN COUNTRY :: TICKET : _____
    A. air   B. house   C. conductor
    D. air   E. arena
       10.____

11. INK : PEN :: PAINT : _____
    A. eraser   B. brush   C. office
    D. typewriter   E. chalk
       11.____

12. SECOND : MINUTE :: MINUTE : _____
    A. day   B. week   C. month
    D. hour   E. year
       12.____

13. EATING : FAT :: DIETING : _____
    A. thin   B. water   C. candy
    D. carbohydrates   E. drinking

13.____

14. SCALES : FISH :: QUILLS : _____
    A. wood   B. coat   C. porcupine
    D. tree   E. fur

14.____

15. SELL : SALE :: ENTERTAIN : _____
    A. enterprise   B. entertain`   C. entertained
    D. entertainment   E. entertainer

15.____

16. I : WE :: HE : _____
    A. them   B. him   C. us
    D. they   E. our

16.____

17. COMMUNICABLE : COMMUNICATION :: DISRUPTIVE : _____
    A. disruption   B. disrupt   C. disruptable
    D. disruptible   E. disrupted

17.____

18. MANAGED : MANAGE :: FLED : _____
    A. flee   B. fled   C. fly
    D. flight   E. flew

18.____

19. LEOPARD : LEOPARDS :: HE : _____
    A. we   B. those   C. they
    D. men   E. his

19.____

20. PHENOMENAL : PHENOMENALLY :: DISCONSOLATE : _____
    A. disconsolately B. dejectedly   C. inconsolably
    D. perniciously   E. hysterically

20.____

21. PRACTICAL : PRACTICE :: BACILLARY : _____
    A. bacille   B. bacillus   C. bacilla
    D. bacilli   E. bacil

21.____

22. MOTIF : MOTIFS :: PARENTHESIS : _____
    A. parenthos   B. parenthesis   C. parentheses
    D. parenthesises   E. parenthesis's

22.____

23. INTUITIVENESS : INTUITIVELY :: MYSTIFICATION : _____
    A. mystificately   B. mystify   C. mystically
    D. mystificate   E. mystificatively

23.____

24. NOTORIETY : NOTORIOUS :: EXEMPLIFICATION : _____
    A. exemplificate   B. exemplificatory C. exemplify
    D. exemplary   E. exemplification

24.____

25. LUXURY : PRIVATION :: SUPERFLUOUS : _____   25.____
    A. depressive   B. deficient   C. abundant
    D. excessive   E. superlative

_____

KEY (CORRECT ANSWERS)

1	D	6.	C	11.	B	16.	D	21.	B
2.	E	7.	A	12.	D	17.	A	22.	C
3.	A	8.	B	13.	A	18.	A	23.	C
4.	C	9.	A	14.	C	19.	C	24.	D
5.	D	10.	E	15.	D	20.	A	25.	B

_____

TEST 14

1. GASOLINE : ENGINE :: BLOOD : _____   1.____
    A. knife   B. heart   C. nose
    D. mouth   E. veins

2. IGLOO : ESKIMO :: TEPEE : _____   2.____
    A. hut   B. Indian   C. home
    D. wigwam   E. wig

3. STEEL : FORK :: WOOD : _____   3.____
    A. forest   B. fire   C. oak
    D. stain   E. chair

4. TONE : HEARING :: COLOR : _____   4.____
    A. blindness   B. brightness   C. hue
    D. sight   E. eyes

5. EDUCATED : KNOW :: WEALTHY : _____   5.____
    A. influence   B. rich   C. own
    D. provide   E. invest

6. CLIENT : LAWYER :: PLAYER : _____   6.____
    A. umpire   B. teammate   C. game
    D. team   E. coach

7. LUMBER : MINE :: STONE : _____   7.____
    A. rock   B. brick   C. quarry
    D. wood   E. roots

8. MONEY : PURSE :: CLOTHING : _____   8.____
    A. purchase   B. suitcase   C. handle
    D. stolen   E. bargain

9. SWEET : SYRUP :: BITTER : _____   9.____
    A. herb   B. sour   C. lemon]
    D. salt   E. viscous

10. SCHOOL : FISH :: SWARM : _____   10.____
    A. bevy   B. bees   C. buffaloes
    D. ants   E. herd

11. BREAK : PLATE :: TEAR : _____   11.____
    A. sew   B. glass   C. repair
    D. cotton   E. suit

12. ARMOR : KNIGHT :: UNIFORM : _____   12.____
    A. general   B. soldier   C. army
    D. dress   E. rank

13. GARDEN : FLOWER :: FOREST : _____   13.____
    A. stamen   B. tree   C. river
    D. leaves   E. plant

14. LEAF : TEA :: BEAN : _____   14.____
    A. cotyledon   B. seed   C. Boston
    D. coffee   E. baked

15. SNOW : SKI :: ICE : _____   15.____
    A. pond   B. slide   C. winter
    D. skate   E. rink

16. BODY : SKELETON :: HOUSE : _____   16.____
    A. foundation   B. plan   C. structure
    D. pile   E. framework

17. AIR : BALLOON :: WATER : _____   17.____
    A. atmosphere   B. cork   C. submarine
    D. float   E. faucet

18. STEER : BEEF :: SWINE : _____   18.____
    A. veal   B. chops   C. pork
    D. steak   E. swill

19. CANDY : SUGAR :: CAKE : _____   19.____
    A. saccharin   B. flour   C. meal
    D. honey   E. cinnamon

20. TOBACCO : POUCH :: FODDER : _____   20.____
    A. silo   B. cattle   C. hogs
    D. silk   E. eggs

21. CUBE : SQUARE :: SPHERE : _____   21.____
    A. oval   B. volume   C. plane
    D. circle   E. area

22. GINGHAM : SUEDE :: LEAD : _____   22.____
    A. sink   B. steel   C. ore
    D. brass   E. platinum

23. SHOE : CALF :: PILLOW : _____   23.____
    A. goose   B. deck   C. bed
    D. buck   E. cotton

24. RAIN : DEW :: SNOW : _____   24.____
    A. moisture   B. dawn   C. cold
    D. humid   E. frost

25. WHIP : SLAP :: CASTIGATE : _____   25.____
    A. flagellate   C. condemn   C. rebuke
    D. excoriate   E. denoun

KEY (CORRECT ANSWERS)

1	B	6.	E	11.	E	16.	E	21.	D
2.	B	7.	C	12.	B	17.	B	22.	E
3.	E	8.	B	13.	B	18.	C	23.	A
4.	D	9.	A	14.	D	19.	B	24.	E
5.	C	10.	B	15.	D	20.	A	25.	C

———

TEST 15

1. SCALES : SALMON :: HAIR : _____
    A. head   B. lobster   C. lair
    D. wolf   E. snake
           1.____

2. FOOT : TOE :: HAND : _____
    A. elbow   B. arm   C. finger
    D. glove   E. leg
           2.____

3. PARACHUTE : AIRPLANE :: JACKET : _____
    A. captain   B. preserver   C. automobile
    D. life   E. ship
           3.____

4. SCHOOL : TEACHER :: HOSPITAL : _____
    A. intern   B. patient   C. orderly
    D. doctor   E. disease
           4.____

5. LAUGHTER : TEARS :: COMICAL : _____
    A. tragic   B. majestic   C. epical
    D. risible   E. comedy
           5.____

6. AMOEBA : PSUEDOPODS :: FINS : _____
    A. shell   B. fish   C. gills
    D. scales   E. mantis
           6.____

7. WAVE : CREST :: CHURCH : _____
    A. cross   B. acme   C. peak
    D. diocese   E. steeple
           7.____

8. RUNG : LADDER :: STEP : _____
    A. leap   B. staircase   C. pace
    D. wall   E. climb
           8.____

9. CLOCK : TIME :: RULER : _____
    A. feet   B. place   C. space
    D. yard   E. measure
           9.____

10. GLARE : SQUINT :: BLOW : _____
    A. overpower   B. punch   C. stare
    D. parry   E. bag
           10.____

11. GENERAL : COMMAND :: KING : _____
    A. prince   B. prime minister   C. power
    D. primacy   E. primate
           11.____

12. DEATH : BIRTH :: CONCLUSION : _____
    A. summary   B. epitaph   C. précis
    D. epilogue   E. introduction
           12.____

13. SPEAKER : HOUSE :: TOASTMASTER : _____   13._____
   A. speech   B. toast   C. jokes
   D. guests   E. banquet

14. VOLCANO : CRATER :: HOUSE : _____   14._____
   A. roof   B. stove   C. powe4r
   D. chimney   E. foundation

15. COAST : TOBOGGAN : REVOLVE : _____   15._____
   A. slide   B. ski   C. sled
   D. slope   E. wheel

16. LIMP : WALK :: STAMMER : _____   16._____
   A. lambaste   B. describe   C. chalk
   D. talk   E. stamp

17. PAPER : TYPIST :: PARCHMENT : _____   17._____
   A. author   B. scribble   C. secretary
   D. papyrus   E. copyist

18. BROTHER : FATHER :: AUNT : _____   18._____
   A. niece`   B. grandmother   C. uncle
   D. mother   E. nephew

19. FACTORY : SMOCK :: KITCHEN : _____   19._____
   A. stove   B. coveralls   C. coverlet
   D. apron   E. smog

20. NAPHTHA : PETROLEUM :: METAL : _____   20._____
   A. liquid   B. mine   C. ore
   D. solid   E. bronze

21. OFFICER : PRIVATE :: FOREMAN : _____   21._____
   A. worker   B. manager   C. boss
   D. union   E. section

22. PROTECT : ATTACK :: DEFEND : _____   22._____
   A. forfend   B. offend   C. preconize
   D. secure   E. shield

23. TODAY : YESTERDAY :: PRESENT : _____   23._____
   A. past   B. tomorrow   C. eternity
   D. future   E. perpetuity

24. SLAVE : BONDS :: KING : _____   24._____
   A. queen   B. armor   C. crown
   D. medals   E. fasceds

25. BICYCLE : MOTORCYCLE :: CARRIAGE : _____   25.____
    A. park   B. horseless   C. wagon
    D. stable   E. automobile

KEY (CORRECT ANSWERS)

1	D	6.	B	11.	D	16.	D	21.	A
2.	C	7.	E	12.	E	17.	E	22.	B
3.	E	8.	B	13.	E	18.	B	23.	A
4.	D	9.	C	14.	D	19.	D	24.	C
5.	A	10.	D	15.	E	20.	C	25.	E

TEST 16

1. DOG : KENNEL :: CATTLE : _____   1._____
   A. steer   B. corral   C. apiary
   D. zoo   E. range

2. HEAL : DOCTOR :: LEND : _____   2._____
   A. bank   B. banker   C. mortgage
   D. principal   E. usurer

3. INFANT : NURSERY :: YOUTH : _____   3._____
   A. school   B. teacher   C. genes
   D. adult   E. experience

4. LEARN : STUDY :: SUCCEED : _____   4._____
   A. education   B. effort   C. attempt
   D. recede   E. master

5. SIX : THREE :: SEXTUPLE : _____   5._____
   A. triple   B. quadruple   C. nothing
   D. quintuple   E. fourfold

6. CURTAIN : WINDOW :: VEIL : _____   6._____
   A. mosque   B. concealment   C. clothes
   D. face   E. privacy

7. METAL : SMITH :: STONE : _____   7._____
   A. quarry   B. mason   C. miner
   D. sculpture   E. vault

8. AVOID : SEEK :: ABSTAIN : _____   8._____
   A. indulge   B. constrain   C. imbue
   D. contain   E. indict

9. JUDGE : TRIAL :: UMPIRE : _____   9._____
   A. team   B. players   C. decision
   D. dispute   E. match

10. INSIST : RECOMMEND :: URGE : _____   10._____
    A. censure   B. coax   C. impel
    D. entreat   E. press

11. SLOPE : MOUNTAIN :: PITCH : _____   11._____
    A. height   B. hill   C. altitude
    D. roof   E. slant

12. CAPE : CONTINENT :: GULF : _____   12._____
    A. ocean   B. sea   C. bay
    D. land   E. river

13. DIAGNOSIS : CLINIC :: DECISION : _____
    A. judge   B. victory   C. trial
    D. defendant   E. jury

13._____

14. MUTINY : ARMY :: HERESY : _____
    A. priest   B. church   C. heretic
    D. anathema   E. establishment

14._____

15. POVERTY : SAVINGS :: DISEASE : _____
    A. germ   B. epidemic   C. vaccination
    D. prevention   E. cleanliness

15._____

16. RING : JEWELRY :: LIPSTICK : _____
    A. mascara   B. makeup   C. beauty parlor
    D. cream   E. lips

16._____

17. FUEL : GASOLINE :: LUBRICANT : _____
    A. oil   B. liquid   C. automobile
    D. wheels   E. water

17._____

18. WHEAT : FLOUR :: ROCK : _____
    A. gravel   B. stone   C. brick
    D. gind   E. cement

18._____

19. TEAM : TRACTOR :: STAIRS : _____
    A. loft   B. lobby   C. elevator
    D. machine   E. electricity

19._____

20. DECIDE : PONDER :: CONCLUDE : _____
    A. deliberate   B. demur   C. hesitate
    D. concur   E. argue

20._____

21. HARE : TORTOISE :: TRAIN : _____
    A. airplane   B. steamboat   C. truck
    D. wagon   E. submarine

21._____

22. REDWOOD : TREE :: CHAIR : _____
    A. seat   B. furniture   C. manufacture
    D. lounge   E. function

22._____

23. POSTCRIPT : LETTER :: AMENDMENT : _____
    A. change   B. addition   C. rescript
    D. law   E. constitutional

23._____

24. SHOES : RUBBERS :: SOCKS : _____
    A. boots   B. shoes   C. spats
    D. rain   E. galoshes

24._____

25. STEAM : HOT :: ICY : _____   25. ____
     A. heat   B. cold   C. stare
     D. icicle   E. snowy

_____

KEY (CORRECT ANSWERS)

1	B	6.	D	11.	D	16.	B	21.	D
2.	B	7.	B	12.	A	17.	A	22.	B
3.	A	8.	A	13.	E	18.	A	23.	D
4.	C	9.	E	14.	B	19.	C	24.	B
5.	A	10.	B	15.	C	20.	A	25.	B

_____

TEST 17

1. SKATE : RINK :: SWIM : _____
   A. gorge
   B. ice
   C. polo
   D. lake
   E. pool

   1.___

2. STORMY : FAIR :: PANICKY : _____
   A. panacea
   B. calm
   C. enervated
   D. pandemonium
   E. hysterical

   2.___

3. STOCKHOLDER : BONDHOLDER :: PROPRIETOR : _____
   A. investor
   B. banker
   C. creditor
   D. debtor
   E. owner

   3.___

4. OPAQUE : STEEL :: TRANSPARENT : _____
   A. paper
   B. brick
   C. apparent
   D. glass
   E. gleam

   4.___

5. CORRECTION OFFICER : WARDEN :: EMPLOYEE : _____
   A. union
   B. foreman
   C. manager
   D. factory
   E. steward

   5.___

6. IMAGINATIVE : FICTION :: AUTHORITATIVE : _____
   A. police
   B. romance
   C. novel
   D. story
   E. record

   6.___

7. TONE : DEAFNESS :: COLOR : _____
   A. sight
   B. picture
   C. muteness
   D. blindness
   E. taste

   7.___

8. FOOD : COMPOTE :: MUSIC : _____
   A. mixture
   B. refrain
   C. jazz
   D. medley
   E. dish

   8.___

9. OAK : STRENGTH :: HORSESHOE : _____
   A. luck
   B. horse
   C. stable
   D. horsepower
   E. size

   9.___

10. RECORD : CONCERT :: PHOTOGRAPH : _____
    A. painting
    B. autograph
    C. art
    D. landscape
    E. picture

    10.___

11. STREET : CITY :: TRAIL : _____
    A. park
    B. woods
    C. winding
    D. sea
    E. precipice

    11.___

12. LOUD : SOFT :: MAROON : _____
    A. yellow
    B. mild
    C. white
    D. pink
    E. red

    12.___

13. BUSY : AMBITIOUS :: INACTIVE : _____　　　　　　　　13._____
    A. invective　　　　B. forthright　　　C. pleasing
    D. preoccupied　　　E. aimless

14. CERTAIN : PROBABLE :: COMPLETE : _____　　　　　14._____
    A. entire　　　　　B. nearly　　　　C. integral
    D. intact　　　　　E. viable

15. PUSH : TOUCH :: TORNADO : _____　　　　　　　　15._____
    A. storm　　　　　B. zephyr　　　　C. cyclone
    D. wind　　　　　E. wave

16. BEVY : GIRLS :: BEVY : _____　　　　　　　　　　16._____
    A. deer`　　　　　B. monkeys　　　C. crowd
    D. larks　　　　　E. men

17. NAME : PERSON :: TITLE : _____　　　　　　　　　17._____
    A. woman　　　　　B. man　　　　C. President
    D. book　　　　　E. judge

18. STEER : RANCH :: MEAT : _____　　　　　　　　　18._____
    A. hogs　　　　　B. viands　　　C. sale
    D. store　　　　　E. butcher

19. PIPE : GAS :: WIRE : _____　　　　　　　　　　　19._____
    A. shock　　　　　B. lamp　　　　C. telephone
    D. electricity　　　E. length

20. NOVICE : GAUCHE :: MASTER : _____　　　　　　　20._____
    A. professional　　B. journeyman　C. artisan
    D. creditable　　　E. adept

21. REGENCY : REGENT :: CHAIRMAN : _____　　　　　21._____
    A. kingdom　　　　B. board of directors　C. office
    D. president　　　E. king

22. FORGET : RECALL :: CONCEAL : _____　　　　　　22._____
    A. kindle　　　　　B. congeal　　　C. publicize
    D. rehearse　　　E. reveal

23. SEE : LOOK :: TOUCH : _____　　　　　　　　　　23._____
    A. eyes　　　　　B. feel　　　　C. watch
    D. hand　　　　　E. taste

24. SUBMARINE : FISH :: AIRPLANE : _____　　　　　24._____
    A. sky　　　　　B. flies　　　　C. bird
    D. ship　　　　　E. helicopter

25. BUILDING : ARCHITECT :: MOTION PICTURE : _____   25.____
    A. director   B. writer   C. producer
    D. monument   E. camera

KEY (CORRECT ANSWERS)

1	E	6.	E	11.	B	16.	D	21.	B
2.	B	7.	D	12.	D	17.	D	22.	E
3.	C	8.	D	13.	E	18.	D	23.	B
4.	D	9.	A	14.	B	19.	D	24.	C
5.	C	10.	D	15.	B	20.	E	25.	A

TEST 18

1. MOO : CATTLE :: CHIRP : _____
   A. birds   B. low   C. sparrows
   D. sing   E. oxen

                                                                                1.____

2. CALICO : COTTON :: SATIN : _____
   A. wool   B. silk   C. gown
   D. shiny   E. dress

                                                                                2.____

3. HISTORY : PREDICTION :: PAST : _____
   A. inspiration   B. prophecy   C. future
   D. sociology   E. present

                                                                                3.____

4. COMPOSE : OPERAT :: CAST : _____
   A. intaglio   B. mold   C. play
   D. marble   E. granite

                                                                                4.____

5. ENEMY : ASSAIL :: ALLY : _____
   A. betray   B. conspire   C. assist
   D. detach   E. control

                                                                                5.____

6. INVENTOR : MACHINE :: SCENARIST : _____
   A. outline   B. book   C. motion picture
   D. scenery   E. author

                                                                                6.____

7. MOUSE : CAT :: SHEEP : _____
   A. goat   B. deer   C. ruminant
   D. wolf   E. lamb

                                                                                7.____

8. FLAME : SPARK :: CATASTROPHE : _____
   A. insignificant   B. calamity   C. tiny
   D. holocaust   E. triviality

                                                                                8.____

9. ILLNESS : INFECTION :: STORM : _____
   A. forecast   B. rain   C. wind
   D. cyclone   E. cloud

                                                                                9.____

10. CLOCK : TIME :: CALENDAR : _____
    A. temperature   B. hour   C. date
    D. week   E. month

                                                                                10.____

11. FEUD : CLAN :: WAR : _____
    A. attrition   B. peace   C. state
    D. U N   E. class

                                                                                11.____

12. SOUND : LOUD :: THING : _____
    A. sharp   B. tiny   C. heavy
    D. scant   E. large

                                                                                12.____

13. DRUM : STICK :: VIOLIN : _____   13.____
    A. pick   B. key   C. music
    D. strings   E. bow

14. BARLEY : GRAIN :: SILVER : _____   14.____
    A. strain   B. gold   C. rock
    D. money   E. metal

15. CHAT : SPEECH :: SNACK : _____   15.____
    A. feast   B. light meal   C. snack
    D. oration   E. snark

16. ARM : JOINT :: GATE : _____   16.____
    A. latch   B. knee   C. axis
    D. hinge   E. jamb

17. GUN : CLUB :: HOUSE : _____   17.____
    A. alarm   B. cave   C. home
    D. mansion   E. protection

18. BOARD : CARPENTER :: PIPE : _____   18.____
    A. saw   B. plumber   C. wrench
    D. jack   E. torsion

19. EXECUTION : LEGAL :: LYNCHING : _____   19.____
    A. deadly   B. lawless   C. mob
    D. hooded   E. clerical

20. INDIVIDUAL : MULTITUDE :: WIRE : _____   20.____
    A. radio   B. electricity   C. cable
    D. telegram   E. communication

21. PERIL : RISK :: SAFETY : _____   21.____
    A. security   B. wariness   C. temerity
    D. discrete   E. danger

22. EXPENSIVE : SCARCE :: CHEAP : _____   22.____
    A. inexpensive   B. plentiful   C. borrowed
    D. rare   E. plethora

23. SWEET : TASTE :: FRAGRANT : _____   23.____
    A. smell   B. aromatic   C. spice
    D. feel   E. sight

24. DIRT : LATHER :: INK : _____   24.____
    A. pen   B. blot   C. eraser
    D. detergent   E. pencil

25. SPOUT : TEAPOT :: NOZZLE : _____   25.____
    A. nose   B. hydrant   C. pistol
    D. bellows   E. socket

    _____

KEY (CORRECT ANSWERS)

1	A	6.	A	11.	C	16.	D	21.	B
2.	B	7.	D	12.	E	17.	B	22.	B
3.	C	8.	E	13.	E	18.	B	23.	A
4.	B	9.	E	14.	E	19.	B	24.	C
5.	C	10.	C	15.	A	20.	C	25.	D

_____

TEST 19

1. MUSIC : MEDLEY :: FRUIT : _____
   A. compote   B. hash   C. grill
   D. stew   E. dessert
   1.____

2. TONGS : ICE :: VISE : _____
   A. grip   B. jaw   C. object
   D. wrench   E. tight
   2.____

3. BURN : BLISTER :: BLOW : _____
   A. punch   B. subdue   C. knockout
   D. push   E. contusion
   3.____

4. YEAR : MONTH :: WEEK : _____
   A. month   B. time   C. hour
   D. day   E. season
   4.____

5. HAND : HANDLE :: FOOT : _____
   A. kick   B. shoe   C. piano
   D. race   E. pedal
   5.____

6. GASOLINE : AUTOMOBILE :: POWDER : _____
   A. keg   B. pistol   C. bullet
   D. dry   E. trigger
   6.____

7. STAIRS : ELEVATOR :: BRIDGE : _____
   A. span   B. ferry   C. suspension
   D. river   E. passage
   7.____

8. WAGE : BONUS :: GRADUATION : _____
   A. college   B. senior   C. diploma
   D. merit   E. honors
   8.____

9. LATE : PENALTY :: PROMPT : _____
   A. payment   B. overdue   C. credit
   D. discount   E. interest
   9.____

10. DOG : KENNEL :: FOWL : _____
    A. chicken   B. aviary   C. kernel
    D. sty   E. coop
    10.____

11. VIOLATION : LAW :: NEGLECT : _____
    A. salutary   B. omission   C. duty
    D. demission   E. volition
    11.____

12. RUST : IRON :: MOLD : _____
    A. mound   B. cheese   C. stale
    D. bronze   E. bread
    12.____

13. TEAMWORK : COORDINATION :: SUBVERSION : _____   13.____
    A. animadversion   B. contorsion   C. destruction
    D. escalation   E. competition

14. COMMISSION : SALESMAN :: ROYALTY : _____   14.____
    A. king   B. court   C. publisher
    D. author   E. invention

15. PANTRY : FOOD :: ARSENAL : _____   15.____
    A. armory   B. drill   C. war
    D. weapons   E. army

16. DEMUR : ACCEPT :: IGNORE : _____   16.____
    A. believe   B. conclude   C. refute
    D. permit   E. recognize

17. ELBOW : ARM :: KNEE : _____   17.____
    A. foot   B. leg   C. action
    D. thigh   E. ankle

18. STREAM : RIVER :: HILL : _____   18.____
    A. precipice   B. chain   C. gorge
    D. elevation   E. mountain

19. LILY : THORN :: TIGER : _____   19.____
    A. lion   B. bush   C. claw
    D. wolf   E. spine

20. TRIUMPH : DEFEAT :: HONOR : _____   20.____
    A. victory   B. defeasance   C. manumission
    D. slavery   E. obloquy

21. FRAME : PICTURE :: FENCE : _____   21.____
    A. cattle   B. pasture   C. enclave
    D. field   E. wire

22. TRANQUILLITY : SERENITY :: DISORDER : _____   22.____
    A. control   B. discipline   C. contrition
    D. order   E. pandemonium

23. OPPOSE : ADVERSARY :: SUPPORT : _____   23.____
    A. enemy   B. sweetheart   C. protagonist
    D. antagonist   E. ally

24. OBSERVE : TELESCOPE :: LISTEN : _____   24.____
    A. camera   B. telegraph   C. lens
    D. telephone   E. spectrum

25. THUNDER : DIN :: LIGHTNING : _____   25._____
    A. bolt   B. clamor   C. light
    D. darkness   E. streak

KEY (CORRECT ANSWERS)

1	A	6.	C	11.	C	16.	E	21.	D
2.	C	7.	B	12.	E	17.	B	22.	E
3.	E	8.	E	13.	C	18.	E	23.	E
4.	D	9.	D	14.	D	19.	C	24.	D
5.	E	10.	E	15.	D	20.	E	25.	C

TEST 20

1. PREVENTION : ACCIDENT :: SANITATION : _____
   A. care   B. garbage   C. infection
   D. cleanliness   E. disease

                                                                                  1.____

2. GRAIN : MAIZE :: WOOD : _____
   A. sand   B. saw   C. millet
   D. sawdust   E. forest

    2.____

3. VOLUME : OIL :: WEIGHT : _____
   A. milk   B. gasoline   C. length
   D. wheat   E. ton

    3.____

4. SUFFOCATE : AIR :: STARVE : _____
   A. meat   B. nourishment   C. breathe
   D. emaciation   E. diet

    4.____

5. LID : COVER :: CONTAINER : _____
   A. pot   B. water   C. boil
   D. retainer   E. strainer

    5.____

6. FICTIONAL : NOVELIST :: FACTUAL : _____
   A. essayist   B. annalist   C. lawyer
   D. records   E. analyst

    6.____

7. TRAIN : DEPOT :: SHIP : _____
   A. automobile   B. liner   C. pier
   D. ship   E. hangar

    7.____

8. WAGON : HORSE :: TRAIN : _____
   A. station   B. carriage   C. railroad cars
   D. locomotive   E. self-propulsion

    8.____

9. OCEAN : GULF :: CONTINENT : _____
   A. land   B. bay   C. sea
   D. peninsula   E. isthmus

    9.____

10. ARRAIGN : INSINUATE :: DEFACE : _____
    A. mutilate   B. mark   C. deform
    D. mar   E. enhance

    10.____

11. DUET : CHORUS :: DUEL : _____
    A. Western   B. death   C. brawl
    D. gang   E. draw

    11.____

12. QUANTITY : LEAST :: QUALITY : _____
    A. best   B. worst   C. most
    D. dimension   E. superior

    12.____

13. HORSE : STABLE :: AIRPLANE : _____   13.____
    A. depot   B. wharf   C. field
    D. airport   E. hangar

14. INITIATE : DUPLICATE :: CREATE : _____   14.____
    A. produce   B. conspire   C. debate
    D. permeate   E. emulate

15. NECK : COLLAR :: WAIST : _____   15.____
    A. stomach   B. girth   C. belt
    D. tie   E. chest

16. ANIMAL : PIG :: FRUIT : _____   16.____
    A. branch   B. onion   C. tomato
    D. cucumber   E. carrot

17. POLE : FISHERMAN :: RIFLE : _____   17.____
    A. policeman   B. soldier   C. hunter
    D. cowboy   E. gangster

18. TUMULT : REPOSE :: SUNSHINE : _____   18.____
    A. noisome   B. darkness   C. gaiety
    D. death   E. winter

19. EXERCISE : TENNIS :: ADDICTION : _____   19.____
    A. dentition   B. heroin   C. aspirin
    D. beer   E. golf

20. WHEEL : CARRIAGE :: RUNNER : _____   20.____
    A. race   B. toboggan   C. towpath
    D. steel   E. wagon

21. FILM : CAMERA :: DISC : _____   21.____
    A. discus   B. record   C. recorder
    D. radio   E. album

22. ESTABLISH : IMPUTE :: CONVICTED : _____   22.____
    A. evicted   B. designed   C. alleged
    D. fugitive   E. covert

23. WORD : LETTER :: NUMBER : _____   23.____
    A. decimal   B. numeral   C. integer
    D. item   E. digit

24. CULTIVATED : WILD :: HOTHOUSE : _____   24.____
    A. greenroom   B. greensward   C. greenhouse
    D. forest   E tender

25. TRUCK : CAB :: PLANE   25.____
     A. jet   B. fuselage   C. cockpit
     D. aileron   E. wing

KEY (CORRECT ANSWERS)

1 E	6. B	11. C	16. C	21. C
2. D	7. C	12. B	17. C	22. C
3. D	8. D	13. E	18. B	23. E
4. B	9. D	14. E	19. B	24. D
5. A	10. B	15. C	20. B	25. C

TESTS IN VERBAL ANALOGIES – 2 BLANKS

— GENERAL INFORMATION

— GENERAL VOCABULARY

DIRECTIONS: Each question in this part consists of two capitalized words which have a certain relationship to each other, followed by five lettered pairs of words in small letters. Choose the letter of the pair of words which are related to each other in the SAME way as the words of the capitalized pair are related to each other. *PRINT THE LETTER OF THE CORRECT ANSWER IN THE SPACE AT THE RIGHT.*

TEST 1

1. CELL : INMATE :: _____ : _____   1._____
   A. walls : jail   B. warden : prison
   C. cage : canary   D. jungle : lion
   E. patient : hospital

2. DOOR : TAXICAB :: _____ : _____   2._____
   A. ticket : aeroplane   B. price : goods
   C. desk : office   D. turnstile : subway
   E. porthole : ship

3. RECONDITE : OPAQUE :: _____ : _____   3._____
   A. concave : convex   B. erudition : profundity
   C. dull : translucent   D. abstract : realistic
   E. abstruse : obtuse

4. BRILLIANCE : GENIUS :: _____ : _____   4._____
   A. intelligence : test   B. father : son
   C. facet : gem   D. heredity : environment
   E. constellation : star

5. VERDICT : JURY :: _____ : _____   5._____
   A. judge : sentence   B. panel : member
   C. nomination : convention   D. criminal : crime
   E. policeman : arrest

6. KNOTS : SHIPS :: _____ : _____   6._____
   A. sea : fathoms   B. suits : divers
   C. miles : automobiles   D. gasoline : aeroplane
   E. milligram : gram

7. GLASSES : VISION :: _____ : _____   7._____
    A. windows : houses   B. defect : myopic
    C. crutches : movement   D. teeth : braces
    E. telescope : astronomer

8. EYE : MIND :: _____ : _____   8._____
    A. toe : foot   B. beacon : lighthouse
    C. lens : camera   D. head : body
    E. vision : thought

9. COSTUME : MASQUERADER :: _____ : _____   9._____
    A. radar : instrument   B. painter : anonymity
    C. cocoon : butterfly   D. camouflage : guerrilla
    E. color : ship

10. PRICE : VALUE :: _____ : _____   10._____
    A. cost : market   B. supply : demand
    C. wholesale : retail   D. net : worth
    E. tax : article

11. FEAR : PANIC :: _____ : _____   11._____
    A. disease : germ   B. storm : hurricane
    C. ship : sink   D. courage : hero
    E. solitude

12. PREDILECTION : AFFINITY :: _____ : _____   12._____
    A. prepossession : prediction B. atom : combination
    C. impartiality : partiality   D. predisposition : relationship
    E. affiliation : preponderance

13. UNCONSCIOUS : CONSCIOUS :: _____ : _____   13._____
    A. passivity : activity   B. sleep : dream
    C. forget : remember   D. coma : comatose
    E. repression : awareness

14. QUIXOTIC : REALISTIC :: _____ : _____   14._____
    A. weak : strong   B. inspired : clumsy
    C. romantic : practical   D. light : heavy
    E. surface : depth

15. INTELLIGENCE : MAN :: _____ : _____   15._____
    A. reason : rationale   B. mind : brain
    C. thought : process   D. instinct : beast
    E. rattle : snake

16. WITTICISM : AMUSING :: _____ : _____   16._____
    A. epigram : metaphor   B. epitaph : mourning
    C. clever : laughable   D. joke : jibe
    E. epithet : insulting

17. HOSTILITY : WAR :: _____ : _____
    A. soldier : battle
    C. company : merger
    E. power : president
    B. passive : active
    D. competition : industry

17._____

18. RADAR : ALARM :: _____ : _____
    A. escape : prison
    C. guns : soldiers
    E. ship : vault
    B. riot : convicts
    D. door : lock

18._____

19. LETTER : CABLE :: _____ : _____
    A. telegraph : code
    C. racing : diving
    E. wading : swimming
    B. word : sentence
    D. parachute : aeroplane

19._____

20. FOOT : STAND :: _____ : _____
    A. ladder : rung
    C. object : touch
    E. walk : run
    B. hearing : ears
    D. hand : grasp

20._____

21. EPIGRAM : ANAGRAM :: _____ : _____
    A. remark : game
    C. epithet : repetition
    E. letter : word
    B. pithy : lengthy
    D. concise : transposed

21._____

22. JUXTAPOSITION : VERTICAL :: _____ : _____
    A. across : horizontal
    C. floor : wall
    E. right angle : rectangle
    B. angle : sphere
    D. side by side : up and down

22._____

23. LIMIT : INFINITY :: _____ : _____
    A. close : far
    C. finite : interminable
    E. time : space
    B. horizon : skyline
    D. boundless : determinate

23._____

24. REFLEX : REACTION :: _____ : _____
    A. eye : blink
    C. tears : crying
    E. thought : speech
    B. motivation : agenda
    D. involuntary : voluntary

24._____

25. LENS : CAMERA :: _____ : _____
    A. pupil : film
    C. retina : eye
    E. speed : focus
    B. light : aperture
    D. telescope : battleship

25._____

KEY (CORRECT ANSWERS)

1	C	6.	C	11.	B	16.	E	21.	D
2.	D	7.	C	12.	D	17.	D	22.	D
3.	E	8.	C	13.	E	18.	E	23.	C
4.	C	9.	D	14.	C	19.	E	24.	B
5.	C	10.	B	15.	D	20.	D	25.	C

TEST 2

1. PAINT : ARTIST :: _____ : _____
   A. clay : model
   B. statue : sculptor
   C. brush : palette
   D. cloth : designer
   E. painting : canvas

1._____

2. SHADE : COLOR :: _____ : _____
   A. primary : secondary
   B. hue : value
   C. beige : brown
   D. yellow : gold
   E. red : pink

2._____

3. EMBEZZLEMENT : THIEF :: _____ : _____
   A. philately : necromancer
   B. student : study
   C. pyromaniac : fire
   D. operation : surgeon
   E. murderer : homicide

3._____

4. DULL : BEAUTIFUL :: _____ : _____
   A. prosaic : aesthetic
   B. lethargic ambitious
   C. behavior : feeling
   D. humorous : brilliant
   E. judicious : sensitivity

4._____

5. PROMISE : RENEGE :: _____ : _____
   A. truth : oath
   B. perfidy : imposture
   C. oath : perjury
   D. inviolability : swear
   E. inaccuracy : falsity

5._____

6. VAGARY : RATIONALITY :: _____ : _____
   A. method : science
   B. irrational : deranged
   C. insanity : sanity
   D. hypothetical : formulated
   E. animal : machine

6._____

7. OBSOLETE : EXTANT :: _____ : _____
   A. jet : aeroplane
   B. fiction : science
   C. loud : gift
   D. gaslight : electricity
   E. horse : carriage

7._____

8. COMPLACEMENT : RESTIVE :: _____ : _____
   A. chaos : satisfaction
   B. doubt : security
   C. dissatisfaction : friction
   D. civilization : jungle
   E. satisfaction : disquietude

8._____

9. AGE : SENILE :: _____ : _____
   A. juvenile : puerile
   B. characteristic : degree
   C. adolescence : childhood
   D. soil : erosion
   E. youth : impulsive

9._____

10. ASTROLOGY : ASTROLOGIST :: _____ : _____   10.____
    A. magic : demonology   B. witchcraft : entomologist
    C. conjure : spirit   D. sorcery : prestidigitator
    E. fetishism : palmist

11. SIGHT : HEARING :: _____ : _____   11.____
    A. touch : hand   B. taste : smell
    C. ears : eyes   D. hearing aid : eyeglasses
    E. aural : oral

12. PARACHUTES : AIR :: _____ : _____   12.____
    A. cork : water   B. rain : umbrellas
    C. clouds : sky   D. shoes : feet
    E. skis : snow

13. ALLEGIANCE : CITIZEN :: _____ : _____   13.____
    A. fealty : fief   B. citizenship : alien
    C. Hippocratic oath : physician   D. contract : marriage
    E. covenant : treaty

14. CELL : ORGANISM :: _____ : _____   14.____
    A. molecule : amoeba   B. growth : osmosis
    C. member : society   D. disease : parasite
    E. leg : foot

15. DECISION : DECLARATION :: _____ : _____   15.____
    A. voting : election   B. interview : census
    C. law : promulgation   D. battle : war
    E. idea : action

16. BULLET : PISTOL :: _____ : _____   16.____
    A. chamber : rifle   B. rapier : blade
    C. shoot : cannon   D. arrow : bow
    E. stone : throw

17. WEIGHT : OUNCE :: _____ : _____   17.____
    A. size : fit   B. dimension : shape
    C. depth : ocean   D. length : measure
    E. distance : meter

18. PLAN : BLUEPRINT :: _____ : _____   18.____
    A. scheme : idea   B. factory : store
    C. salesman : customer   D. plot : conspiracy
    E. cave : rock

19. DISPLACEMENT : HOUR :: _____ : _____   19.____
    A. gravity : speed   B. millesecond : light
    C. force : pull   D. time : depth
    E. space : time

20. PERIPHERY : CIRCLE :: _____ : _____   20.____
    A. planet : sun   B. perimeter : circumference
    C. hypotenuse : angle   D. earth : satellite
    E. solar system : planet

21. AEON : CENTURY :: _____ : _____   21.____
    A. decade : generation   B. years : score
    C. hundred : hundreds   D. mile : foot
    E. ounce : pound

22. WEAPON : FELON :: _____ : _____   22.____
    A. cavalry : horses   B. soldier : sword
    C. drill : dentist   D. whistle : dog
    E. writer : pen

23. SLUM : CITY :: _____ : _____   23.____
    A. illness : hospital   B. plague : populace
    C. ulcer : cancer   D. island : ocean
    E. poverty : impoverished

24. INDICT : CONVICT :: _____ : _____   24.____
    A. evidence : indication   B. accuse : condemn
    C. penalize : blame   D. absolve : punish
    E. volunteer : draft

25. WITNESS : TESTIMONY :: _____ : _____   25.____
    A. pedestal : speech   B. accused : alibi
    C. graph : lie detector   D. interpreter : translation
    E. swallow : summer

KEY (CORRECT ANSWERS)

1	D	6.	D	11.	B	16.	D	21.	D
2.	C	7.	D	12.	E	17.	E	22.	C
3.	D	8.	E	13.	C	18.	D	23.	B
4.	A	9.	E	14.	C	19.	E	24.	B
5.	C	10.	D	15.	C	20.	B	25.	B

TEST 3

1. CONVIVIALITY : SECLUSION :: _____ : _____   1.____
   A. denial : acceptance   B. austere : sensuous
   C. monastery : monk   D. gregariousness : asceticism
   E. secluded : remote

2. DISSENT : GROUP :: _____ : _____   2.____
   A. motion : meeting   B. discord : partisan
   C. rebellion : government   D. disbanding : party
   E. commitment : withdrawal

3. MUSIC : COLOR :: _____ : _____   3.____
   A. sound : reflection   B. symphony : color wheel
   C. intensity : pitch   D. vibration : light
   E. rhyme : harmony

4. WING : AEROPLANE :: _____ : _____   4.____
   A. pinwheel : toy   B. pilot : controls
   C. sail : boat   D. fender : automobile
   E. ski shoes : skis

5. SKIN : SNAKE :: _____ : _____   5.____
   A. wood : fire   B. goat : milk
   C. pluck – chicken   D. fur : bear
   E. feather : ostrich

6. TEAR : WOUND :: _____ : _____   6.____
   A. break : crack   B. arm : cast
   C. bruise : heal   D. paper : body
   E. rip : mend

7. CLIP : PAPER :: _____ : _____   7.____
   A. staple : machine   B. sharpener : pencil
   C. stamp : letter   D. sew : cloth
   E. stamp : mail

8. BREAK : CONCUSSION :: _____ : _____   8.____
   A. leg : temple   B. brain : foot
   C. hole : bullet   D. head : neck
   E. arm : head

9. HOMICIDE : FRATRICIDE :: _____ : _____   9.____
   A. death : dishonor   B. man : brother
   C. father : son   D. murder : man
   E. child : murder

10. INSTRUMENT : OCTAVE :: _____ : _____   10.____
    A. violin : music   B. range : singer
    C. piano : scale   D. one : seven
    E. stanza : poem

11. CLIENT : ATTORNEY :: _____ : _____   11.____
    A. jury : judge   B. audience : actor
    C. patient : physician   D. customer : store
    E. adviser : advised

12. DOMICILE : HIVE :: _____ : _____   12.____
    A. domestic : habitat   B. abode : hiatus
    C. man : bee   D. ant : hill
    E. sanctuary : wilderness

13. STONE : SNAKE :: _____ : _____   13.____
    A. lizard : lair   B. ocean : amphibian
    C. mineral : reptile   D. mummy : body
    E. water : goldfish

14. SLEIGH : SNOW :: _____ : _____   14.____
    A. element : vehicle   B. ride : winter
    C. ice : skate   D. canoe : river
    E. hounds : ranger

15. SUNDAY : JULY :: _____ : _____   15.____
    A. month : day   B. foot : inch
    C. hour : clock   D. vacation : holiday
    E. week : month

16. FIRE ESCAPE : TENANT :: _____ : _____   16.____
    A. siren : air raid   B. aeroplane : parachute
    C. net : acrobat   D. scream : child
    E. web : spider

17. DANCE : BALLETOMANE :: _____ : _____   17.____
    A. actor : audience   B. drama : review
    C. race : parlay   D. ballet : dancer
    E. coins : numismatist

18. WINDOW : PORTHOLE :: _____ : _____   18.____
    A. hatch : cabin   B. door : starboard
    C. sailor : navy   D. house : boat
    E. submarine : telescope

19. PRECURSOR : SUCCESSOR :: _____ : _____   19.____
    A. predecessor : forerunner   B. prince : king
    C. helicopter : jet   D. kerosene : electric
    E. prophecy : event

20. ORE : BOAT :: _____ : _____   20.____
    A. paddle : canoe   B. stick : hockey
    C. mallet : croquet   D. mined : manufactured
    E. mineral : vegetable

21. ASYLUM : COUNTRY :: _____ : _____   21.____
    A. expatriate : exile   B. hospitality : host
    C. prisoner : prison   D. board : parole
    E. inmate : institution

22. CONJUGATION : DECLENSION :: _____ : _____   22.____'
    A. forms : language   B. adverb : pronoun
    C. type : kind   D. verb : noun
    E. transitive : intransitive

23. PENINSULA : ISLAND :: _____ : _____   23.____
    A. mountainous : flat   B. state : city
    C. connected : surrounded   D. populated : isolated
    E. channel : isthmus

24. FELINE : CAT :: _____ : _____   24.____
    A. supine : man   B. asinine : donkey
    C. domesticated : wild   D. bovine : cow
    E. anthropoid : anthropology

25. WHEEL : AXLE :: _____ : _____   25.____
    A. man : invention   B. track : parallel
    C. horizontal : vertical   D. metronome : pendulum
    E. compartment : train

KEY (CORRECT ANSWERS)

1	D	6.	D	11.	C	16.	C	21.	B
2.	C	7.	D	12.	C	17.	E	22.	D
3.	D	8.	E	13.	C	18.	D	23.	C
4.	C	9.	B	14.	D	19.	D	24.	D
5.	C	10.	C	15.	E	20.	D	25.	D

TEST 4

1. POETRY : PROSE :: _____ : _____
   - A. art : fiction
   - B. meter : rhyme
   - C. narration : style
   - D. stanza : chapter
   - E. clause : sentence

   1.____

2. DEHYDRATE : DROWN :: _____ : _____
   - A. illness : death
   - B. parch : thirst
   - C. abundance : surfeit
   - D. suffocation : evaporation
   - E. desert : ocean

   2.____

3. TREE : BRANCH :: _____ : _____
   - A. sprout : potato
   - B. seed : plant
   - C. flower : petal
   - D. root : earth
   - E. moss : stone

   3.____

4. RHINESTONE : DIAMOND :: _____ : _____
   - A. semi-precious : precious
   - B. bullion : gold
   - C. pretense : fraud
   - D. simulated : genuine
   - E. private : general

   4.____

5. CONDIMENT : THYME :: _____ : _____
   - A. saccharine : sugar
   - B. candy : dextrose
   - C. seasoning : herb
   - D. synthetic : genuine
   - E. natural : manufactured

   5.____

6. INCHOATE : EMBRYONIC :: _____ : _____
   - A. disappearing : appearing
   - B. plant : seed
   - C. incipient : rudimentary
   - D. unknown : unseen
   - E. death : birth

   6.____

7. APATHY : EMPATHY :: _____ : _____
   - A. sympathy : identification
   - B. peasant : worker
   - C. indifference : understanding
   - D. peon : peonage
   - E. happiness : sadness

   7.____

8. CAT : PANTHER :: _____ : _____
   - A. shark : whale
   - B. lion : tamer
   - C. cat : mouse
   - D. worm : snake
   - E. shark : carnivorous

   8.____

9. INSULT : DUEL :: _____ : _____
   - A. sprint : pistol
   - B. fencing : sport
   - C. hat : ring
   - D. challenge : contest
   - E. sword : rapier

   9.____

10. RITE : RIGHT :: _____ : _____   10._____
    A. manner : might   B. ceremony : correct
    C. kinsman : kind   D. inauguration : irate
    E. sworn : swerve

11. REGRESS : EGRESS :: _____ : _____   11._____
    A. worsen : withdraw   B. down : up
    C. fantasy : reality   D. swing : gate
    E. retrogress : digress

12. BETTER : BEST :: _____ : _____   12._____
    A. among : between   B. first : second
    C. perfect : excellent   D. penultimate : ultimate
    E. more : many

13. INSIGNIA : ARMY :: _____ : _____   13._____
    A. judge : robe   B. road : sign
    C. crest : clan   D. fairy : wand
    E king : scepter

14. LAX : PROTOCOL :: _____ : _____   14._____
    A. lazy : perfect   B. individual : political
    C. dinner : banquet   D. order : disorder
    E. loose : discipline

15. HYMN : NOTE :: _____ : _____   15._____
    A. poem : rhume   B. change : paean
    C. story : sentence   D. brushstroke : painting
    E. song : music

16. ADVERTISEMENT : BILLBOARD :: _____ : _____   16._____
    A. canvas : paint   B. wallpaper : wall
    C. pen : ink   D. wood : mineral
    E. picture : frame

17. PARSIMONY : PRODIGALITY :: _____ : _____   17._____
    A. extravagance : waste   B. cupidity : profusion
    C. lavish : starve   D. avarice : stinginess
    E. dissipate : begrudge

18. SEGMENT : COMPLEX :: _____ : _____   18._____
    A. add : divide   B. totality : universe
    C. number : sum   D. decimal : fraction
    E. multiply : equate

19. MODERATION : HYPERBOLE :: _____ : _____   19._____
    A. iambic pentameter : blank verse B. exaggeration : understatement
    C. temper : embellish   D. dearth : sparsity
    E. dissonance : cacophony

20. PROPELLER : HELICOPTER :: _____ : _____   20.____
    A. nut : bolt   B. electricity : fan
    C. fan : belt   D. carriage : wheel
    E. hammer : nail

21. LINER : PASSENGER :: _____ : _____   21.____
    A. tourist : class   B. fleet : navy
    C. trawler : tug   D. whaler : vessel
    E. freighter : cargo

22. ORIENTAL : OCCIDENTAL :: _____ : _____   22.____
    A. south : north   B. car : rickshaw
    C. west : east   D. Peking : Venice
    E. nationality : country

23. NARCOTICS : SMUGGLER :: _____ : _____   23.____
    A. pirate : high seas   B. illegal : market
    C. contraband : neutral   D. stolen : property
    E. goods : illegal

24. MAGIC : RELIGION :: _____ : _____   24.____
    A. man : God   B. charm : statue
    C. priest : sorcerer   D. natural : supernatural
    E. experience : manifestation

25. PEDESTRIAN : EQUESTRIAN :: _____ : _____   25.____
    A. horse : rider   B. person : sculptor
    C. walk : ride   D. citizen : knight
    E. bridle path : sidewalk

KEY (CORRECT ANSWERS)

1	D	6.	C	11.	A	16.	B	21.	E
2.	E	7.	C	12.	D	17.	B	22.	D
3.	C	8.	D	13.	C	18.	C	23.	C
4.	D	9.	D	14.	E	19.	C	24.	B
5.	C	10.	B	15.	C	20.	C	25.	C

TEST 5

1. THUNDER : LIGHTNING :: _____ : _____
    A. sleet : fog
    C. rain : snow
    E. snow : ice
    B. storm : winter
    D. snowflake : snowball

1._____

2. TELEPHONE : RING :: _____ : _____
    A. bell : belfry
    C. town : crier
    E. cuckoo : clock
    B. sound : curfew
    D. clock : chime

2._____

3. CAFFEINE : COFFEE :: _____ : _____
    A. tobacco : nicotine
    C. alcohol : wine
    E. tea : leaf
    B. nicotine : pipe
    D. stimulant : depressant

3._____

4. RADIO : TELEVISION :: _____ : _____
    A. phonograph : record
    C. stereo : sound
    E. cinema : concert
    B. film : tape
    D. aural : visual

4._____

5. HEAT : FIRE :: _____ : _____
    A. hunger : food
    C. tree : leaf
    E. seed : plant
    B. wood : flame
    D. sound : music

5._____

6. BULB : LIGHT :: _____ : _____
    A. image : mirror
    C. film : camera
    E. sun : rays
    B. words : book
    D. writing : paper

6._____

7. WINTER : OVERCOAT :: _____ : _____
    A. fall : leaves
    C. North Pole : igloo
    E. bathing suit : swimming
    B. summer : sunglasses
    D. India : sari

7._____

8. ESPIONAGE : SPY :: _____ : _____
    A. feet : chiropodist
    C. politics : government
    E. business : Wall Street
    B. obstetrics : pediatrician
    D. surgery : doctor

8._____

9. DETONATE : BOMB :: _____ : _____
    A. grenade : explode
    C. stop : action
    E. trigger : revolver
    B. useless : weapon
    D. violence : war

9._____

10. COURIER : MESSENGER :: _____ : _____
    A. delegate : country   B. speech : politician
    C. carrier : pigeon   D. plenipotentiary : ambassador
    E. run : walk

11. BUS : TERMINAL :: _____ : _____
    A. cow : barn   B. traveler : destination
    C. baseball : home plate   D. train : depot
    E. field : hangar

12. RIBBON : TYPEWRITER :: _____ : _____
    A. refrigerator : freezer   B. bookcase : book
    C. telephone : dial   D. bureau : drawer
    E. wire : telephone

13. VARIABLE : CONSTANT :: _____ : _____
    A. economy : gross national product
    B. element : temperament
    C. velocity : wind
    D. same : change
    E. fluctuation : rate

14. PROVINCIAL : URBAN :: _____ : _____
    A. peasant : peon   B. prince : pauper
    C. suburb : city   D. capital : state
    E. town : country

15. VELOCITY : LIGHT :: _____ : _____
    A. linear : dimension   B. fathom : ocean
    C. time : hour   D. speed : sound
    E. force : gravity

16. AGENT : EMISSARY :: _____ : _____
    A. foreign : intrigue   B. correspondent : journalist
    C. welfare : social worker   D. CIA : intelligence
    E. briefing : member

17. HEATING : AIR CONDITIONING :: _____ : _____
    A. ice : fire   B. refrigeration : cooking
    C. insulation : prefabrication D. winter : summer
    E. degree : temperature

18. PLASTIC : LEATHER :: _____ : _____
    A. tin : aluminum   B. raincoat : handbag
    C. cotton : wool   D. synthetic : genuine
    E. nylon : orlon

19. FAUCET : SINK :: _____ : _____   19.____
    A. pipe : water   B. spray : hose
    C. hose : garden   D. valve : tank
    E. liquid : solid

20. DISCREET : JUDICIOUS :: _____ : _____   20.____
    A. man : judge   B. fool : seer
    C. wise : rash   D. prudence : sagacity
    E. discriminate : indiscriminate

21. ORTHODOX : PARADOX :: _____ : _____   21.____
    A. true : false   B. familiar : strange
    C. doctrinaire : contradiction   D. reason : unreason
    E. usual : exceptional

22. NEFARIOUS : DEED :: _____ : _____   22.____
    A. evil : doer   B. heinous : villainous
    C. crime : wrong   D. flagrant : behavior
    E. iniquitous : atrocious

23. STATE : GOVERNOR :: _____ : _____   23.____
    A. taxpayer : citizen   B. senator : state
    C. city : mayor   D. president : country
    E. Assembly Chamber : Speaker

24. COMMISSION : AGENT :: _____ : _____   24.____
    A. percentage : part   B. remuneration : reward
    C. expense : income   D. fee : attorney
    E. salary : recompense

25. TRAFFIC : STREET :: _____ : _____   25.____
    A. tires : automobiles   B. skaters : rink
    C. sidewalk : pedestrian D. path : horse
    E. signal : policeman

KEY (CORRECT ANSWERS)

1	E	6.	E	11.	D	16.	B	21.	C
2.	D	7.	B	12.	E	17.	D	22.	D
3.	C	8.	D	13.	C	18.	D	23.	C
4.	D	9.	E	14.	C	19.	D	24.	D
5.	D	10.	D	15.	D	20.	D	25.	B

TEST 6

1. VOCABULARY : VERNACULAR :: _____ : _____   1._____
    A. argot : slang   B. idiom : words
    C. region : colloquialism   D. usage : indigenous
    E. locale : accent

2. ALMANAC : STATISTIC :: _____ : _____   2._____
    A. census : population   B. dictionary : definition
    C. anthology : bibliography   D. thesaurus : quotation
    E. encyclopedia : synonym

3. CHAIR : CUSHION :: _____ : _____   3._____
    A. paper : pencil   B. horse : carriage
    C. lawn : grass   D. horse : saddle
    E. clock : time

4. LOCALE : INDIGENOUS :: _____ : _____   4._____
    A. orchids : tropics   B. inherent : inborn
    C. plant : greenhouse   D. city : native
    E. transient : permanent

5. USE : DISUSE :: _____ : _____   5._____
    A. engine : water power   B. siren : shelter
    C. television : newspaper   D. bottle : container
    E. car : carriage

6. TILE : FLOOR :: _____ : _____   6._____
    A. room : wall   B. enamel : paint
    C. beam : ceiling   D. sidewalk : pavement
    E. road : dirt

7. FACTUAL : FICTIVE :: _____ : _____   7._____
    A. prose : poetry   B. newspaper : book
    C. non-fiction : fiction   D. number : word
    E. handwriting : graphology

8. NOVOCAINE : TOOTH :: _____ : _____   8._____
    A. pain : insensitize   B. needle : injection
    C. sterile : syringe   D. anesthetic : area
    E. ache : pull

9. ADDICTION : HABIT :: _____ : _____   9._____
    A. affliction : preference   B. cancer : smoking
    C. practice : frequent   D. drug : coffee
    E. unwonted : rare

10. HEXAGON : PARAGON :: _____ : _____
    A. six : one
    B. angle : curve
    C. six-sided : model
    D. octagon : diamond
    E. septennial : period

10.____

11. PARIAH : PARASITE :: _____ : _____
    A. despised : antagonistic
    B. shepherd : flock
    C. disease : carrier
    D. insect : cell
    E. outcast : sycophant

11.____

12. PROTAGONIST : ANTAGONIST :: _____ : _____
    A. prologue : epilogue
    B. play : message
    C. hero : villain
    D. against : for
    E. evil : good

12.____

13. NOMAD : COLONIST :: _____ : _____
    A. caravan : tent
    B. tribe : indigent
    C. casual : enduring
    D. settle : rove
    E. explore : pioneer

13.____

14. DEMUR : DEMURE :: _____ : _____
    A. decline : disavow
    B. adverb : adjective
    C. hesitate : humble
    D. restrain : refrain
    E. inhibit : inhibition

14.____

15. ENIGMA : PERPLEX :: _____ : _____
    A. falsify : disguise
    B. conundrum : bewilder
    C. mystery : Sphinx
    D. baffle : explanation
    E. ennui : enosis

15.____

16. ICONOCLAST : CHAUVINIST :: _____ : _____
    A. anarchist : patriot
    B. agnostic : heretic
    C. soldier : revolutionary
    D. topple : government
    E. Loyalist : Tory

16.____

17. NUMBER : WORD :: _____ : _____
    A. sum : fraction
    B. decimal : comma
    C. letter : fraction
    D. period : sentence
    E. clause : ratio

17.____

18. SUM : ADDITION :: _____ : _____
    A. multiplication : table
    B. add : arithmetic
    C. part : whole
    D. words : sentence
    E. product : multiplication

18.____

19. STOICAL : BOMBASTIC :: _____ : _____
    A. pain : noise
    B. enthusiasm : exuberance
    C. impassive : inflated
    D. mediocre : outstanding
    E. hermit : pedant

19.____

20. DIVER : DRIVER :: _____ : _____   20.____
    A. road : sea   B. league : fathom
    C. ship : car   D. depth : distance
    E. subterranean : surface

21. FAUNA : FLORA :: _____ : _____   21.____
    A. faun : deer   B. plant : flower
    C. lion : jungle   D. seaweed : octopus
    E. cow : milk

22. WATER : DELUGE :: _____ : _____   22.____
    A. river : ocean   B. exhaust : fume
    C. suffocate : drown   D. wind : cyclone
    E. pressure : atmosphere

23. CONCAVE : CONVEX :: _____ : _____   23.____
    A. up : down
    B. hemisphere : globe
    C. bowl : ball
    D. earth : cave
    E. bulging and curved : hollow and curved

24. DIAMETER : CIRCUMFERENCE :: _____ : _____   24.____
    A. perimeter :parallel   B. hypotenuse : rectangle
    C. earth : equator   D. line : curve
    E. semi-circle : circle

25. ABSOLUTE : RELATIVE :: _____ : _____   25.____
    A. dogmatic : vacillatory   B. all : few
    C. certain : decisive   D. affinity : infinity
    E. pure : contaminated

―――――――

KEY (CORRECT ANSWERS)

1	D	6.	C	11.	E	16.	A	21.	C
2.	B	7.	C	12.	C	17.	B	22.	D
3.	D	8.	D	13.	C	18.	E	23.	C
4.	D	9.	E	14.	C	19.	C	24.	D
5.	E	10.	C	15.	B	20.	E	25.	A

―――――――

TEST 7

1. CHIMERA : MIRAGE :: _____ : _____
   A. illusion : actuality
   B. delusion : desert
   C. vision : mental image
   D. fantasy : phenomenon
   E. fact : fancy

   1.____

2. CONCENTRIC : ROUNDABOUT :: _____ : _____
   A. sphere : circuit
   B. turn : circumference
   C. coil : spiral
   D. circumnavigation : world
   E. radius : center

   2.____

3. VOICE : SONG :: _____ : _____
   A. music : instrument
   B. singer : speaker
   C. body : mime
   D. symphony : concert
   E. athlete : running

   3.____

4. MISANTRHROPY : MISOGYNY :: _____ : _____
   A. miserlinesss : polygamy
   B. female : male
   C. egotism : cynicism
   D. hatred : incivility
   E. mankind : women

   4.____

5. PHILANTHROPY : PHILOLOGY :: _____ : _____
   A. humanitarianism : literature
   B. legend : linguistics
   C. culture : altruism
   D. patriot : anglophile
   E. speech : welfare

   5.____

6. PHONETICIAN : POLEMICIST :: _____ : _____
   A. refutation : principle
   B. sound : dispute
   C. aggressive : controversy
   D. interpreter : anarchist
   E. friendly : hostile

   6.____

7. MENDICANT : MARAUDER :: _____ : _____
   A. cadge : plunder
   B. beggar : masquerader
   C. raider : parasite
   D. poor : rich
   E. settle : roam

   7.____

8. POST OFFICE : STAMP :: _____ : _____
   A. calendar : date
   B. business : letter
   C. tailor : mend
   D. restaurant : dinner
   E. delivery : mail

   8.____

9. MESMERISM : INDUCTION :: _____ : _____
   A. magician : rabbit
   B. hypnotic : hagiologic
   C. magnetism : attraction
   D. psychic : phenomenon
   E. conduction : electricity

   9.____

10. ROPE : HANGING :: _____ : _____
    A. guillotine : executioner
    C. air : suffocation
    E. burning : fire
    B. gas : asphyxiation
    D. epidemic : holocaust

10.____

11. GILL : FISH :: _____ : _____
    A. beak : bird
    C. lung : man
    E. claw : cat
    B. arm : octopus
    D. stinger : bee

11.____

12. PIT : PROTUBERANCE :: _____ : _____
    A. extension : prominence
    C. river :ditch
    E. depth : length
    B. mountain : canyon
    D. abyss : projection

12.____

13. MEASURE : SURFACE :: _____ : _____
    A. gram : time
    C. square rod : area
    E. ocean : depth
    B. pound : ounce
    D. space : league

13.____

14. RED : STOP :: _____ : _____
    A. yellow : fever
    C. black : death
    E. blue : sky
    B. white : truce
    D. red : green

14.____

15. PROFIT : LOSS :: _____ : _____
    A. deterioration : improvement
    C. enter : ledger
    E. debit : credit
    B. debt : debit
    D. black : red

15.____

16. SAND : HOURGLASS :: _____ : _____
    A. minute : time
    C. salt : shaker
    E. ship : ocean
    B. bottle : milk
    D. sun dial : sun

16.____

17. KEY : DOOR :: _____ : _____
    A. raise : window
    C. nail : picture
    E. latch : key
    B. combination : safe
    D. hanger : coat

17.____

18. DEPUTIZE : DEPUTY :: _____ : _____
    A. office : appoint
    C. position : order
    E. elect : governor
    B. administer : administration
    D. inauguration : president

18.____

19. TEAM : DOGS :: _____ : _____
    A. sled : snow
    C. race : horse
    E. sheep : flock
    B. herd : cattle
    D. people : group

19.____

20. OCEAN : ATLANTIC :: _____ : _____   20.____
    A. island : coast   B. straits : Gibraltar
    C. peninsula : Malta   D. cape : Africa
    E. Danube : river

21. GEOGRAPHY : HISTORY :: _____ : _____   21.____
    A. locale : situation   B. space : time
    C. navigation : course   D. individual : ancestry
    E. dimension : depth

22. LOG : CAPTAIN :: _____ : _____   22.____
    A. ledger : bookkeeper   B. compass : direction
    C. fort : cavalry   D. deck : crew
    E. biography : historian

23. INCITE : REVOLT :: _____ : _____   23.____
    A. water : flood   B. ax : tree
    C. ignite : fire   D. mass : riot
    E. flame : gasoline

24. DEPORTATION : EXPATRIATION :: _____ : _____   24.____
    A. criminal : soldier   B. export : import
    C. illegal : legal   D. involuntary : voluntary
    E. punishment : crime

25. INHUME : EXHUME :: _____ : _____   25.____
    A. inhale : exhale   B. bury : disinter
    C. corporeal : spirit   D. autopsy : funeral
    E. burial : cremation

_____

KEY (CORRECT ANSWERS)

1	D	6.	B	11.	C	16.	C	21.	B
2.	A	7.	A	12.	D	17.	B	22.	C
3.	C	8.	D	13.	C	18.	E	23.	C
4.	E	9.	C	14.	B	19.	B	24.	D
5.	A	10.	B	15.	D	20.	B	25.	B

_____

TEST 8

1. GAME : CHESS :: _____ : _____   1._____
    A. hiking : walking   B. sport : swimming
    C. crossword : puzzle   D. gambling : cards
    E. chance : skill

2. FOX : HOUND :: _____ : _____   2._____
    A. horses : chase   B. mouse : cat
    C. detectives : thieves   D. jaguar : ocelot
    E. fire engine : fire

3. ZOOLOGY : ANIMAL :: _____ : _____   3._____
    A. philology : philosophy   B. phytology : plant
    C. penology : penalty   D. training : lion
    E. phrenology : head

4. PHOTOSTAT : DOCUMENT :: _____ : _____   4._____
    A. several : one   B. telegraph : transmission
    C. image : photograph   D. copy : original
    E. device : photography

5. PAGE : PAGEANT :: _____ : _____   5._____
    A. leaf : book   B. errand : palace
    C. words : folio   D. attendant : exhibition
    E. table : tableau

6. PAGODA : GONDOLA :: _____ : _____   6._____
    A. temple : boat   B. Italy : India
    C. water : land   D. boat : tower
    E. vessel : building

7. DULCET : DULCIMER :: _____ : _____   7._____
    A. quiet : organ   B. song : paean
    C. melodious : instrument   D. surcease : bagpipe
    E. modulate : choir

8. DUPERY : DUPLEX :: _____ : _____   8._____
    A. pretend : decay   B. credulity : complex
    C. delude : duple   D. swindle : victimize
    E. trickery : twofold

9. LOQUACITY : GARRULITY :: _____ : _____   9._____
    A. prattle : talkative   B. verbosity : volubility
    C. idle :gossip   D. speech : eloquence
    E. prolific : proliferation

10. METEROROLOGIST : CLAIRVOYANT :: _____ : _____   10._____
    A. weather : oracle   B. climate : air
    C. forecast : prophecy   D. practical : phenomenal
    E. table : crystal ball

11. SEMAPHORIC : SOPHOMORIC :: _____ : _____   11._____
    A. sophistication : absurdity   B. sophist : casuist
    C. casuistry : reasoning   D. signal : student
    E. process : specious

12. HIATUS : SOUND :: _____ : _____   12._____
    A. whisper : vowel   B resonant : vocal
    C. break : sustain   D. omission : emission
    E. memory : lapses

13. MERCURY : THERMOMETER :: _____ : _____   13._____
    A. umbrella : rain   B. air : vacuum
    C. gas : automobile   D. ink : pen
    E. parachute : jumper

14. VICARIOUS : PLEASURE :: _____ : _____   14._____
    A. sympathetic : displacement   B. participating : feeling
    C. substitutional : gratification   D. subliminal : joy
    E. fantasy : pain

15. PLEBISCITE : PLEBEIAN :: _____ : _____   15._____
    A. issue : obscure   B. election : popular
    C. vote : citizen   D. quorum : representatives
    E. plague : populace

16. PLACARD : PLACATE :: _____ : _____   16._____
    A. pacific : pacify   B. notice : appease
    C. poster : propaganda   D. agreement : compromise
    E. place : please

17. NIRVANA : MECCA :: _____ : _____   17._____
    A. Islamic : Utopia   B. Hindu : Arabian
    C. heaven : center   D. Buddhism : Mohammedanism
    E. fantasy : reality

18. SPECTRUM : SPECULATION :: _____ : _____   18._____
    A. image : idea   B. array : meditation
    C. varying : thought   D. sequence : continuous
    E. reflecting : reflect

19. DEXTROSE : GLUCOSE :: _____ : _____   19._____
    A. organic : compound   B. hydrogen : water
    C. coal : carbon   D. liquid : solid
    E. pure : impure

20. CITADEL : CITY :: _____ : _____   20.____
    A. state : capital   B. stronghold : municipality
    C. fortress : command   D. protected : protector
    E. strategic : locale

21. FACTOR : CHARACTERISTIC :: _____ : _____   21.____
    A. corporeal : body   B. paper : wood
    C. gene : gender   D. composition : author
    E. ventricle : heart

22. SPECTRUM : SPECTACLES :: _____ : _____   22.____
    A. color wheel : rotation   B. vision : eyeglasses
    C. mirror : image   D. compendium : exhibit
    E. reflector : sight

23. RHETORICAL : PRAGMATICAL :: _____ : _____   23.____
    A. question : fact   B. abstract : equation
    C. stylized : factual   D. florid : dogma
    E. doctrinaire : philosophy

24. CONTRACTION : ABSTRACTION :: _____ : _____   24.____
    A. abate : abhstruse   B. dwindle : inattentive
    C. decree : summarize   D. diminution : difficult
    E. reduction : removal

25. FRANC : FRANCE :: _____ : _____   25.____
    A. peseta : Cuba   B. drachma : Hong Kong
    C. escudo : Spain   D. rupee : India
    E. krona : Czechoslovakia

_____

KEY (CORRECT ANSWERS)

1	B	6.	A	11.	D	16.	B	21.	C
2.	B	7.	C	12.	D	17.	D	22.	E
3.	B	8.	E	13.	D	18.	B	23.	C
4.	D	9.	B	14.	D	19.	B	24.	E
5.	D	10.	C	15.	B	20.	B	25.	D

_____

TEST 9

1. SOLILOQUY : OBLOQUY :: _____ : _____
   A. Hamlet : deprecatory
   B. language : defamatory
   C. loneliness : contrariness
   D. monologue : calumny
   E. actor : politician

1.____

2. GRAPHITE : CARBON :: _____ : _____
   A. charcoal : coal
   B. mercury : quicksilver
   C. combustible : substance
   D. air : pressure
   E. anthracite : coal

2.____

3. PROCRASTINATE : OBVIATE :: _____ : _____
   A. delaying : disposal
   B. postpone : prevent
   C. lazy : forestall
   D. afraid : obstacle
   E. trifling : erasing

3.____

4. SEQUACIOUS : SEQUENTIAL :: _____ : _____
   A. systematic : methodical
   B. subservient : slave
   C. following : event
   D. legal : process
   E. alienate : organize

4.____

5. PERFORATE : HOLE :: _____ : _____
   A. separation : boring
   B. piercing : knife
   C. weld : joint
   D. union : merger
   E. deteriorate : process

5.____

6. OPACITY : WALL :: _____ : _____
   A. pellucidity : cloud
   B. diaphanousness : cellophane
   C. hyaline : muscle
   D. perspicacity : lucidity
   E. draperies : window

6.____

7. OVAL : EGG :: _____ : _____
   A. adhesive : tape
   B. hexagonal : pentagon
   C. square : circle
   D. rectangular : book
   E. circumference : globe

7.____

8. ONUS : LAGNIAPPE :: _____ : _____
   A. harbinger : spring
   B. debt : debtor
   C. obstacle : clearing
   D. burden : gratuity
   E. omen : guilt

8.____

9. WOOD : SAP :: _____ : _____
   A. rain : snow
   B. plane : safety belt
   C. sky : clouds
   D. calendar : date
   E. ice : water

9.____

10. APOSTIL : APOSTLE :: _____ : _____   10.____
    A. pistil : plant   B. annotation : advocate
    D. footnote : following   D. deception : disciple
    E. atheist : theologist

11. OBSEQUIOUS : BEGGAR :: _____ : _____   11.____
    A. mendicant : suppliant   B. inane : witless
    C. destitute : solicitor   D. fatuous : dullard
    E. penurious : spendthrift

12. APPLIQUÉ : APPLIED :: _____ : _____   12.____
    A. wood : saw   B. eraser : erasure
    C. brick : cemented   D. wheel : spin
    E. book : read

13. RHINOCEROS : MAMMAL :: _____ : _____   13.____
    A. tomato : vegetable   B. snake : animal
    C. rhinestone : diamond   D. paleography : extinct species
    E. rhinoplasty : surgery

14. POUND : LIRA :: _____ : _____   14.____
    A. Lisbon : Monte Carlo   B. Gibraltar : Tangier
    C. Tel Aviv : Sicily   D. Guatemala : South Africa
    E. Denmark : Haiti

15. PERIODICAL : STORY :: _____ : _____   15.____
    A. article : column   B. cart : wheel
    C. newspaper : journal   D. magazine : cartridge
    E. quarterly : book

16. MACHINATE : PLOT :: _____ : _____   16.____
    A. scheme : expedite   B. contrivance : contrive
    C. conspire : cabal   D. conspiracy : intrigue
    E. object : plan

17. FILM : PROJECTOR :: _____ : _____   17.____
    A. tank : oil   B. flame : welder
    C. torch : fire   D. beam : searchlight
    E. forest : timber

18. CYLINDER : ENGINE :: _____ : _____   18.____
    A. pine : cone   B. close : call
    C. head : ax   D. chair : rung
    E. angle : line

19. MERCURIAL : SATURNINE :: _____ : _____   19.____
    A. planet : position   B. volatile : taciturn
    C. Mercury : Saturn   D. mood : fluid
    E. undependable : stolid

20. TIME : SEASON :: _____ : _____   20.____
    A. space : season   B. hybrid : herb
    C. measure : mite   D. predict : plant
    E. seasoning : thyme

21. RATIO : ANALOGY :: _____ : _____   21.____
    A. numbers : equation   B. quotient : proportion
    C. mathematical : verbal   D. fraction : word
    E. computation : anagram

22. ANCHOR : ANCHORITE :: _____ : _____   22.____
    A. secure : withdraw   B. ship : mausoleum
    C. sailor : salacious   D. secrete : drop
    E. article : manufacturer

23. DERAIL : ENGINEER :: _____ : _____   23.____
    A. track : train   B. abdicate : king
    C. execute : warden   D. crash : aeroplane
    E. revolution : anarchist

24. DRAM : TON :: _____ : _____   24.____
    A. peck : bushel   B. rod : pound
    C. gill : fathom   D. gallon : cord
    E. ounce : inch

25. NOM DE PLUME : PEN NAME :: _____ : _____   25.____
    A. nomenclature : title   B. appellation : given name
    C. pseudonym : assumed name   D. surname : first name
    E. title : aristocrat

———

KEY (CORRECT ANSWERS)

1	D	6.	B	11.	D	16.	C	21.	C
2.	E	7.	D	12.	C	17.	D	22.	A
3.	B	8.	D	13.	E	18.	C	23.	B
4.	A	9.	E	14.	C	19.	B	24.	A
5.	C	10.	B	15.	D	20.	E	25.	C

———

TEST 10

1. SENTIMENTALISM : COMPASSION :: _____ : _____
   A. anti-climax : letdown
   B. elevated : commonplace
   C. bathos : pathos
   D. insincere : old fashioned
   E. understated : overstated

   1.____

2. SAND : DESERT :: _____ : _____
   A. door : knob
   B. engine : propulsion
   C. wax : candle
   D. tape : magnetic
   E. photograph : image

   2.____

3. TOOTHPASTE : TUBE :: _____ : _____
   A. file : cabinet
   B. drop : eye
   C. piece : mosaic
   D. solvent : substance
   E. serum : syringe

   3.____

4. SAVANT : SIMPLETON :: _____ : _____
   A. dolt : seer
   B. save : spend
   C. scholar : dunce
   D. detailed : disarranged
   E. thinking : impulsiveness

   4.____

5. SAFARI : ANIMAL :: _____ : _____
   A. voyage : vessel
   B. pilgrimage : shrine
   C. automobile : race
   D. hounds : hunt
   E. excursion : trip

   5.____

6. PATRIMONY : MATRIMONY :: _____ : _____
   A. patriarchy : matriarchy
   B. father : mother
   C thriftiness : marriage
   D. heritage : union
   E. acrimony : conjunction

   6.____

7. DANCE : BALLET :: _____ : _____
   A. music : orchestra
   B. literature : publisher
   C. art : collage
   D. creativity : inspiration
   E. painting : painter

   7.____

8. GOLF : IRON :: _____ : _____
   A. racket : tennis
   B. mineral : game
   C. badminton : shuttlecock
   D. hockey : ice
   E. jai alai : mallet

   8.____

9. EX : ISM :: _____ : _____
   A. Latin : Greek
   B. process : behavior
   C. prefix : suffix
   D. act : from
   E. past : present

   9.____

10. GENERAL : ARMY :: _____ : _____
   A. president : military
   C. executive : company
   E. equestrian : cavalry
   B. factory : foreman
   D. laborer : field

10.____

11. EARTH : ROTATION :: _____ : _____
   A. globe : axis
   C. balloon : ascension
   E. ladder : descend
   B. planet : satellite
   D. sphere : circumference

11.____

12. MAGAZINE : ADVERTISEMENT :: _____ : _____
   A. placard : notice
   C. title : book jacket
   E. reading : selling
   B. wall : poster
   D. leaflet : sentence

12.____

13. CLOWN : CIRCUS :: _____ : _____
   A. playwright : theater
   C. midget : giant
   E. mummer : festivity
   B. humor : arena
   D. drama : actor

13.____

14. HORSE : BRIDLE :: _____ : _____
   A. ship : rope
   C. escalator : stairs
   B. skis : poles
   D. paddle : canoe

14.____

15. ANTIDOTE : ANECDOTE :: _____ : _____
   A. account : remedy
   C. nullification : narration
   E. enmity : affection
   B. action : counteraction
   D. medicinal : mercurial

15.____

16. TENOR : TYPE :: _____ : _____
   A. innate : temperament
   C. singer : song
   E. aspect : acuity
   B. distinguished : personified
   D. demeanor : character

16.____

17. WATER : POWER :: _____ : _____
   A. gravity : force
   C. sieve : straining
   E. atomic : bomb
   B. electricity : illumination
   D. stroke : brush

17.____

18. FLUOROSCOPE : TUBERCULOSIS :: _____ : _____
   A. barometer : temperature
   C. seismograph : earthquake
   E. x-ray : pulsation
   B. thermometer : pressure
   D. lubritorium : laboratory

18.____

19. SEPTUM : SPECTRUM :: _____ : _____
   A. enclosing : parietal
   C. partition : series
   E. fencing : parading
   B. division : rescission
   D. wall : ghastly

19.____

20. DECADENT : CIRCUMSPECT :: _____ : _____   20._____
    A. period : proper   B. cadence : credo
    C. impoverished : wealthy   D. depraved : respectful
    E. recidivistic : prudent

21. CLUB : MEMBERS :: _____ : _____   21._____
    A. party : guests   B. clan : crest
    C. flag : country   D. family : children
    E. feline : cat

22. ORBIT : EARTH :: _____ : _____   22._____
    A. sign : street   B. route : avenue
    C. furrow : plow   D. ring : bull
    E. crash : aeroplane

23. SAVINGS : BANK :: _____ : _____   23._____
    A. stipend : income   B. wall : plug
    C. socket : bulb   D. stocks : bonds
    E. records : file

24. DROLL : DROMEDARY :: _____ : _____   24._____
    A. boar : camel   B. diversion : pachyderm
    C. fig : forest   D. court : desert
    E. plant : person

25. HYPHENATED : ABBREVIATED :: _____ : _____   25._____
    A. quotes : parentheses   B. decimal : fraction
    C. separation : partition   D. discrete : abridged
    E. separated : slang

KEY (CORRECT ANSWERS)

1	C	6.	D	11.	C	16.	D	21.	D
2.	C	7.	C	12.	B	17.	B	22.	C
3.	E	8.	C	13.	E	18.	C	23.	E
4.	C	9.	C	14.	B	19.	C	24.	D
5.	B	10.	C	15.	C	20.	E	25.	D

TEST 11

1. INTERPOSE : INTRUDE :: _____ : _____
   A. interfere : impute
   B. intervene : intercede
   C. arbitrate : argue
   D. meditate : mediate
   E. space : species

2. MALADROIT : GAUCHE :: _____ : _____
   A. right : left
   B. evil : sinful
   C. clever : stupid
   D. depraved : foolish
   E. inept : tactless

3. PRIMITIVE : CIVILIZED :: _____ : _____
   A. jungle : forest
   B. atavistic : masochistic
   C. cave : dwelling
   D. animal : man
   E. wild : domesticated

4. SYMBOL : WORD :: _____ : _____
   A. x : division
   B. $: pound
   C. - : hyphen
   D. y : geometry
   E. & : sum

5. CURRENT : FLOW :: _____ : _____
   A. lighter : match
   B. electricity : gas
   C. fire : flame
   D. conductor : ignition
   E. train : automobile

6. DEMONOLOGY : PHARMACOLOGY :: _____ : _____
   A. demon : farmer
   B. devil : druggist
   C. medieval : primitive
   D. dispensed : compounded
   E. Faustian : Freudian

7. FUNCTIONAL : ORNAMENTAL :: _____ : _____
   A. elevator : escalator
   B. floor : parquet
   C. filigree : scroll
   D. wreath : nosegay
   E. head : hair

8. BRANCH : TREE :: _____ : _____
   A. pin : clasp
   B. stone : setting
   C. cell : prison
   D. annex : building
   E. island : mainland

9. CLOCK : RADIO :: _____ : _____
   A. time : number
   B. light : lamp
   C. ticking : talking
   D. hand : dial
   E. time : space

1._____

2._____

3._____

4._____

5._____

6._____

7._____

8._____

9._____

10. PRESIDENT : UNITED STATES :: _____ : _____   10. _____
    A. Queen Elizabeth : England   B. king : Belgium
    C. president : Bolivia   D. governor : state
    E. king : Italy

11. MILLIMETER : CENTIMETER :: _____ : _____   11. _____
    A. gram : kilogram   B. dekameter : decimeter
    C. mile : kilometer   D. micron : microbe
    E. Centigrade : Fahrenheit

12. METALLURGY : METEOROLOGY :: _____ : _____   12. _____
    A. weight : measure   B. alloys : atmosphere
    C. technology : science   D. archaic : present
    E. metal : meteor

13. MÉTIER : MELEE :: _____ : _____   13. _____
    A. strong : weak   B. profession : struggle
    C. mixed : confusion   D. vocation : trade
    E. expert : novice

14. MEDITERRANEAN : PACIFIC :: _____ : _____   14. _____
    A. Baltic : Indian   B. Atlantic : Caribbean
    C. Arctic : Gulf of Mexico   D. Black Sea : Persian Gulf
    E. Antarctic : Andaman Sea

15. PAROXYSM : PARRICIDE :: _____ : _____   15. _____
    A. filial : fraternal   B. mind : body
    C. attack : murder   D. sudden : poison
    E. diseased : ;dead

16. BUSINESS : EXPEDITER :: _____ : _____   16. _____
    A. travel : interfere   B. experiment : catalyst
    C. manuscript : publisher   D. hasten : rush]
    E. energy : expend

17. COBALT : NICKEL :: _____ : _____   17. _____
    A. calcium : enamel   B. copper : penny
    C. carbon : diamond   D. pure : impure
    E. iodine : chlorine

18. FIRE : ANDIRON :: _____ : _____   18. _____
    A. tire : puncture   B. gas : leak
    C. clay : mold   D. element : support
    E. paper : perforate

19. FLOOD : RAIN :: _____ : _____   19. _____
    A. river : overflowing   B. raining : excessively
    C. monsoon : wind   D. cyclone : hurricane
    E. earthquake : volcano

20. CYLINDRICAL : COLUMN :: _____ : _____   20.____
    A. triangular : obelisk   B. conic : funnel
    C. hexagonal : star   D. cyanic : bluish
    E. rhombus : parallelogram

21. POISON : EMETIC :: _____ : _____   21.____
    A. carbolic acid : milk   B. catalyst : venomous
    C. infect : defect   D. arsenic : anecdote
    E. nicotine : cigarette

22. POIGNANT : SENTIENT :: _____ : _____   22.____
    A. pungent : perceptive   B. biting : feeling
    C. sensitive : emotional   D. keen : piercing
    E. arouse : display

23. ELECTION : ELECTOR :: _____ : _____   23.____
    A. vote : voter   B. process : participant
    C. choice : chosen   D. president : people
    E. primary : privilege

24. ELK : ASIA :: _____ : _____   24.____
    A. camel : South America   B. beaver : Egypt
    C. mosquito : malaria   D. moose : North America
    E. Australia : kangaroo

25. MAH JONGG : TILES :: _____ : _____   25.____
    A. cards : bridge   B. chess : pieces
    C. Russian roulette : dice   D. tennis : court
    E. letters : scrabble

KEY (CORRECT ANSWERS)

1	B	6.	B	11.	A	16.	B	21.	A
2.	E	7.	B	12.	B	17.	E	22.	A
3.	E	8.	D	13.	B	18.	D	23.	B
4.	C	9.	D	14.	A	19.	C	24.	D
5.	B	10.	C	15.	C	20.	B	25.	B

TEST 12

1. DECADE : SCORE :: _____ : _____
   A. century : millennium
   B. planet : astronomy
   C. year : twenty
   D. month : year
   E. one : two

2. DICHOTOMY : SCHIZOPHRENIA :: _____ : _____
   A. altruism : megalomania
   B. neurosis : psychosis
   C. persecution : paranoia
   D. extraversion : claustrophobia
   E. disease : symptom

3. LONDON : ENGLAND :: _____ : _____
   A. Estopil : Portugal
   B. Pnom Penh : Laos
   C. Barcelona : Spain
   D. Saigon : South Vietnam
   E. Venezuela : Caracas

4. POLICEMAN : GENDARME :: _____ : _____
   A. official : citizen
   B. United States : France
   C. officer : attendant
   D. New York : Louisiana
   E. west : east

5. ANTELOPE : TROTTER :: _____ : _____
   A. orangutan : broncho
   B. Wales : United States
   C. caribou : marmoset
   D. ewe : ram
   E. steeplechaser : pacer

6. FALCON : PHEASANT :: _____ : _____
   A. termite : cockroach
   B. chanticleer : rooster
   C. bald eagle : grouse
   D. peacock : hen
   E. vulture : hawk

7. ELECTION : CONCEDE :: _____ : _____
   A. victor : accede
   B. grant : scholarship
   C. war : surrender
   D. state : cede
   E. prison : confess

8. FEAR : DIFFIDENCE :: _____ : _____
   A. qualm : irresolution
   B. fright : stampede
   C. awe : trust
   D. sanguine : apprehensive
   E. nightmare : alarm

9. LASSITUDE : FATIGUE :: _____ : _____
   A. laziness : weariness
   B. continence : ennui
   C. enfeebled : haggard
   D. exertion : tiredness
   E. lethargy : exhaustion

1. ____
2. ____
3. ____
4. ____
5. ____
6. ____
7. ____
8. ____
9. ____

10. DOOM : DESTINY :: _____ : _____   10.____
    A. fate : predestination   B. appointed : office
    C. elect : fated   D. exigency : inevitability
    E. lot : choice

11. DISAVOWAL : NEGATION :: _____ : _____   11.____
    A. veto : ignore   B. contradiction : convention
    C. cancel : canker   D. denial : disclaimer
    E. gainsay : contradict

12. PATOIS : NEOLOGIST :: _____ : _____   12.____
    A. brogue : jargonist   B. empathy : psychiatrist
    C. dialect : Anglicism   D. country : patriot
    E. gazette : journalist

13. LATENCY : DORMANCY :: _____ : _____   13.____
    A. lurk : abeyance   B. concealed : potential
    C. quiescence : indolence   D. escape : observation
    E. suppress : inertia

14. INTERPOLATE : AMALGAMATE :: _____ : _____   14.____
    A. fusion : blend   B. commingle : miscellany
    C. interpretation : commingling D. adulterate : compound
    E. mix : potpourri

15. HARMONIST : CONTRAPUNTIST :: _____ : _____   15.____
    A. instrumentalist : organist   B. quartet : counterpoint
    C. lute : lutenist   D. singer : composition
    E. celloo : violoncello

16. FIENDISH : INCUBI :: _____ : _____   16.____
    A. devilish : ghoulish   B. demoniacal : fabulous
    C. hobgoblin : spook   D. ghoulish : spirits
    E. gnome : salamander

17. QUARRY : PREY :: _____ : _____   17.____
    A. jointure : appanage   B. sporting : blood
    C. contest : play   D. divert : entertain
    E. chase : animal

18. TRENCH : DITCH :: _____ : _____   18.____
    A. carve : chisel   B. furrow : moat
    C. engraving : offset   D. slit : seam
    E. etch : wrinkle

19. ORCHARD : VINEYARD :: _____ : _____   19.____
    A. bower : pergola   B. market : agriculture
    C. greenhouse : gardening   D. wine : apple
    E. fertilizer : vintage

20. BEMUSEMENT : INAPTNESS :: _____ : _____   20.____
    A. oblation : immolation   B. babbling : idiocy
    C. fatuity : inanity   D. shallowness :asininity
    E. thralldom : freedom

21. COUNTERFEIT : FORGERY :: _____ : _____   21.____
    A. imitate :duplication   B. mimicking : parrot
    C. satirize : parody   D. semblance : adaptation
    E. echo : mountain

22. TORT : WRONG :: _____ : _____   22.____
    A. parking : offense   B. smuggle : contraband
    C. breach : violation   D. void : marriage
    E. annulment : invalidation

23. PHANTOM : APPARITION :: _____ : _____   23.____
    A. hallucination : illusion   B. phantasm : phantasmagorical
    C. fancy : visual   D. error : deceptive
    E. ghost : appear

24. SLUMBER : HIBERNATE :: _____ : _____   24.____
    A. doze : somnolence   B. vegetate : dormant
    C. loaf : loiter   D. dawdler : truant
    E. eater : opium

25. DISSONANCE : DISCORDANT :: _____ : _____   25.____
    A. incoherent : unconsolidated   B. unfit : absurd
    C. slacken : looseness   D. instrument : orchestra
    E. incongruity : discrepant

_____

KEY (CORRECT ANSWERS)

1	E	6.	C	11.	D	16.	D	21.	D
2.	C	7.	C	12.	A	17.	A	22.	A
3.	D	8.	A	13.	C	18.	B	23.	A
4.	B	9.	E	14.	D	19.	A	24.	C
5.	A	10.	A	15.	A	20.	A	25.	E

_____

TEST 13

1. SAILOR : PIRATE :: _____ : _____
   A. transient : permanent
   B. mate : captain
   C. plant : fungus
   D. police : thief
   E. wolf : prey

   1._____

2. SPRINTER : GUN :: _____ : _____
   A. butterfly hunter : net
   B. fencer : sword
   C. writer : pen
   D. dog : whistle
   E. fighter : bell

   2._____

3. WRINKLE : FOLD :: _____ : _____
   A. tear : cut
   B. paper : refuse
   C. wrinkle : smooth
   D. steal : lose
   E. sprinkle : rub

   3._____

4. WIND : GALE :: _____ : _____
   A. storm : sea
   B. contraction : dilation
   C. atmospheric pressure : clear day
   D. breeze : gale
   E. affection : passion

   4._____

5. FRAME : PICTURE :: _____ : _____
   A. sash : window
   B. setting : diamond
   C. shell : egg
   D. painting : canvas
   E. border : exile

   5._____

6. TRAIN : WHISTLE :: _____ : _____
   A. air raid : siren
   B. swimmer : bell buoy
   C. singer : tune
   D. car : horn
   E. ship : anchor

   6._____

7. REFUGEE : HAVEN :: _____ : _____
   A. child : bed
   B. exile : sanctuary
   C. berth : stowaway
   D. fish : bowl
   E. prisoner : dungeon

   7._____

8. WAIT : LOITER :: _____ : _____
   A. bum : thief
   B. late : laggard
   C. regress : ingress
   D. diligent : tardy
   E. work : puttr

   8._____

9. SHRUB : PRUNE :: _____ : _____
   A. beard : shave
   B. lawn : mow
   C. wool : shear
   D. hair : trim
   E. scissors :: cut

   9._____

10. FAÇADE : BUILDING :: _____ : _____   10. _____
    A. personality : qualities   B. aspect : appearance
    C. vestibule : apartment   D. demeanor : character
    E. front : affront

11. PARCHED : DESERT :: _____ : _____   11. _____
    A. captive : jail   B. penurious : slum
    C. withered : plant   D. inundated : floor
    E. glum : outlook

12. PARAGRAPH : GIST :: _____ : _____   12. _____
    A. play : outcome   B. matter : particle
    C. molecule : atom   D. matter : essence
    E. epitome : paraphrase

13. BUOY : DETOUR :: _____ : _____   13. _____
    A. ship : hurricane   B. canal : road
    C. storm : accident   D. ocean : road
    E. warning : signal

14. MOTORIST : ROAD SIGN :: _____ : _____   14. _____
    A. telegraph operator : Morse code
    B. vocabulary : alphabet
    C. English : pronunciation
    D. bicyclist : roadblock
    E. reader : punctuation

15. SYNONYM : SAME :: _____ : _____   15. _____
    A. antonym : unlike   B. metaphor : poetry
    C. triangle : pyramid   D. antonym : opposite
    E. metonymy : versification

16. LEG : KNEE :: _____ : _____   16. _____
    A. angle : elbow   B. compound sentence : conjunction\
    C. hand : wrist   D. ribs : breastbone
    E. simile : metaphor

17. SUPPLENESS : ACROBAT :: _____ : _____   17. _____
    A. paint : artist   B. imagination : artist
    C. grace : chess-player   D. fleetness : runner
    E. strength : detective

18. LAUGH : SMILE :: _____ : _____   18. _____
    A. grumble : scowl   B. express : restrain
    C. cry : sigh   D. lament : condole
    E. entice : endow

19. ANARCHY : CHAOS :: _____ : _____   19.____
    A. hierarchy : peace   B. disturbance : problem
    C. government : order   D. oppression : confusion
    E. dictator : democrat

20. CEILING : PILLAR :: _____ : _____   20.____
    A. steel : girder   B. apex : climax
    C. tree : trunk   D. society : law
    E. prices : subsidy

21. EMOTION : REASON :: _____ : _____   21.____
    A. deference : thought   B. anger : spite
    C. intemperate : critical   D. devotion : fondness
    E. fulmination : recrimination

22. PROSPEROUS : PRODIGAL :: _____ : _____   22.____
    A. rich : gorgeous   B. wealth : prosperous
    C. well-to-do : heedless   D. poor : frugal
    E. lachrymose : indolent

23. FISH : MERMAID :: _____ : _____   23.____
    A. horse : centaur   B. fish : nymph
    C. horse : man   D. crocodile : dragon
    E. shark : whale

24. SOLDIER : KHAKI :: _____ : _____   24.____
    A. sum : gold   B. soldier : whisper
    C. king : purple   D. grass : green
    E. cork : bottle

25. WEIGHT : PAPER :: _____ : _____   25.____
    A. stopper : door   B. sound : whisper
    C. length : inch   D. anchor : ship
    E. cork : bottle

KEY (CORRECT ANSWERS)

1	C	6.	D	11.	B	16.	C	21.	C
2.	E	7.	B	12.	D	17.	D	22.	D
3.	A	8.	E	13.	D	18.	A	23.	A
4.	E	9.	D	14.	E	19.	C	24.	C
5.	B	10.	D	15.	D	20.	E	25.	D

TEST 14

1. LOOM : DISASTER :: _____ : _____
   A. impend : catastrophe   B. question : puzzle
   C. imminent : eminent   D. howl : storm
   E. hurt : penalty

2. STUDY : GRANT :: _____ : _____
   A. honor : medal   B. merit : scholarship
   C. student : bonus   D. matrimony : dowry
   E. research : fellowship

3. BURGLAR : ALARM :: _____ : _____
   A. snake : hiss   B. trespasser : bark
   C. crossing : bell   D. air raid : siren
   E. ship : buoy

4. FEELING : INTUITION :: _____ : _____
   A. discretion : improvidence   B. spirit : spiritualism
   C. reason : rationalization   D. sophistry : logic
   E. wisdom : sophistication

5. REMORSELESS : COMPASSION :: _____ : _____
   A. unscrupulous : qualms   B. intrepid : rashness
   C. opportunist : opportunity   D. querulous : lamentation
   E. impenitent : sin

6. SECULAR : ALTRUISTIC :: _____ : _____
   A. scientist : missionary   B. mundane : spiritual
   C. municipal : ecclesiastical D. pecuniary : musical
   E. student : teacher

7. POSTERIOR : SIMULTANEOUS :: _____ : _____
   A. posthumous : following   B. now : there
   C. consecutive : ensuing   D. subsequent : coincidental
   E. prolonged : before

8. EPILOGUE : PROLOGUE :: _____ : _____
   A. glossary : index   B. preface : table of contents
   C. progeny : proletariat   D. footnote : emendation
   E. appendix : preface

9. CONDONE : ERROR :: _____ : _____
   A. extenuate : crime   B. placate : pardon
   C. expiate : sin   D. moderate : tone
   E. reprisal : retaliation

1.____

2.____

3.____

4.____

5.____

6.____

7.____

8.____

9.____

10. PACT : FEUD :: _____ : _____
    A. alliance : organization   B. treaty : covenant
    C. conciliation : revolution   D. entreaty : parity
    E. concord : discord

10.____

11. ENTHUSIASTIC : FERVOR :: _____ : _____
    A. affectionate : adumbration   B. calm : listless
    C. eager : sentimentality   D. glib : fluency
    E. fond : infatuation

11.____

12. GANG : HIGHJACK :: _____ : _____
    A. rat : gnaw   B. monkey : mimic
    C. reader : browse   D. trooper : lurk
    E. wolf : prowl

12.____

13. REWARD : CAPTURE :: _____ : _____
    A. deed : crime   B. play : plot
    C. criminal : reward   D. dance : movement
    E. emolument : incentive

13.____

14. OVAL : CIRCLE :: _____ : _____
    A. line : perimeter   B. triangle : square
    C. square : diamond   D. circle : square
    E. rectangle : square

14.____

15. SEA : OCEAN :: _____ : _____
    A. land : water   B. village : suburb
    C. cape : continent   D. stream : river
    E. city : country

15.____

16. GRADE : MOUNTAIN :: _____ : _____
    A. altitude : hill   B. pitch : roof
    C. shingles : roof   D. depth : valley
    E. height : hill

16.____

17. VEGETABLES : PORTION :: _____ : _____
    A. medicine : dose   B. oatmeal : spoon
    C. bread : loaf   D. water : glass
    E. fish : vitamins

17.____

18. FAILURES : EXAMINATION :: _____ : _____
    A. water : faucet   B. impurities : filter
    C. remedies : petition   D. quality : denier
    E. wheat : chaff

18.____

19. EARTH : AXIS :: _____ : _____
    A. wheel : hub   B. state : nation
    C. mountain : sea   D. earth : sun
    E. orbit : firmament

19.____

20. TERSE : TURGID :: _____ : _____   20._____
    A. cow : pig   B. state : nation
    C. mountain : sea   D. tremendous : prodigious
    E. slim : obese

21. SKY : CLOUD :: _____ : _____   21._____
    A. crime : sex   B. sun : shade
    C. mind : prejudice   D. ugly : thought
    E. knowledge : obtuse

22. INCONSTANT : VACILLATION :: _____ : _____   22._____
    A. unstable : stability   B. aberrant : constancy
    C. variable : wind   D. capricious : vagary
    E. vacillating : steadfastness

23. CLIMAX : BATTLE :: _____ : _____   23._____
    A. prelude : interlude   B. emergency : decision
    C. coup d'etat : revolution D. apex : flight
    E. crisis : disease

24. FAILURE : TIMOROUSNESS :: _____ : _____   24._____
    A. sagacity : experience   B. study : mastery
    C. heredity : wisdom   D. smarting : ointment
    E. experiment : hypothesis

25. AFFIRMATION : REPORT :: _____ : _____   25._____
    A. acknowledgment : rumor   B. testify : certify
    C. probably : possible   D. reputation : gossip
    E. servility : dependability

_____

KEY (CORRECT ANSWERS)

1	A	6.	B	11.	E	16.	B	21.	C
2.	E	7.	D	12.	E	17.	A	22.	D
3.	B	8.	E	13.	E	18.	B	23.	E
4.	D	9.	A	14.	E	19.	A	24.	A
5.	A	10.	E	15.	D	20.	E	25.	A

_____

TEST 15

1. FEATHERS : PLUMAGE :: _____ : _____   1.____
    A. skin : hide   B. New York State : The United States
    C. fur : hair   D. drawers : bureau
    E. pillows : bed

2. EAST : ORIENT :: _____ : _____   2.____
    A. mysterious : orient   B. north : polar
    C. west : occident   D. south : tropic
    E. equator : latitude

3. DEFTNESS : PIANIST :: _____ : _____   3.____
    A. thought : teacher   B. easel : artist
    C. fleetness : runner   D. grace : ballplayer
    E. skill : boxer

4. UNIFORM : SOLDIER :: _____ : _____   4.____
    A. dungarees : child   B. screen : fireplace
    C. wings : airman   D. clothing : man
    E. domino : masquerader

5. WOOD : LATTICE :: _____ : _____   5.____
    A. metal : auto radiator   B. tile : fireplace
    C. wood : door   D. iron : grille
    E. steel : building

6. UMBRELLA : RAIN :: _____ : _____   6.____
    A. roof : snow   B. screen : insects
    C. sewer : water   D. aspirin : cold
    E. hood : coat

7. RELAX : BODY :: _____ : _____   7.____
    A. slacken : rope   B. empty : ballast
    C. conciliation : strike   D. sleep : fatigue
    E. knockout : boxer

8. MUSIC : SCORE :: _____ : _____   8.____
    A. music : anthology   B. penmanship : handwriting
    C. paper : portfolio   D. poetry : verse
    E. song : paean

9. STORM : SUBSIDE :: _____ : _____   9.____
    A. snow : rain   B. revolution : quell
    C. attack : die   D. degree : cool
    E. fight : rumpus

10. NORTH STAR : VANE :: _____ : _____   10.____
    A. air pressure : barometer   B. sun : sextant
    C. honesty : hypocrisy   D. constancy : capriciousness
    E. mirror : mirage

11. AGNOSTIC : ATHEIST :: _____ : _____   11.____
    A. orthodox : heterodox   B. unbeliever : iconoclast
    C. vague : defiant   D. heretic : pagan
    E. questionable : definite

12. SMITH : SMITHY :: _____ : _____   12.____
    A. druggist :drug store   B. chemist : laboratory
    C. captain : ship   D. sickly : sickliness
    E. miser : miserliness

13. SECOND : TIME :: _____ : _____   13.____
    A. inch : space   B. pound : weight
    C. minute : day   D. point : line
    E. steak : potatoes

14. SINGLE : PROTEAN :: _____ : _____   14.____
    A. cursed : hallowed   B. inexorable : austere
    C. unvarying : transient   D. reasonableness : sensibility
    E. varying : steadfast

15. PRESCIENCE : ORACLE :: _____ : _____   15.____
    A. blunderbuss : soldier   B. priesthood : deity
    C. highness : prince   D. unimpressiveness : gnome
    E. omniscience : seer

16. ACID : CARBOY :: _____ : _____   16.____
    A. disillusionment : life   B. water : jug
    C. destructiveness : railway   D. solution : mineral
    E. discipline : army

17. REDRESS : LAWSUIT :: _____ : _____   17.____
    A. refugee : homeland   B. recuperation : vacation
    C. bail : sentence   D. cajole : jailor
    E. joy : sorrow

18. PEREMPTORY : POSITIVE :: _____ : _____   18.____
    A. demented : vexed   B. ancient : old
    C. ineluctable : indefeasible   D. celibate : without relatives
    E. generosity : parsimony

19. ZEAL : ASSIDUOUSLY :: _____ : _____   19.____
    A. determination : flatteringly B. error : not thoroughly
    C. ardor : elusively   D. perfunctory : diligently
    E. indolence

121

20. VENT : IRE :: _____ : _____   20.____
    A. pardon : prisoner   B. slake : thirst
    C. devour : food   D. loose : tight
    E. unshackle : fetters

21. VIRTUOSO : TYRO :: _____ : _____   21.____
    A. sophistication : ingenuity B. knowledge : rudiments
    C. end : beginning   D. complexity : elementary
    E. bellicosity : ingenuousness

22. SOLUTION : CRYSTALLIZATION :: _____ : _____   22.____
    A. seedling : towering oak   B. ponder : puzzle
    C. hypothesis : premise   D. gestation : birth
    E. answer : question

23. FREEDOM : TYRANNY :: _____ : _____   23.____
    A. leisure class : aristocracy B. democracy : autocracy
    C. tyranny : nobility   D. mob : despot
    E. poverty : wealth

24. WATER : SPONGE :: _____ : _____   24.____
    A. spore : sponge   B. ink : blotter
    C. water : wet   D. pen : pencil
    E. margin : hole

25. GOSSIP : HAMLET :: _____ : _____   25.____
    A. village : reputation   B. press : nation
    C. gossip : newspaper   D. truth : story
    E. chapter : book

KEY (CORRECT ANSWERS)

1	B	6.	B	11.	E	16.	B	21.	B
2.	C	7.	A	12.	B	17.	B	22.	D
3.	E	8.	D	13.	A	18.	B	23.	B
4.	E	9.	D	14.	C	19.	E	24.	B
5.	D	10.	D	15.	E	20.	E	25.	B

TEST 16

1. DESIST : CONTINUE :: _____ : _____
   A. supply : produce
   B. advance : hesitate
   C. perform : undertake
   D. lose : possess
   E. recur : cease

1.____

2. DESTINATION : VOYAGE :: _____ : _____
   A. success : talent
   B. goal : motivation
   C. triumph : victory
   D. consequence : misdeed
   E. objective : campaign

2.____

3. OAK : ACORN :: _____ : _____
   A. vegetable : earth
   B. bird : egg
   C. muscle : cell
   D. flight : motion
   E. crime : implication

3.____

4. POUND : PIERCE :: _____ : _____
   A. club : sword
   B. cut : parry
   C. thrust : pierce
   D. cut : break
   E. break : crack

4.____

5. PAW : CAT :: _____ : _____
   A. wing : robin
   B. egg : chicken
   C. hoof : horse
   D. hole : chipmunk
   E. purr : kitten

5.____

6. CLOCK : HOURGLASS :: _____ : _____
   A. matter : mind
   B. church : temple
   C. oak : scorn
   D. cannon : catapult
   E. temple : foundation

6.____

7. LETTER : TELEGRAM :: _____ : _____
   A. tortoise : hare
   B. truth : lie
   C. essay : thesis
   D. word : number
   E. modesty : egotism

7.____

8. LAW : SOCIETY :: _____ : _____
   A. law : jury
   B. rules : baseball
   C. jury : sentence
   D. prisoner : cell
   E. prisoner : law

8.____

9. PRAISE : DEJECTION :: _____ : _____
   A. relaxation : recreation
   B. precipice : mountain
   C. laziness : obesity
   D. diploma : graduate
   E. rest : fatigue

9.____

10. MEMBER : LEAGUE :: _____ : _____
    A. appurtenance : object
    C. nucleus : cell
    E. fiber : fabric
    B. obstinate : deadlock
    D. leverage : aggregate

10.____

11. CHARACTER : DISSIPATION :: _____ : _____
    A. signature : forgery
    C. food : fasting
    E. task : fatigue
    B. landscape : flatness
    D. rock : erosion

11.____

12. BLACKMAIL : VICTIM :: _____ : _____
    A. death : suffer
    C. war : prisoner
    E. ransom : captive
    B. money : prisoner
    D. money : kidnapper

12.____

13. TREASON : STATE :: _____ : _____
    A. treason : institution
    C. orthodoxy : atheism
    E. heresy : church
    B. institution : state
    D. atheism : agnosticism

13.____

14. ACCOMPLISHMENT : PLAN :: _____ : _____
    A. moth : larva
    C. community : plan
    E. train : community
    B. accomplishment : community
    D. populace : community

14.____

15. AVIARY : BIRDS :: _____ : _____
    A. jungle : monkeys
    C. nest : birds
    E aquarium : fish
    B. estuary : monkeys
    D. museum : monkeys

15.____

16. ORANGE : SPHERE :: _____ : _____
    A. sphere : triangle
    C. wheel : circle
    E. round : orange
    B. square : house
    D. round : sphere

16.____

17. CONSPIRATORS : PLOT :: _____ : _____
    A. general : army
    C. priest : religion
    E. government : people
    B. farm : produce
    D. architect : house

17.____

18. SMASHED : CRACKED :: _____ : _____
    A. irretrievable : mislaid
    C. found : lost
    E. invisible : seen
    B. mend : break
    D. present : gone

18.____

19. FAULT : GUILT :: _____ : _____
    A. apparently : secretly
    C. more : less
    E. guilt : punishment
    B. rather : quite
    D. nearly : hardly

19.____

20. APPARENTLY : REALLY :: _____ : _____   20.____
    A. hardship : emergency   B. from : to
    C. by : of   D. angrily : satirically
    E. off : down

21. SELF-SATISFACTION : PRAISE :: _____ : _____   21.____
    A. grief : sadness   B. dying : grave
    C. peace : lose   D. evil : chastisement
    E. weeping : punishment

22. LAUGH : TITTER :: _____ : _____   22.____
    A. condemn : complain   B. jail : sentence
    C. sigh : weep   D. laughter : anger
    E. brightness : fancy

23. HYPOTHESIS : PROBLEM :: _____ : _____   23.____
    A. medicine : illness   B. cause : disaster
    C. prognosis : disease   D. forecast : humidity
    E. warning : detour

24. WOOL : SUIT :: _____ : _____   24.____
    A. bullion : coin   B. voice : words
    C. mint : money   D. soup : dessert
    E. print : periodical

25. BUS : DEPOT :: _____ : _____   25.____
    A. apiary : bees   B. grain : barn
    C. birds : aviary   D. subway : kiosk
    E. ships : drydock

KEY (CORRECT ANSWERS)

1	D	6.	D	11.	D	16.	C	21.	E
2.	E	7.	A	12.	E	17.	D	22.	A
3.	B	8.	B	13.	E	18.	A	23.	C
4.	A	9.	E	14.	A	19.	B	24.	A
5.	C	10.	E	15.	E	20.	B	25.	C

TEST 17

1. CHARCOAL : WOOD :: _____ : _____   1.____
    A. steel : iron   B. oxygen : nitrogen
    C. bread : yeast   D. coke : coal
    E. skeleton : body

2. TRIANGLE : SQUARE :: _____ : _____   2.____
    A. pyramid : cube   B. square : parallelogram
    C. triangle : cone   D. hexagon : pentagon
    E. cone : cylinder

3. APRICOT : FIG :: _____ : _____   3.____
    A. raisin : prune   B. grape : raisin
    C. wine : alcohol   D. privet : barberry
    E. cherry : wine

4. NATIONALIZATION : SOCIALISM :: _____ : _____   4.____
    A. taxation : totalitarianism   B. independence : agriculture
    C. entreprenueur : laissez-faire D. serfdom : feudalism
    E. freedom : dictatorship

5. ICHTHYOLOGIST : MARINE LIFE :: _____ : _____   5.____
    A. philologist : stamps   B. entomologist : words
    C. theologian : astronomy   D. ornithologist : horticulture
    E. archeologist : antiquity

6. PILOT : SEXTANT :: _____ : _____   6.____
    A. mason : awl   B. reader : novel
    C. ploughman : scythe   D. teacher : quadrant
    E. woodman : axe

7. POTATO : PECK :: _____ : _____   7.____
    A. bullion : silver   B. ring : gold
    C. gold : ore   D. diamond : carat
    E. bushel : oat

8. INTRODUCTION : CONCLUSION :: _____ : _____   8.____
    A. motor : housing   B. engine : caboose
    C. cabin : train   D. power : freight
    E. beginning : commencement

9. PEWTER : LEAD :: _____ : _____   9.____
    A. brass : copper   B. tin : foil
    C. urn : copper   D. zinc : iron
    E. coin : silver

10. LAGOON : BAY :: _____ : _____
    A. island : peninsula
    C. brook : river
    E. stream : outlet
    B. cove : bay
    D. ocean : gulf

10.____

11. BICARBONATE : GASTRIC ACIDITY :: _____ : _____
    A. steam : engine
    C. ulcer : cancer
    E. hope : despair
    B. apathy : despair
    D. praise : depression

11.____

12. DEAN : STUDENTS :: _____ : _____
    A. guide : tourists
    C. scientists : knowledge
    E. leader : paratroop team
    B. doctor : patients
    D. minister : congregation

12.____

13. HOMICIDE : MURDER :: _____ : _____
    A. weakness : act
    C. untruth : lie
    E. hallucination : nightmare
    B. prevaricate : deny
    D. accident : assault

13.____

14. EGOTISM : SELFISH :: _____ : _____
    A. hardihood : hardy
    C. solitude : indifference
    E. great : greater
    B. fortitude : force
    D. friendship : friend

14.____

15. CERTAINLY : SURELY :: _____ : _____
    A. rarely : generally
    C. probably : perhaps
    E. incidentally : fortuitous
    B. necessity : invention
    D. surely ; accidentally

15.____

16. CARICATURE : PORTRAIT :: _____ : _____
    A. imitate : lampoon
    C. paraphrase : verbatim
    E. likeness : sketch
    B. quotation : allusion
    D. similarity : likeness

16.____

17. LUXURY : LETHARGY :: _____ : _____
    A. because : out
    C. necessity : invention
    E. opulence : affluence
    B. emergency : effect
    D. hardship : luck

17.____

18. THAT IS : SUCH AS :: _____ : _____
    A. like : i.e.
    C. for instance : especially
    E. viz. : ibid.
    B. namely : for example
    D. to wit : thus

18.____

19. PROVIDED THAT : AGREEMENT :: _____ : _____
    A. granted that : nevertheless
    C. relying upon : enmity
    E. in accordance with : depending
    B. except : consent
    D. on condition that : acceptance

19.____

20. IN FACT : INDEED :: _____ : _____   20.____
    A. really : consequently   B. statement : hyperbole
    C. average : extraordinary   D. truly : forsooth
    E. reality : fiction

21. PHLEGMATIC : STOLIDITY :: _____ : _____   21.____
    A. dry : moderation   B. degenerate : perversity
    C. accident : recklessness   D. headlong : impetuosity
    E. quiet : tacit

22. RESPECTED : RESPECTFUL :: _____ : _____   22.____
    A. intend : pretend   B. proud : haughty
    C. reverend : reverent   D. kneeling :pious
    E. sycophant : king

23. OVERDOSE : HEAPING MEASURE :: _____ : _____   23.____
    A. potion : beverage   B. of : off
    C. approach : accost   D. too : very
    E. copious : scanty

24. CONTIGUOUS : CLOSE :: _____ : _____   24.____
    A. wit : approach   B. off : from
    C. next : by   D. warmth : glow
    E. adjacent : sequence

25. SOLO : ENSEMBLE :: _____ : _____   25.____
    A. each : everybody   B. ocean : wave
    C. ball of wool : skein   D. spool : thread
    E. house : beams

KEY (CORRECT ANSWERS)

1	D	6.	E	11.	D	16.	C	21.	D
2.	A	7.	D	12.	D	17.	C	22.	C
3.	A	8.	B	13.	C	18.	B	23.	D
4.	D	9.	A	14.	A	19.	D	24.	C
5.	E	10.	C	15.	C	20.	D	25.	A

TEST 18

1. SUPERSTITION : TALISMAN :: _____ : _____   1._____
   - A. belief : peaceful
   - B. charm : talisman
   - C. savage : barbarian
   - D. ritual : savage
   - E. experiment : antitoxin

2. MARTIAL : HALCYON :: _____ : _____   2._____
   - A. belligerent : growling
   - B. warlike : peaceful
   - C. warlike : mournful
   - D. Mars : sun
   - E. worried : soothed

3. WHEAT : CHAFF :: _____ : _____   3._____
   - A. wine : dregs
   - B. dross : ore
   - C. lead : gold
   - D. humanity : dregs
   - E. wisdom : cunning

4. RIDDLE : ENIGMA :: _____ : _____   4._____
   - A. string : labyrinth
   - B. matador : bull
   - C. alternative : dilemma
   - D. haze : labyrinth
   - E. ancient : sphinx

5. ELATION : PASSED :: _____ : _____   5._____
   - A. disapproval : approved
   - B. emotion : success
   - C. dejected : failed
   - D. angry : rejected
   - E. dejection : failed

6. GREYHOUND : FLEETNESS :: _____ : _____   6._____
   - A. bloodhound : odor
   - B. hen : cowardice
   - C. truck : commodious
   - D. Pekingese :affectation
   - E. bulldog : pugnacity

7. LEAGUE : TEAM :: _____ : _____   7._____
   - A. federation : union
   - B. city : borough
   - C. gender : girls
   - D. congregation : sect
   - E. organization : club

8. LABOR : WAGES :: _____ : _____   8._____
   - A. ambition : honor
   - B. examination : marks
   - C. diligence : bonus
   - D. study : diploma
   - E. course : promotion

9. ENVY : GREEN :: _____ : _____   9._____
   - A. depressed : yellow
   - B. rage : red
   - C. fright : chalk
   - D. red : henna
   - E. cadaverous : ashen

10. MOTOR : IGNITION :: _____ : _____   10.____
    A. ambition : aspiration   B. lamp : light
    C. spur : horse   D. man : stimulus
    E. dynamo : switch

11. WEALTHY : INDIGENT :: _____ : _____   11.____
    A. graceful : gauche   B. poised : sad
    C. secretive : clandestine   D. melancholy : lugubrious
    E. thoughtless : inadvertent

12. MASTERPIECE : CONNOISSEUR :: _____ : _____   12.____
    A. art : artificer   B. edition : critic
    C. patrician : plebeian   D. séance : clairvoyant
    E. caviar : gourmet

13. BLACKBOARD : PENMANSHIP :: _____ : _____   13.____
    A. statue : sphinx   B. masterpiece : signature
    C. geography : cartography   D. medicine : cardiograph
    E. obelisk : hieroglyphic

14. MELANCHOLY : EFFUSIVE :: _____ : _____   14.____
    A. downcast : exuberant   B. beaver : eager
    C. lavish : exultant   D. abundant : parsimonious
    E. dispersal : congregation

15. INDIVIDUAL : MULTITUDE :: _____ : _____   15.____
    A. cerebrum : nucleus   B. strait : peninsula
    C. nucleus : cell   D. island : archipelago
    E. Africa : Australia

16. COOLIE : RICKSHAW :: _____ : _____   16.____
    A. teacher : prodigy   B. horse : carriage
    C. ass : Ford   D. Shetland : pony
    E. hen : egg

17. SPEAR : KNIGHT :: _____ : _____   17.____
    A. marine : sailor   B. pirate : ship
    C. book : writer   D. carbine : soldier
    E. test tube : chemist

18. RED : BLACK :: _____ : _____   18.____
    A. Fascists :; Nazis   B. Communists : Fascists
    C. Liberals : Blackshirts   D. Whites : Brownshirts
    E. subversive : patriotic

19. FATHOM : DEPTH :: _____ : _____   19.____
    A. carat : weight   B. rod : farm
    C. speed : knot   D. acre : distance
    E. pennyweight : diamond

20. DULL : SHREWD :: _____ : _____   20._____
    A. knife : blade   B. obtuse : acute
    C. chisel : hammer   D. opaque : transparent
    E. perspicuous : perspicacious :

21. COLLAPSE : REGIME :: _____ : _____   21._____
    A. fame : disgrace   B. illness : woman
    C. founder : ship   D. incarcerate : criminal
    E. holocaust : earthquake

22. STATUE : SCULPTOR :: _____ : _____   22._____
    A. art : sculptor   B verse : poet
    C. prelude : musician   D. house : architect
    E. chisel : craftsman

23. CULMINATION : INCEPTION :: _____ : _____   23._____
    A. lamb : cub   B. pod : seed
    C. senility : puerility   D. novice : fundamental
    E. maturity : infancy

24. REMOTE : PONDEROUS :: _____ : _____   24._____
    A. recondite : bulky   B. protracted : laden
    C. distant : momentous   D. hence : pensive
    E. yonder : onerous

25. DISORDER : POLICE :: _____ : _____   25._____
    A. money : miser   B. stoic : emotion
    C. humility : arrogant   D. dilemma : solution
    E. flood : levee

KEY (CORRECT ANSWERS)

1	C	6.	E	11.	A	16.	B	21.	C
2.	B	7.	A	12.	E	17.	D	22.	B
3.	A	8.	D	13.	E	18.	B	23.	E
4.	D	9.	B	14.	A	19.	A	24.	A
5.	E	10.	E	15.	E	20.	B	25.	E

TEST 19

1. SHEEP : MUTTON :: _____ : _____   1.____
    A. youth : age   B. sheep : lamb
    C. beef : steer   D. beef : veal
    E. pig : pork

2. BULL : PICADOR :: _____ : _____   2.____
    A. song : vocalist   B. cow : matador
    C. speaker : heckler   D. victim : executioner
    E. eye : mote

3. WHIG : TORY :: _____ : _____   3.____
    A. Socialist : Monarchist B. Liberal : Conservative
    C. Democrat : Republican   D. patriot : traitor
    E. Republican : Conservative

4. SPARSE : DENSE :: _____ : _____   4.____
    A. clever : shrewd   B. bald : stupid
    C. obtuse : acute   D. California : New York
    E. Nevada : Java

5. FREQUENTLY : SELDOM :: _____ : _____   5.____
    A. happy : sad   B. always : never
    C. never : always   D. intermittently : occasionally
    E. constantly : ubiquitously

6. BULLET : TRIGGER :: _____ : _____   6.____
    A. rope : pulley   B. drawer : handle
    C. light : bulb   D. current : switch
    E. gun : holster

7. DISASTER : PREMONITION :: _____ : _____   7.____
    A. event : prophecy   B. fact : opinion
    C. religion : faith   D. life : dream
    E. expectation : hope

8. COASTLINE : STATUE :: _____ : _____   8.____
    A. oblong : square   B. trapezoid : parallel
    C. irregular : symmetrical D. area : perimeter
    E. solid : sphere

9. DISEASE : IMMUNITY :: _____ : _____   9.____
    A. obligation : debt   B. custom : conformity
    C. tax : exemption   D. change : adaptation
    E. transgression : pardon

10. GLANCE : SCRUTINIZE :: _____ : _____   10.____
    A. watch : search   B. look : see
    C. ponder : examine   D. eye : sight
    E. touch : grasp

11. MUSCLE : CRAMP :: _____ : _____   11.____
    A. stone : crack   B. pain : throb
    C. order : cancel   D. machine : jam
    E. lightning : flash

12. PLATEAU : PLAIN :: _____ : _____   12.____
    A. lake : river   B. country : state
    C. order : cancel   D. peak : gorge
    E. mountain : valley

13. POODLE : KENNEL :: _____ : _____   13.____
    A. pugilist : ring   B. canary : cage
    C. tiger : zoo   D. bird : nest
    E. fish : tackle

14. WALL : MASON :: _____ : _____   14.____
    A. cement : bricklayer   B. friendship : stranger
    C. cure : doctor   D. magic : magician
    E. picture : painter

15. AUTOMOBILE : BRAKE :: _____ : _____   15.____
    A. doer : thinker   B. horse : ride
    C. society : detergent   D. man : conscience
    E. carburetor : choke

16. ARCTIC : GELID :: _____ : _____   16.____
    A. penicillin : cure   B. invigoration : exhilaration
    C. tropical : luxuriant   D. cold : muddy
    E. disturbed : halcyon

17. BIGOTRY : TOLERANCE :: _____ : _____   17.____
    A. urgency : exigency   B. ribaldry : prodigality
    C. profession : avocation   D. unselfish : selfish
    E. parsimony : magnanimity

18. ENCORE : CATCALL :: _____ : _____   18.____
    A. amnesia : oblivion   B. felon : miscreant
    C. constantly : bow   D. applause : ridicule
    E. generosity : lechery

19. PRECIPITOUS : DISCONSOLATE :: _____ : _____   19.____
    A. melancholy : unhappy   B. askew : explicit
    C. nebulous : credulous   D. intrinsic : fatuous
    E. headlong : dejected

20. LETHARGIC : ABSTEMIOUS :: _____ : _____   20.____
    A. torpid : temperate   B. pusillanimous : absent
    C. militant : irascible   D. dogmatic : truculent
    E. latent : gregarious

21. TRESPASS : WANDER :: _____ : _____   21.____
    A. examine : glance   B. sprawl : recline
    C. gorge : eat   D. destroy : mar
    E. perjure : relate

22. OBLIGATION : ABSOLVE :: _____ : _____   22.____
    A. honor : retract   B. debt : regain
    C. duty : resent   D. position : retract
    E. blame : exculpate

23. CONTEMPT : SNUB :: _____ : _____   23.____
    A. retaliation : injury   B. superiority : scorn
    C. understanding : praise   D. approbation : applause
    E. amusement : grimace

24. CONVINCE : GULLIBLE :: _____ : _____   24.____
    A. cheat : unassuming   B. insult : sensitive
    C. steal : starved   D. suffer : fatigued
    E. fear :frightened

25. SPECIES : HYBRID :: _____ : _____   25.____
    A. mixture : blend   B. metal : alloy
    C. plant : flower   D. rock : metal
    E. block : chip

KEY (CORRECT ANSWERS)

1	E	6.	D	11.	D	16.	C	21.	E
2.	C	7.	A	12.	E	17.	E	22.	E
3.	B	8.	C	13.	B	18.	D	23.	D
4.	E	9.	C	14.	E	19.	E	24.	B
5.	B	10.	E	15.	D	20.	A	25.	B

TEST 20

1. EXPEDITE : DEFER :: _____ : _____
   A. dilatory : summary
   B. extempore : temporize
   C. catalyze : protract
   D. retard : precocious
   E. procrastination : punctuality

   1.____

2. PRIVATE : GENERAL :: _____ : _____
   A. monkey : man
   B. amoeba : man
   C. fellow : professor
   D. army : navy
   E. captain : admiral

   2.____

3. TREATMENT : CURE :: _____ : _____
   A. benign : malign
   B. patronize : admire
   C. destroy : injure
   D. positive : absolute
   E. temporary : titanic

   3.____

4. ASCETISM : MODERATION :: _____ : _____
   A. possibility : probability
   B. contrition : attrition
   C. conservatism : liberalism
   D. coercion : persuasion
   E. induction : deduction

   4.____

5. ESTIMATION : ADULATION :: _____ : _____
   A. anathema : curse
   B. acme : vertex
   C. acumen : perspicacity
   D. amenable : agreeable
   E. deference : obsequiousness

   5.____

6. VIOLENCE : ANGER :: _____ : _____
   A. hope : happiness
   B. dream : analysis
   C. venture : ambition
   D. hate : harm
   E. caress : love

   6.____

7. DESTITUTE : DEVOID :: _____ : _____
   A. politician : politics
   B. private : sergeant
   C. affluent : forceful
   D. obliteration : extirpation
   E. construction : building

   7.____

8. VACILLATE : CHANGE :: _____ : _____
   A. vacate : rent
   B. trend : graph
   C. endure : stamina
   D. index : chart
   E. fluctuate : move

   8.____

9. LAUGH : JOKE :: _____ : _____
   A. moral : story
   B. painting : sketch
   C. caboose : train
   D. pain :; headache
   E. film : negative

   9.____

10. STUDY : LEARNING :: _____ : _____   10.____
    A. reading : writing   B. umpire : game
    C. vaccine : diphtheria   D. planning : execution
    E. perspiration : exercise

11. ACT : PLAY :: _____ : _____   11.____
    A. novel : hero   B. sonnet : sextet
    C. essay : tone   D. canto : epic
    E. ballad : troubadour

12. POEM : PASTORAL :: _____ : _____   12.____
    A. science : curriculum   B. chauvinism : Pan-Slavism
    C. miser : cupidity   D. monastery : monk
    E. crystal ball : medium

13. SOCIETY : DERELICT :: _____ : _____   13.____
    A. magazine : rejection slip B. ship : jetsam
    C. prison : convict   D. sea : flotsam

14. CONDENSATION : NOVEL :: _____ : _____   14.____
    A. dew : moisture   B. article : summary
    C. microcosm : world   D. conclusion : thesis
    E. beans : coffee

15. RELIGION : RITUAL :: _____ : _____   15.____
    A. society : etiquette   B. wisdom : education
    C. rules : game   D. protocol : diplomacy
    E. science : truth

16. WHEEL : AXLE :: _____ : _____   16.____
    A. hoof : horse   B. runner : sled
    C. top : string   D. ramrod : rifle
    E. propeller : wing

17. CIRCLE : QUADRANT :: _____ : _____   17.____
    A. polygon : hexagon   B. sphere : hemisphere
    C. duality : modality   D. acute angle : obtuse angle
    E. triangle : rectangle

18. LETTER : POSTCRIPT :: _____ : _____   18.____
    A. introduction : theme   B. antithesis : synthesis
    C. stanza : poem   D. bill : amendment
    E. summary : report

19. NEUROSIS : PSYCHOSIS :: _____ : _____   19.____
    A. fear : dread   B. aggression : war
    C. nervousness : reaction   D. demises : disease
    E. illness : treatment

20. NOTICEABLE : FLAGRANT :: _____ : _____   20.____
   A. scribe : inscribe   B. spiritual : material
   C. agnostic : prognosis   D. moderate : extremist
   E. heathen : pagan

21. MATCH : FLAME :: _____ : _____   21.____
   A. eating : appendicitis   B. grass : lawn mower
   C. typewriter : ribbon   D. friction : heat
   E. night : day

22. LEAK : PLUMBER :: _____ : _____   22.____
   A. dividends : stocks   B. salary :laborer
   C. robbery : thief   D. wind : sail
   E. sickness : doctor

23. BULB : TULIP :: _____ : _____   23.____
   A. pistil : stamen   B. tree : leaf
   C. acorn : oak   D. root : grass
   E. rose : thorn

24. ROOF : RAIN :: _____ : _____   24.____
   A. Dr. Salk : polio   B. storm window : cold
   C. disease : vaccination   D. thermos : heat
   E. vitamin D : rickets

25. PROBLEM : SOLUTION :: _____ : _____   25.____
   A. crossword puzzle : design   B. frame : window
   C. door : key   D. suitcase : handle
   E. password : sentry

KEY (CORRECT ANSWERS)

1	C	6.	C	11.	D	16.	C	21.	D
2.	C	7.	D	12.	B	17.	B	22.	E
3.	D	8.	E	13.	D	18.	D	23.	C
4.	C	9.	D	14.	C	19.	B	24.	B
5.	E	10.	C	15.	A	20.	D	25.	C

TEST 21

1. DRIZZLE : DRENCH :: _____ : _____
    A. crawl : creep
    B. freeze : jell
    C. freshen : clean
    D. splash : inundate
    E. drift : swim

    1.____

2. TEPID : TORRID :: _____ : _____
    A. turgid : horrid
    B. cool : frigid
    C. livid : lurid
    D. pool : placid
    E. tumid : turbid

    2.____

3. MILLENNIUM : CENTURY :: _____ : _____
    A. year : month
    B. month : day
    C. minute : second
    D. hour : minute
    E. decade : year

    3.____

4. ALPHA : OMEGA :: _____ : _____
    A. coda : prelude
    B. elephant : tail
    C. glossary : appendix
    D. prologue : epilogue
    E. plot : denouement

    4.____

5. CHRONOMETER : CALENDAR :: _____ : _____
    A. pedometer : hydrometer
    B. daylight saving : standard time
    C. beat : measure
    D. sun-dial : candle power
    E. chronicle : anachronism

    5.____

6. BROOM : MOP :: _____ : _____
    A. baseball bat : baseball
    B. pencil : eraser
    C. wall : brick
    D. pencil : pen
    E. water : wash

    6.____

7. BREAD : BISCUIT :: _____ : _____
    A. pie : dessert
    B. salad : dressing
    C. steak : lamb chops
    D. chicken : egg
    E. cake : cookies

    7.____

8. SAWDUST : FLOUR :: _____ : _____
    A. sand : powder
    B. bread : wood
    C. table: chair
    D. sky : water
    E. rain : snow

    8.____

9. GILLS : LUNGS :: _____ : _____
    A. water : air
    B. fins : feet
    C. mouth : ears
    D. tail : feathers
    E. wings : arms

    9.____

10. FATHER : DAUGHTER :: _____ : _____   10.____
    A. aunt : nephew   B. uncle : niece
    C. nephew : niece   D. mother : daughter-in-law
    E. minor : adult

11. RIBS : UMBRELLA :: _____ : _____   11.____
    A. rafters : roof   B. roof : rafters
    C. garret : house   D. spokes : hub
    E. skeleton : frame

12. MERIDIAN : SETTING :: _____ : _____   12.____
    A. start : finish   B. pinnacle : climax
    C. maturity : homestretch   D. baptism : birth
    E. culminate : terminate

13. HARBINGER : SPRING :: _____ : _____   13.____
    A. fight : might   B. telegram : event
    C. dawn : day   D. tail : comet
    E. spring : winter

14. ART : CUBISM :: _____ : _____   14.____
    A. scenery : play   B. mustache : face
    C. drape : window   D. setting : ring
    E. poem : epic

15. STATION : TRAIN :: _____ : _____   15.____
    A. lair : fox   B. home : parent
    C. dock : ship   D. whistle : cab
    E. haven : refugee

16. OPPOSITE : ANTONYM :: _____ : _____   16.____
    A. bell : bellows   B. false : pseudonym
    C. same : homonym   D. botanist : biologist
    E. same : synonym

17. MASTER : SLAVE :: _____ : _____   17.____
    A. soldier : civilian   B. policeman : prisoner
    C. omnipotent : vassal   D. captain : tar
    E. native : alien

18. ORDINATION : PRIEST :: _____ : _____   18.____
    A. promulgation : list   B. matriculation : student
    C. election : candidate   D. promotion : officer
    E. inauguration : president

19. AIR : DIRIGIBLE :: _____ : _____   19.____
    A. locomotive : steam   B. wagon : horse
    C. water : boat   D. lion : tiger
    E. gasoline : taxi

20. IMMORTALITY : MORTALITY :: _____ : _____   20.____
    A. second : minute   B. hour : minute
    C. era : decade   D. month : day
    E. infinite : finite

21. GOVERNMENT : ORDER :: _____ : _____   21.____
    A. anarchy : chaos   B. beast : beauty
    C. government : law   D. rule : order
    E. totalitarian : mob

22. WAIL : WHIMPER :: _____ : _____   22.____
    A. lament : cry   B. guffaw : laugh
    C. face : mouth   D. chuckle : snicker
    E. smirk : simper

23. CONDUCT : CONSCIENCE :: _____ : _____   23.____
    A. promoter : event   B. victory : leader
    C. ship : navigator   D. state : army
    E. nation : patriotism

24. FABULOUS : REAL :: _____ : _____   24.____
    A. descendant : ancestor   B. medieval : prehistoric
    C. dragon : dinosaur   D. creditable : veritable
    E. amphibian : reptile

25. FRIGHTFUL : HORRID :: _____ : _____   25,____
    A. death : demise   B. resistance : invasion
    C. asylum : insane   D. life : breath
    E. might : right

KEY (CORRECT ANSWERS)

1	D	6.	D	11.	A	16.	E	21.	A
2.	B	7.	E	12.	E	17.	C	22.	B
3.	E	8.	A	13.	C	18.	E	23.	C
4.	D	9.	B	14.	E	19.	C	24.	C
5.	C	10.	B	15.	C	20.	E	25.	A

TEST 22

1. LITERAL : FREE :: _____ : _____
   A. intrinsic : extrinsic
   B. communicate : express
   C. hews : hearsay
   D. translate : paraphrase
   E. simile : metaphor

   1.____

2. CITADEL : VAULT :: _____ : _____
   A. virtue : disgrace
   B. building : foundation
   C. tower : dungeon
   D. prop : cornice
   E. head : foot

   2.____

3. EXPOSITION : PRECIS :: _____ : _____
   A. genuine : synthetic
   B. tome : epitaph
   C. synopsis : compendium
   D. volume : booklet
   E. obese : slender

   3.____

4. IMPLICIT : EXPLICIT :: _____ : _____
   A. suggestion : recommendation
   B. innuendo : assertion
   C. state : hint
   D. allusion : insinuation
   E. indirect : devious

   4.____

5. HOG : PORK :: _____ : _____
   A. lion : jackal
   B. beef : stew
   C. deer : venison
   D. mutton : sheep
   E. lamb : chops

   5.____

6. PHILOLOGIST : LANGUAGE :: _____ : _____
   A. ornithologist : birds
   B. biologist : cells
   C. pediatrician : feet
   D. botanist : animals
   E. etymologist : insects

   6.____

7. DIME : DOLLAR :: _____ : _____
   A. decade : century
   B. time : number
   C. little : much
   D. penny : dime
   E. decalogue : trilogy

   7.____

8. RECTANGLE : OVAL :: _____ : _____
   A. acre : rod
   B. square : circle
   C. sphere : cube
   D. cube : sphere
   E. hexagon : pentagon

   8.____

9. POPE : PAPACY :: _____ : _____
   A. leader : executive
   B. clansman : tribe
   C. king : monarchy
   D. president : democracy
   E. queen : aristocracy

   9.____

10. MYRIAD : SPARSE :: _____ : _____
    A. many : few
    B. major : minor
    C. minority : plurality
    D. plethora : innumerable
    E. predominant : sporadic
    10._____

11. RELIGION : RITES :: _____ : _____
    A. government : army
    B. men : men
    C. manuscript : thesis
    D. legislature : judiciary
    E. table : legs
    11._____

12. FALL : RISE :: _____ : _____
    A. callow : mature
    B. light : murky
    C. diurnal : nocturnal
    D. moon : sun
    E. dusk : dawn
    12._____

13. SYMPATHY : SORROW :: _____ : _____
    A. pain : agony
    B. ointment : burn
    C. powder : face
    D. water : fire
    E. medicine : doctor
    13._____

14. TRIUMPH : EXULTATION :: _____ : _____
    A. war : victory
    B. calamity : distress
    C. tidings : jubilation
    D. emergency : desolation
    E. news : gratification
    14._____

15. DISSIPATION : DEPRAVITY :: _____ : _____
    A. callowness : inexperience
    B. attempt : achievement
    C. repetition : monotony
    D. familiarity : recognition
    E. interest : boredom
    15._____

16. SPECTACLES : VISION :: _____ : _____
    A. statement : contention
    B. canoe : paddle
    C. hero : worship
    D. airplane : locomotion
    E. hay : horse
    16._____

17. RAZOR : BLADE :: _____ : _____
    A. lighter : fluid
    B. keys : typewriter
    C. cup : coffee
    D. book : page
    E. pencil : lead
    17._____

18. BOOK : COVER :: _____ : _____
    A. window : door
    B. ink : crayon
    C. body : skin
    D. write : compose
    E. spelling : grammar
    18._____

19. LINKS : CHAIN :: _____ : _____
    A. sugar : cane
    B. warp : woof
    C. strands : rope
    D. train : cars
    E. rivers : ocean
    19._____

20. CORRAL : CATTLE :: _____ : _____   20._____
    A. dog : kennel   B. fish : aquarium
    C. mortuary : people   D. apiary : bees
    E. breviary : priest

21. MOVEMENT : SYMPHONY :: _____ : _____   21._____
    A. notes : staff   B. harmony : counterpoint
    C. melody : harmony   D. key : piano
    E. act : play

22. STAR : GALAXY :: _____ : _____   22._____
    A. kennel : dog   B. shelf : book
    C. sea : fish   D. regiment : soldier
    E. molecule : atom

23. BITTER : SOUR :: _____ : _____   23._____
    A. disliking : liking   B. pink : red
    C. frigid : cool   D. enthusiastic : approving
    E. apathetic : disapproving

24. DRUNK : DRINK :: _____ : _____   24._____
    A. arisen : arise   B. rung : ring
    C. stroke : strike   D. sang : sing
    E. clang : cling

25. SUNSET : SUNRISE :: _____ : _____   25._____
    A. coming : going   B. ten : five
    C. evening : morning   D. spring : autumn
    E. despair : hope

KEY (CORRECT ANSWERS)

1	D	6.	A	11.	E	16.	D	21.	E
2.	C	7.	A	12.	E	17.	E	22.	E
3.	D	8.	B	13.	B	18.	C	23.	D
4.	B	9.	C	14.	B	19.	C	24.	B
5.	C	10.	A	15.	C	20.	D	25.	C

TEST 23

1. LAMPOON : SATIRIZE :: _____ : _____   1.____
   A. inveigh : impound   B. inculpate : exculpate
   C. asperse : discredit   D. accede : exceed
   E. condone : condign

2. ESOTERIC : ABSTRUSE :: _____ : _____   2.____
   A. dulcet : tame   B. cavalier :; finical
   C. feigned : restricted   D. recondite : elementary
   E. anomalous : abnormal

3. NOBLESSE OBLIGE : OBLIGATION OF GENEROUS BEHAVIOR   3.____
   ASSOCIATED WITH HIGH RANK ::
   A. obliquity : defamatory language B. junto : hunt
   C. scourge : dereliction   D. sequester : set apart
   E. colander : calendar

4. DEROGATE : DETRACT :: _____ : _____   4.____
   A. adumbrate : outline   B. reticulate : reformulate
   C. obtrude : obtest   D. obvert : obviate
   E. abrogate : validate

5. MAUDLIN : FUDDLED :: _____ : _____   5.____
   A. tractable : spineless   B. fusty : musty
   C. climacteric : released   D. donative : illative
   E. fictile : fictive

6. NIMBUS : ATMOSPHERE :: _____ : _____   6.____
   A. Zeitgeist : spirit of the time B. lintel : vertical support
   C. atoll : treeless plain   D. cloak : cloister
   E. cloisonné : filigree-work

7. IMPUGN : CALL IN QUESTION :: _____ : _____   7.____
   A. enervate : give impetus to B. roil : convulse
   C. asseverate : affirm   D. essay : assay
   E. digest : diffuse

8. ADIPOSE : FATTY :: _____ : _____   8.____
   A. voracious : veracious   B. clamorous : glamorous
   C. fricative : forced   D. vaunted : truckle
   E. bellicose : mangy

9. CANARD : HOAX :: _____ : _____   9.____
   A. fatuity : crassness   B honorarium : fee
   C. torpor : trudgen   D. trull : trumpet
   E. truffle : trousseau

10. DEMEAN : CONDUCT ONESELF :: _____ : _____   10._____
    A. eviscerate : thin out   B. skulk : hulk
    C. decoct : prepare by boiling   D. concoct : evict
    E. rescind : abstain

11. CREPUSCULAR : GLIMMERING :: _____ : _____   11._____
    A. consummate : inchoate   B. plethoric : insufficient
    C. callow : mature   D. decuman : tenth
    E. decumbent : lambent

12. NEXUS : LINK :: _____ : _____   12._____
    A. tarantella : dance of the spiders   B. covert : bevy
    C. argot : dragon   D. eidolon : image
    E. efflux : effluvium

13. CAVIL : CARP :: _____ : _____   13._____
    A. acerbate : retaliate   B. deprecate : depreciate
    C. dub : dress   D. cadge : lie
    E. comprise : constrain

14. DISCREPANT : DISCORDANT :: _____ : _____   14._____
    A. bovine : piglike   B. sidereal : starry
    C. perspicuous : ambiguous   D. browsing : carousing
    E. declivitous : narrow

15. HIERARCHY : ORGANIZATION OF OFFICIALS ACCORDING TO RANK ::   15._____
    _____ : _____
    A. heresy : hexapla   B. purveyor : overseer
    C. minion : dominion   D. métier : calling
    E. administration : oligarchy

16. EXECRATE : CURSE :: _____ : _____   16._____
    A. abjure : appeal to   B. vouchsafe : contemplate
    C. rail : revile   D. exorcise : criticize
    E. ablactate : abominate

17. CONTUMACIOUS : HEADSTRONG :: _____ : _____   17._____
    A. extirpative : invective   B. inchoate : nascent
    C. disinterested : prejudiced   D. veracious : mendacious
    E. abandoned : manumitted

18. RIGMAROLE : PROLIX TALK :: _____ : _____   18._____
    A. satrap : executive   B. apostasy : denunciation
    C. apogee : perigee   D. allotropy : allusion
    E. chaldron : chalice

19. DISCOUNTENANCE : DISCONCERT :: _____ : _____   19._____
    A. extrapolate : disengage   B. preen : sleek
    C. bandy : banter   D. cense : ascribe
    E. cite : proscribe

20. OBLATE : FLATTENDED AT THE POLES :: _____ : _____   20.____
    A. complaisant : priggish   B. myopic : farsighted
    C. awry : convex   D. slatternly : slovenly
    E. slavish : sleazy

21. ETHOS : FUNDAMENTAL SPIRIT OF A CULTURE :: _____ : _____   21.____
    A. jape : hiatus   B. salaam : obeisance
    C. gravamen : greeting   D. chanticleer : fox
    E. ablation : inhalation

22. BESET : ASSAIL :: _____ : _____   22.____
    A. comport : frolic   B. slake : allay
    C. parry : join   D. revet : review
    E. remonstrate : concur

23. BELEAGUERED : BESIEGED :: _____ : _____   23.____
    A. sullied : inflamed   B. seminal : originative
    C. viable : moribund   D. amorphous : remanent
    E. quintan : fourth

24. NONAGE : MINORITY :: _____ : _____   24.____
    A. cameo : miniature   B. spaniel : fawning person
    C. pediment : obstacle   D. flacon : flag
    E. marasca : wine

25. PROPITIATE : PLACATE :: _____ : _____   25.____
    A. scarify : cleanse   B. hector : befriend
    C. chaffer : bargain   D. improvise : intercalate
    E. decollate : decode

KEY (CORRECT ANSWERS)

1	C	6.	A	11.	D	16.	C	21.	B
2.	E	7.	C	12.	D	17.	B	22.	B
3.	D	8.	C	13.	C	18.	A	23.	B
4.	A	9.	B	14.	B	19.	B	24.	B
5.	B	10.	C	15.	D	20.	D	25.	C

TEST 24

1. EXALTANT : GRATIFIED :: _____ : _____
   A. intensive : extensive
   B. fabulous : large
   C. physical : mental
   D. nervous : depressed
   E. insane : neurotic

2. TERSE : SUCCINCT :: _____ : _____
   A. unctuous : smooth
   B. cowardly : obsequious
   C. stalwart : pusillanimous
   D. valiant : verve
   E. viscous : suave

3. ACUTE : ACERB :: _____ : _____
   A. refreshing : refreshment
   B. flabby : flaccid
   C. brusque : brisk
   D. pungent : bitter
   E. morbid : morbidity

4. ATTORNEY : CLIENT :: _____ : _____
   A. doctor : nurse
   B. executive : subordinate
   C. student : teacher
   D. merchant : marine
   E. broker : investor

5. DIME : DOLLAR :: _____ : _____
   A. multitude : myriads
   B. second : hour
   C. youth : senescence
   D. decade : century
   E. penny : dime

6. EXONERATE : CHARGE :: _____ : _____
   A. prescription : sickness
   B. repent : sin
   C. release : bail
   D. presentment : jury
   E. acquit : crime

7. ARITHMETIC : NUMBERS :: _____ : _____
   A. science : experiments
   B. language : words
   C. center : arc
   D. social science : history
   E. spelling : phonetics

8. SEETHE : SMOLDER :: _____ : _____
   A. precipice : precipitous
   B. engulf : convulse
   C. holocaust : flagrant
   D. burn : wound
   E. puncture : incise

9. SPHINX : ENIGMA :: _____ : _____
   A. guess : choose
   B. oracle : treacle
   C. maturation : condensation
   D. dilemma : puzzle
   E. portent : foretell

1._____
2._____
3._____
4._____
5._____
6._____
7._____
8._____
9._____

10. NUN : MINISTRATION :: _____ : _____
    A. thief : theft
    C. pirate : ship
    E. boss : efficiency
    B. electors : president
    D. doctor : treatment

10.____

11. LEDGE : MINARET :: _____ : _____
    A. windmill : water
    C. forest : meadow
    E. supine : horizontal
    B. smokestack : chimney
    D. woof : warp

11.____

12. SUBTERFUGE : CLANDESTINE :: _____ : _____
    A. affluence : parsimony
    C. generosity : altruism
    E. deceit : furtive
    B. notoriety : flagrant
    D. perennial : decennial

12.____

13. DIFFIDENT : SANGUINE :: _____ : _____
    A. pompous : pomposity
    C. signature : calligraphy
    E. alto : contralto
    B. archaic : archeological
    D. cursory : consummate

13.____

14. SENESCENCE : YOUTH :: _____ : _____
    A. fertility : fruition
    C. maturation : incipience
    E. field marshal : lieutenant
    B. materialism : existentialisms
    D. imbecile : moron

14.____

15. ENERVATING : STIMULATING :: _____ : _____
    A. effective : effectual
    C. listless : motivating
    E. energizing : forcible
    B. active : thinking
    D. cold : hot

15.____

16. TRANSIENT : EVANESCENT :: _____ : _____
    A. permanent : temporary
    C. fleeting : ephemeral
    E. passing : perceptible
    B. casual : persistent
    D. temporary : permanent

16.____

17. COMMON MAN : ELITE :: _____ : _____
    A. Democrat : Republican
    C. serf : fief
    E. plebeian : patrician
    B. Communist : Conservative
    D. vassal : lord

17.____

18. ANOMALY : IRREGULAR :: _____ : _____
    A. applause : approval
    C. remuneration : payable
    E. emulation : insidious
    B. inordinacy : excessive
    D. provocation : irritate

18.____

19. SPONTANEOUS : IMPROMPTU :: _____ : _____
    A. unrehearsed : prepared
    C. premeditated : unpremeditated
    E. unconstrained : improvised
    B. simultaneous : pithy
    D. extemporaneous : contemporaneous

19.____

20. INDIGENCE : POVERTY :: _____ : _____   20._____
    A. indigenous : spontaneous   B. reticence : verbosity
    C. philately : numismatics   D. cumulative : accretive
    E. culvert : bridge

21. ENCOMIUM : PRAISE :: _____ : _____   21._____
    A. eulogy : mirth   B. tirade : tears
    C. sycophancy : music   D. philippic : abuse
    E. intrepidity : fear

22. INGENUOUS : URBANE :: _____ : _____   22._____
    A. ingenious : artful   B. credulous : unctuous
    C. naïve : provincial   D. benign : benignant
    E. cantankerous : peevish

23. WARP : WOOF :: _____ : _____   23._____
    A. citadel : tower   B. spire : dungeon
    C. steeple : ledge   D. peak : summit
    E. cone : roof

24. CAPTAIN : CREW :: _____ : _____   24._____
    A. President : Congress   B. Speaker : Senate
    C. manager : team   D. minister : hierarchy
    E. principal : P.T.A.

25. LACONIC : GRANDILOQUENT :: _____ : _____   25._____
    A. verbose : taciturn   B. garrulous : pompous
    C. meagre : replete   D. pithy : bombastic
    E. concise : precise

KEY (CORRECT ANSWERS)

1	D	6.	E	11.	D	16.	C	21.	D
2.	A	7.	B	12.	E	17.	E	22.	B
3.	D	8.	E	13.	D	18.	B	23.	C
4.	E	9.	D	14.	C	19.	E	24.	C
5.	D	10.	D	15.	C	20.	D	25.	D

TEST 25

1. CRIME : SHERIFF :: _____ : _____   1.____
    A. hospital : intern   B. disease : doctor
    C. money : miser   D. prescription : illness
    E. fine : offense

2. MONEY : QUARTER :: _____ : _____   2.____
    A. dime : half dollar   B. leaves : forest
    C. garden : trees   D. tree : oak
    E. maple : ash

3. DEFERENTIAL : SYCOPHANTIC :: _____ : _____   3.____
    A. suave : unctuous   B. innocuous : iniquitous
    C. precocious : prehensile   D. self-respecting : ostentatious
    E. diffident : cringing

4. HOUSES : BROKER :: _____ : _____   4.____
    A. money : treasurer   B. ships : purser
    C. landlords : tenants   D. churches : sexton
    E. insurance : agent

5. COMPENSATION : LOSS :: _____ : _____   5.____
    A. ransom : captivity   B. lawsuit : case
    E. restitution : destituition   D. settlement : law
    E. penalty : punishment

6. HOUSE : BLUEPRINT :: _____ : _____   6.____
    A. epitome : prologue   B. plot : play
    B. story : outline   D. plan : architecture
    E. epitaph : epilogue

7. SHEEP : EWE :: _____ : _____   7.____
    A. duck : goose   B. buck : deer
    C. daughter : mother   D. mare : gelding
    E. antelope : doe

8. DESTINATION : VOYAGE :: _____ : _____   8.____
    A. goal : aim   B. triumph : battle
    C. campaign : army   D. results : deeds
    E. success : failure

9. DESIST : CONTINUE :: _____ : _____   9.____
    A. suggest : affirm   B. recur : abate
    C. lose : hold   D. proscribe : prescribe
    E. retrogression : recidivism

10. SPEECH : GARBLED :: _____ : _____   10._____
    A. sight : blind   B. odor : foul
    C. preach : censorious   D. writing : legible
    E. walk : stumbling

11. FAVORITISM : NEPOTISM :: _____ : _____   11._____
    A. good : bad   B. plebeians : patricians
    C. democracy : communism   D. despotism : dictatorship
    E. military rule : civil rule

12. TRESPASS : WANDER :: _____ : _____   12._____
    A. stray : conjure   B. drink : carouse
    C. search : examine   D. incline : decline
    E. swear : perjure

13. INCONSISTENCY : INCONGRUITY :: _____ : _____   13._____
    A. incontrovertible : ineffable   B. antithesis : oxymoron
    C. evasion : implausibility   D. irresolution : illicit
    E. discrete : indistinct

14. DECLARE : ASSEVERATE :: _____ : _____   14._____
    A. plead : ask   B. annul : rescind
    C. request : demand   D. persuade : coax
    E. repeat : entreat

15. METAL : ALLOY :: _____ : _____   15._____
    A. associate : ally   B. species : hybrid
    C. element : compound   D. admixture : substance
    E. metal : nonmetal

16. VOTES : CAMPAIGNING :: _____ : _____   16._____
    A. sales : advertising   B. savings : banking
    C. liquor : drinking   D. troops : leading
    E. weakness : strength

17. APPROVAL : APPLAUSE :: _____ : _____   17._____
    A. perjury : boos   B. pleasure : pain
    C. disdain : affront   D. age : wrinkle
    E. grimace : awry

18. WARDROBE : COSTUME :: _____ : _____   18._____
    A. suits : closet   B. team : baseball
    C. melody : harmony   D. repertoire : opera
    E. chest : drawers

19. AFFLUENCE : FRUGALITY :: _____ : _____   19._____
    A. capitalism : socialism   B. erudition : reprise
    C. logic : irrationality   D. profusion : austerity
    E. effluence : confluence

20. FIELD : FALLOW :: _____ : _____
    A. crop : barren
    B. property : useless
    C. purchase : unnecessary
    D. visitor : unwelcome
    E. worker : unemployed

    20.____

21. MURDER : EXECUTE :: _____ : _____
    A. punish : revenge
    B. walk : trespass
    C. insult : offend
    D. rob : confiscate
    E. take : accept

    21.____

22. THRESHOLD : LINTEL :: _____ : _____
    A. depression : recovery
    B. perigee : apogamy
    C. earth : sky
    D. appanage : station
    E. nadir : zenith

    22.____

23. LEVER : CROWBAR :: _____ : _____
    A. pulley : ladder
    B. hand : clock
    C. pendulum : swing
    D. balance : seesaw
    E. weight : fulcrum

    23.____

24. BLAME : VINDICATE :: _____ : _____
    A. duty : refrain
    B. promise : renege
    C. debt : honor
    D. responsibility : release
    E. position : retract

    24.____

25. TAX : EXEMPTION :: _____ : _____
    A. crime : pardon
    B. custom : practice
    C. debt : bankruptcy
    D. disease : immunity
    E. travel : deduction

    25.____

KEY (CORRECT ANSWERS)

1	B	6.	C	11.	D	16.	A	21.	D
2.	D	7.	E	12.	E	17.	C	22.	E
3.	D	8.	D	13.	B	18.	D	23.	C
4.	E	9.	C	14.	C	19.	D	24.	D
5.	A	10.	E	15.	B	20.	E	25.	D

TESTS IN VERBAL ANALOGIES - CLASSICS

DIRECTIONS: Each question in this part consists of two capitalized words which have a certain relationship to each other, and a third capitalized word which is followed by five lettered words in small letters. Choose the letter of the word which is related in the SAME way to the third capitalized word as the first two capitalized words are related to each other. *PRINT THE LETTER OF THE CORRECT ANSWER IN THE SPACE AT THE RIGHT.*

TEST 1

1. JOCASTA : OEDIPUS :: CLYTEMNESTRA : _____   1.____
    A. Electra   B. Orestes   C. Anchises
    D. Polyneices   E. Antigone

2. "LYSISTRATA" : ARISTOPHANES :: "ANDROMACHE" : _____   2.____
    A. Euripides   B. Sophocles   C. Aristotle
    D. Aeschylus   E. Plato

3. "THE KNIGHTS" : CLEON :: "THE FROGS" : _____   3.____
    A. Aesculapius   B. Aeschylus   C. Dionysus
    D. Aristophanes   E. Euripides

4. "FATHER OF TRAGIC DRAMA" : AESCHYLUS :: "TENTH MUSE" : _____ 4.____
    A. Terpsichore   B. Medea   C. Sappho
    D. Lesbos   E. Andromache

5. ODE : PINDAR :: PASTORAL : _____   5.____
    A. Theocritus   B. Alcaeus   C. Artemis
    D. Sappho   E Simonides

6. TERENCE : "THE SELF TORMENTOR" :: PLAUTUS : _____   6.____
    A. "The Adelphi"   B. "The Maid of Andros"
    C. "The Mother-in-Law"   D. "Amphitryon"
    E. "The Eunuch"

7. "ON THE NATURE OF THINGS" : LUCRETIUS :: PLAUTUS : _____   7.____
    A. Catullus   B. Virgil   C. Alcaeus
    D. Baucis   E. Keats

8. "METAMORPHOSES" : OVID :: "EPODES" : _____   8.____
    A. Homer   B. Horace   C. Livy
    D. Cicero   E. Polybius

9. "PARALLEL LIVES" : PLUTARCH :: "SATIRICON" : _____   9.____
    A. Tacitus   B. Seneca   C. Petronius
    D. Apuleius   E. Marcus Aurelius

10. ALEXANDER : CAESAR :: THESEUS : _____   10.____
    A. Cicero   B. Demosthenes   C. Romulus
    D. Augustus   E. Justinian

11. "EARLY ROSY-FINGERED DAWN" : AURORA :: "FULL-ARMED FROM   11.____
    THE FOREHEAD OF ZEUS" : _____
    A. Athena   B. Rhea   C. Aphrodite
    D. Alcmena   E. Arachne

12. ELECTRA : SOPHOCLES :: IPHIGENIA : _____   12.____
    A. Aeschylus   B. Euripides   C. Aristophanes
    D. Tauris   E. Plato

13. ANACREON : PINDAR :: HERODOTUS : _____   13.____
    A. Thucydides   B. Cicero   C. Laocöön
    D. Alcaeus   E. Praxiteles

14. "THE REPUBLIC" : "THE DIALOGUES" :: "OEDIPUS AT COLONUS" : _____   14.____
    A. "Antigone"   B. Sophocles   C. "The Wasps"
    D. Aristophanes   E. "The Trojan Women"

15. AESCHYLUS : EURIPIDES :: PLAUTUS : _____   15.____
    A. Lucretius   B. comedy   C. Terence
    D. Seneca   E. tragedy

16. EURIPIDES : ELECTRA : AESCHYLUS : _____   16.____
    A. Medea   B. Orestia   C. Amalthaea
    D. Baccae   E. Camilla

17. MELPOMENE :TRAGEDY :: CLIO : _____   17.____
    A. comedy   B. dance   C. music
    D. history   E. astronomy

18. ORPHEUS : EURYDICE :: OSIRIS : _____   18.____
    A. Thalia   B. Hermes   C. Isis
    D. Iphigenia   E. Atellana

19. AEETES : MEDEA :: AGAMEMNON : _____   19.____
    A. Clytemnestra   B. Hippolyte   C. Lachesis
    D. Electra   E. Adrastea

20. AESCHINES : ORATORY :: MENANDER : _____   20.____
    A. poetry   B. medicine   C. philosophy
    D. drama   E. history

21. ZENO : PHILOSOPHY :: POLYBIUS : _____   21.____
    A. medicine   B. drama   C. oratory
    D. history   E. poetry

22. VIRGIL : POETRY :: QUINTILIAN : _____   22.____
    A. politics   B. morality   C. oratory
    D. religion   E. warfare

23. DECAPITATION : MEDUSA :: DOG : _____   23.____
    A. Helena   B. Eros   C. Cyclops
    D. Pleiades   E. Hecuba

24. TANTALUS : GRAPES :: SISYPHUS : _____   24.____
    A. reflection   B. fire   C. beheading
    D. conscience   E. rocks

25. PENELOPE : ODYSSEUS :: PERSEPHONE : _____   25.____
    A. Xenophon   B. Persius   C. Osiris
    D. Homer   E. Hades

───────────

KEY (CORRECT ANSWERS)

1	B	6.	D	11.	A	16.	B	21.	D
2.	A	7.	A	12.	B	17.	D	22.	C
3.	B	8.	B	13.	A	18.	C	23.	E
4.	C	9.	C	14.	A	19.	D	24.	E
5.	A	10.	C	15.	C	20.	D	25.	E

───────────

TEST 2

1. DIODORUS : EPICTETUS :: ARISTOPHANES : _____   1.____
   A. Strabo   B. Aesop   C. Xenophon
   D. Democritus   E. Plutarch

2. TRAGEDY : SOPHOCLES :: COMEDY : _____   2.____
   A. Aeschylus   B. Euripides   C. Parmenides
   D. theatre   E. Aristophanes

3. SILVER AGE (BEGINNING) : TIBERIUS :: SILVER AGE (END : _____   3.____
   A. Hadrian   B. Trajan   C. Augustus
   D. Otho   E. Livius Andronicus

4. LAIUS : OEDIPUS :: PELEUS : _____   4.____
   A. Achates   B. Admetus   C. Aegeus
   D. Achilles   E. Aeolus

5. EROS : LOVE :: APOLLO : _____   5.____
   A. thunder   B. beauty   C. Mercury
   D. light   E. the sea

6. DIANA : MOON :: GAEA : _____   6.____
   A. love   B. earth   C. thunder
   D. muse   E. Uranus

7. JUVENAL : SENECA :: CICERO : _____   7.____
   A. Tiberius   B. Sallust   C. Martial
   D. Quintilian   E. Tacitus

8. DEMOSTHENES : HYPERIDES :: PARMENIDES : _____   8.____
   A. Bacchylides   B. Philoxenus   C. Xenophanes
   D. oratory   E. Timotheus

9. SOPHOCLES : EURIPIDES :: EUPOLIS : _____   9.____
   A. tragedy   B. epic poetry   C. Antimachus
   D. Cratinus   E. Panyasis

10. "NATURAL HISTORY" : PLINY THE ELDER :: "INSTITUTIO ORATORIA" :   10.____
    _____
    A. Pliny the Younger   B. Emperor Titus   C. Lucullus
    D. Quintilian   E. Demosthenes

11. JUVENAL : SATIRE :: MARTIAL : _____   11.____
    A. comedy   B. tragedy   C. essay
    D. history   E. epigram

12. CALLIOPE : EPIC SONG :: CLIO : _____   12.____
    A. history   B. tragedy   C. sacred song
    D. lyric song   E. poetry

13. THALIA : COMEDY :: URANIA : _____   13.____
    A. meditation   B. remembrance   C. earth
    D. song   E. astronomy

14. REMEMBRANCE : MNEME :: SONG : _____   14.____
    A. Euterpe   B. Melpomene   C. Erato
    D. Erythea   E. Aoide

15. CRONUS : HERA :: URANUS : _____   15.____
    A. Rhea   B. Gaea   C. Urania
    D. Mnemosyne   E. Ganymede

16. POSEIDON : SEA :: HEPHAESTUS : _____   16.____
    A. earth   B. fertility   C. light
    D. fire   E. wisdom

17. HOMER : 900 BC :: CLEOPATRA : _____   17.____
    A. Antony   B. 117 AD   C. 14 AD
    D. 500 BC   E. 30 BC

18. HELLENISTIC PERIOD : HELLENIC PERIOD :: 300 BC : _____   18.____
    A. 900 BC   B. 30 BC   C. 80 BC
    D. 50 BC   E. 529 AD

19. HELLENIC PERIOD : HIPPOCRATES :: HELLENISTIC PERIOD : _____   19.____
    A. Alexander the Great   B. Lacöön   C. Phidias
    D. Myron   E. Archimedes

20. ATHENS : SPARTA :: DEMOCRACY : _____   20.____
    A. city-state   B. republic   C. diarchy
    D. tyranny   E. oligarchy

21. PENELOPE : HOMER :: JASON : _____   21.____
    A. Aeschylus   B. Medea   C. Creon
    D. Aristophanes   E. Euripides

22. JUPITER : JUNO :: CRONUS : _____   22.____
    A. Rhea   B. Hera   C. Hades
    D. Hestia   E. Demeter

23. HISTORY : PLUTARCH :: ORATORY : _____   23.____
    A. Hortensius   B. Livy   C. Ennius
    D. Horace   E. Vergil

24. GALEN : MEDICINE :: PYTHAGORAS : _____   24._____
    A. philosophy   B. literature   C. mathematics
    D. Euclid   E. drama

25. DRACO : SOLON :: CLISTHENES : _____   25._____
    A. Xenophon   B. Eratosthenes   C. Aristarchus
    D. Epicurus   E. Pericles

KEY (CORRECT ANSWERS)

1	D	6.	B	11.	E	16.	D	21.	E
2.	E	7.	B	12.	A	17.	E	22.	A
3.	B	8.	C	13.	E	18.	D	23.	A
4.	D	9.	D	14.	E	19.	E	24.	C
5.	D	10.	D	15.	D	20.	C	25.	E

TEST 3

1. DEFEAT OF TROY : "THE TROJAN WOMEN" :: VICTORY OF SPARTA : _____   1.____
    A. "Hellenica"   B. "The Suppliants"   C. "The Phormioi"
    D. Aristophanes   E. "Hippolytus"

2. LOSS OF SIGHT : OEDIPUS :: RESTORATION OF SIGHT : _____   2.____
    A. Plutus   B. Achilles   C. Philoctetus
    D. Apollo   E. Sophocles

3. ODYSSEUS : PENELOPE :: HECTOR : _____   3.____
    A. Home   B. "Iliad"   C. Andromache
    D. Achilles   E. Priam

4. THREE CANTICAS : HELL, PURGATORY , AND PARADISE :: FIFTH   4.____
    CIRCLE : _____
    A. swamp of Styx   B. "The Inferno"   C. plains of Abraham
    D. After-Life   E. presence of God

5. SUPPLIANTS FLEEING FROM EGYPT : AESCHYLUS :: SUPPLIANTS   5.____
    BURYING THEIR DEAD : _____
    A. Sophocles   B. Euripides   C. mothers of Thebes
    D. "Promethus Bound"   E. "The Suppliants"

6. PARADISE : NINE HEAVENS :: PURGATORY : _____   6.____
    A. damned souls   B. spirit of Beatrice
    C. mountain of seven terraces   D. first circle of Hell
    E. the supernal light

7. LAST HOURS OF SOCRATES : "PHAEDRO" :: LAST HOURS OF   7.____
    AEGISTHUS : _____
    A. Plato   B. "Oresteia"   C. "Oedipus Rex"
    D. "Electra"   E. "Oedipus at Colonus"

8. AN OLLD MAN RESTORED TO YOUTH :: "THE KNIGHTS" :: TWO OLD   8.____
    MEN FOUND A CITY : _____
    A. "The Frogs"   B. "The Birds"
    C. "The Wasps"   D. "The Two Boys from Syracuse"
    E. "The Clouds"

9. THEOLOGY AS A SCIENCE : THOMAS AQUINAS :: ETHICS AS A   9.____
    GEOMETRIC METHOD : _____
    A. Socrates   B. Spinoza   C. Virgil
    D. Horace   E. Boethius

10. TWO KINGS CLAIM A CITY : KING JOHN :: TWO WOMEN CLAIM A   10.____
    CHILD : _____
    A. King Solomon   B. Old Testament   C. King Saul
    D. King Herod   E. King David

11. ORESTES' REPENTANCE : EURIPIDES :: ORESTES' TRIUMPH : _____   11.____
    A. Aeschylus   B. Anacreon   C. Sophocles
    D. "Electra"   E. "Oresteia"

12. SPARTA : MENELAUS :: TROY : _____   12.____
    A. Agamemnon   B. Hector   C. Priam
    D. "The Iliad"   E. Ulysses

13. DARK AGES : BOETHIUS :: MIDDLE AGES : _____   13.____
    A. Saint Augustine   B. Saint Ambrose
    C. Abelard   D. "Kalevala"
    E. "The Consolation of Philosophy"

14. GREEK TRAGEDY : "THE TROJAN WOMEN" :: GREEK SCIENTIFIC   14.____
    WORK : _____
    A. Plato   B. "Timaeus"   C. "Rhesus"
    D. "Troades"   E. "Plutarch's Lives"

15. MOUNTAINS : OREADS :: WATERS : _____   15.____
    A. Dryads   B. Naiads   C. nymphs
    D. Eumenides   E. Sirens

16. DIALOGUES : LUCIAN :: DIALOGUES : _____   16.____
    A. Plato   B. Plutarch   C. Seneca
    D. "Parallel Lives"   E. Terence

17. CREON : HAEMON :: OEDIPUS : _____   17.____
    A. Antigone   B. Sophocles   C. Polynices
    D. Tiresias   E. Colonus

18. CARNIVOROUS GIANTS : CYCLOPS :: CARNIVOROUS SEA-   18.____
    MONSTER : _____
    A. Calypso   B. Charybdis   C. Laestrygonians
    D. Scylla   E. Gorgon

19. DEATH OF SONS : "MEDEA" :: DEATH OF SONS : _____   19.____
    A. "Oedipus Tyrannus"   B. Sophocles
    C. "Oedipus at Colonus"   D. "Phoenissae"
    E. Polynices and Eteocles

20. ENCHANTRESS : CIRCE :: GIANT : _____   20.____
    A. "Odyssey"   B. Medusa   C. Centaur
    D. Polyphemus   E. Gorgon

21. ITHACA : LAERTES :: CORINTH : _____   21.____
    A. Demetrius   B. Philon   C. Creon
    D. Midas   E. Eupolemus

22. ACHILLES : PARIS :: ORPHEUS : _____   22.____
    A. Maenads   B. Graeae   C. Eurydice
    D. "Iliad"   E. Excalibur

23. EROS : LOVE :: DEMETER : _____   23.____
    A. wine   B. grain   C. earth
    D. Homeric hymn   E. Ceres

24. FATHER OF THE MUSES : ZEUS :: MOTHER OF THE MUSES : _____   24.____
    A. Melpomene   B. Leda   C. Aphrodite
    D. Euterpe   E. Mnemosyne

25. VOYAGE ON A DUNG BEETLE : "PEACE" :: TRIAL OF A DOG : _____   25.____
    A. "Plutus"   B. "The Wasps"   C. "The Persians"
    D. Aristophanes   E. "Acharnians"

KEY (CORRECT ANSWERS)

1	A	6.	C	11.	C	16.	B	21.	C
2.	A	7.	D	12.	C	17.	C	22.	A
3.	C	8.	B	13.	C	18.	D	23.	B
4.	A	9.	B	14.	B	19.	D	24.	E
5.	B	10.	A	15.	B	20.	D	25.	B

TEST 4

1. SACRIFICE OF POLYXENA : "HECUBA" :: SACRIFICE BY
   AGAMEMNON : _____
      A. Euripides   B. "Bacchae"   C. "Oresteia"
      D. "Iphigenia in Aulis"   E. "Troades"

   1.____

2. TUTOR OF ACHILLES : PHOENIX :: VICTIM OF ACHILLES : _____
      A. Hector   B. Patroclus   C. Hephaestus
      D. Paris   E. "Iliad"

   2.____

3. TWELE LABORS : HERACLES :: WEAVING A SHROUD : _____
      A. Hera   B. Hippolyta   C. Penelope
      D. Pandora   E. Cybele

   3.____

4. FLOWERS SPRINGING FROM BLOOD : HYACINTHUS :: A WINGED
   HORSE SPRINGING FROM BLOOD : _____
      A. Hermes   B. Pegasus   C. Medusa
      D. Tantalus   E. Persephone

   4.____

5. DESTRUCTION ON THE SEA : SIRENS :: TURNING MEN TO SWINE : _____
      A. Odysseus   B. Medusa   C. Scylla
      D. Circe   E. Homer

   5.____

6. RIVER :STYX :: ISLAND : _____
      A. Helicon   B. Delphi   C. Scheria
      D. Pelion   E. Charybdis

   6.____

7. SHIPWRECK : ODYSSEUS :: SHIP'S COLLAPSE : _____
      A. Argo   B. Pelias   C. Hesiod
      D. Jason   E. Rhodius

   7.____

8. DESCENT TO HADES : "THE FROGS" :: RETURN FROM HADES : _____
      A. Dionysius   B. "Charon"   C. "Knights"
      D. "Phalaris"   E. "Menippus"

   8.____

9. COMEDY : THALIA :: MIME : _____
      A. Polyhymnia   B. Calliope   C. Terpsichore
      D. Mnemosyne   E. tragedy

   9.____

10. MT. OLYMPUS : GODS :: MT. HELICON : _____
      A. oracles   B. Laestrygonians   C. nymphs
      D. muses   E. Phaeacians

   10.____

11. IRONY : "OEDIPUS" :: VENGEANCE : _____
      A. "Seven Against Thebes"   B. "Promethus Bound"
      C. "Medea"   D. Aeschylus
      E. oracle of Delphi

   11.____

12. TRANSFORMATION INTO A COW : IO :: APPEARANCE AS A BULL : _____   12.____
    A. Hermione   B. Phoenix   C. Europa
    D. Minos   E. Hera

13. HYPNOS : SLEEP :: HELIUS : _____   13.____
    A. astronomy   B. healing   C. prophecy
    D. sun   E. thunder

14. PELEUS : ACHILLES :: TANTALUS : _____   14.____
    A. Thetis   B. Hippolytus   C. Pelops
    D. fruit   E. Hippodameia

15. EPHIALTES : APOLLO :: ETOCLES : _____   15.____
    A. Hermes   B. Oedipus
    C. Hades   D. "Seven Against Thebes"
    E. Polynices

16. ELECTRA : CHRYSOTHEMIS :: ANTIGONE : _____   16.____
    A. Haemon   B. Ismene   C. Helen of Troy
    D. Oedipus   E. Creon

17. SELENE : MOON :: DIONYSUS : _____   17.____
    A. sleep   B. fire   C. vegetation
    D. music   E. Bacchus

18. GRAEAE : PHORCYS :: CHARITIES : _____   18.____
    A. three sisters   B. Perseus   C. Zeus
    D. the Graces   E. Auxo

19. FABLE : AESOP :: SATYR-PLAY : _____   19.____
    A. Hesiod   B. Archilochus   C. Homer
    D. Euripides   E. "The Cyclops"

20. TRAGIC INDICTMENT OF WAR : "THE TROJAN WOMEN" :: COMIC   20.____
    INDICTMENT OF WAR : _____
    A. "The Persians" B. "Lysistrata"   C. "Peace"
    D. Aristophanes   E. Terence

21. FOOD STOLEN FROM THE GODS : TANTALUS :: FIRE STOLEN FROM   21.____
    THE GODS : _____
    A. Pegasus   B. Promethus   C. Hephaestus
    D. Aeschylus   E. Hermes

22. URANUS : KRONOS :: KRONOS : _____   22.____
    A. Rhea   B. Gaea   C. Eros
    D. Poseidon   E. heaven

23. MAN WITH HORSE'S BODY : CENTAUR :: SPIRIT WITH GOAT'S   23.____
    LEGS : _____
       A. Lotus-Eaters   B. Graeae   C. Gorgon
       D. Satyr   E.Cyclops

24. BLOOD-SUCKING MONSTERS : FURIES :: WINGED MONSTERS : _____   24.____
       A. Hecatoncheires   B. Eumenides   C. Minotaurs
       D. Erinyes   E. Harpies

25. MT. OLYMPUS : ZEUS :: DELPHI : _____   25.____
       A. Pythian priestess   B. Odysseus   C. Oedipus
       D. Mt. Pelion   E. Ossa

———————

KEY (CORRECT ANSWERS)

1	D	6.	C	11.	C	16.	B	21.	B
2.	A	7.	D	12.	C	17.	C	22.	D
3.	C	8.	E	13.	D	18.	C	23.	D
4.	C	9.	A	14.	C	19.	D	24.	E
5.	D	10.	D	15.	E	20.	B	25.	A

———————

TEST 5

1. JONAH : WHALE :: NOAH : _____
   A. two of each species   B. Shem   C. ark
   D. flood   E. Mount Ararat

2. "THE LOVE OF MONEYH IS THE ROOT OF ALL EVIL" : BIBLE :: "TURN,
   THEREFORE, THY FACE TOWARDS THE HOLY TEMPLE OF
   MECCA" : _____
   A. Koran   B. Science and Health   C. New Testament
   D. "The Sheik"   E. Apocrypha

3. "...FOR THINE IS THE KINGDOM AND THE POWER AND THE GLORY
   FOREVER AND EVER, AMEN" : KING JAMES VERSION :: LEAD US NOT
   INTO TEMPTATION BUT DELIVER US FROM EVIL, AMEN" : _____
   A. Ten Commandments   B. Old Testament
   C. Church of England   D. Douay Bible
   E. Genesis

4. CAIN : ABEL :: ADAM : _____
   A. Eve   B. Lilith   C. Methuselah
   D. the Serpent   E. the Garden of Eden

5. "GLORIA PATRI" : "AVE MARIA" :: "GLORY BE TO THE FATHER" : _____
   A. Confession   B. Old Testament
   C. Hail, Mary   D. prayer
   E. The Sermon on the Mount

6. BACH : HYMN :: ST. GREGORY : _____
   A. incantation   B. chant   C. psalm
   D. ode   E. prayer

7. "THE POMP AND VARIETY OF THIS WICKED WORLD" : CATECHISM ::
   "THOU SHALT NOT COMMIT ADULTERY" : _____
   A. New Testament   B. Lord's Prayer   C. Beatitudes
   D. The Divine Comedy E. Ten Commandments

8. ABRAHAM : SARAH :: JESUS : _____
   A. The Maccabees   B. Mary   C. Adam
   D. Jonah   E. Moses

9. "THERE WAS A MAN SENT FROM GOD WHOSE NAME WAS JOHN" :
   JOHN :: "TAKE THINE EASE, EAT, DRINK, AND BE MERRY" : _____
   A. Genesis   B. Matthew   C. Luke
   D. Pilate   E. Acts

10. APOCRYPHA : ALEXANDRIAN JEWS :: DOUAY : _____
    A. Christian Scientists B. Lutherans   C. Mormons
    D. Roman Catholics   E. Jehovah's Witnesses

1._____
2._____
3._____
4._____
5._____
6._____
7._____
8._____
9._____
10._____

11. WITH ALL MY WORLDLY GOODS I THEE ENDOW" : MARRIAGE
    CEREMONY :: "BLESS US O LORD, AND THESE THY GIFTS..." : _____
    A. morning prayer   B. confession   C. grace
    D. Ave, Maria   E. the Seder

11.____

12. OLD TESTAMENT : GENESIS :: NEW TESTAMENT : _____
    A. Psalms   B. Koran   C. Leviticus
    D. Ecclesiastes   E. Numbers

12.____

13. SAMSON : DELILAH :: JACOB : _____
    A. Sarah   B. Leah   C. Eve
    D. Naomi   E. Rebecca

13.____

14. ARISTOTLE : PHILOSOPHY :: THEOCRITUS : _____
    A. poetry   B. drama   C. oratory
    D. Homer   E. religion

14.____

15. GREEK ORATORY : DEMOSTHENES :: LATIN ORATORY : _____
    A. Terence   B. Seneca   C. Cicero
    D. Plautus   E. Vergil

15.____

16. PHILIP : ALEXANDER :: ABRAHAM : _____
    A. Cleopatra   B. Isaac   C. Moses
    D. Plato   E. Aristophanes

16.____

17. WOODEN HORSE : TROY :: RAM'S HORNS : _____
    A. Canaan   B. Hector   C. Joshua
    D. Jericho   E. Rome

17.____

18. FIRST ROMAN TRIUMVIRATE : CAESAR,K POMPEIUS AND CRASSUS ::
    SECOND ROMAN TRIUMVIRATE : _____
    A. Diocletianus, Maximus, and Tacitus
    B. Octavius, Antonius, and Lepidus
    C. Caesar, Antony, and Brutus
    D. Florianius, Probus, and Carus
    E. Aristotle, Plato, and Socrates

18.____

19. WESTERN WORLD IN 4TH CENTURY B.C. : ROME :: EASTERN WORLD
    IN 4TH CENTURY A.D. : _____
    A. Istanbul   B. Athens   C. Turkey
    D. Alexandria   E. Constantinople

19.____

20. PHILOSOPHY : PLATO :: HISTORY : _____
    A. Herodotus   B. Pindar   C. Zeus
    D. Odysseus   E. Tantalus

20.____

21. LUCRETIUS : HORACE :: EPICURUS : _____
    A. Menander   B. Euripides   C. Hesiod
    D. Homer   E. Nero

21.____

22. DRAMA : TERENCE :: BIOGRAPHY : _____
    A. Cato   B. Statius   C. Plutarch
    D. Plautus   E. Agamemnon

22.____

23. SATURN : TIME :: MARS : _____
    A. love   B. war   C. speed
    D. fertility   E. hunting

23.____

24. JUPITER : ZEUS :: NEPTUNE : _____
    A. Hermes   B. Poseidon   C. Pluto
    D. Demeter   E. Cupid

24.____

25. BACCHUS : WINE :: EROS : _____
    A. Cupid   B. the sea   C. the sun
    D. wisdom   E. love

25.____

KEY (CORRECT ANSWERS)

1	C	6.	B	11.	C	16.	B	21.	C
2.	A	7.	E	12.	D	17.	D	22.	C
3.	D	8.	B	13.	D	18.	B	23.	B
4.	D	9.	C	14.	A	19.	D	24.	D
5.	C	10.	D	15.	C	20.	B	25.	C

TEST 6

1. FOOD : AMBROSIA :: DRINK : _____
   A. aphrodisia   B. aqua   C. ichor
   D. néctar   E. hemlock

   1._____

2. VENUS : APHRODITE :: MINERVA : _____
   A. Diana   B. Athena   C. Ares
   D. Juno   E. Vesta

   2._____

3. JUPITER : JUNO :: OSIRIS : _____
   A. Rhea   B. Kronos   C. Hestia
   D. Isis   E. Priam

   3._____

4. FABLES : AESOP :: DRAMA : _____
   A. Aeschylus   B. Plato   C. Thucydides
   D. comedy   E. prayer

   4._____

5. DAMON : PYTHIAS :: PLEIADES : _____
   A. Romulus   B. Esau   C. Orestes
   D. Laertes   E. Caligula

   5._____

6. CYCLOPS : ONE EYE :: MEDUSA : _____
   A. many arms   B. lyre   C. head of serpents
   D. many heads   E. body of a snake

   6._____

7. CZAR : RUSSIA :: ARCHON : _____
   A. Athens   B. Afghanistan   C. Persia
   D. Macedonia   E. Rome

   7._____

8. SABINES : ITALY :: THE LORELEI : _____
   A. France   B. Rome   C. Greece
   D. Rubens   E. Germany

   8._____

9. PATHENON : ATHENS :: NOTRE DAME : _____
   A. Lyons   B. Normandy   C. Paris
   D. Brittany   E. Lourdes

   9._____

10. "THE MAID" : JOAN OF ARC :: "PRINCE OF POETS" : _____
    A. Palestrina   B. Homer   C. "Aeneid"
    D. Vergil   E. Euripides

    10._____

11. AHAB : ELIJAH :: KING : _____
    A. poet   B. prophet   C. prince
    D. whale   E. Egypt

    11._____

12. CENTAUR : HEAD OF MAN AND BODY OF HORSE :: MINOTAUR : _____   12.____
    A. head of snakes   B. head of bull and body of man
    C. unicorn   D. body of serpent
    E. Sagittarius

13. "THE VALLEY OF THE SHADOW OF DEATH" : OLD TESTAMENT ::   13.____
    "...SALT OF THE EARTH" : _____
    A. Koran   B. Bible   C. New Testament
    D. Jesus   E. Shakespeare

14. OCEANUS BRITANNICUS : OCEANUS HIBERNICUS :: ENGLISH   14.____
    CHANNEL : _____
    A. Red Sea   B. Irish Sea   C. Mediterranean Sea
    D. Dead Sea   E. Black Sea

15. CAMBORICUM : CAMBRIDGE :: MANCUNIUM : _____   15.____
    A. London   B. Middlesex   C. Edinburgh
    D. Oxford   E. Manchester

16. ANGLO-SAXONS : ENGLAND :: VIKINGS : _____   16.____
    A. Rome   B. Germany   C. Greece
    D. Phoenecia   E. Scandinavia

17. ACROPOLIS : PARTHENON :: SPHINX : _____   17.____
    A. Pyramids   B. Tower of Pisa
    C. Cologne   D. Colosseum
    E. Seven Wonders of the World

18. "AS DAWN'S LEFT HAND WAS IN THE SKY" : OMAR KHAYYAM ::   18.____
    "ROSY-FINGERED DAWN" : _____
    A. Theocritus   B. Homer   C. Ovid
    D. Vergil   E. Horace

19. MICHELANGELO : ROME :: GIOTTO : _____   19.____
    A. Pisa   B. Venice   C. Naples
    D. Florence   E. Palermo

20. ORESTES : AGAMEMNON :: ORPHEUS : _____   20.____
    A. Zeus   B. Apollo   C. Demeter
    D. Ares   E. Vesta

21. DANTE : "DIVINE COMEDY" :: BOCACCIO : _____   21.____
    A. "Dialogues"   B. "Lives"   C. "Decameron"
    D. "Iliad"   E. "The Persian Wars"

22. NAPOLEON : ELBA :: DANTE : _____   22.____
    A. Sicily   B. Malta   C. Ravenna
    D. Sardinia   E. Cyprus

23. CYMBELINE : ENGLAND :: CYCLOPS : _____   23.____
    A. Troy   B. Thrace   C. Sparta
    D. Olympus   E. one-eyed giant

24. CLIO : HISTORY :: URANIA : _____   24.____
    A. poetry   B. tragedy   C. religion
    D. astronomy   E. dance

25. NERO : ROME :: ALEXANDER : _____   25.____
    A. Rhodes   B. Cyprus   C. Macedonia
    D. Troy   E. Philip

_____

KEY (CORRECT ANSWERS)

1	D	6.	C	11.	B	16.	E	21.	C
2.	B	7.	A	12.	B	17.	A	22.	C
3.	D	8.	E	13.	C	18.	B	23.	B
4.	A	9.	C	14.	B	19.	D	24.	D
5.	C	10.	D	15.	E	20.	B	25.	C

_____

TEST 7

1. HECTOR : PARIS :: ROMULUS : _____ 1.___
   A. Prian B. Vergil C. Homer
   D. Claudius E. Remus

2. LILLIPUTIANS : SWIFT :: PYGMIES : _____ 2.___
   A. Homer B. Horace C. Seneca
   D. Sophocles E. Pygmalion

3. ACHILLES : HEEL :: TANTALUS : _____ 3.___
   A. heart B. temptation C. Sodom
   D. greed E. gold

4. TERPSICHORE : DANCE :: THALIA : _____ 4.___
   A. music B. comedy C. song
   D. sleep E. wine

5. NILE : EGYPT :: STYX : _____ 5.___
   A. Greece B. Olympus C. Hell
   D. Israel E. Norway

6. HYDRA : MANY HEADS :: PAN : _____ 6.___
   A. invisibility B. goat legs C. Roman god
   D. Hermes E. gargoyle

7. DAPHNE : PINE TREE :: SYRINX : _____ 7.___
   A. thunder B. reed pipe C. frog
   D. sheep E. horse

8. ZEUS : CLOUDS :: CRONUS : _____ 8.___
   A. Sun God B. ocean C. lightning
   D. mythology E. Rain God

9. URANUS : SKY :: GAEA : _____ 9.___
   A. moon B. Pluto C. rain
   D. Earth E. forest

10. PAN : ALL :: ANDROGNO : _____ 10.___
    A. man-woman B. oak-man C. fountain
    D. manhood lost E. constellation

11. "...BUT WHEN I GO TO ROOM, I DO AS ROME DOES" : ST. AUGUSTINE :: 11.___
    "OH, THAT ROME HAD BUT ONE HEAD, THAT I MIGHT STRIKE IT OFF AT
    A BLOW!" : _____
    A. Romulus B. St. Ambrose C. Antony
    D. Caligula E. Caesar

12. ULYSSES : PENELOPE :: CUPID : _____
    A. Psyche   B. heart   C. Myrrha
    D. darts   E. Aphrodite
                                                      12._____

13. PYGMALION : GALATEA :: OEDIPUS : _____
    A. Adonis   B. Penelope   C. Hermaphrodite
    D. Jocasta   E. Sappho
                                                       13._____

14. STYX : RIVER :: OLYMPUS : _____
    A. ocean   B. continent   C. valley
    D. mountain   E. oracle
                                                       14._____

15. GOTHS : TEUTONS :: FRANKS : _____
    A. Romans   B. Lombards   C. barbarians
    D. Saxons   E. Charlemagne
                                                       15._____

16. LOT'S WIFE : SODOM AND GOMORRAH :: EURYDICE : _____
    A. Bedlam   B. Hell   C. heavens
    D. Elysian Fields   E. Bethlehem
                                                        16._____

17. EVE : TREE OF KNOWLEDGE :: PANDORA : _____
    A. long hair   B. bow and arrow   C. Tantalus
    D. box   E. Adam
                                                       17._____

18. CLEOPATRA : ASP :: SOCRATES : _____
    A. Plato   B. arsenic   C. hemlock
    D. peyote   E. curare
                                                       18._____

19. HANNIBAL : ALPS :: JOSHUA : _____
    A. Jericho   B. plagues   C. Jerusalem
    D. wall   E. Red Sea
                                                       19._____

20. BABYLON : GARDENS :: RHODES : _____
    A. Acropolis   B. Colossus   C. Parthenon
    D. Pyramids   E. Troy
                                                     20._____

21. HERCULES : AUGAEAN STABLES :: ATLAS : _____
    A. Zeus   B. strength   C. Golden Apples
    D. universe   E. oceans
                                                     21._____

22. ATTIC ERA : MENANDER :: SILVER AGE : _____
    A. Julius Caesar   B. Gracchi   C. Herodotus
    D. Apollonius   E. Persius
                                                    22._____

23. ZENO : EPICURUS :: EUCLID : _____
    A. Phidias   B. Praxiteles   C. Xenophon
    D. Eratosthenes   E. Pythagoras
                                                   23._____

24. CATO : GALBA :: CICERO : _____   24.____
    A. Crassus   B. Carbo   C. Caecilius
    D. Catiline   E. Catullus

25. THUCYDIDES : XENOPHON :: PLUTARCH : _____   25.____
    A. Justinian   B. Seneca   C. Suetonius
    D. Pliny   E. Ovid
                                  _____

KEY (CORRECT ANSWERS)

1	E	6.	A	11.	D	16.	B	21.	D
2.	A	7.	B	12.	A	17.	D	22.	E
3.	B	8.	C	13.	D	18.	C	23.	D
4.	B	9.	D	14.	D	19.	D	24.	D
5.	C	10.	A	15.	B	20.	B	25.	C

TEST 8

1. OEDIPUS : MURDER OF LAIUS :: MEDEA : _____   1.____
   A. murder of father   B. murder of Jason   C. murder of mother
   D. murder of Creon   E. murder of Idyia

2. GOLDEN FLEECE : JASON :: GOLDEN APPLE : _____   2.____
   A. Calliope   B. Minerva   C. Rhea
   D. Athena   E. Aphrodite

3. HERACLES : MURDER OF NESSUS :: ORESTES : _____   3.____
   A. murder of Electra   B. Euripides
   C. murder of Antigone   D. murder of Clytemnestra
   E. murder of Julius Caesar

4. "OEDIPUS REX" : PROPHECY OF THE DEPHIC ORACLE :: "ORESTIA" : _____   4.____
   A. song of the Sirens   B. curse of Medusa
   C. prophecy of Zeus   D. curse of the house of Atreus
   E. oath of Hera

5. KING OF ARGOS : PELASGUS :: KING OF THEBES : _____   5.____
   A. Laius   B. Tiresias   C. Creon
   D. Admetus   E. Heracles

6. MURDER OF HER CHILDREN : MEDEA :: SACRIFICE OF HIS   6.____
   DAUGHTER : _____
   A. Agamemnon   B. Creusa   C. Atreus
   D. Menelaus   E. Helen

7. ORESTES : ELECTRA :: CREON : _____   7.____
   A. Medea   B. Niobe   C. Creusa
   D. Jocasta   E. Daphne

8. PELOPONNESIAN WARS : "THE KNIGHTS" :: TROJAN WAR : _____   8.____
   A. "Orestia"   B. "The Trachiniae"   C. "Agamemnon"
   D. "Euripides"   E. "Philoctetes"

9. DENUNCIATION OF WAR : "THE TROJAN WOMEN" :: REFUSAL TO BURY   9.____
   THE DEAD : _____
   A. Aristophanes   B. "The Wasps"   C. "Lysistrata"
   D. "The Frogs"   E. "The Suppliants"

10. THE LAST HOURS OF OEDIPUS : COLONUS :: ORESTES' MURDER OF   10.____
    HIS MOTHER : _____
    A. Athens   B. Argos   C. Mycenae
    D. Attica   E. Thebes

11. "SEVEN AGAINST THEBES" : SONS OF OEDIPUS :: "PROMETHUS   11.____
    BOUND : _____
    A. Clytemnestra   B. Hippolytus   C. Aristophanes
    D. "Acharnians"   E. Zeus

12. "I AM A HUMAN BEING; I CONSIDER NOTHING HUMAN FOREIGN TO   12.____
    ME" : "THE SELF-TORMENTOR" :: "FORTUNE FAVORS THE BRAVE :
    _____
    A. Terence   B. "The Women of Andros"
    C. "Phormio"   D. "The Brothers"
    E. "The Eunuch

13. LOVERS : PHAEDRA AND HIPPOLYTUS :: ENEMIES : _____   13.____
    A. Electra and Orestes   B. Tweedledum and Tweedledee
    C. Troilus and Cressida   D. Creusa and Medea
    E. Diana and Endymion

14. STRANGLING OF TWO SERPENTS : HERACLES :: DRIVING HIS FATHER'S   14.____
    CHARIOT TOO NEAR THE SUN : _____
    A. Perseus   B. Phaethon   C. Orchomenus
    D. Orpheus   E. Daedalus

15. ODYSSEUS : ODYSSEY: :: ACHILLES : _____   15.____
    A. Homer   B. "Lysistrata"   C. "Iliad"
    D. Hector   E. "Agamemnon"

16. FERTILITY : PAN :: WINE : _____   16.____
    A. Apollo   B. roses   C. Dionysus
    D. Ares   E. Muses

17. IMMORTALITY OF THE SOUL : "PHAEDRO" :: IDEAL STATE : _____   17.____
    A. "Dialogues"   B. "Republic"   C. Plato
    D. Socrates   E. "Laws"

18. PHRYGIA : MIDAS :: CRETE : _____   18.____
    A. Priam   B. Troy   C. Minos
    D. Hector   E. Creon

19. MIDDLE COMEDY : BURLESQUES :: OLD COMEDY : _____   19.____
    A. tragedy   B. biographies   C. satire
    D. politics   E. Aristophanes

20. HEEL : ACHILLES :: ROCK : _____   20.____
    A. Odysseus   B Pan   C. Sisyphus
    D. Apollo   E. Hades

21. "AGAMEMNON" : "ORESTIA" :: "LAIUS" : _____   21.____
    A. "Seven Against Thebes"   B. "The Birds"
    C. Aeschylus   D. "Oedipus a Colonus"
    E. Sophocles

22. ARGO : BOAT :: ARGOS : _____   22. _____
    A. king   B. god   C. mythology
    D. Jason   E. city

23. ZEUS : HESTIA :: ARES : _____   23. _____
    A. Isis   B. Eros   C. Eris
    D. Sirens   E. Aphrodite

24. EPHEMERIS : ALMANAC :: ENCOMIUM : _____   24. _____
    A. Pindar   B. "Mice"   C. legend
    D. eulogy   E. play

25. POLITICAL SATIRE : ARISTOPHANES :: POLITICAL SPEECHES : _____   25. _____
    A. Demophilus   B. Plato   C. Demosthenes
    D. Plutarch   E. Lycophron

KEY (CORRECT ANSWERS)

1	D	6.	A	11.	E	16.	C	21.	A
2.	E	7.	D	12.	C	17.	B	22.	E
3.	D	8.	A	13.	D	18.	C	23.	C
4.	D	9.	E	14.	B	19.	C	24.	D
5.	E	10.	C	15.	B	20.	C	25.	C

TESTS IN VERBAL ANALOGIES - HISTORY

DIRECTIONS: Each question in this part consists of two capitalized words which have a certain relationship to each other, and a third capitalized word which is followed by five lettered words in small letters. Choose the number of the word which is related in the SAME way to the third capitalized word as the first two capitalized words are related to each other. *PRINT THE LETTER OF THE CORRECT ANSWER IN THE SPACE AT THE RIGHT.*

TEST 1

1. CYRUS : CAMBYSES :: PHILIP : _____   1._____
   A. Menelaus   B. Homer   C. Agamemnon
   D. Miletos   E. Alexander

2. BONAPARTE : WATERLOO :: CUSTER : _____   2._____
   A. Black Cloud   B. Indians   C. Appomattox
   D. Little Big Horn   E. General Ludendorff

3. "LITTLE FLOWER" : FIORELLO H. LA GUARDIA : "HAPPY WARRIOR" : _____   3._____
   A. Franklin D. Roosevelt   B. Wendell Willkie
   C. Alfred E. Smith   D. Joseph McCarthy
   E. Stephen Douglas

4. AUGUSTUS : LIVIA :: CLAUDIUS : _____   4._____
   A. Minerva   B. Agrippina   C. Julia
   D. Josephine   E. Messalina

5. KING CHRISTIAN : PEACE OF LUBECK :: KING ADOLPHUS : _____   5._____
   A. Treaty of Verdun   B. Peace of Prague
   C. Munich Conference   D. Treaty of Versailles
   E. Peace of Augsburg

6. LORD HOWARD : ENGLISH FLEET :: KING PHILIP : _____   6._____
   A. French Revolution   B. Dutch Revolt
   C. Moslems   D. Spanish Armada
   E. Duke of Marlborough

7. LORD GODOLPHIN : VOLPONE :: FRANCOIS MARIE AROUET : _____   7._____
   A. Jean Christophe   B. Samuel Clemens
   C. Francisco Franco   D. Rousseau
   E. Voltaire

8. WASHINGTON : DELAWARE :: PATTON : _____   8._____
   A. Mississippi   B. Danube   C. Amazon
   D. Elbe   E. Ebro

177

9. MONTGOMERY : WORLD WAR ii :: CAIUS MARIUS : _____   9.____
    A. Social Wars   B. Punic Wars
    C. Jugurthine War   D. "Sacred War"
    E. Peloponnesian War

10. NAPOLEON : CORSICA :: JOSEPHINE : _____   10.____
    A. Lorraine   B. Prague   C. Santo Domingo
    D. Paris   E. Martinique

11. ELIZABETH : ANN BOLEYN :: CATHERINE : _____   11.____
    A. Marie Louise   B. Isabella   C. Mary
    D. Marie Antoinette   E. Joan of Arc

12. LINCOLN : "GREAT EMANCIPATOR" :: CLAY : _____   12.____
    A. "Man of the Half Century"   B. "The Plumed Knight"
    C. "The Little Giant"   D. "The Silver-Tongued Orator"
    E. "Great Pacificator

13. LINCOLN : JOHNSON :: JEFFERSON : _____   13.____
    A. Sparkman   B. Wallace   C. Nixon
    D. Burr   E. Humphrey

14. JULY REVOLUTION : 1830 :: CRIMEAN WAR : _____   14.____
    A. 1854   B. 1861   C. 1812
    D. 1898   E. 1876

15. HUNGARY LOUIS KOSSUTH :: RUSSIA : _____   15.____
    A. Ivan the Terrible   B. Catherine the Great   C. Nicholas I
    D. Peter the Great   E. Alexander I

16. GARIBALDI : ANITA :: HENRY II : _____   16.____
    A. Alberta   B. Gertrude   C. Eleanor
    D. Marie   E. Isabella

17. SAINT-SIMON : SOCIALISM :: GARIBALDI : _____   17.____
    A. Anarchism   B. Liberalism   C. Republicanism
    D. Conservatism   E. Fascism

18. POPE URBAN II : FIRST CRUSADE :: BARBAROSSA : _____   18.____
    A. Storming of the Bastille   B. War of the Roses
    C. Peace of Utrecht   D. October Days
    E. Third Crusade

19. WELFS : POPES :: WAIBLINGS : _____   19.____
    A. politicians   B. merchants   C. autocrats
    D. emperors   E. autocrats

20. LEGNANO : FREDERICK BARBAROSSA :: STALINGRAD : _____   20.____
    A. Normandy   B. Paulus   C. von Rundstedt
    D. von Schleicher   E. Hindenburg

21. NORSEMEN : VIKINGS :: MONGOLS : _____   21.____
    A. Franks   B. Atilla   C. Vandals
    D. Magyars   E. Visigoths

22. ROMAN EMPEROR : CHARLEMAGNE :: KING OF THE FRANKS : _____   22.____
    A. "Iron Crown"   B. Pepin   C. Martel
    D. Clovis   E. Theodosius

23. ABBASID DYNASTY : BAGHDAD :: OMMIAD DYNASTY : _____   23.____
    A. Alexandria   B. Baghdad   C. Syria
    D. Damascus   E. Constantinople

24. ARAB EMPIRE : HAROUN-AL-RASCHID :: BYZANTINE EMPIRE : _____   24.____
    A. Mohammed   B. Saladin   C. Justinian
    D. St. Thomas Aquinas E. Odoacer

25. BERBERS : NORTH AFRICA :: MORISCOS : _____   25.____
    A. Moors   B. Italy   C. Spain
    D. South America   E. Mexico

───────────

KEY (CORRECT ANSWERS)

1	E	6.	D	11.	B	16.	C	21.	D
2.	D	7.	E	12.	E	17.	B	22.	B
3.	C	8.	D	13.	D	18.	E	23.	D
4.	B	9.	C	14.	A	19.	D	24.	C
5.	B	10.	E	15.	C	20.	B	25.	C

───────────

TEST 2

1. ALARIC : VISIGOTHS :: THEODORIC : _____
   A. Huns
   B. Vandals
   C. Lombards
   D. Franks
   E. Ostrogoths

   1.____

2. AUGUSTUS : MAECENAS :: JULIUS CAESAR : _____
   A. Caligula
   B. Catullus
   C. Octavian
   D. Ovid
   E. Tacitus

   2.____

3. CONSTANTINOPLE : ISTANBUL :: TYRE : _____
   A. Baghdad
   B. Cairo
   C. Carthage
   D. Miletos
   E. Alexandria

   3.____

4. TIBERIUS : GAIUS :: NAPOLEON : _____
   A. Jerome
   B. Nelson
   C. Barras
   D. Alexander
   E. Murat

   4.____

5. FIRST TRIUMVIRATE : POMPEY :: SECOND TRIUMVIRATE : _____
   A. Sulla
   B. Cicero
   C. Caesar
   D. Crassus
   E. Antony

   5.____

6. COMMODUS : MILITARY EMPERORS :: CALIGULA : _____
   A. Social Reformers
   B. Soldiers
   C. New Frontiers
   D. Roman Liberals
   E. Political Emperors

   6.____

7. GREECE : MILETOS :: FRANCE : _____
   A. Burgundy
   B. Paris
   C. Toulon
   D. Cologne
   E. Lorraine

   7.____

8. WATER : THALES :: FIRE : _____
   A. Pompeii
   B. Hipparchus
   C. Nero
   D. Heracleitos
   E. Herodotus

   8.____

9. HUGH CAPET : FRANCE :: HAROLD : _____
   A. Italy
   B. Hastings
   C. Saxony
   D. England
   E. Greece

   9.____

10. MAGYARS : OTTO :: GOLDEN HORDE : _____
    A. Genghis Khan
    B. Tamerlane
    C. Hunyadi
    D. Osman I
    E. Kublai Khan

    10.____

11. EUGENE DEBS : NORMAL THOMAS :: R. NIXON : _____
    A. F. Roosevelt
    B. A. Stevenson
    C. J. Kennedy
    D. T. Dewey
    E. H. Humphrey

    11.____

12. "THE POOR MEN OF LYON" : PETER WALDO :: "BEGGING BROTHERS :
    ____
    A. St. Paul   B. Gregory   C. Abelard
    D. St. Francis   E. Zoroaster   12.____

13. AGRIPPINA : NERO :: MARIE ANTOINETTE : ____
    A. Louis XIV   B. Louis XV   C. Louis XVI
    D. Louis XVII   E. Louis XVIII   13.____

14. JANUARY 21, 1793 : LOU9IS xvi :: JULY 28, 1794 : ____
    A. Napoleon   B. Philip   C. Robespierre
    D. Jacobins   E. July 13, 1789   14.____

15. LEOPOLD II : MARIE ANTOINETTE :: CESARE BORGIA : ____
    A. Elizabeth I   B. Maria Louisa   C. Eleanor of Aquitane
    D. Maria Theresa   E. Lucrezia Borgia   15.____

16. GETTYSBURG : CIVIL WAR :: KÖNIGGRATZ : ____
    A. Franco-Prussian War   B. Seven Years' War
    C. Thirty Years' War   D. Hundred Years' War
    E. Seven Weeks' War   16.____

17. HENRY II : BECKET :: CHARLES I : ____
    A. Laud   B. Adolphus   C. Richelieu
    D. Mazarin   E. Cranmer   17.____

18. HERNANDO : BARTOLOMEO :: CORTEZ : ____
    A. Amalie   B. Pizarro   C. Verrazano
    D. Diaz   E. Francisco   18.____

19. BUDDHA : GAUTAMA :: CONFUCIUS : ____
    A. Mao Tse-tung   B. Lao-tse   C. Kung Fu-tze
    D. Tai-tsung   E. Thucydides   19.____

20. CAVALIERS : ANGLICANS :: ROUNDHEADS : ____
    A. Mohammedans   B. Anglicans   C. Popes
    D. Puritans   E. Catholics   20.____

21. "RED-BEARD" : FREDERICK :: "BLACK PRINCE" : ____
    A. Othello   B. Edward   C. Charles
    D. Lear   E. Richard   21.____

22. FASCISTS : ITALY :: FREE CORPS : ____
    A. America   B. Prussia   C. France
    D. Germany   E. Corsica   22.____

23. LATERAN TREATY : MUSSOLINI :: NINETY-FIVE THESES : ____
    A. Philip   B. St. Peter   C. Paul
    D. Peale   E. Luther   23.____

24. S.A. : ERNST ROHM :: S.S. : _____   24.____
    A. Bruning   B. President Ebert   C. Gustav Stresemann
    D. von Hindenburg   E. Heinrich Himmler

25. NEW JERSEY : WOODROW WILSON :: NEW YORK : _____   25.____
    A. Robert F. Wagner   B. F.H. LaGuardia   C. General U.S. Grant
    D. Grover Whalen   E. Grover Cleveland

KEY (CORRECT ANSWERS)

1	E	6.	E	11.	D	16.	E	21.	B
2.	B	7.	C	12.	D	17.	A	22.	D
3.	E	8.	D	13.	D	18.	D	23.	E
4.	A	9.	D	14.	C	19.	C	24.	E
5.	E	10.	B	15.	E	20.	D	25.	E

TEST 3

1. TROTSKY : RED ARMY :: DENIKIN : _____
    - A. Jacobins
    - B. Bolshevists
    - C. Cadets
    - D. Don Cossacks
    - E. Menshevists

    1._____

2. GERMANY : GESTAPO :: RUSSIA : _____
    - A. Troika
    - B. Cheka
    - C. White Army
    - D. Duma
    - E. Kremlin

    2._____

3. LABOR PARTY : BRITAIN :: UNITED SOCIALIST PARTY : _____
    - A. Austria
    - B. Belgium
    - C. United States
    - D. France
    - E. Germany

    3._____

4. BOSTON : TEA :: CANTON : _____
    - A. Treaty Port
    - B. Rice
    - C. Opium
    - D. Bamboo
    - E. Silk

    4._____

5. EMPEROR FERDINAND : PRINCE METTERNICH :: EMPEROR FRANCIS
    JOSEPH : _____
    - A. Rasputin
    - B. Rainier
    - C. Prince Schwarzenberg
    - D. Talleyrand
    - E. Francis Kossuth

    5._____

6. ROBESPIERRE : JACOBINS :: CHARLES X : _____
    - A. Huguenots
    - B. Bonapartists
    - C. Ultras
    - D. Bourbons
    - E. Socialists

    6._____

7. NAPOLEON : JOSEPHINE :: BONAPARTE : _____
    - A. Oberon
    - B. du Barry
    - C. Barras
    - D. Beauharnais
    - E. Bovary

    7._____

8. "REIGN OF TERROR" : ROBESPIERRE :: "RED TERROR" : _____
    - A. Zapata
    - B. Lenin
    - C. Sun Ya-sen
    - D. Kornilov
    - E. Atilla

    8._____

9. PRUSSIA : VON MOLTKE :: UNITED STATES : _____
    - A. Thomas E. Dewey
    - B. Paul Robeson
    - C. Omar Bradley
    - D. William O'Dwyer
    - E. Huey Long

    9._____

10. ENGLAND : CHURCHILL :: PRUSSIA : _____
    - A. Mazarin
    - B. Frederick William
    - C. Gambetta
    - D. Cavour
    - E. Bismarck

    10._____

11. "SEPTEMBER MASSACRES" : PARIS :: "OCTOBER DAYS" : _____
    - A. Alexandria
    - B. Prague
    - C. Versailles
    - D. Congo
    - E. St. Bartholomew's Day

    11._____

12. FULTON : STEAMBOAT :: WATT : _____   12.____
    A. reaper   B. steam bath   C. steam engine
    D. electricity   E. spinning jenny

13. ELIZABETH : RUSSIA :: MARIA THERESA : _____   13.____
    A. Italy   B. Spain   C. France
    D. Austria   E. England

14. HENRY VII : HENRY TUDOR :: ALEXANDER VI : _____   14.____
    A. Alexander I   B. Alexander the Great C. Roderigo Borgia
    D. Julius II   E. Lorenzo il Magnifico

15. BATTLE OF AGINCOURT : FRANCE :: "BATTLE OF HASTINGS" : _____   15.____
    A. Ireland   B. Battle of Balaclava   C. Burgundy
    D. England   E. Normandy

16. EGYPTIANS :HIEROGLYPHICS :: SUMERIANS : _____   16.____
    A. clay tablets   B. Druids   C. Sanskrit
    D. cuneiform writing E. Rosetta Stone

17. U.S. GRANT : MANHATTAN :: CHRISTOPHER COLUMBUS : _____   17.____
    A. Spain   B. San Juan   C. Mexico
    D. Italy   E. Santo Domingo

18. JUAREZ : MEXICO :: BOLIVAR : _____   18.____
    A. Colombia   B. Peru   C. Bolivia
    D. Venezuela   E. Uruguay

19. LINCOLN : SLAVERY :: TSAR ALEXANDER II : _____   19.____
    A. Orthodox Church   B. mirs   C. pogroms
    D. serfdom   E. capitalism

20. HUNS : ATILLA :: RED SHIRTS : _____   20.____
    A. Alaric   B. Nazis   C. Garibaldi
    D. Ottomans   E. Fascists

21. CONSERVATISM : DISRAELI ::" LIBERALISM : _____   21.____
    A. Peel   B. Canning   C. Marquess of Salisbury
    D. Balfour   E. Gladstone

22. BOURBON DYNASTY : ORLEANS DYNASTY :: RURIK DYNASTY : _____   22.____
    A. Franco dynasty   B. Tsang dynasty   C. Ming dynasty
    D. Hapsburg dynasty E. Romanov dynasty

23. ATOM BOMB : WORLD WAR II :: POISON GAS : _____   23.____
    A. trench warfare   B. Finnish Uprising C. World War I
    D. Civil War   E. Boer War

24. MADERO : DIAZ DYNASTY : SUN YAT-SEN : _____   24.____
    A. Han dynasty   B. Shang dynaty   C. Chou dynasty
    D. Manchu dynasty   E. Ch'in dynasty

25. SIR ARUTHUR EVANS : CRETE :: HEINRICH SCHLIEMANN : _____   25.____
    A. Mesopotamia   B. Egypt   C. Rome
    D. Athens   E. Troy

_____

KEY (CORRECT ANSWERS)

1	D	6.	C	11.	C	16.	D	21.	E
2.	B	7.	D	12.	C	17.	E	22.	E
3.	D	8.	B	13.	D	18.	D	23.	C
4.	C	9.	C	14.	C	19.	D	24.	D
5.	C	10.	E	15.	D	20.	C	25.	E

_____

TEST 4

1. DRAVIDIANS : INDUS VALLEY :: HITTITES : _____   1.____
   A. Haiti   B. Russia   C. Turkey
   D. Palestine   E. Gaul

2. CHALDEAN EMPIRE : NEBUCHADNEZZAR :: PERSIAN EMPIRE : _____   2.____
   A. Darius   B. Zarathustra   C. David
   D. Ahab   E. Karnak

3. MONTEZUMA : AZTEC :: JUAREZ : _____   3.____
   A. Spanish   B. Mexican   C. Mayan
   D. Zapotec   E. Bandito

4. FIRST CASTE : BRAHMINS :: FOURTH CASTE : _____   4.____
   A. knights   B. warriors   C. serfs
   D. Nirvana   E. Vedas

5. CODE OF CIVIL LAW : JUSTINIAN :: FOURTEEN POINTS : _____   5.____
   A. Six Points   B. Wilson   C. Hitler
   D. F.D. Roosevelt   E. Marx

6. ALLAH : MOHAMMED :: ATON : _____   6.____
   A. Osiris   B. Brahma   C. Confucius
   D. Amenhotep IV   E. Odin

7. JERUSALEM : DAVID :: BABYLON : _____   7.____
   A. Solon   B. Assurbanipal   C. Philip of Macedon
   D. Hammurabi   E. Hannibal

8. ROMAN EMPIRE : CONSTANTINE :: FRANKISH KINGDOM : _____   8.____
   A. Otto   B. Clovis   C. Theodoric
   D. Alaric   E. Odoacer

9. "CHARLES THE HAMMER" : MOSLEMS :: "CHARLES THE GREAT" : _____   9.____
   A. Huns   B. Ostrogoths   C. Visigoths
   D. Lombards   E. Turks

10. WELCH : MCCARTHY :: DARROW : _____   10.____
    A. Mencken   B. Cohn   C. Bryan
    D. Stevens   E. T. Roosevelt

11. UNITED NATIONS : GOLDWATER :: LEAGUE OF NATIONS : _____   11.____
    A. Willkie   B. Wilson   C. Clemenceau
    D. Lodge   E. Debs

12. ENGLAND : WELLINGTON :: PRUSSIA : _____   12.____
    A. Metternich   B. Blucher   C. Castlereagh
    D. von Fritsch   E. Stresemann

13. ROMANS : CHRISTIANS :: MOGULS : _____   13.____
    A. Chinese   B. Hindus   C. Sassanids
    D. Moslems   E. Huguenots

14. FRANK COSTELLO : ESTES KEFAUVER :: ALGER HISS : _____   14.____
    A. Clarence Darrow   B. Vito Genovese   C. Margaret Chase Smith
    D. Richard Nixon   E. Whittaker Chambers

15. REPUBLICANS : DEMOCRATS :: TORIES : _____   15.____
    A. Socialists   B. Ultras   C. Liberals
    D. House of Lords   E. Fascists

16. DEPRESSION : WORLD WAR I :: THERMIDOREAN REACTION : _____   16.____
    A. Seven Years' War   B. Reign of Terror   C. Hundred Years' War
    D. Boer War   E. World War II

17. LOUIS XIV : BAROQUE :: LOUIS XV : _____   17.____
    A. Period   B. Bach   C. Gothic
    D. Gold   E. Rococo

18. TEUTONIC KNIGHTS : BATTLE ON THE ICE :: SWEDES : _____   18.____
    A. Northwest Passage   B. Battle of White Mountain
    C. Battle of Salamis   D. Great Northern War
    E. Prussian Purge

19. PELOPONNESIAN WAR : GOLDEN AGE :: GREAT NORTHERN WAR : _____   19.____
    A. Middle Ages   B. Dark Ages   C. Renaissance
    D. Age of Reason   E. Bronze Age

20. WORLD WAR I : SGT. YORK :: WORLD WAR II : _____   20.____
    A. Eisenhower   B. MacArthur   C. Audie Murphy
    D. General Patton   E. Ernie Pyle

21. "BLACK HAND" : ITALY :: "ORDER OF HARMONIOUS FISTS" : _____   21.____
    A. Constantinople   B. Ireland   C. Japan
    D. China   E. Mafia

22. DUKE WILLIAM : NORMANDY :: DON JUAN : _____   22.____
    A. Italy   B. France   C. Belgium
    D. Spain   E. Prussia

23. SPARTA : DORIANS :: ATHENS : _____   23.____
    A. Aryans   B. Phoenicians   C. Ionians
    D. Aegeans   E. Corinthians

24. JESUS : NAZARETH :: SAUL : _____   24.____
    A. Galilee   B. Jerusalem   C. David
    D. Tarsus   E. Nicaea

25. HAMMURABIAN CODE : BABYLON :: HITTITE CODE : _____   25.____
    A. Greece   B. Egypt   C. Persia
    D. Assyria   E. Macedonia

KEY (CORRECT ANSWERS)

1	C	6.	D	11.	D	16.	B	21.	D
2.	A	7.	D	12.	B	17.	E	22.	D
3.	D	8.	B	13.	B	18.	D	23.	C
4.	C	9.	D	14.	D	19.	D	24.	D
5.	B	10.	C	15.	C	20.	C	25.	C

TEST 5

1. EGYPT : TUTANKHAMEN :: MESOPOTAMIA : _____   1._____
   A. Ptolemy   B. Sargon I   C. Shalmaneser
   D. Sennacherib   E. Seleucus

2. BATTLE OF CRECY : ;1347 :: BATTLE OF RUNNYMEDE : _____   2._____
   A. 1607   B. 1485   C. 1215
   D. 1642   E. 1304

3. NILE : EGYPT :: TIGRIS : _____   3._____
   A. Babylon   B. Hwang-ho   C. Nile
   D. Mesopotamia   E. Euphrates

4. AMORITES : MESOPOTAMIA :: HYKSOS : _____   4._____
   A. Jordan   B. Greece   C. Egypt
   D. Huns   E.. Carthage

5. EGYPTIANS : PAPYRUS :: PHOENICIANS : _____   5._____
   A. pottery   B. numerical system   C. calendar
   D. alphabet   E. clay tablets

6. BATTLE OF MARATHON : DARIUS :: BATTLE OF ACTIUM : _____   6._____
   A. Tiberius   B. Trojan War   C. Antony
   D. Caesar   E. Livy

7. GREECE : SPARTA :: MESOPOTAMIA : _____   7._____
   A. Corinth   B. Crete   C. Sumer
   D. Assyria   E. Lydia

8. HEBREWS : HOSEA :: PERSIANS : _____   8._____
   A. Zosimus   B. Zebadiah   C. Zarathustra
   D. Zadok   E. Zebedee

9. "ATHENA" : PHIDIAS :: "DISCUS THROWER" : _____   9._____
   A. Ictinus   B. Calicrates   C. Pericles
   D. Myron   E. Scopas

10. AHMOSE : EIGHTEENTH DYNASTY :: THUTMOSE III : _____   10._____
    A. Aramaean Empire   B. Amon-Re Dynasty   C. Age of Pyramids
    D. The New Kingdom   E. Babylonian Empire

11. EGYPT : KARNAK :: CRETE : _____   11._____
    A. Athens   B. Thrace   C. Cnossos
    D. Ziggurat   E. Rhodes

12. RED SQUARE : COMMUNISM :: MECCA : _____   12._____
    A. Medina   B. Mohammed   C. Islam
    D. Kaaba   E. Dardanelles

13. SCIPO : ROMANS :: HANNIBAL : _____   13.____
    A. Sumerians   B. Spartans   C. Hittites
    D. Semites   E. Carthaginians

14. ASSYRIA : SARGON II :: EGYPT : _____   14.____
    A. Menelaus   B. Gracchus   C. Ptolemy
    D. Occam   E. Ezekiel

15. FIRST PUNIC WAR : 254 B.C. :: BATTLE OF PHARSALUS : _____   15.____
    A. 49 A.D.   B. 211 B.C.   C. 134 B.C.
    D. 48 B.C.   E. 180 B.C.

16. MESOPOTAMIA : BABYLONIAN EMPIRE :: INDIA : _____   16.____
    A. Indus-Valley Empire   B. Indo-Aryan Empire
    C. Hashid Empire   D. Mauryan Empire
    E. Mayan Empire

17. CAESAR : "IMPERATOR" :: OCTAVIAN : _____   17.____
    A. "lictor"   B. "consul"   C. "fasces"
    D. "princeps"   E. "pontifex maximus"

18. ROMAN EMPIRE : VESPASIAN :: BYZANTINE EMPIRE : _____   18.____
    A. Genghis Khan   B. Theodoric   C. Julian
    D. Belisarius   E. Jugurtha

19. NATIONALISM : SEVENTEENTH CENTURY : MANORIALISM : _____   19.____
    A. Age of Reason   B. Renaissance   C. Middle Ages
    D. Golden Age of Rome E. Periclean Age

20. CALVINISM : SWITZERLAND :: LUTHERANISM : _____   20.____
    A. Spain   B. Russia   C. Germany
    D. France   E. Sweden

21. FLORENCE : MEDICI :: MILAN : _____   21.____
    A. Naples   B. Gregory   C. Urban
    D. Visconti   E. Buonarroti

22. BOHEMIA : HUS :: ENGLAND : _____   22.____
    A. Luther   B. John of Gaunt   C. Germany
    D. Wycliffe   E. Lollards

23. LORENZO : PIERO II :: DAVID : _____   23.____
    A. Joseph   B. Saul   C. Solomon
    D. Goliath   E. Samuel

24. JULIUS II : RENAISSANCE :: INNOCENT III : _____   24.____
    A. "Fall of Rome" B. Age of Reason   C. Middle Ages
    D. Reformation   E. Dark Ages

25. SAXONS : KING HAROLD I :: NORSEMEN : _____   25.____
    A. "Sven of the Hammer"   B. Lars the Heart
    C. Thor   D. Harold Blue-Tooth
    E. Orgone

KEY (CORRECT ANSWERS)

1	B	6.	C	11.	C	16.	D	21.	D
2.	C	7.	C	12.	C	17.	D	22.	D
3.	D	8.	C	13.	E	18.	D	23.	C
4.	C	9.	D	14.	C	19.	C	24.	C
5.	D	10.	D	15.	D	20.	C	25.	D

TEST 6

1. 1870 : KIMBERLEY DIAMONDS :: 1886 : _____
   A. H.L. Moss pearls   B. La Prince oysters   C. Halley's Comet
   D. Rand gold   E. Comstock Lodge

   1._____

2. DELCASSE : FASHODA AFFAIR :: HORATIO GATES : _____
   A. Lincoln Assassination   B. Conway Cabal
   C. Guy Fawkes Gunpowder Plot   D. Sorge Affair
   E. Trent Affair

   2._____

3. ENGLAND : CHARTIST MOVEMENT :: FRANCE : _____
   A. Jacquerie   B. Paris Commune   C. Reform Bill of 1832
   D. Flight to Varennes E. Peace of Frankfort

   3._____

4. FRANCE : FOURIER :: AMERICA : _____
   A. Earl Grey   B. Franklin   C. Owen
   D. Jefferson   E. Henry

   4._____

5. ADAM SMITH : "NATURAL LAWS" :: THOMAS MALTHUS : _____
   A. "bullets, not ballots"   B. "circulatory system"   C. "law of peace"
   D. "iron law"   E. "economic right"

   5._____

6. ENGLAND : WILLIAM GLADSTONE :: IRELAND : _____
   A. Daniel Ryan   B. Peter Graves   C. Charles Parnell
   D. Thomas Hood   E. Frederick Taylor

   6._____

7. RUSSIAN CAMPAIGN : 1812 :: BATTLE OF NATIONS : _____
   A. 1872   B. 1756   C. 1800
   D. 1840   E. 1814

   7._____

8. LOUIS NAPOLEON : LOMBARDY :: GIUSEPPE GARIBALDI : _____
   A. Piedmont   B. "Young Italy"
   C. Sardinian Kingdom   D. Kingdom of the Two Sicilies
   E. New Venetian Kingdom

   8._____

9. FRANCO-PRUSSIAN WAR : 1870 :: AUSTRO-PRUSSIAN WAR : _____
   A. 1815   B. 1864   C. 18870
   D. 1866   E. 1915

   9._____

10. CHARLES RIVER : PAUL REVERE :: BOSTON NECK : _____
    A. Wallace Hastings   B. William Dawes   C. Samuel Adams
    D. Nathan Hale   E. Massachusetts

    10._____

11. YANKEES : PUTNAM :: REDCOATS : _____
    A. Garrick   B. Howe   C. Cromwell
    D. Butler   E. Green Mountain Boys

    11._____

12. BATTLE OF SARATOGA : BENEDICT ARNOLD :: BATTLE OF BUNKER   12.____
    HILL : _____
    A. Revolutinary War   B. Battle of Chickamauga
    C. Cornwallis   D. Burgoyne
    E. Wolfe

13. GUY CARLTON : BATTLE OF VALCOUR ISLAND :: SIR HENRY   13.____
    CLINTON : _____
    A. Battle of Blenheim   B. Battle of Brandywine Creek
    C. Battle of Breed Hill   D. Battle of Saratoga
    E. Battle of Monmouth

14. MARY HAYES : "MOLLY PITCHER" :: JOHN BURGOYNE : _____   14.____
    A. "Johnny English"   B. "Big John"   C. "Honest John"
    D. "Gentleman Johnny" E. "Journeyman John"

15. "DESERT FOX" : ROMMEL :: "SWAMP FOX" : _____   15.____
    A. Horatio Hornblower B. Gen. Wayne   C. Francis Marion
    D. Fabius Cunctator   E. T.E. Lawrence

16. LINCOLN'S ARMY : CHARLESTON :: GATES' ARMY : _____   16.____
    A. Plains of Abraham   B. Fort Sumter   C. Philadelphia
    D. Camden   E. Princeton

17. TICONDEROGA : GREEN MOUNTAIN BOYS :: KING'S MOUNTAIN : _____   17.____
    A. Cherry Creek Raiders   B. Loyalists
    C. Oregon Raiders   D. Marion's Mountaineers
    E. Watauga Men

18. CORNWALLIS : YORKTOWN :: TARLETON : _____   18.____
    A. Chesapeake Bay   B. Virginia   C. Greene's Point
    D. Cowpens   E. New York

19. MOUNT VERNON : WASHINGTON :: AIX-LA-CHAPELLE : _____   19.____
    A. Napoleon   B. Louis XVI   C. Charlemagne
    D. Martel   E. Rousseau

20. GREAT WALL OF CHINA : CH'IN DYNASTY :: CHURCH OF HAGIA   20.____
    SOPHIA : _____
    A. Rurik Empire   B. Roman Revolution C. Byzantine Empire
    D. Council of Basle   E. Babylonian Empire

21. BATTLE OF ADRIANOPLE : VISIGOTHS :: CHERRY VALLEY MASSACRE :   21.____
    _____
    A. Smith Colony   B. American Loyalists C. Colonial Army
    D. Minute Men   E. Mohawk Uprising

22. STAMP ACT : 1765 :: INTOLERABLE ACTS : _____   22.____
    A. 1781   B. 1767   C. 1771
    D. 1774   E. 1779

193

23. UNITED STATES : "UNCLE SAM" :: ENGLAND : _____   23. ____
    A. "Duke of York"   B. "Punch"   C. "Tiny Tim:
    D. "John Bull"   E. "Johnny Reb"

24. TREATY OF NANKING : ENGLAND :: TREATY OF PORTSMOUTH : _____   24. ____
    A. F.D. Roosevelt   B. New Hampshire   C. United States
    D. Russia   E. Japan

25. QUISLING : NORWAY :: CZECHOSLOVAKIA : _____   25. ____
    A. Benes   B. Dollfuss   C. Starhemberg
    D. Hacha   E. Henlein

——————

KEY (CORRECT ANSWERS)

1	D	6.	C	11.	B	16.	D	21.	B
2.	B	7.	E	12.	D	17.	E	22.	D
3.	B	8.	D	13.	E	18.	D	23.	D
4.	C	9.	D	14.	D	19.	C	24.	C
5.	D	10.	B	15.	C	20.	C	25.	E

——————

TEST 7

1. DAMASCUS : TIGLATH-PILESER :: EGYPT : _____   1.____
   A. Hannibal   B. Darius   C. Essarhaddon
   D. Nebuchadnezzar   E. Nasser

2. ARISTOCRATS : ISOCRATES :: DEMOCRATS : _____   2.____
   A. Cyaxares   B. Cynics   C. Cleisthenes
   D. Demosthenes   E. republicans

3. "PLAINS" : NOBLES :: "SHORE" : _____   3.____
   A. dictators   B. farmers   C. serfs
   D. merchants   E. slaves

4. BATTLE OF CARCHEMISH : NECHO II :: BATTLE OF ZAMA : _____   4.____
   A. Ramad-Ahmid   B. Hannibal   C. Ramses I
   D. Assurbanipal   E. Aristides

5. TYCHO : JOHANN :: BRAHE : _____   5.____
   A. Hart   B. Bruhn   C. Kiepler
   D. Copernicus   E. Huygens

6. MEROVINGIANS : CLOVIS :: CAROLINGIAN : _____   6.____
   A. William the Silent   B. Charlemagne   C. Charles Martel
   D. Pepin the Short   E. Charles the Bold

7. FRANCE : HOUSE OF VALOIS :: ENGLAND : _____   7.____
   A. House of Commons   B. House of Usher   C. House of Lancaster
   D. House of Windsor   E. House of Hanover

8. INDIANS : BOW AND ARROW :: PHILISTINES : _____   8.____
   A. pepper   B. stones   C. iron spikes
   D. poison darts   E. iron cross

9. BON HOMME RICHARD : AMERICA :: SERAPIS : _____   9.____
   A. Greece   B. Spaiin   C. Arabia
   D. England   E. Scotland

10. CHERRY VALLEY MASSACRE : INDIANS :: BOSTON MASSACRE : _____   10.____
    A. Loyalists   B. Americans   C. British
    D. Patriots   E. Boston Tea Party

11. 1763 : FRENCH AND INDIAN WAR :: 1688 : _____   11.____
    A. Seven Years' War   B. Hundred Years' War   C. Spanish-American War
    D. Glorious Revolution   E. War of the Roses

12. NINETY-FIVE THESES : 1517 :: THIRTY-NINE ARTICLES : _____   12.____
    A. 1800   B. 1643   C. 1570
    D. 1850   E. 1816

13. PETER THE GREAT : 1682 :: CATHERINE II : _____   13._____
    A. 1714   B. 1730   C. 1762
    D. 1800   E. 1700

14. ENGLAND : PETITION OF RIGHT :: AMERICAN COLONIES : _____   14._____
    A. legislative union
    B. Olive Branch Petition
    C. Tennis Court Oath
    D. Bill of Rights
    E. Declaration of the Rights of Man and of the Citizen

15. ENGLAND : DRAKE :: UNITED STATES : _____   15._____
    A. Washington   B. Prescott   C. Arnold
    D. Jones   E. Montgomery

16. CATHOLICISM : QUEEN MARY I :: PROTESTANTISM : _____   16._____
    A. Catherine the Great   B. Wilhelmina   C. Marie Louise
    D. Elizabeth I   E. Queen Anne

17. FRANCE : HUGUENOTS :: SCOTLAND : _____   17._____
    A. Baptists   B. Puritans   C. Presbyterians
    D. Lutheran   E. Dutch Reformed

18. DOMINICANS : ST. DOMINIC :: FRIARS : _____   18._____
    A. St. Peter   B. Peter Waldo   C. Becket
    D. Baedeker   E. Francis of Assisi

19. DAYS OF THE PRINCIPATE : AUGUSTUS :: DAYS OF THE REPUBLIC :   19._____
    _____
    A. Constantine   B. Justinian   C. Octavian
    D. Caesar   E. Seneca

20. CLAUDIUS : NERO :: TIBERIUS : _____   20._____
    A. Vespasian   B. Caligula   C. Hadrian
    D. Otho   E. Trajan

21. OLD KINGDOM : KHUFU :: MIDDLE KINGDOM : _____   21._____
    A. Horus   B. Osiris   C. Minos
    D. Midas   E. Ramses III

22. SENNACHERIB : NINEVAH :: NECHO II : _____   22._____
    A. Sparta   B. Jonah   C. Greece
    D. Palestine   E. Egypt

23. ELAMITE KINGDOM : CYAXERES :: MEDIA KINGDOM : _____   23._____
    A. Xenophon   B. Darius   C. Cyrus
    D. Aeschylus   E. Claudius

24. HENRY IV : RICHELIEU :: LOUIS XIV : _____   24.____
    A. Sully   B. Talleyrand   C. Fontaine
    D. Mazarin   E. Moliere

25. SEVEN YEARS' WAR : TREATY OF PARIS :: WAR OF THE SPANISH   25.____
    SUCCESSION : _____
    A. Peace of Campo Formio   B. Treaty of Westphalia
    C. Treaty of Berlin   D. Treaty of Utrecht
    E. Treaty of Verdun

_____

KEY (CORRECT ANSWERS)

1.	C	6.	D	11.	D	16.	D	21.	E
2.	C	7.	C	12.	C	17.	C	22.	D
3.	D	8.	C	13.	C	18.	E	23.	C
4.	B	9.	D	14.	B	19.	D	24.	D
5.	C	10.	C	15.	D	20.	B	25.	D

_____

TEST 8

1. HITLER : LINZ :: MARX : _____
    A. Petrograd   B. Cologne   C. Leningrad
    D. Berlin   E. Moscow

    1._____

2. C.C.C. : UNITED STATES :: LABOR SERVICE : _____
    A. France   B. England   C. Russia
    D. Germany   E. Switzerland

    2._____

3. MUSSOLINI : "BLACK SHIRTS" :: HITLER : _____
    A. "Black Shirts"   B. "Red Shirts"   C. Gestapo
    D. S.S.   E. "Brown Shirts"

    3._____

4. GERMANY : "SIEGFRIED LINE" :: FRANCE : _____
    A. West Wall   B. "Hot Line"   C. "Maginot Line"
    D. Arch of Triumph E. Berlin Wall

    4._____

5. OCTAVIA : ANTONY :: JULIA : _____
    A. Augustus   B. Antony   C. Romulus
    D. Pompey   E. Caesar

    5._____

6. GALLIC WARS : CAESAR :: BATTLE OF POITIERS : _____
    A. Edward the Black Prince   B. Ferdinand II
    C. Charles IV   D. Louis XI
    E. George III

    6._____

7. 81 A.D. : DOMITIAN :: 138 A.D. : _____
    A. Marcus Aurelius B. Nero   C. Caligula
    D. Antoninus Pius   E. Claudius

    7._____

8. HENRY IV : "EDICT OF NANTES" :: CONSTANTINE : _____
    A. Concordat of Worms   B. Salesian Law
    C. Edict of Constantine   D. Rule of St. Benedict
    E. "Edict of Milan"

    8._____

9. "SICILIAN VESPERS MASSACRE" : ITALY :: "ST. BARTHOLOMEW'S
    DAY MASSACRE : _____
    A. England   B. Ireland   C. France
    D. Germany   E. Sweden

    9._____

10. JAPAN : MUTSUHITO :: RUSSIA : _____
    A. Turgenev   B. Miliukov   C. Peter the Great
    D. Leeuwenhoek   E. Alexander I

    10._____

11. GERMANY : ROMMEL :: ENGLAND : _____
    A. Arnold   B. Brooke   C. Mountbatten
    D. Montgomery   E. Alexander

    11._____

12. "DER FÜHRER" : HITLER :: "IL DUCE" : _____

    A. Badoglio   B. Caesar   C. Tito
    D. Augustus   E. Mussolini

13. TORAH : HEBREWS :: KORAN : _____

    A. Egyptians   B. Mongols   C. Mormons
    D. Mohammedans   E. Buddhists

14. RED RUSSIANS : LENIN :: WHITE RUSSIANS : _____

    A. Leon Trotsky   B. Alexander Kerensky   C. Kropotkin
    D. General Kornilov E. Price Lvov

15. UNIVERSITY OF BOLOGNA : LAW :: UNIVERSITY OF PADUA : _____

    A. Theology   B. Trivium   C. Philosophy
    D. Medicine   E. Quadrivium

16. GUADALCANAL : GENERAL MAC ARTHUR :: STALINGRAD : _____

    A. Marshal Budenny   B. Marshal Voroshilov
    C. General Zhukov   D. Field Marshal Paulus
    E. General Tukachevsky

17. COLUMBUS : AMERICA :: DA GAMA : _____

    A. Russia   B. Spain   C. France
    D. India   E. Holland

18. INDIA : JOSEPH DUPLEIX :: CANADA : _____

    A. Cartier   B. Champlain   C. Duquesne
    D. La Salle   E. Montcalm

19. MOUNTAINS : POLAND :: PLAINS : _____

    A. U.S.S.R.   B. Hungary   C. Finland
    D. Greece   E. Rumania

20. POLAND AND HUNGARY : MORAVIA :: DANUBE BASIN AND
    MACEDONIA : _____

    A. Vardar Valley   B. Salonika   C. Budapest
    D. the Iron Gate   E. Wallachia

21. CZECHOSLOVAKIA : SLOVAKIA :: ITALY : _____

    A. Midi   B. Mezzogiorno   C. Po Valley
    D. Central Valley   E. Trieste

22. (BEFORE WORLD WAR II)
    GERMANY : RUMANIA :: GREAT BRITAIN : _____

    A. Norway   B. Eire   C. France
    D. Sweden   E. Belgium

23. TRUMAN PLAN : U.S.A. :: MONNET PLAN : _____

    A. France   B. Belgium   C. U.S.S.R.
    D. Luxembourg   E. West Germany

24.	REPUBLIC OF INDIA : GANDHI :: PAKISTAN : _____	24._____
	A.	Sukarno	B.	Mohammed Ayub Khan
	C.	Mohammed Ali Jinnah	D.	Macapagal
	E.	Nehru

25.	PERSIA : IRAN :: MESOPOTAMIA : _____	25._____
	A.	Baghdad	B.	Jordan	C.	Syria
	D.	Iraq	E.	Kuwait

KEY (CORRECT ANSWERS)

1	B	6.	A	11.	D	16.	C	21.	C
2.	D	7.	D	12.	E	17.	D	22.	B
3.	E	8.	E	13.	D	18.	E	23.	A
4.	C	9.	C	14.	E	19.	B	24.	B
5.	D	10.	C	15.	D	20.	C	25.	D

TESTS IN VERBAL ANALOGIES - LITERATURE

DIRECTIONS: Each question in this part consists of two capitalized words which have a certain relationship to each other, and a third capitalized word which is followed by five lettered words in small letters. Choose the number of the word which is related in the SAME way to the third capitalized word as the first two capitalized words are related to each other. *PRINT THE LETTER OF THE CORRECT ANSWER IN THE SPACE AT THE RIGHT.*

TEST 1

1. "THE LAST HURRAH" : JAMES CURLEY :: "LONG DAY'S JOURNEY INTO   1.____
    NIGHT" : _____
    A. "Strange Interlude"   B. Eugene O'Neill
    C. Maxwell Anderson   D. Arthur Miller
    E. "Desire Under the Elms"

2. SHYLOCK : PORTIA :: HAMLET : _____   2.____
    A. Juliet   B. Coriolanus   C. Ophelia
    D. Macbeth   E. Marlowe

3. WORDSWORTH : FROST :: WYCHERLEY : _____   3.____
    A. John Keats   B. Charles Lamb   C. Sir Francis Bacon
    D. Maxwell Anderson   E. Edgar Allan Poe

4. "THE YOUNG LIONS" : DWIGHT D. EISENHOWER :: "THE RED BADGE OF   4.____
    COURAGE" : _____
    A. "Gone With the Wind"   B. Ross Lockridge, Jr.
    C. "From Here to Eternity"   D. George Washington
    E. Robert E. Lee

5. "A CHRISTMAS CAROL" : REPENTANCE :: "LORD OF THE FLIES" : _____   5.____
    A. "Catcher in the Rye"   B. William Golding
    C. the superficiality of civilization   D. the essential goodness of people
    E. the wages of sin

6. "HASTE MAKES WASTE" : "HE WHO HESITATES IS LOST" :: "BIRDS   6.____
    OF A FEATHER FLOCK TOGETHER" : _____
    A. "A stitch in time saves nine"
    B. "Opposites attract"
    C. "Waste not, want not"
    D. "A penny saved is a penny earned"
    E. "The early bird catches the worm"

7. "OLIVER TWIST" : "BARNABY RUDGE" :: "OTHER VOICES, OTHER   7.____
   ROOMS" : _____
   A. "The Grass Harp"   B. Tennessee Williams
   C. "Dark at the Top of the Stairs"   D. "House Divided"
   E. "Fanny Hill"

8. COMMA : SEMI-COLON :: PERIOD : _____   8.____
   A. colon   B. apostrophe   C. question mark
   D. quotation mark   E. dash

9. "ODE TO A GRECIAN URN" : "THE RAVEN" :: BEAUTY : _____   9.____
   A. Edgar Allan Poe   B. loneliness   C. elation
   D. "The Bells"   E. religious fervor

10. BAUDELAIRE : RIMBAUD :: EDMUND WILSON : _____   10.____
    A. Dwight MacDonald B. Keats   C. "Flowers of Evil"
    D. Jean Genet   E. Henry Miller

11. FRANK HARRIS : OSCAR WILDE :: CARL SANDBURG : _____   11.____
    A. George Washington   B. "The Fog"
    C. Abraham Lincoln   D. Franklin D. Roosevelt
    E. Thomas Jefferson

12. FAGIN : SCROOGE :: IAGO : _____   12.____
    A. Othello   B. Brutus   C. Lady Macbeth
    D. Polonius   E. Ariel

13. F. SCOTT FITZGERALD : RING LARDNER :: LEON URIS : _____   13.____
    A. Matthew Arnold   B. "End As a Man"   C. James Baldwin
    D. Stephen Crane   E. Hart Crane

14. DOSTOEVSKI : PASTERNACK :: ZOLA : _____   14.____
    A. Tolstoy   B. "Nana"   C. Verlaine
    D. "War and Peace"   E. Ehrenberg

15. "A FAREWELL TO ARMS" : FOR WHOM THE BELL TOLLS" :: BARBARY   15.____
    SHORE: : _____
    A. "The Old Man and the Sea"   B. "Breakfast at Tiffany's"
    C. "On the Road"   D. "The Thin Red Line"
    E. "Deer Park"

16. "PARADISE LOST" : "AREOPAGITICA" :: "ANNABEL LEE" : _____   16.____
    A. Poe   B. Milton   C. "The Gold Bug"
    D. "Paradise Regained" E. censorhip

17. HORATIO ALGER : EDGAR RICE BURROUGHS :: SUCCESS : _____   17.____
    A. adventure   B. "Tarzan of the Apes" C. honesty
    D. ambition   E. riches

18. "A WATCHED POT NEVER BOILS" : PATIENCE :: "FOOLS RUSH IN   18.____
    WHERE ANGELS FEAR TO TREAD" : _____
    A. fearlessness   B. caution   C. deceit
    D. speed   E. candor

19. COLETTE : GIGI :: MARGARET MITCHELL : _____   19.____
    A. Lorna Doone   B. Rebecca   C. Tom Swift
    D. Scarlett O'Hara   E. Constance Chatterley

20. "BLACK SPRING" : "NEXUS" :: "DUBLINERS" : _____   20.____
    A. "Juno and the Paycock"   B. J.M. Synge
    C. "Finnegan's Wake"   D. "Memoirs of Hecate County"
    E. "The Quare Fellow"

21. RICHARD WRIGHT : JAMES BALDWIN :: "NATIVE SON" : _____   21.____
    A. "Uncle Tom's Children"   B. "Giovanni's Room"
    C. "Black Boy"   D. Langston Hughes
    E. Countee Cullen

22. MELLORS : "LADY CHATTERLEY'S LOVER" :: WARDEN : _____   22.____
    A. "The Naked and the Dead"   B. "From Here to Eternity"
    C. "Raintree County"   D. "An American Tragedy"
    E. "Compulsion"

23. "VANITY FAIR" : "BABBITT" :: "1984" : _____   23.____
    A. "Night Must Fall"   B. George Orwell
    C. "Death Takes a Holiday"   D. "Things to Come"
    E. "Lost Horizon"

24. ROBERT BROWNING : "SONNETS FROM THE PORTUGUESE" ::   24.____
    PERCY B. SHELLEY : _____
    A. "Frankenstein"
    B. Keats
    C. Southey
    D. "Miniver Cheevy"
    E. "On Hearing the First Cuckoo in Spring"

25. "PAUL REVERE'S RIDE" : "ABRAHAM LINCOLN WALKS AT MIDNIGHT" ::   25.____
    HENRY W. LONGFELLOW : _____
    A. William Cullen Bryant   B. Allen Ginsberg
    C. William Carlos Williams   D. Robert Frost
    E. Vachel Lindsay

KEY (CORRECT ANSWERS)

1 B	6. B	11. C	16. C	21. B
2. C	7. A	12. C	17. A	22. B
3. D	8. C	13. C	18. B	23. D
4. E	9. B	14. C	19. D	24. A
5. C	10. A	15. E	20. C	25. E

TEST 2

1. "WHEN I WAS ONE AND TWENTY, I HEARD A WISE MAN SAY...":
   "THEY ALSO SERVE WHO ONLY STAND AND WAIT" :: A.E. HOUSEMAN :
   _____
   A. John Milton   B. Adlai E. Stevenson   C. Barry Goldwater
   D. Robert Burns   E. Henry Purcell

   1.____

2. WILLIAM INGE : JOHN OSBORNE :: KENNETH PATCHEN : _____
   A. Henry W. Longfellow   B. Dante G. Rossetti
   C. John Betjeman   D. Sidney Kingsley
   E. Sean O'Casey

   2.____

3. "THE FARMER'S HOTEL" : "APPOINTMENT IN SAMARRA" :: "THE
   THREEPENNY OPERA" : _____
   A. John O'Hara   B. "Tea and Sympathy"
   C. "The Congo"   D. "Mother Courage"
   E. "The Saint of Bleecker Street"

   3.____

4. OPHELIA : JULIET :: TINY TIME : _____
   A. William M. Thackeray   B. Sidney Carton
   C. Maggio   D. Dr. Jekyll
   E. Rhett Butler

   4.____

5. T.S. ELIOT : GERTRUDE STEIN :: CARL SANDBURG : _____
   A. Mark Twain   B. Victor Hugo   C. Charles Dickens
   D. Nikolai Gogol   E. Karl Marx

   5.____

6. "PICNIC" : "BUS STOP" :: "CAMINO REAL" : _____
   A. "Night Life"   B. "Born Yesterday"
   C. "Bells are Ringing"   D. "Cat on a Hot Tin Roof"
   E. "Member of the Wedding"

   6.____

7. WILLIAM FAULKNER : "ON THE TERRACE" :: WILLIAM SHAKESPEARE :
   _____
   A. "Troilus and Cressida"   B. "All's Well that Ends Well"
   C. "A Midsummer Night's Dream"   D. "Dr. Faustus"
   E. "A Comedy of Errors"

   7.____

8. HEMINGWAY : FITZGERALD :: NORMAL MAILER : _____
   A. Eugene O'Neill   B. James Jones   C. Edward Albee
   D. "The Young Lions" E. World War II

   8.____

9. SOPHOCLES : OEDIPUS :: EURIPIDES : _____
   A. Electra   B. Caligula   C. Antigone
   D. Hermes   E. Medea

   9.____

10. "THE GREAT GATSBY" : "TENDER IS THE NIGHT" :: "THE FALL" : _____   10.____
    A. "A Farewell to Arms"   B. "This Side of Paradise"
    C. "The Stranger"   D. "Deer Park"
    E. "Another Country"

11. "UNDER MILKWOOD" : DYLAN THOMAS :: "MURDER IN THE CATHEDRAL :   11.____
    _____
       A. Bertholt Brecht   B. F. Garcia Lorca   C. "The Cocktail Party"
       D. Baudelaire   E. T.S. Eliot

12. REGAN : LEAR :: OPHELIA : _____   12.____
    A. Laertes   B. Polonius   C. Horatio
    D. Hamlet   E. Henry V

13. "AN AMERICAN TRAGEDY" : "OF TIME AND THE RIVER" :: THEODORE   13.____
    DREISER : _____
       A. Thomas Wolfe   B. Gertrude Stein   C. "Sister Carrie"
       D. Sherwood Anderson   E. Robert Sherwood

14. HELEN : MENELAUS :: MEDEA : _____   14.____
    A. her children   B. Greek Chorus   C. Orestes
    D. Jason   E. Aeneas

15. STANISLAVSKI : BRECHT :: "AN ACTOR PREPARES" : _____   15.____
    A. method acting
    B. Bolshoi Theatre
    C. "Brecht on Brecht"
    D. "The Galilei Magic Mountain"
    E. House Un-American Activities Committee

16. KAFKA : "HELLAS" :: BRECHT : _____   16.____
    A. "Barrack Room Ballads"   B. "Flowers of Evil"
    C. Mallarmé   D. St. John Perse
    E. Rolla

17. MAYAKOVSKY : RUSSIAN REVOLUTION :: YEVTUSHENKO : _____   17.____
    A. Pasternack   B. pre-Czarist poetry
    C. revolutionary movement   D. Post-Impressionism
    E. modern Russia

18. ANDRE MALRAUX : FRENCH CABINET :: LAWRENCE DURRELL : _____   18.____
    A. "The Alexandria Quartet"   B. "Justice"
    C. Croix de Guerre   D. diplomacy
    E. Pulitzer Prize

19. ALDOUS HUXLEY : "BRAVE NEW WORLD" :: EDWARD BELLAMY : _____   19.____
    A. "Erewhon"   B. "The Disappearance"
    C. "Doors of Perception"   D. "1984"
    E. "Looking Backward"

20. GRAHAM GREENE : "THE LIVING ROOM" :: EVELYN WAUGH : _____   20.____
    A. "Miss Lonelyhearts"   B. "The Loved One"   C. religion
    D. "Point Counterpoint" E. "The Hollow Men"

21. OEDIPUS : FREUD :: ORPHEUS : _____   21.____
    A. Tennessee Williams   B. Eurydice   C. Cocteau
    D. Calliope   E. Aeschylus

22. MARGARET MITCHELL : SCARLETT O'HARA :: DAPHNE DU MAURIER :   22.____
    _____
      A. Mata Hari   B. Marie Antoinette   C. Lucretia Borgia
      D. Rebecca   E. Simone de Beauvoir

23. SELECTION : ANTHOLOGY :: SENTENCE : _____   23.____
    A. phrase   B. compendium   C. paragraph
    D. letter   E. appendix

24. THE CHILD OF NATURE : ROUSSEAU :: THE NOBLE SAVAGE : _____   24.____
    A. Herman Melville   B. Thoreau   C. Chateaubriand
    D. Geronimo

25. "YARROW REVISITED" : SIR WALTER SCOTT :: "THE HOURS" : _____   25.____
    A. Mary, Queen of Scots   B. Fitzgerald
    C. Longfellow   D. Pound
    E. Yeats

KEY (CORRECT ANSWERS)

1	A	6.	D	11.	E	16.	A	21.	C
2.	C	7.	D	12.	B	17.	E	22.	D
3.	D	8.	B	13.	A	18.	D	23.	C
4.	B	9.	E	14.	D	19.	E	24.	C
5.	A	10.	C	15.	D	20.	B	25.	B

TEST 3

1. LEWIS CARROLL : THE RED QUEEN :: J.M. BARRIE : _____   1.____
   A. Winnie the Pooh   B. The March Hare
   C. Peter Pan   D. Pogo
   E. The Manchurian Candidate

2. JEAN GENET : "THE MAIDS" :: MOLIERE : _____   2.____
   A. "The Glass Menagerie"   B. "The Importance of Being Earnest"
   C. "The Bourgeois Gentleman" D. Ben Jonson
   E. "Elizabeth and Essex"

3. HOMER : "THE ODYSSEY" :: NATHANIEL HAWTHORNE : _____   3.____
   A. "The Iliad"   B. "Blithedale Romance"
   C. "Remembrance of Things Past" D. "Evangeline"
   E. "Ivanhoe"

4. FIGURATIVE MIGRATION : "ORLANDO" :: LITERAL MIGRATION : _____   4.____
   A. "The Lemming"   B. "The Grapes of Wrath
   C. Thomas Wolfe   D. Thomas Hardy
   E. "Buddenbrooks"

5. "DAS KAPITAL" : KARL MARX :: "ANNA KARENINA" : _____   5.____
   A. Hitler   B. "Mein Kampf"
   C. Dostoevski   D. Swinburne
   E. "Communist Manifesto"

6. "SHALL I COMPARE THEE TO A SUMMER'S DAY?" : IAMABIC VERSE ::   6.____
   "DO NOT GO GENTLY INTO THAT GOOD NIGHT" : _____
   A. sonnet   B. trochaic verse   C. stanza
   D. heroic couplet E. free verse

7. HUCKLEBERRY FINN : SAMUEL CLEMENS :: TOBERMORY : _____   7.____
   A. Saki   B. Thomas Mann   C. Tom Sawyer
   D. H.H. Munro   E. Oscar Wilde

8. "SOME ARE BORN GREAT, SOME ACHIEVE GREATNESS, AND SOME   8.____
   HAVE GREATNESS THRUST UPON THEM" : "TWELFTH NIGHT" ::
   "JOURNEYS END IN LOVERS MEETING, EVERY WISE MAN'S SON DOTH
   KNOW" : _____
   A. "All's Well that Ends Well"   B. William Shakespeare
   C. "The Tempest"   D. "Twelfth Night"
   E. "Richard III"

9. ADAGE : PROVERB :: PARABLE : _____   9.____
   A. axiom   B. maxim   C. by-law
   D. paradox   E. allegory

10. "GOLDEN BOY" : CLIFFORD ODETS :: "THE CLOUD" : _____   10.____
    A. John M. Synge   B. Sean O'Casey   C. Percy B. Shelley
    D. Robert Browning   E. William Wordsworth

11. "THY CHILDREN LIKE OLIVE PLANTS ROUND ABOUT THY TABLE" :   11.____
    THE OLD TESTAMENT :: "THIS NIGHT THY SOUL SHALL BE REQUIRED
    OF THEE" : _____
    A. "There was a man sent from God, whose name was John"
    B. The Bible
    C. "Dr. Faustus"
    D. The New Testament
    E. Judas

12. "THE FAR WEST" : BRET HARTE :: "SPOON RIVER ANTHOLOGY" : _____   12.____
    A. William Faulkner   B. Sherwood Anderson   C. James T. Farrell
    D. Edgar Lee Masters   E. William Saroyan

13. THE MOSCOW ART THEATRE : RUSSIA :: THE ABBEY PLAYERS : _____   13.____
    A. Denmark   B. England   C. Ireland
    D. Wales   E. Stratford-on-Avon

14. "EARLY TO BED, EARLY TO RISE" : BENJAMIN FRANKLIN :: "THE   14.____
    QUALITY OF MERCY IS NOT STRAINED" : _____
    A. Dickens   B. sonnet   C. Shakespeare
    D. Marlowe   E. Portia

15. JOHN GALSWORTHY : ENGLISH UPPER CLASS :: BRENDAN BEHAN :   15.____
    _____
    A. Sean O'Casey   B. Victorian England   C. Parnell
    D. Irish lower classes   E. French royalty

16. "THE AUTOBIOGRAPHY OF ALICE B. TOKLAS" : GERTRUE STEIN ::   16.____
    "SHIP OF FOOLS" : _____
    A. Daphne Du Maurier   B. Carson McCullers   C. Katherine Anne Porter
    D. George Sand   E. Charlotte Bronte

17. "LIFE IS JUST A BOWL OF CHERRIES" : "MY LOVE IS LIKE A RED, RED   17.____
    ROSE" :: METAPHOR : _____
    A. alliteration   B. simile   C. antithesis
    D. trochee   E. phrase

18. "PETER PIPER PICKED A PECK OF PICKLED PEPPERS" : BUZZING   18.____
    BEE :: ALLITERATION : _____
    A. anapest   B. Iamb   C. hexameter
    D. onomatopoeia   E. gerund

19. POGO : WALT KELLY :: CHARLIE BROWN : _____   19.____
    A. Shel Silverstein   B. Jules Feiffer   C. Charles Schulz
    D. Peter Arno   E. H.T. Webster

20. "ONCE UPON A MIDNIGHT DREARY, WHILE I PONDERED, WEAK AND WEARY..." : TROCHEE :: "THEY ALSO SERVE WHO ONLY STAND AND WAIT" : _____

    A. iamb   B. anapest   C. dactyl

    D. onomatopoeia   E. preterite

20._____

21. ROMAIN ROLLAND : MALLARMÉ :: THOMAS MANN : _____

    A. Verlaine   B. Karl Marx   C. Bismarck

    D. Heine   E. Zola

21._____

22. "MY LIFE AND HARD TIMES" : JAMES THURBER :: "THE ROAD TO MILTOWN" : _____

    A. Robert Benchley   B. S.J. Perelman   C. Mark Twain

    D. Art Buchwald   E. Peter De Vries

22._____

23. "THE SEVEN YEAR ITCH" : "NO TIME FOR SERGEANTS" :: GEORGE AXELROD : _____

    A. Mac Hyman   B. Jesse Stuart   C. A.B. Guthrie

    D. Al Capp   E. Zane Grey

23._____

24. COLD AND ICY : WET AND DRY :: SYNONYM : _____

    A. metaphor   B. similie   C. dichotomy

    D. antonym   E. syllable

24._____

25. "PLAYBOY" : "EROS" :: "THE SATURDAY EVENING POST" : _____

    A. "Life"   B. "Time"

    C. "The Ladies' Home Journal   D. "Colliers"

    E. "Redbook"

25._____

KEY (CORRECT ANSWERS)

1	C	6.	E	11.	D	16.	C	21.	D
2.	C	7.	D	12.	D	17.	B	22.	B
3.	B	8.	D	13.	C	18.	D	23.	A
4.	B	9.	E	14.	C	19.	C	24.	C
5.	C	10.	C	15.	D	20.	A	25.	D

TEST 4

1. "THE NATION" : "NATIONAL REVIEW" :: "THE REPORTER" : _____ 1.____
   A. "The New Republic"   B. "U.S. News and World Report"
   C. "Popular Mechanics"   D. "Look"
   E. "The New York Times"

2. TUGBOAT ANNIE : NORMAL R. RAINE :: SCATTERGOOD BAINES : _____ 2.____
   A. Jack Kerouac   B. Clarence B. Kelland
   C. Normal Rockwell   D. Ben Hibbs
   E. Alexander Botts

3. KRAZY KAT : GEORGE HERMANN :: CASPER MILQUETOAST : _____ 3.____
   A. Thomas Nast   B. Don Marquis   C. H.T. Webster
   D. Ham Fisher   E. Bud Fisher

4. SAMUEL JOHNSON : JAMES BOSWELL :: FRANKLIN D. ROOSEVELT : _____ 4.____
   A. Robert Sherwood   B. Sherwood Anderson
   C. Theodore White   D. Walter Lippmann
   E. John Crosby

5. "THE OLD BUNCH" : "COMPULSION" :: "THE GOOD EARTH" : _____ 5.____
   A. "The Bad Seed"   B. "Dragon Seed"   C. "Dragonwyck"
   D. "Forever Amber"   E. "The Razor's Edge"

6. "DON JUAN IN HELL" : "MAN & SUPERMAN" :: "THE BIG MONEY : _____ 6.____
   A. John Dos Passos   B. "U.S.A."
   C. "Manhattan Transfer"   D. "Caesar and Cleopatra"
   E. "Pygmalion"

7. TROILUS : CRESSIDA :: ORLANDO : _____ 7.____
   A. Juliet   B. Viola   C. Pythias
   D. Beatrice   E. George Sand

8. "WHERE THE BEE SUCKS, THERE SUCK I" : PICK "" "FIND A NEW 8.____
   MASTER, BE A NEW MAN" : _____
   A. Malvolio   B. Bottom   C. Ariel
   D. Caliban   E. Prospero

9. "SURELY YOU DON'T BELIEVE THOSE ARE REAL TEARS" : LEWIS 9.____
   CARROLL :: "THERE ARE MORE THINGS IN HEAVEN AND EARTH…THAN
   ARE DREAMT OF IN YOUR PHILOSOPHY" : _____
   A. Dickens   B. Shakespeare   C. Milton
   D. Kant   E. Mann

10. O. HENRY : WILLIAM S. PORTER :: LEWIS CARROLL : _____ 10.____
    A. H.H. Munro   B. George Eliot   C. George Sand
    D. Isak Dinesen   E. Charles L. Dodgson

11. HAMLET : GERTRUDE :: OEDIPUS : _____
    A. Helen   B. Antigone   C. Medea
    D. Jocasta   E. Diana

11.____

12. H. RIDER HAGGARD : "SHE" :: RAY BRADBURY : _____
    A. "Fahrenheit 451"   B. "Flaming Creatures"
    C. "Isaac Asimov"   D. "Galaxy"
    E. "When Worlds Collide"

12.____

13. HERMAN MELVILLE : "MOBY DICK" :: PHILIP WYLIE : _____
    A. "Typee"   B. "Sex Without Guilt"
    C. "Opus 21"   D. "Look Back in Anger"
    E. "Wastelands"

13.____

14. "LOLITA" : "PNIN" :: "HAWAII" : _____
    A. "The Manchurian Candidate"   B. "Tales of the South Pacific"
    C. "Gavgin   D. Nabokov
    E. "The Sand Pebbles"

14.____

15. WILLY LOMAN : ARTHUR MILLER :: HARRY HOPE : _____
    A. Eugene O'Neill   B. Bertholt Brecht   C. William Inge
    D. Alfred Jarry   E. Harold Pinter

15.____

16. "THE CARETAKER" : "THE DUMBWAITER" :: "THE TIME OF YOUR
    LIFE : _____
    A. "The Telephone"
    B. "The Milk Train Doesn't Stop Here Any More"
    C. "Hello, Out There"
    D. "The Connection"
    E. "Fiddler on the Roof"

16.____

17. "ENDGAME" : BECKETT :: "THE BALD SOPRANO" : _____
    A. Ghelderode   B. Genet   C. Richardson
    D. Gelber   E. Ionesco

17.____

18. "GOOD FENCES MAKE GOOD NEIGHBORS" : FROST :: "NOT WITH
    A BANG BUT A WHIMPER" : _____
    A. e.e. cummings   B. Carl Sandburg   C. Allen Ginsberg
    D. T.S. Eliot   E. George Seurat

18.____

19. "A ROSE IS A ROSSE IS A ROSE" : GERTRUDE STEIN :: "I AM THE
    MASTER OF MY FATE, I AM THE CAPTAIN OF MY SOUL" : _____
    A. Wordsworth   B. Stevenson   C. Southey
    D. Henley   E. Swinburne

19.____

20. "EVE OF ST. AGNES" : KEATS :: "ODE TO A GRECIAN URN" : _____
    A. Marlowe   B. Burns   C. Shelley
    D. Blake   E. Bacon

20.____

21. BECKY THATCHER : JIM :: QUILTY : _____   21.____
    A. Lolita   B. Justine   C. Mark Twain
    D. Madame De Farge   E. Heathcliff

22. "CALL OF THE WILD" : "MARTIN EDEN" :: "TOM JONES" : _____   22.____
    A. Henry Fielding   B Jack London
    C. "David Copperfield"   D. "Joseph Andrews"
    E. "The Red and the Black"

23. "TESS OF THE D'URBERVILLES" : THOMAS HARDY :: "JURGEN" : _____   23.____
    A. James Whitcomb Riley   B. Edward Everett Hale
    C. James Branch Cabell   D. Henry Wadsworth Longfellow
    E. Edward Arlington Robinson

24. IVANHOE : SIR WALTER SCOTT :: HESTER PRYNNE : _____   24.____
    A. Nathaniel Hawthorne   B. F. Scott Fitzgerald
    C. James Fenimore Coloper   D. Jerome K. Jerome
    E. Emily Bronte

25. IZAAK WALTON : FISHING :: HAVELOCK ELLIS : _____   25.____
    A. cooking   B. clothing   C. fine arts
    D. sex   E. war

_____

KEY (CORRECT ANSWERS)

1	B	6.	B	11.	D	16.	C	21.	A
2.	B	7.	B	12.	A	17.	E	22.	D
3.	C	8.	D	13.	C	18.	D	23.	C
4.	A	9.	B	14.	B	19.	D	24.	A
5.	B	10.	E	15.	A	20.	C	25.	D

_____

TEST 5

1. "THE PHYSICIAN IN SPITE OF HIMSELF" : MOLIERE :: "CLOUDS" : _____   1.____
   A. Aristippus   B. Aristotle   C. Aristophanes
   D. "Birds"   E. Averroes

2. MURDER IN THE CATHEDRAL" : T.S. ELIOT :: "PELLEAS AND   2.____
   MELISANDE" : _____
   A. Shakespeare   B. G.B. Shaw   C. Dumas
   D. Maeterlinck   E. Congreve

3. D'ARTAGNAN : "THE THREE MUSKETEERS" :: BECKY SHARP : _____   3.____
   A. "Little Women"   B. "Tom Sawyer"
   C. "Daisy Miller"   D. "This Side of Paradise"
   E. "Vanity Fair"

4. "ARS AMORIS" : OVID :: "RUBAIYAT" : _____   4.____
   A. Zola   B. Omar Khayyam
   C. Henry Miller   D. Edward Fitzgerald
   E. Edward Bulwer Lytton

5. TOUCHSTONE : "AS YOU LIKE IT" :: ROXANNE : _____   5.____
   A. "All's Well That Ends Well"   B. "The Bourgeois Gentleman
   C. Sheridan   D. "Cyrano de Bergerac"
   E. Edmond Rostand

6. "AUTOBIOGRAPHY OF ALICE B. TOKLAS" : GERTRUDE STEIN :: "THE   6.____
   ENORMOUS ROOM" : _____
   A. Graham Greene   B. EvelynWaugh   C. "Three Lives"
   D. Virginia Woolf   E. e.e. cummings

7. SHERLOCK HOLMES : A.C. DOYLE :: ARTFUL DODGER : _____   7.____
   A. Fagin   B. Watson   C. Jules Verne
   D. Dickens   E. Saki

8. "THE YOUNG VISITORS" : DAISY ASHFORD :: "JUDE THE OBSCURE :   8.____
   _____
   A. Nan Hardwick   B. Tess of the D'Urbervilles
   C. Thomas Hardy   D. Irwin Shaw
   E. Sherwood Anderson

9. SIR TOBY BELCH : "TWELFTH NIGHT" :: SIR MULBERRY HAWK : _____   9.____
   A. "Nicholas Nickleby"   B. "Great Expectations"
   C. Oliver Twist   D. "A Midsummer Night's Dream"
   E. "The Blithedale Romance"

10. "TWICE TOLD TALES" : "THE SCARLET LETTER" .. "THE DEERSLAYER" :   10.____
    ____
    A. "The House of the Seven Gables"
    B. "Mosses From an Old Manse"
    C. Edgar Allan Poe
    D. "The Last of the Mohicans"
    E. Hawthorne

11. BABBIT : SINCLAIR LEWIS :: SALLY BOWLES : _____   11.____
    A. "Main Street"   B. Christopher Isherwood
    C. Henry James   D. Mark Twain
    E. Irwin Wallace

12. MAT BURKE : "ANNA CHRISTIE" :: DION ANTHONY : _____   12.____
    A. "Strange Interlude"   B. "Mourning Becomes Electra"
    C. Eugene O'Neill   D. Nina Leeds
    E. "The Great God Brown"

13. "RUY BLAS" : VICTOR HUGO :: "COMEDIE HUMAINE" : _____   13.____
    A. Dante   B. Balzac   C. Zola
    D. Merimee   E. Anatole France

14. ALEXANDER PUSHKIN : CHATEAUBRIAND :: GOGOL : _____   14.____
    A. Johann Gottsched   B. Goethe   C. Goldini
    D. Lamartine   E. Gorki

15. "BARRACK ROOM BALLADS" : KIPLING :: "THE FOUR HORSEMEN OF   15.____
    THE APOCALYPSE" : _____
    A. Vincente Blasco Ibanez   B. Erich Maria Remarque
    C. "Blood and Sand"   D. "Kim"
    E. Le Sage

16. POLONIUS : OPHELIA :: BABANTIO : _____   16.____
    A. Goneril   B. Juliet   C. Desdemona
    D. Gertrude   E. Shakespeare

17. "ARIA DA CAPO" : EDNA ST. VINCENT MILLAY :: "LURIA" : _____   17.____
    A. Elizabeth Barrett Browning   B. Robert Browning
    C. Amy Lowell   D. Edith Sitwell
    E. "Sonnets From the Portuguese"

18. "DEATH COMES FOR THE ARCHBISHOP" : "THE POET ASSASSINATED ::   18.____
    WILLA CATHER : _____
    A. "The Lost Lady"   B. Guillaume Appolinaire
    C. Luis de Camoens   D. F.G. Lorca

19. THE FOREST OF ARDEN : SHAKESPEARE :: SHERWOOD FOREST : _____   19.____
    A. Robin Hood   B. Sir Walter Raleigh
    C. Sir Walter Scott   D. Robert Louis Stevenson
    E. Sir John Suckling

20. ROMEO : JULIET :: LYSANDER : _____   20.____
    A. Hermia   B. Viola
    C. Olivia   D. "A Midsummer Night's Dream"
    E. Bottom

21. "PORTRAIT OF THE ARTIST AS A YOUNG MAN" : JAMES JOYCE ::   21.____
    "PORTRAIT OF A LADY" : _____
    A. William James   B. Henry James   C. Sir Hugh Walpole
    D. Gilbert Osmond   E. Stephan Dedalus

22. "SALAMMBO" : FLAUBERT :: "GIL BLAS" : _____   22.____
    A. "Madame Bovary"   B. Dr. Sangrado   C. de Sade
    D. Le Sage   E. Anthony Trollope

23. LILLIPUTIANS : JONATHAN SWIFT :: THE TROLLS : _____   23.____
    A. dwarfs of northern mythology   B. "Gulliver's Travels"
    C. Asa Knowles   D. Ibsen
    E. Galsworthy

24. THE KARAMAZOV BROTHERS : DOSTOEVSKI :: THE CHEERYBLE   24.____
    BROTHERS : _____
    A. Wilkie Collins   B. James Farrell   C. George Meredith
    D. George Eliot   E. Charles Dickens

25. EMILIA : IAGO :: CALPURNIA : _____   25.____
    A. Antony   B. Julius Caesar   C. Caligula
    D. MacDuff   E. Desdemona

KEY (CORRECT ANSWERS)

1	C	6.	E	11.	B	16.	C	21.	B
2.	D	7.	D	12.	E	17.	B	22.	D
3.	E	8.	C	13.	B	18.	B	23.	D
4.	B	9.	A	14.	D	19.	C	24.	E
5.	D	10.	D	15.	A	20.	A	25.	B

TEST 6

1. "DON QUIXOTE DE LA MANCHA" : CERVANTES :: "DON JUAN IN HELL" :   1.____
    ____
    A. Eliot   B. G.B. Shaw   C. W. Saroyan
    D. L. Durrell   E. Sancho Panza

2. "BLOOD OF A POET" : "THE INFERNAL MACHINE" :: "GIGI" : _____   2.____
    A. Cocteau   B. Colette   C. "Les Infants Terribles"
    D. "The Innocents" E. "Cheri"

3. MAGWITCH : "GREAT EXPECTATIONS" :: DAISY BUCHANAN : _____   3.____
    A. Dickens   B. "Oliver Twist"   C. "Green Mansions"
    D. "Leaves of Grass" E. "The Great Gatsby"

4. "PENDENNIS" : THACKERAY :: "TRISTAM SHANDY" : _____   4.____
    A. Laurence Sterne B. Stendhal   C. John Sterling
    D. C. LaFarge   E. George Eliot

5. PROUST : "REMEMBRANCE OF THINGS PAST" :: BURTON : _____   5.____
    A. "Finnegan's Wake"   B. "Anatomy of Melancholy"
    C. "Diary of an Opium Eater" D. "Pleasures and Days"
    E. "Eve of St. Agnes"

6. ANATOLE FRANCE : "PENGUIN ISLAND" :: ANTOINE DE SAINT-EXUPÉRY :   6.____
    ____
    A. "Swann's Way"   B. St. Mael   C. "The Little Prince"
    D. Keats   E. "Etudes de la Nature"

7. "THE RAVEN" : POE :: "EVANGELINE" : _____   7.____
    A. Wordsworth   B. Longfellow
    C. "The Legend of Sleepy Hollow" D. Glaspell
    E. Whittier

8. "THE WORLD IS TOO MUCH WITH US" : WORDSWORTH :: "TIGER,   8.____
    TIGER, BURNING BRIGHT : _____
    A. Coleridge   B. Blake   C. Shelley
    D. Keats   E. Yeats

9. "EVE'S DIARY" : MARK TWAIN :: "THE UGLY DUCKLING" : _____   9.____
    A. Hans Christian Andersen   B. Robert Penn Warren
    C. Lord Dunsany   D. "The Tin Soldier"
    E. Saint-Exupery

10. "THE DIVINE COMEDY" : DANTE :: "LA GIOCANDA" : _____   10.____
    A. D'Annunzio   B. Verga   C. Manzoni
    D. Leopardi   E. Carducci

11. "DUBLINERS" : JAMES JOYCE :: "DEAD SOULS" : _____
    A. Gorki   B. Gogol   C. "The Overcoat"
    D. Sidney Kingsley   E. Dostoevski   11.____

12. "DEATH IN THE AFTERNOON" : HEMINGWAY :: "DEATH IN VENICE" : _____
    A. Thomas Mann   B. "Buddenbrooks"   C. Thomas Hardy
    D. Gustave Aschenbach E. Willa Cather   12.____

13. "SMOKE AND STEEL" : CARL SANDBURG :: "THE DEATH OF THE HIRED MAN" : _____
    A. Poe   B. Longfellow   C. Robert Frost
    D. "Excelsior"   E. "Chicago Poems"   13.____

14. "THE EVE OF ST. AGNES" : "THE EVE OF ST. JOHN" :: KEATS : _____
    A. Yeats   B. Sir Walter Raleigh   C. Blake
    D. Sir Walter Scott   E. Coleridge   14.____

15. "TOM JONES" : HENRY FIELDING :: "ETHAN FROME" : _____
    A. Edith Wharton   B. Thomas Macaulay   C. Thomas Carlyle
    D. "Esther Waters"   E. Henry Esmond   15.____

16. "ETHAN BRAND" : HAWTHORNE :: "NOTRE DAME DE PARIS" : _____
    A. Victor Hugo   B. Alexander Pope   C. Quasimodo
    D. Andre Maurois   E. Flaubert   16.____

17. TITANIA : SHAKESPEARE :: ANITRA : _____
    A. Antonio   B. Mallarmé   C. Ibsen
    D. Moliere   E. Congreve   17.____

18. ROBERT BROWNING : ELIZABETH BARRETT :: WILLIAM ROSE BENET : _____
    A. Charlotte Bronte   B. Daisy Ashford   C. Elinor Wylie
    D. Virginia Woolf   E. Edith Sitwell   18.____

19. "THE FIFTH DECADE OF CANTOS" : EZRA POUND :: "THE LUSIAD" : _____
    A. Mor Jokai   B. Valera y Alcala   C. Jose Maria de Pereda
    D. "Blood Wedding"   E. Luis de Camoens   19.____

20. "OF HUMAN BONDAGE" : SOMERSET MAUGHAM : "THE WAY OF ALL FLESH" : _____
    A. Charles Reade   B. Anthony Trollope   C. Samuel Butler
    D. "Erewhon"   E. Victor Hugo   20.____

21. PHILIP CAREY : SOMERSET MAUGHAM :: MARGUERITE GAUTHIER : _____
    A. Balzac   B. Alexandre Dumas (père)
    C. Alexandre Dumas (fils)   D. "Le Demi-Monde"
    E. George du Maurier   21.____

22. PENROD : BOOTH TARKINGTON :: TRILBY : _____   22.____
    A. Longfellow   B. Mark Twain   C. George du Maurier
    D. "Peter Ibbetson"   E. "Peer Gynt"

23. "MAJOR BARBARA" : G.B. SHAW :: "THE MAKING OF AMERICANS" : _____   23.____
    A. Sherwood Anderson   B. Irwin Shaw
    C. Ernest Hemingway   D. Gertrude Stein
    E. "Man and Superman"

24. ICHABOD CRANE : "THE LEGEND OF SLEEPY HOLLOW" :: MRS.   24.____
    MALAPROP : _____
    A. "School for Scandal"   B. Sheridan
    C. "She Stoops to Conquer"   D. "The Rivals"
    E. "The Imaginary Invalid"

25. "PETER PAN" : J.M. BARRIE :: "TONIGHT WE IMPROVISE" : _____   25.____
    A. Philip Barry   B. Luigi Pirandello
    C. Sir James Matthew Barrie   D. John Gay
    E. "Hotel Universe"

KEY (CORRECT ANSWERS)

1	B	6.	C	11.	B	16.	A	21.	C
2.	E	7.	B	12.	A	17.	C	22.	C
3.	E	8.	B	13.	C	18.	C	23.	D
4.	A	9.	A	14.	D	19.	E	24.	D
5.	B	10.	A	15.	A	20.	C	25.	B

TEST 7

1. "SONG OF MYSELF" : WALT WHITMAN :: "ROAN STALLION" : _____   1.____
   A. Archibald MacLeish   B. Edward Arlington Robinson
   C. William Rose Benet   D. Robert Frost
   E. Robinson Jeffers

2. "TAMERLANE" : EDGAR ALLAN POE :: "TOWER OF IVORY" : _____   2.____
   A. Robert Lowell   B. "Annabel Lee"   C. Carl Sandburg
   D. Archibald MacLeish   E. Alexander Pope

3. "IT CAN'T HAPPEN HERE" : SINCLAIR LEWIS :: "THE STRANGE CASE   3.____
   OF DR. JEKYLL AND MR. HYDE" : _____
   A. A.C. Doyle   B. Ray Bradbury   C. Mrs. Shelley
   D. "Frankenstein"   E. R.L. Stevenson

4. "PARADISE LOST" : MILTON :: "BLEAK HOUSE" : _____   4.____
   A. Dickens   B. Conrad
   C. Chaucer   D. "Paradise Regained"
   E. "Sonnet on His Blindness"

5. "THE HOUSE OF THE SEVEN GABLES" : HAWTHORNE :: "THE HOUSE   5.____
   OF MIRTH" : _____
   A. Hermann Hess   B. Edith Wharton   C. Thomas Hardy
   D. "Scarlet Letter"   E. Thomas Mann

6. "THE IDIOT" : DOSTOEVSKI :: "STEPPENWOLFE" : _____   6.____
   A. Gogol   B. Hermann Hesse
   C. Bjornson   D. "Crime and Punishment"
   E. Mayakovsky

7. "SEA GARDEN" : HILDA DOOLITTLE :: "THE HOUSE OF LIFE" : _____   7.____
   A. Christina Georgina Rossetti   B. Edith Sitwell
   C. Osbert Sitwell   E. Dante Gabriel Rossetti
   E. Sacheverell Sitwell

8. "THE WEARY BLUES" : LANGSTON HUGHES :: "GIANTS IN THE EARTH" :   8.____
   _____
   A. Pearl Buck   B. "Simple Speaks His Mind
   C. O.E. Rolvaag   D. Katherine Anne Porter
   E. Daphne DuMaurier

9. MARY ANN EVANS : GEORGE ELIOT :: WILLIAM S. PORTER : _____   9.____
   A. William Carlos Williams   B. George Sand
   C. Emlyn Williams   D. O. Henry
   E. Saki

10. ELIZA GANT : THOMAS WOLFE :: ELIZA DOOLITTLE : _____   10.____
    A. "Look Homeward, Angel"   B. Thomas Hardy
    C. G.B. Shaw   D. "Pygmalion"
    E. Charles Dickens

11. POLONIUS : LAERTES :: BANQUO : _____   11.____
    A. MacDuff   B. Horatio   C. "Macbeth"
    D. Fleance   E. Iago

12. THE MISSISSIPPI RIVER : MARK TWAIN :: THE RIVER LIFFEY : _____   12.____
    A. Sean O'Casey   B. Galsworthy   C. "Quiet Flows the Don"
    D. James Joyce   E. St. John Gogarty

13. "THE ALCHEMIST" : BEN JONSON :: "THE DUCHESS OF MALFI" : _____   13.____
    A. John Webster   B. Voltaire
    C. Molière   D. "The Duke's Children"
    E. Marlowe

14. "THE PICTURE OF DORIAN GRAY" : OSCAR WILDE :: "SISTER CARRIE :   14.____
    _____
    A. Sherwood Anderson
    B. Sinclair Lewis
    C. Thomas Wolfe
    D. Theodore Dreiser
    E. "The Importance of Being Earnest"

15. "LITTLE DORRIT" : DICKENS :: "MOLL FLANDERS" : _____   15.____
    A. Daniel DeFoe   B. George Eliot   C. "Robinson Crusoe"
    D. Thomas Hardy   E. Sir Thomas More

16. "ADONAIS" : SHELLEY :: "IN MEMORIAM" : _____   16.____
    A. Tennyson   B. Kipling   C. Robert Browning
    D. Whittier   E. "Ode to a Skylark"

17. "SONS AND LOVERS" : D.H. LAWRENCE :: "FATHERS AND SONS" : _____   17.____
    A. Turgenev   B. Congreve
    C. "A Son of the Middle Border" D. Jack London
    E. William Dean Howells

18. "A FAREWELL TO ARMS" : HEMINGWAY :: "ABSALOM, ABSALOM" : _____   18.____
    A. John Dos Passos B. John Steinbeck   C. Gertrude Stein
    D. William Faulkner E. Theodore Dreiser

19. JOHN PEEL : "FINNEGAN'S WAKE" :: MOLLY BLOOM : _____   19.____
    A. Samuel Beckett   B. "Dubliners"   C. Sean O'Casey
    D. James Joyce   E. "Ulysses"

20. FRIAR TUCK : SIR WALTER SCOTT :: FRIAR LAWRENCE : _____   20.____
    A. "Ivanhoe"   B. Shakespeare   C. Sir John Falstaff
    D. "Robin Hood"   E. Laurence Sterne

21. ELMER GANTRY : SINCLAIR LEWIS :: CLYDE GRIFFITHS : _____
    A. "Tobacco Road"   B. "Gone With the Wind"
    C. John Steinbeck   D. Theodore Dreiser
    E. William Faulkner
                                                    21._____

22. "FAR FROM THE MADDING CROWD" : HARDY :: "A FAREWELL TO ARMS" : _____
    A. F. Scott Fitzgerald   B. Ernie Pyle   C. Eugene O'Neill
    D. "The Sun Also Rises" E. Ernest Hemingway
                                                      22._____

23. "CONFESSIONS" : ST. AUGUSTINE :: "IMITATION OF CHRIST"
    A. Thomas Aquinas   B. Thomas a Kempis
    C. "Summa Theologicae"   D. Bede the Venerable
    E. Sainte-Beuve
                                                    23._____

24. "LA PUCELLE D'ORLEANS" : VOLTAIRE :: "SAINT JOAN" : _____
    A. Schiller   B. Charles VII   C. "Jeanne d'Arc"
    D. Anatole France   E. Bernard Shaw
                                                    24._____

25. "TURN OF THE SCREW" : "THE INNOCENTS" :: "THE WAVES" : _____
    A. "The Trial"   B. "The Castle"   C. "The Heiress"
    D. Henry James   E. "Jacob's Room"
                                                      25._____

KEY (CORRECT ANSWERS)

1	E	6.	B	11.	D	16.	A	21.	D
2.	D	7.	D	12.	D	17.	A	22.	E
3.	E	8.	C	13.	A	18.	D	23.	B
4.	A	9.	D	14.	D	19.	E	24.	E
5.	B	10.	C	15.	A	20.	B	25.	E

TEST 8

1. LITTLE BOY BLUE : EUGENE FIELD :: LITTLE BILLEE : _____   1.____
   A. Hawthorne   B. Tennyson
   C. "Little Eva"   D. Thackeray
   E. Harriet Beecher Stowe

2. "RIGHT YOU ARE IF YOU THINK YOU ARE" : PIRANDELLO :: "LILIOM" : _____   2.____
   A. Molière
   B. "Six Characters in Search of an Author"
   C. Maeterlinck
   D. Molnar
   E. Milne

3. "LADY WINDERMERE'S FAN" : OSCAR WILDE :: "THE LADY OR THE TIGER :   3.____
   _____
   A. Ellen Glasgow   B. Robert Gissing
   C. Frank Stockton   D. "The Lady of the Lake"
   E. Sir Walter Scott

4. MR. CHIPS : JAMES HILTON :: PUDD'NHEAD WILSON : _____   4.____
   A. Ben Franklin   B. Mark Twain   C. Charles Dickens
   D. Lewis Carroll   E. Mrs. Wiggs

5. "PICTURES OF THE FLOATING WORLD" : AMY LOWELL :: "THE VISION   5.____
   OF SIR LAUNFAL" : _____
   A. James Russell Lowell   B. John Greenleaf Whittier
   C. "For Lancelot Andrews"   D. Longfellow
   E. Robert Penn Warren

6. MINIVER CHEEVY : EDWARD ARLINGTON ROBINSON :: ALFRED J.   6.____
   PRUFROCK : _____
   A. Stephen Vincent Benet   B. Dylan Thomas
   C. George Dillon   D. "What's O'Clock"
   E. T.S. Eliot

7. "THE GRAPES OF WRATH" : JOHN STEINBECK :: "THE BRIDGE OF SAN   7.____
   LUIS REY" : _____
   A. Thornton Wilder   B. Robert Sherwood   C. John Hersey
   D. "A Bell for Adano" E. Willa Cather

8. POLLY PEACHUM : JOHN GAY :: LITTLE LORD FAUNTLEROY : _____   8.____
   A. "Beggar's Opera"   B. Francis H. Burnett   C. Mack the Knife
   D. Zoe Atkins   E. Jesse L. Williams

9. MRS. JERVIS : RICHARDSON :: MRS. DALLOWAY : _____   9.____
   A. Louis Bromfield   B. Daphne DuMaurier
   C. Virginia Woolf   D. "A Room of One's Own"
   E. Amy Lowell

10. SCARLETT O'HARA : MARGARET MITCHELL :: ALICE ADAMS : _____   10.____
    A. Martin Flavin   B. Marc Connelly
    C. Booth Tarkington   D. "They Knew What They Wanted"
    E. Sidney Howard

11. "GARGANTUA" : RABELAIS :: "NOSTROMO" : _____   11.____
    A. "Pantagruel"   B. Rudyard Kipling
    C. Joseph Conrad   D. Victor Hugo
    E. "Notre Dame de Paris"

12. "EMMA" : JANE AUSTEN :: "THE TRAGICAL HISTORY OF DR. FAUSTUS" :   12.____
    _____
    A. Oliver Goldsmith   B. James Boswell   C. Christopher Marlowe
    D. Edmund Burke   E. "Peregrine Pickle"

13. "GUNGA DIN" : RUDYARD KIPLING :: "THE BROKEN VASE" (LA VASE   13.____
    BRISE) : _____
    A. B. Bjornson   B. Paul Heyse   C. "Just-so Stores"
    D. Sully Pudhomme   E. Andre Gide

14. "THE FAIR MAID OF PERTH" : SIR WALTER SCOTT :: "THE FAERIE   14.____
    QUEENE" : _____
    A. Spenser   B. Chaucer
    C. Keats   D. "The Shepherd's Calendar"
    E. Byron

15. "EMILE" : JEAN JACQUES ROUSSEAU :: "THE AMERICAN SCHOLAR" : _____   15.____
    A. Carlyle   B. Wordsworth   C. "Nature"
    D. Coleridge   E. Emerson

16. ANDREW FAIRSERVICE : "ROB ROY" :: SIR JOHN FALSTAFF : _____   16.____
    A. "All's Well That Ends Well"   B. "Love's Labor Lost"
    C. Shakespeare   D. "Merry Wives of Windsor"
    E. "Much Ado About Nothing"

17. ELSIE DINSMORE : MARTHA FINLEY :: MR. PIM : _____   17.____
    A. J.M. Synge   B. A.A. Milne
    C. "The Dover Road"   D. Hans Christian Andersen
    E. "The Pied Piper"

18. "RETURN OF THE DRUSES" : ROBERT BROWNING :: "REVOLT OF THE   18.____
    ANGELS" : _____
    A. Marcel Proust   B. Anatole France
    C. Jonathan Swift   D. "Return of the Native"
    E. Henry James

19. "PALE HORSE, PALE RIDER" : KATHERINE ANNE PORTER :: "PAMELA, OR   19.____
    VIRTUE REWARDED" : _____
    A. Samuel Richardson   B. Henry Fielding   C. "Joseph Andrews"
    D. Stephen Hawes   E. "Ship of Fools"

224

20. CALIBAN : SHAKESPEARE :: QUASIMODO : _____   20.____
    A. Balzac   B. Victor Hugo
    C. Hans Berghof   D. "The Hunchback of Notre Dame"
    E. Thomas Mann

21. "PEREGRINE PICKLE" : SMOLLETT :: "HASTY PUDDING : _____   21.____
    A. Lord Reginald Hastings   B. Joel Barlow
    C. Mark Twain   D. Humphrey Chimpden Earwicker
    E. Marmaduke Howard

22. "RETURN OF PETER GRIMM" : BELASCO :: "EBB TIDE" : _____   22.____
    A. Robert Herrick   B. Robert Louis Stevenson
    C. Hermann Hesse   D. Wallace Irwin
    E. Percy Lewis

23. "THE SILENCE OF COLONEL BRAMBLE" : ANDRE MAUROIS :: "STRAIT   23.____
    IS THE GATE" : _____
    A. Emile Herzog   B. Francois Mauriac   C. Andre Gide
    D. Graham Greene   E. "The Immoralist"

24. "JUSTINE" : DONATIEN DE SADE :: "VENUS IN FURS" : _____   24.____
    A. Simone de Beauvoir   B. Leopold von Sacher-Masoch
    C. Stéphane Mallarmé   D. Garcilaso de la Vega
    E. "The Second Sexé

25. "RASPUTIN THE HOLY DEVIL" : RENÉ FULOP-MILLER :: "WILHELM   25.____
    MEISTER" : _____
    A. Gunter Grass   B. Goethe
    C. "The Sorrows of Werther"   D. Gottfried Keller
    E. Heinrich Heine

KEY (CORRECT ANSWERS)

1	D	6.	E	11.	C	16.	D	21.	B
2.	D	7.	A	12.	C	17.	B	22.	B
3.	C	8.	B	13.	C	18.	B	23.	C
4.	B	9.	C	14.	A	19.	A	24.	B
5.	A	10.	C	15.	E	20.	B	25.	A

TEST 9

1. "BATEAU IVRE" : RIMBAUD :: "FLEUR DE MAL" : _____   1._____
    A. Verlaine   B. Mallarmé   C. Rolla
    D. Baudelaire   E. St. John Perse

2. "THE KILLERS" : HEMINGWAY :: "THE ICE PALACE" : _____   2._____
    A. O. Henry   B. Saki   C. Sinclair Lewis
    D. Thomas Wolfe   E. F. Scott Fitzgerald

3. JAMES BOND : IAN FLEMING :: SHERLOCK HOLMES : _____   3._____
    A. Watson   B. Arthur Conan Doyle C. Peter Wimsey
    D. Dr. Moriarty   E. Edgar Allan Poe

4. "SHALL I COMPARE THEE TO A SUMMER'S DAY" : SHAKESPEARE ::   4._____
    "HOW DO I LOVE THEE? LET ME COUNT THE WAYS" : _____
    A. Spenser   B. Defoe
    C. Elizabeth Barrett Browning   D. Edna St. Vincent Millay
    E. Marlowe

5. SIR WALTER RALEIGH : ELIZABETHAN AGE :: JONATHAN SWIFT : _____   5._____
    A. 18th century   B. Victorian Era   C. England
    D. "Gulliver's Travels"   E. Dean Swift

6. BILLY BUDD : MELVILLE :: HESTER PRYNNE : _____   6._____
    A. Poe   B. Hawthorne   C. Cooper
    D. "Typee"   E. "Scarlet Letter"

7. LAERTES : POLONIUS :: HAMLET : _____   7._____
    A. Gertrude   B. Horatio   C. Rosencrantz
    D. King Hamlet   E. Shakespeare

8. "BLOOD WEDDING" : LORCA :: "THE MARQUIS OF LUNBRIA" : _____   8._____
    A. Quiroga   B. Unanumo   C. Borges
    D. Cervantes   E. Bazán

9. DON JUAN : SHAW :: POLLY PEACHUM : _____   9._____
    A. Twain   B. Brecht   C. Alcott
    D. "Mother Courage" E. Stevenson

10. "UNDER MILKWOOD" : DYLAN THOMAS :: "THE BALLAD OF READING   10._____
    GAOL" : _____

11. "THE MAN WHO DIED" : LAWRENCE :: "MELANCTHA" : _____   11._____
    A. Gertrude Stein   B. Hemingway   C. de Maupassant
    D. O. Henry   E. T.S. Eliot

12. "THE MYTH OF SISYPHUS" : CAMUS :: "NAUSEA" : _____   12.____
    A. Beckett   B. "Andorra"   C. Sartre
    D. Pinter   E. Richardson

13. "ENDGAME" : "OUR LADY OF THE FLOWERS" :: BECKETT : _____   13.____
    A. Artaud   B. Genet   C. Werfel
    D. "Waiting For Lefty"   E. Schnitzler

14. CHRISTOPHER MARLOWE : "THE TRAGICAL HISTORY OF DOCTOR   14.____
    FAUSTUS" :: GEOFFREY CHAUCER : _____
    A. "The Burning Babe"   B. Ben Jonson
    C. "Complaint of a Lover Rebuked" D. "The Canterbury Tales"
    E. Elizabethan Era

15. "LORD RANDAL : BALLAD :: "THE PASSIONATE SHEPHERD TO HIS   15.____
    LOVE : _____
    A. sonnet   B. Shakespeare   C. Joohn Lyly
    D. lyric   E. quatrain

16. "OF MARRIAGE AND SINGLE LIFE" : FRANCIS BARON :: "GO AND   16.____
    CATCH A FALLING STAR" : _____
    A. Charles Lamb   B. John Donne
    C. Michael Drayton   D. Robert Herrick
    E. "When I was One and Twenty"

17. FIRST LINE : "WHY SO PALE AND WAN, FOND LOVER?" :: LAST LINE :   17.____
    _____
    A. Sir John Suckling
    B. "Why so dull and mute, young sinner?"
    C. "And I am one and twenty and oh, 'tis true, 'tis true"
    D. "Out upon it, I have loved"
    E. "When I lie tangled in her hair and fettered to her eye"

18. "COLOSSUS OF MAROUSSI" : HENRY MILLER :: "SEA AND SARDINIA :   18.____
    _____
    A. "Laurence Hope"   B. Lawrence Durrell   C. "Etruscan Places"
    D. D.H. Lawrence   E. T.E. Lawrence

19. "SHALL I WASTING IN DESPAIR" : GEORGE WITHER :: "TO ALTHEA,   19.____
    FROM PRISON : _____
    A. "To His Coy Mistress"   B. "Hymn to Diana"
    C. "Thomas More"   D. Richard Lovelace
    E. George Herbert

20. "MOURNING BECOMES ELECTRA" : EUGENE O'NEILL :: "ELECTRA" :   20.____
    _____
    A. Euripides   B. Sophocles   C. Eumenides
    D. "Antigone"   E. "Prometheus Bound"

21. "PROFILES IN COURAGE" : AMERICAN POLITICS :: "TWILIGHT IN   21.____
    ITALY : _____
      A. war   B. travel   C. Italian politics
      D. The Holy See   E. D.H. Lawrence

22. "HECATE COUNTY" : WILSON :: YOKNAPATAWPHA COUNTY : _____   22.____
      A. Miller   B. Steinbeck   C. Faulkner
      D. Twain   E. Caldwell

23. THOMAS WOLFE : SHERWOOD ANDERSON :: EVELYN WAUGH : _____   23.____
      A. Willa Cather   B. James Joyce   C. Robert Sherwood
      D. "The Loved One"   E. G.K. Chesterton

24. ENGLAND : T.S. ELIOT :: SPAIN : _____   24.____
      A. Gertrude Stein   B. "The Wasteland"   C. Robert Graves
      D. Italy   E. Ezra Pound

25. "A DOLL'S HOUSE : IBSEN :: "PURPLE DUST" : _____   25.____
      A. "The Master Builder"   B. O'Casey
      C. Galsworthy   D. Synge
      E. "Juno and the Paycock"

KEY (CORRECT ANSWERS)

1	D	6.	B	11.	A	16.	B	21.	B
2.	E	7.	D	12.	C	17.	C	22.	C
3.	B	8.	B	13.	B	18.	D	23.	E
4.	C	9.	B	14.	D	19.	D	24.	C
5.	A	10.	E	15.	E	20.	B	25.	B

TEST 10

1. THE CAPULETS : SHAKESPEARE :: THE SHOPESES : _____   1._____
    A. "Romeo and Juliet"   B. Yerby   C. Hemingway
    D. Faulkner   E. the Montagues

2. VIOLA : POPEYE :: ORLANDO : _____   2._____
    A. Temple Drake   B. Miranda   C. Faulkner
    D. Mercurio   E. Cordelia

3. FLAUBERT : "MADAME BOVARY" :: DUMAS : _____   3._____
    A. Hugo   B. "Père Goriot"   C. "Camille"
    D. "Salammbo"   E. Balzac

4. "THE VILLAGE" : GEORGE CRABBE :: "THE SUNFLOWER" : _____   4._____
    A. William Blake   B. Lord Chesterfield C. Oscar Wilde
    D. Robert Burns   E. Thomas Percy

5. KATHERINE ANNE PORTER :: "SHIP OF FOOLS" :: JAMES BOSWELL : _____   5._____
    A. Benjamin Franklin
    B. "Decline and Fall of the Roman Empire"
    C. Samuel Johnson
    D. "The Traveler"
    E. "The Life of Samuel Johnson"

6. "...IN A CLOAKROOM AT VICTORIA STATION" : OSCAR WILDE :: "THIS IS   6._____
    THE WAY THE WORLD ENDS...." : _____
    A. "Burnt Norton"
    B. C.S. Lewis
    C. T.S. Eliot
    D. "...And waiting for a knock upon the door"
    E. W.H. Auden

7. "GOOD NIGHT, SWEET LADIES, GOOD NIGHT" : "HAMLET" :: "O BRAVE   7._____
    NEW WORLD, THAT HAS SUCH PEOPLE IN'T!" : _____
    A. George Orwell   B. "Richard III"
    C. "The Tempest"   D. Aldous Huxley
    E. "The Merchant of Venice"

8. "BLOW, BLOW, THOU WINTER WIND" : "AS YOU LIKE IT" :: "WHO IS   8._____
    SYLIVA? WHAT IS SHE?" : _____
    A. Shakespeare's Sonnets
    B. "She Stoops to Conquer"
    C. Christopher Marlowe
    D. "Where the bee sucks, there suck I"
    E. "The Two Gentlemen of Verona"

9. "IT WAS A LOVER AND HIS LASS" : WILLIAM SHAKESPEARE :: "DRINK TO
ME ONLY WITH THINE EYES..." : _____
   A. Thomas Kyd
   B. "We are such stuff as dreams are made on..."
   C. Ben Jonson
   D. William Shakespeare
   E. George Peele

9.____

10. "TELL ME, WHERE IS FANCY BRED,...?" : "THE MERCHANT OF VENICE" ::
"O MISTRESS MINE, WHERE ARE YOU ROAMING?" : _____
   A. "Twelfth Night"   B. Thomas Wyatt
   C. "Antony and Cleopatra"   D. "It is a tale told by an idiot..."
   E. "Cymbeline"

10.____

11. 'ODE TO THE WEST WIND" : PERCY B. SHELLEY :: "ODE TO EVENING :
_____
   A. John Keats
   B. William Collins
   C. William Wordsworth
   D. "I met a traveler from an antique land..."
   E. "Ode to a Skylark"

11.____

12. "HOW SOON HATH TIME.... STOLEN ON HIS WING MY THREE AND
TWENTIETH YEAR!" : JOHN MILTON :: "...IT WAS MY THIRTIETH YEAR TO
HEAVEN" : _____
   A. Brendan Behan
   B. "Lycidas"
   C. Edgar Arlington Robinson
   D. Dylan Thomas
   E. "Do Not Go Gently Into That Good Night"

12.____

13. GONERIL : LEAR :: CALPURNIA : _____
   A. Prospero   B. Fagin   C. Miranda
   D. Brutus   E. Cordelia

13.____

14. SERGIUS O'SHAUGHNESSY : NORMAN MAILER :: DAISY MILLER : _____
   A. "Washington Square"   B. Arnold Bennett
   C. William James   D. Henry James
   E. "The Deer Park"

14.____

15. SEAN O'CASEY : "THE PLOUGH AND THE STARS" :: SOMERSET
MAUGHAM : _____
   A. "Riders to the Sea"   B. "The Wave"   C. G.K. Chesterton
   D. "Our Betters"   E. "The Forsyte Saga"

15.____

16. ALICE : TOM SAWYER :: THE MAD HATTER : _____
   A. the Red Queen   B. Samuel Clemens   C. Lewis Carroll
   D. Huckleberry Finn   E. Peter Pan

16.____

17. MARY ANN EVANS : GEORGE ELIOT :: ARMANDINE LUCILE DUPON : _____ 17.____
    A. Gertrude Stein   B. "Silas Marner"   C. Cassandra
    D. Evelyn Waugh   E. George Sand

18. "THE SEAGULL" : CHEKHOV :: "THE LOWER DEPTHS" : _____ 18.____
    A. Ostrovski   B "The Idiot"   C. Gorki
    D. Gogol   E. Borodin

19. "IL CINQUE MAGGIO" : MANZONI :: "WOMEN OF THE PHARISEES" : _____ 19.____
    A. Mauriac   B. Carducci   C. Gide
    D. Malraux   E. "The Immoralist"

20. SIR WALTER SCOTT : WILLIAM MAKEPEACE THACKERAY :: "THE LADY 20.____
    OF THE LAKE" : _____
    A. Samuel Butler   B. "Adam Bede"
    C. "Silas Marner"   D. "Vanity Fair"
    E. "The Lay of the Last Minstrel"

21. CLYDE GRIFFITH : DREISER :: BILL SYKES : _____ 21.____
    A. Brecht   B. "A Christmas Carol"   C. Dickens
    D. Fagin   E. Hood

22. "DR. JEKYLL AND MR. HYDE" : "MASTER OF BALLANTRAE" :: THE 22.____
    CHARTERHOUSE OF PARMA" : _____
    A. Stendahl   B. "The Three Musketeers"
    C. "The Count of Monte Cristo"   D. Stevenson
    E. "The Red and the Black"

23. ANNE BRONTE : CHARLOTTE BRONTE :: "THE TENANT OF WILDFELL 23.____
    HALL" : _____
    A. "Wuthering Heights"   B. "Jude the Obscure"
    C. "Anthony Adverse"   D. "Return of the Native"
    E. "The Professor

24. HEATHCLLIFFE : CATHY :: ALEX D'URBERVILLE : _____ 24.____
    A. the Earnshaws   B. Marguerite Gautier   C. Eustacia Vye
    D. Thrushcross Grange E. Jane Austen

25. "UNDER FIRE" : "JEAN CHRISTOPHE :: "MRS. DALLOWAY : _____ 25.____
    A. "Men of Good Will"   B. Romain Rolland
    C. "Jacob's Room"   D. "The Heart of the Matter"
    E. Virginia Woolf

231

KEY (CORRECT ANSWERS)

1	D	6.	C	11.	B	16.	D	21.	C
2.	B	7.	C	12.	D	17.	E	22.	E
3.	C	8.	E	13.	D	18.	C	23.	E
4.	A	9.	C	14.	D	19.	C	24.	C
5.	E	10.	A	15.	D	20.	D	25.	D

TEST 11

1. HARRY HOPE : "THE ICEMAN COMETH" :: CAPTAIN QUEEG : _____   1.____
    A. "Winesburg, Ohio"   B. "Ile"   C. "An American Tragedy"
    D. Eugene O'Neill   E. "The Caine Mutiny"

2. "RICHARD CORY" : E.A. ROBINSON :: "THE BRIDGE" : _____   2.____
    A. Edgar Lee Masters   B. "Four Quartets"
    C. Hart Crane   D. Bret Harte
    E. William Carlos Williams

3. GAUTIER : CHATEAUBRIAND :: COLERIDGE : _____   3.____
    A. Honoré   B. Maeterlinck   C. T.S. Eliot
    D. Sir Robert Peel   E. Trollope

4. VILLON : RABELAIS :: VICTOR HUGO : _____   4.____
    A. René Descartes   B. La Rochefoucauld   C. Corneille
    D. Perrault   E. Edmond Rostand

5. "R.U.R." : CAPEK :: "RIGHT YOU ARE IF YOU THINK YOU ARE : _____   5.____
    A. "Six Characters in Search of an Author"
    B. Pirandello
    C. Toller
    D. Gorki
    E. Pratolini

6. "THE HOUSE OF BERNARDA ALBA" : LORCA :: "SEVEN RED SUNDAYS :   6.____
    _____
    A. Remarque   B. "Pro Patria"   C. Sender
    D. "Blood Wedding"   E. Koestler

7. "METAMORPHOSIS" : HOFKA :: "A PIECE OF STRING" : _____   7.____
    A. Poe   B. "A String of Pearls"
    C. Chekhov   D. "The Hunter Gracchus"
    E. de Maupassant

8. "DOWN AND OUT IN PARIS IN LONDON" : "LAFCADIO'S ADVENTURES" :   8.____
    _____
    A. "The Counterfeiters"   B. "Brave New World"
    C. Georges Bidet   D. Jules Romains
    E. Andre Gide

9. SIGRID UNDSET : NORWAY :: HENRYK SIENKIEWICZ : _____   9.____
    A. Germany   B. Lithuania   C. "Quo Vadis"
    D. Poland   E. "Kristin Lavransdatter"

10. "THE TELL-TALE HEART" : "THE BLACK CAT" :: "THE CITY IN THE SEA :   10.____

    A. "The Prairie Finder"   B. "The Village Blacksmith"
    C. "The Haunted Palace"   D. "The Pioneers"
    E. Edgar Allan Poe

11. LENORE : "THE RAVEN" :: NATTY BUMPPO : _____   11.____
    A. "The Purloined Letter"   B. "The Gold Bug"
    C. "The Deerslayer"   D. James Fenimore Cooper
    E. "The Masque of the Red Death"

12. "MOBY DICK" : MELVILLE :: "THE MARBLE FAUN" : _____   12.____
    A. Hawthorne   B. "Omoo"   C. Poe
    D. Lanier   E. Whittier

13. "POOR RICHARD'S ALMANAC" : FRANKLIN :: "THE RIGHTS OF MAN" :   13.____

    A. Montesquieu   B. "The Age of Reason"
    C. Jefferson   D. Lanier
    E. Madison

14. "HELLO, OUT THERE" : SAROYAN :: "THE BATHHOUSE" : _____   14.____
    A. Glaspell   B. Mayakovsky
    C. O'Neill   D. "Twenty-Seven Wagons Full of Cotton"
    E. Williams

15. "LA VIDA ES SUEÑO" ("LIFE IS BUT A DREAM") : PEDRO CALDERÓN DE   15.____
LA BRCA :: "EL MEJOR ALCALDE EL REY" ("THE KING, THE GREATEST
ALCALDE") : _____
    A. Luis Vas de Camoëns   B. "Yerma"
    C. José Ortega y Gasset   D. Giorgio Vasari
    E. Lope Félix De Vega Carpio

16. PHILIP FRENEAU : THOMAS PAINE :: JEAN COCTEAU : _____   16.____
    A. "The Cocktail Party"   B. "Orpheus and Eurydice"
    C. Benjamin Franklin   D. William Congreve
    E. Ramon J. Sender

17. "LITTLE WOMEN" : LOUISA MAY ALCOTT :: "MISS LONELYHEARTS : _____   17.____
    A. Michael Gold   B. "The Day of the Locust"
    C. Nathaniel West   D. Meyer Levin
    E. John Dos Passos

18. "GRONGAR HILL" : JOHN DYER :: "EAST CORKER" : _____   18.____
    A. Andrew Marvell   B. T.S. Eliot   C. Robert Herrick
    D. John Donne   E. "Holy Sonnets"

19. "THE DUCHESS OF MALFI" : JOHN WEBSTER :: "THE PASSIONATE   19.____
    SHEPHERD TO HIS LOVE" : _____
    A. Christopher Marlowe   B. Earl of Rochester
    C. "The Jew of Malta"   D. "Sodom"
    E. John Bunyan

20. "GULLIVER'S TRAVELS" : JONATHAN SWIFT :: "THE RAPE OF THE LOCK" :   20.____
    _____
    A. "The Dunciad"   B. Joseph Addison   C. Edgar Allan Poe
    D. George Eliot   E. Alexander Pope

21. "TIGER, TIGER, BURNING BRIGHT..." : WILLIAM BLAKE :: "GATHER YE   21.____
    ROSEBUDS WHILE YE MAY..." : _____
    A. Thomas Hood
    B. Robert Herrick
    C. John Milton
    D. William Shakespeare
    E. "Shall I compare thee to a summer's day..."

22. IZAAK WALTON : FISHING :: HELEN GURLEY BROWN : _____   22.____
    A. hunting   B. food preparation
    C. Albert Ellis   D. sex
    E. "The Compleat Angler"

23. UPTON SINCLAIR : BUSINESS MONOPOLIES :: PHILIP WYLIE : _____   23.____
    A. sex   B. mothers   C. crime
    D. Lanny Budd   E. "The Disappearance"

24. "IT'S A GREAT DAY FOR BANANAFISH" : "CATCHER IN THE RYE" ::   24.____
    "THE DIAMOND AS BIG AS THE RITZ" : _____
    A. "Franny and Zooey"   B. F. Scott Fitzgerald
    C. "The Last Tycoon"   D. Sinclair Lewis
    E. Eugene O'Neill

25. ALFRED TENNYSON : JOHN KEATS :: GEORGE JEAN NATHAN : _____   25.____
    A. Percy B. Shelley   B. "The American Mercury"
    C. Kenneth Tynan   D. "The Spectator"
    E. Olin Downes

KEY (CORRECT ANSWERS)

1	E	6.	C	11.	C	16.	E	21.	B
2.	C	7.	E	12.	A	17.	C	22.	D
3.	E	8.	E	13.	D	18.	B	23.	B
4.	E	9.	D	14.	B	19.	A	24.	C
5.	B	10.	C	15.	E	20.	E	25.	C

TEST 12

1. JEAN COCTEAU : OPIUM :: ALEXANDER TROCCI : _____   1._____
   A. Richard Burton   B. Thomas De Quincey   C. heroin
   D. hashish   E. marijuana

2. STRATFORD-ON-AVON : WILLIAM SHAKESPEARE :: NEW ENGLAND : _____   2._____
   A. James Joyce   B. Mark Twain   C. Robert Frost
   D. Virginia Woolf   E. Robert Browning

3. "THE SLEEPING BEAUTY" : CHARLES PERRAULT :: JOSEPH ANDREWS :   3._____
   _____
   A. Herman Melville   B. Henry Fielding   C. Thomas Jones
   D. John Gay   E. "Moll Flanders"

4. "THIS PROPERTY IS CONDEMNED" : "THE CRUCIBLE" :: TENNESSEE   4._____
   WILLIAMS : _____
   A. Arthur Miller   B. "Cat on a Hot Tin Roof"
   C. "A View From the Bridge"   D. William Inge
   E. Arthur Laurents

5. MAXIM DE WINTER : REBECCA :: MOLL FLANDERS : _____   5._____
   A. Captain Marvel   B. Lorna Doone   C. Captain Singleton
   D. Captain Hook   E. Daniel Defoe

6. SIMONOV : "DAYS AND NIGHTS" :: SHOLOOV : _____   6._____
   A. "Bread and Wine"   B. Ehrenburg
   C. "The Thaw"   D. "A City of Night"
   E. "And Quiet Flows the Don"

7. EDITH SITWELL : EMILY DICKINSON :: WILLIAM COWPER : _____   7._____
   A. Gerard Manley Hopkins   B. "Carrion Comfort"
   C. Laurence Sterne   D. Richard Steele
   E. Marianne Moore

8. VERLAINE : RIMBAUD :: COLERIDGE : _____   8._____
   A. William Wordsworth
   B. John Evelyn
   C. Siegfried Sassoon
   D. "Chant d'Automne"
   E. "The Rime of the Ancient Mariner"

9. VOLTAIRE : PREVOST :: "THE FOX" : _____   9._____
   A. "Manon Lescaut"   B. "Candide"
   C. "Camille"   D. Jean Francois-Marie Arouet
   E. Rousseau

10. "PENGUIN ISLAND" : ANATOLE FRANCE :: "THE INSPECTOR-GENERAL" :   10.____
    ____
    A. Gogol   B. "Ghosts"   C. Gorki
    D. "Dead Souls: E. Kropotkin

11. "FOR BRUTUS IS AN HONORABLE MAN" : IRONY :: "ALL IN A HOT   11.____
    AND COPPER SKY" : ____
    A. hyperbole   B. inversión   C. Shakespeare
    D. metaphor   E. Coleridge

12. HYPERBOLE : EXAGGERATION :: IDYL : ____   12.____
    A. false God   B. "...down to a sunless sea..."
    C. imagery   D. inertia
    E. pastoral poem

13. QUINTET : FIVE-LINE STANZA :: OXYMORON : ____   13.____
    A. nonsense verse   B. paradox   C. quartet
    D. paradigm   E. antithesis

14. SPONDEE : PYRRHIC :: TWO ACCENTED SYLLABLES : ____   14.____
    A. one unaccented syllable
    B. two unaccented syllables
    C. three accented syllables
    D. one accented and one unaccented syllable
    E. one accented syllable

15. TWO SUCCESSIVE RHYMING LINES : COUPLET :: A PAUSE IN OR AT   15.____
    THE END OF A VERSE : ____
    A. caesura   B. trochee   C. metrical silence
    D. dactyl   E. anapest

16. "LYCIDAS" : CLEGY :: "O WILD WEST WIND" : ____   16.____
    A. onomatopoeia   B. Percy B. Shelley C. John Milton
    D. dactylic trimeter E. apostrophe

17. ALLUSION : REFERENCE :: CACOPHONY : ____   17.____
    A. repetition of the same consonant
    B. repetition of the same word
    C. intentional misspelling
    D. variation in meter
    E. dissonance

18. FREE VERSE : IRREGULAR RHYTHMICAL PATTERN :: ALLEGORY : ____ 18.____
    A. prolonged metaphor   B. repeated last lines
    C. grisly verse   D. blank verse
    E. repeated similes

19. PERFECT QUATRAINS : "THE RUBAIYAT" :: ODE : _____   19._____
    A. idyl   B. "Thyrsis"
    C. Dryden   D. "The Fog"
    E. "A Song for St. Cecilia's Day"

20. "STONE WALLS DO NOT A PRISON MAKE" : PARADOX :: "THERE IS   20._____
    DEATH IN THAT GLASS" : _____
    A. litotes
    B. catalexis
    C. simile
    D. "...Ask not for whom the bell tolls..."
    E. metonymy

21. SIMILE : AN EXPRESSED COMPARISON :: TERCET : _____   21._____
    A. an unexpressed comparison   B. ottava rima
    C. metaphor   D. iambic verse
    E. a three-line stanza

22. EIGHT IAMBIC PENTAMETER LINES FOLLOWED BY ONE VERSE OF   22._____
    IAMBIC HEXAMETER : SPENSERIAN STANZA :: FOUR IAMBIC
    PENTAMETER LINES WITH SKIP RHYME : _____
    A. terza rima   B. quadroon   C. "Rubaiyat" stanza
    D. ironic verse   E. synecdoche

23. SIX-LINE STANZA : SESTET :: RUN-ON LINE : _____   23._____
    A. gnomic verse   B. enjambment   C. scansion
    D. couplet   E. hyperbole

24. "O DEATH WHERE ISD THEY STING? : ST. PAUL :: "SHE WALKS IN   24._____
    BEAUTY LIKE THE NIGHT" : _____
    A. "Childe Harold"   B. Blake   C. Shelley
    D. "Don Juan"   E. Byron

25. STOKE POGES : THOMAS GRAY :: STRAWBERRY HILL : _____   25._____
    A. Sir Walter Scott   B. Lord Byron   C. Horace Walpole
    D. Thomas Carlyle   E. Oliver Goldsmith

KEY (CORRECT ANSWERS)

1	C	6.	E	11.	D	16.	E	21.	E
2.	C	7.	C	12.	E	17.	E	22.	C
3.	B	8.	C	13.	E	18.	A	23.	B
4.	A	9.	A	14.	B	19.	E	24.	E
5.	C	10.	A	15.	A	20.	E	25.	C

TEST 13

1. SUICIDE : OPHELIA :: SUFFOCATION : _____   1.____
   A. Juliet   B. Gertrude   C. Desdemona
   D. Lady Mabeth   E. Olivia

2. KING IN BATTLE : HENRY VI :: KING IN EXILE : _____   2.____
   A. King HamletqB.   B. King Lear   C. Prospero
   D. Henry V   E. Richard II

3. MOSCA : VOLPONE :: FTATATITA : _____   3.____
   A. Mary Queen of Scots   B. Voltaire
   C. Queen Elizabeth   D. "The Fox"
   E. Cleopatra

4. BLUNDERING KNIGHT WHO LEARNS WISDOM : "PARZIVAL" :: WARRIOR   4.____
   KNIGHT WHO BECOMES MAD : _____
   A. Arthur   B. "El Cid"   C. "Orlando Furioso"
   D. "The Wasps"   E. "Song of Roland"

5. MURDEROUS JEALOUSY : "OTHELLO" :: FAMILY RIVALRY : _____   5.____
   A. "The Taming of the Shrew"
   B. "The Capulets and the Montagues"
   C. "Romeo and Juliet"
   D. The Merchant of Venice"
   E. "Electra"

6. ORESTES AND HERMIONE : RACINE :: HAEMON AND ANTIGONE : _____   6.____
   A. Sophocles   B. "Andromaque"   C. Socrates
   D. Pindar   E. Aeschylus

7. THE DEFEAT OF EGYPT : "ANTONY AND CLEOPATRA" :: ROMAN   7.____
   CONSPIRACY : _____
   A. Brutus   B. "Julius Caesar"
   C. Triumvirate   D. Marcus Aurelius
   E. "Caesar and Cleopatra"

8. OBERON : KING OF THE FAIRIES :: HIPPOLYTA : _____   8.____
   A. Queen of the Amazon   B. King of the Lilliputians
   C. Queen of the Fairies   D. "A Midsummer Night's Dream"
   E. Queen of Denmark

9. KNIGHTS OF THE ROUND TABLE : "LE MORTE D'ARTHUR :: KNIGHTS OF   9.____
   THE PYRENEES : _____
   A. Rodrigo Diaz   B. "El Cantor del Mil Cid"
   C. War with the Moors   D. "Song of Roland"
   E. John of Salisbury

10. NATASHA : ;TOLSTOY :: FRANCESCA : _____ 10._____
    A. "The Divine Comedy"   B. "Dolce Stil Nuova"
    C. Chaucer   D. Boethius
    E. Dante

11. ISLAND OF SYCORAX : "THE TEMPEST" :: ISLAND OF LESBOS : _____ 11._____
    A. "Daphnis and Chloe"   B. Longus
    C. "Ode to Lesbia"   D. "Troilus and Cressida"
    E. Sappho

12. CONFESSION OF OPIUM ADDICTION : DE QUINCEY :: CONFESSION 12._____
    OF A SINFUL LIFE : _____
    A. Thomas Aquinas   B. Saint Augustine
    C. Saint Therese   D. Thomas a Kempis
    E. Saint Francis of Assissi

13. MARRIAGE : "DOLL'S HOUSE" :: CHRISTIANITY : _____ 13._____
    A. "Utopia"   B. Sir Thomas More
    C. Gargantua and Pantagruel D. Ibsen
    E. "Hedda Gabler"

14. DEATH BY POISON : "HAMLET" :: DEATH THROUGH GRIEF : _____ 14._____
    A. "Richard II"   B. "King Lear"
    C. "Henry V"   D. "History of King Richard III"
    E. Shakespeare

15. CRISIS AT CAPE HORN : "TWO YEARS BEFORE THE MAST" :: MUTINOUS 15._____
    CRISIS AT SEA : _____
    A. "Pitcairn Island"   B. "Typee"   C. Melville
    D. "Moby Dick"   E. Captain Bligh

16. THE ALBATROSS : "ANCIENT MARINER" :: THE WHALE : _____ 16._____
    A. Coleridge   B. "Moby Dick"   C. Melville
    D. "Silas Marner"   E. "Omoo"

17. VOYAGE TO INDIA : "THE LUSIAD" :: VOYAGE TO THE SOUTH SEAS : _____ 17._____
    A. Camoens   B. "Pioneers"   C. "Typee"
    D. Captain Ahab   E. Vasco da Gama

18. SHIPWRECK AT ILLYRIA : "TWELFTH NIGHT" :: SHIPWRECK AT 18._____
    OGYGIA : _____
    A. Ulysses   B. "Aeneid"
    C. "Iliad"   D. "Mutiny on the Bounty"
    E. "Odyssey"

19. "MOON AND SIXPENCE" : GAUGUIN :: "MURDER IN THE CATHEDRAL : 19._____

    A. T.S. Eliot   B. Thomas Aquinas   C. Thomas a Kempis
    D. Somerset Maugham   E. Thomas a Becket

20. THE DEVIL TESTS A MAM'S INTEGRITY : "FAUST" :: THE DEVIL IS   20.____
    DISGUISED AS A YEOMAN : ____
    A. Goethe   B. "Don Juan in Hell"   C. Dante
    D. "Canterbury Tales"   E. Chaucer

21. A WOMAN'S SUICIDE : "ANNA KARENINA" :: A STUDENT'S MURDER :   21.____
    ____
    A. Dostoevski   B. "War and Peace"
    C. Raskolnikov   D. "The Brothers Karamazov"
    E. "Crime and Punishment"

22. DRAMA OF STALIN : "THE PATH TO VICTORY" :: DRAMA OF NAPOLEON :   22.____
    ____
    A. Shaw   B. "The French Revolution"
    C. "Man of Destiny"   D. Tolstoi
    E. Sardou

23. AUTOBIOGRAPHY OF A STATESMAN : BENJAMIN FRANKLIN ::   23.____
    AUTOBIOGRAPHY OF A NOVELIST : ____
    A. Hemingway   B. Fitzgerald   C. Stein
    D. Virginia Woolf   E. Thomas Wolfe

24. CHRISTMAS CELEBRATED IN LONDON : DICKENS :: CHRISTMAS   24.____
    CELEBRATED IN WALES : ____
    A. Bernard Shaw   B. "A Christmas Carol"
    C. James Joyce   D. Dylan Thomas
    E. "A Child's Christmas in Wales"

25. LIFE IN NORTH CAROLINA : THOMAS WOLFE :: LIFE IN MISSISSIPPI : ____ 25.____
    A. Mark Twain   B. William Faulkner
    C. "Life on the Mississippi"   D. John Steinbeck
    E. John Dos Passos

KEY (CORRECT ANSWERS)

1	C	6.	A	11.	A	16.	B	21.	E
2.	C	7.	B	12.	B	17.	C	22.	C
3.	E	8.	A	13.	A	18.	E	23.	C
4.	C	9.	D	14.	B	19.	E	24.	D
5.	C	10.	E	15.	A	20.	D	25.	B

TESTS IN VERBAL ANALOGIES - MATHEMATICS

DIRECTIONS: Each question in this part consists of two capitalized words which have a certain relationship to each other, and a third capitalized word which is followed by five lettered words in small letters. Choose the number of the word which is related in the SAME way to the third capitalized word as the first two capitalized words are related to each other. *PRINT THE LETTER OF THE CORRECT ANSWER IN THE SPACE AT THE RIGHT.*

TEST 1

1. CENTER OF DISTRIBUTION : SPREAD OF DISTRIBUTION :: MEAN : _____   1._____
    A. average   B. standard score   C. normal distribution
    D. standard deviation   E. mode

2. STRAIGHT LINE : FIRST DEGREE EQUATION :: PARABOLA : _____   2._____
    A. second degree equation   B. circle
    C. third degree equation   D. linear equation
    E. hyperbola

3. CUBE : SQUARE :: _____ : CIRCLE   3._____
    A. rectangle   B. ellipse   C. cone
    D. sphere   E. cylinder

4. RECTANGLE : _____ :: ELLIPSE : CIRCLE   4._____
    A. rhombus   B. triangle   C. square
    D. trapezoid   E. cube

5. VOLUME : CUBIC UNITS :: _____ : SQUARE UNITS   5._____
    A. length   B. weight   C. height   D. area   E. width

6. CONE : CYLINDER :: PYRAMID : _____   6._____
    A. prism   B. sphere   C. cube   D. ellipse   E. circle

7. SINE : _____ :: TANGENT : COTANGENT   7._____
    A. secant   B. cosine   C. chord   D. altitude   E. radius

8. ADDITION : O :: MULTIPLICATION : _____   8._____
    A. 2   B. 2   C. 0   D. 3   E. 10

9. SUBTRACTION : ADDITION :: _____ : MULTIPLICATION   9._____
    A. square root   B. inversion   C. division
    D. involution   E. evolution

10. TRIANGLE : EQUILATERAL :: QUADRILATERAL : _____   10.____
    A. square   B. rectangle   C. isosceles
    D. circle   E. right triangle

11. TRIANGLE : EQUILATERAL :: QUADRILATERAL : _____   11.____
    A. 540°   B. 90°   C. 60°   D. 120°   E. 180°
12. HEXAGON : 6 :: _____ : 5   12.____
    A. decagon   B. quadrilateral   C. pentagon
    D. square   E. octagon

13. CIRCLE : ELLIPSE :: _____ : ELLIPSOID   13.____
    A. sphere   B. cube   C. rectangle
    D. cone   E. cylinder

14. 2 : 3 :: 5 : _____   14.____
    A. 6   B. 8   C. 7½   D. 9½   E. 8½

15. MULTIPLICATION : _____ :: ADDITION : SUM   15.____
    A. quotient   B. product   C. remainder
    D. difference   E. factor

16. DIVIDEND : DIVISOR :: _____ : SUBTRAHEND   16.____
    A. addend   B. sum   C. factor
    D. quotient   E. minuend

17. QUADRATIC : _____ :: SECOND DEGREE : FIRST DEGREE   17.____
    A. cubic   B. quartic   C. linear
    D. conditional   E. quintic

18. PARALLELOGRAM : RECTANGLE :: _____ : SQUARE   18.____
    A. rhombus   B. triangle   C. circle
    D. quadrilateral   E. trapezoid

19. CYLINDER : RECTANGLE :: _____ : CIRCULAR SECTOR   19.____
    A. cube   B. sphere   C. cone   D. square   E. triangle

20. CONGRUENCE :; EQUALITY :: SIMILARITY : _____   20.____
    A. inequality   B. proportionality   C. ratio
    D. equivalence   E. partition

21. SQUARE : SQUARE ROOT :: _____ : SUBTRACTION   21.____
    A. multiplication   B. division   C. addition
    D. cube root   E. exponent

22. 6x : 10x :: _____ : 15   22.____
    A. 10x   B. 9x   C. 9   D. 12   E. 12x

244

23. CUBE : TETRAHEDRON :: SQUARE : _____   23. ____
    A. quadrilateral   B. triangle   C. parallelogram
    D. rectangle   E. sphere

24. MULTIPLICATION : _____ :: ADDITION : INVERSE   24. ____
    A. reciprocal   B. identity   C. opposite
    D. product   E factpr

25. SQUARE ROOT : SQUARE YARD :: 1 : _____   25. ____
    A. 3   B. 6   C. 9   D. 12   E. 27

KEY (CORRECT ANSWERS)

1	D	6.	A	11.	E	16.	E	21.	C
2.	A	7.	B	12.	C	17.	C	22.	C
3.	D	8.	B	13.	A	18.	A	23.	B
4.	C	9.	C	14.	C	19.	C	24.	A
5.	D	10.	A	15.	B	20.	B	25.	C

TEST 2

1. CIRCUMFERENCE : _____ :: _____ : 1
   A. radius   B. diameter   C. area   D. chord   E. tangent   1._____

2. CUBIC FOOT : CUBIC YARD :: 1 : _____
   A. 3   B. 6   C. 9   D. 12   E. 27   2._____

3. REGULAR POLYGON : _____ :: CIRCLE : CIRCUMFERENCE
   A. area   B. perimeter   C. radius
   D. apothem   E. diameter   3._____

4. SINE : OPPOSITE LEG :: _____ : ADJACENT LEG
   A. tangent   B. cotangent   C. secant
   D. cosecant   E. cosine   4._____

5. PLANE : LINE :: SPHERE : _____
   A. circle   B. square   C ellipse
   D. rectangle   E. cylinder   5._____

6. _____ : SQUARE OF RADIUS :: π : 1
   A. circumference   B. diameter   C. perimeter
   D. area   E. volume   6._____

7. HYPERBOLA : _____ :: ELLIPSE : SUM
   A. product   B. quotient   C. remainder
   D. factor   E. difference   7._____

8. SLOPE : _____ :: DIRECTION : ANGLE
   A. inclination   B. tangent   C. cosine
   D. right angle   E. depression   8._____

9. REGULAR POLYGON : POLYGON :: _____ QUADRILATERAL
   A. rectangle   B. square   C. rhombus
   D. parallelogram   E. pentagon   9._____

10. VOLUME : _____ :: WEIGHT : POUNDS
    A. inches   B. square feet   C. gallons
    D. ounces   E. yards   10._____

11. VOLUME : QUART :: AREA : _____
    A. foot   B. cubic inch   C. ouce
    D. acre   E. liter   11._____

12. CENTIMETER : _____ :: INCH : GALLON
    A. liter   B. foot   C. quart   D. hectare   E. ounce   12._____

13. ROD : ACRE :: _____ : HECTARE
    A. liter   B. quart   C. meter   D. ounce   E. knot   13._____

14. KNOT : _____ :: POUND : WEIGHT
    A. length   B. speed   C. volume   D. height   E. distance

15. GRAM : WEIGHT :: LIGHT YEAR : _____
    A. time   B. speed   C. density   D. distance   E. height

16. POSITIVE EXPONENT : LARGE NUMBER :: _____ : SMALL NUMBER
    A. power   B. negative exponent   C. zero exponent
    D. fractional exponent   E. logarithm

17. MEDIAN : MID-POINT :: ALTITUDE : _____
    A. side   B. right angle   C. acute angle
    D. angle-bisector   E. vertex

18. VERTEX : POINT :: EDGE : _____
    A. line   B. side   C. curve   D. square   E. face

19. FRACTION : WHOLE NUMBER :: _____ : INTEGER
    A. real number   B. complex number   C. rational number
    D. irrational number   E. digit

20. ARITHMETIC SERIES : DIFFERENCE :: GEOMETRIC SERIES : _____
    A. sum   B. product   C. ratio
    D. factory   E. remainder

21. INSCRIBED ANGLE : CENTRAL ANGLE :: _____ : 1
    A. 2   B. ½   C. 1   D. ¼   E. 3

22. REGULAR : POLYGON :: _____ : TRIANGLE
    A. isosceles   B. scalene   C. right
    D. equilateral   E. obtuse

23. SUPPLEMENT : _____ :: STRAIGHT ANGLE : RIGHT ANGLE
    A. interior angle   B. vertical angle   C. complement
    D. corresponding   E. external

24. SQUARE : RIGHT ANGLE :: EQUILATERAL TRIANGLE : _____
    A. 30° angle   B. 60° angle   C. straight angle
    D. acute angle   E. obtuse angle

25. EVEN NUMBER : ODD NUMBER :: 2N : _____
    A. n   B. n+1   C. 2n+2   D. n+2   E. 2n+1

14._____

15._____

16._____

17._____

18._____

19._____

20._____

21._____

22._____

23._____

24._____

25._____

KEY (CORRECT ANSWERS)

1	B	6.	D	11.	D	16.	B	21.	B
2.	E	7.	E	12.	A	17.	B	22.	D
3.	B	8.	A	13.	C	18.	A	23.	C
4.	E	9.	B	14.	B	19.	C	24.	B
5.	A	10.	C	15.	D	20.	C	25.	E

TESTS IN VERBAL ANALOGIES - SCIENCE

DIRECTIONS: Each question in this part consists of two capitalized words which have a certain relationship to each other, and a third capitalized word which is followed by five lettered words in small letters. Choose the number of the word which is related in the SAME way to the third capitalized word as the first two capitalized words are related to each other. *PRINT THE LETTER OF THE CORRECT ANSWER IN THE SPACE AT THE RIGHT.*

TEST 1

1. ACID : HYDRONIUM ION :: BASE : _____   1.____
   A. hydrogen ion   B. hydrogen gas   C. sodium ion
   D. hydroxide ion   E. water

2. SINGLE BOND : ALKANE :: TRIPLE BOND : _____   2.____
   A. alkene   B. alkyne   C. aryl   D. alkyl   E. aromatic

3. DECOMPOSITION : ANALYSIS :: COMBINATION : _____   3.____
   A. single replacement   B. double replacement   C. metathesis
   D. synthesis   E. hydrolysis

4. AMALGAM : MERCURY :: BRASS : _____   4.____
   A. silver   B. copper   C. gold   D. tin   E. lead

5. BASIC ANHYDRIDE : CaO :: ACIDIC ANHYDRIDE : _____   5.____
   A. MgO   B. Na_2O`   C. HCl   D. SO_2 E. H_2O_2

6. ELECTRON : BETA PARTICLE :: _____ : ALPHA PARTICLE   6.____
   A. proton   B. neutron   C. helium ion
   D. hydrogen ion   E. gamma ray

7. BESSEMER CONVERTER : STEEL :: BLAST FURNACE : _____   7.____
   A. alloy   B. zinc   C. spiegeleisen
   D. iron   E. aluminum

8. CARBOXYL GROUP : ACID :: HYDROXYL GROUP : _____   8.____
   A. aldehyde   B. ester   C. hydrocarbon
   D. ether   E. alcohol

9. IRON : HABER PROCESS :: _____ : CONTACT PROCESS   9.____
   A. manganese dioxide   B. platinum   C. aluminum oxide
   D. sulfur   E. sulfuric acid

10. COKE : BITUMINOUS COAL :: _____ : WOOD
    A. boneblack   B. carbon black   C. lampblack
    D. charcoal   E. graphite

10.____

11. 100°C : 0°C :: 373°K : _____°K
    A. 100   B. 0   C. 273   D. 20   E. 212

11.____

12. COLLOIDAL SUSPENSION : TWO PHASE :: SOLUTION : _____
    A. 1 phase   B. 2 phase   C. 3 phase
    D. no phase   E. more than 3 phase

12.____

13. CONDENSATION : VAPOR :: _____ : LIQUID
    A. sublimation   B. evaporation   C. solidification
    D. coagulation   E. sedimentation

13.____

14. SEDIMENTATION : SUSPENDED SOLIDS :: FILTRATION : _____
    A. suspended solids   B. dissolved solids   C. microorganisms
    D. dissolved gases   E. colloids

14.____

15. BORON STEEL : CONTROL ROD :: GRAPHITE : _____
    A. moderator   B. heat exchanger   C. fuel element
    D. radiation shield   E. fission

15.____

16. FISSION : URANIUM ISOTOPE :: FUSION : _____
    A. hydrogen isotope   B. radium isotope   C. cobalt-60
    D. uranium isotope   E. lead isotope

16.____

17. COVALENCE : ELECTRON SHARING :: ELELCTROVALENCE : _____
    A. proton transfer   B. neutrón sharing   C. proton sharing
    D. electron transfer E. alpha emission

17.____

18. BETATRON : ELECTRONS :: CYCLOTRON : _____
    A. protons   B. neutrons   C. electrons
    D. gamma rays   E. cyclopropane

18.____

19. EFFLORESCENCE : WASHING SODA :: DELIQUESCENCE : _____
    A. baking soda   B. sal soda   C. table salt
    D. caustic soda   E. sodium carbonate

19.____

20. EXOTHERMIC : HEAT LIBERATION :: _____ : HEAT ABSORPTION
    A. isothermic   B. diathermic   C. endothermic
    D. adiabatic   E. kinetic

20.____

21. ELECTROLYTE : NaCl :: NONELECFTROLYTE : _____
    A. NaOH   B. HCl   C. KNO_3 D. HNO_3 E. CH_3OH

21.____

22. GRAM : MASS :: _____ : VOLUME
    A. pound   B. meter   C. liter   D. dyne   E. newton

22.____

23. $CH_4 : C_nH_{2n+2} :: C_2H_4 :$ _____   23.____
   A. C_NH_n B. C_nH_{2n} C. C_nH_{2n-2} D. C_nH_{2n-6} E. C_nH_{4n}

24. HYDROCARBON : C_6H_{14} :: CARBOHYDRATE : _____   24.____
   A. CH_3CHO B. $C_{12}H_{22}O_{11}$ C. C_6H_{12}
   D. $C_6H_{13}COOH$ E. $(C_2H_5)_2O$

25. OXIDATION : $Cl^- - e \rightarrow Cl$ :: REDUCTION : _____   25.____
   A. $Na \rightarrow Na^+ + e$ B. $H^+ + OH^- \rightarrow H_2O$ C. $Fe^{++} - e \rightarrow Fe^{+++}$
   D. $Cu^{++} + 2e \rightarrow Cu$ E. $_{90}Th^{234} \rightarrow _{91}Pa^{234} + e$

———————

KEY (CORRECT ANSWERS)

1	D	6.	C	11.	C	16.	A	21.	E
2.	B	7.	D	12.	A	17.	D	22.	C
3.	D	8.	E	13.	C	18.	A	23.	B
4.	B	9.	B	14.	A	19.	D	24.	B
5.	D	10.	D	15.	A	20.	C	25.	D

———————

TEST 2

1. ALLOTROPE : ISOTOPE :: DIAMOND : _____
   A. carbón-14   B. graphite   C. boneblack
   D. coke   E. charcoal
   1._____

2. PERMANENT HARD WATER : $CaSO_4$ :: TEMPORARY HARD WATER : _____
   A. $CaCO_3$ B. $MgCl_2$ C. $Mg(HCO_3)_2$
   D. $MgSO_4$ E. $CaCl_2$
   2._____

3. MONOMER : SIMPLE MOLECULE :: COMBINATION OF SIMPLE
   MOLECULES : _____
   A. isomer   B. monosaccharide   C. polymer
   D. isotope   E. vapor
   3._____

4. ALUMINUM : BAUXITE :: IRON : _____
   A. galena   B. chalcocite   C. cassiterite
   D. cryolite   E. hermatite
   4._____

5. SLAG : FLUX :: _____ : CaO
   A. $CaCO_3$ B. SiO_2 C. $CaSiO_3$ D. Fe_3O_4 E. CO
   5._____

6. CHLORIC ACID : CHLORATE :: _____ : CHLORITE
   A. hydrochloric acid   B. hypochlorous acid   C. perchloric acid
   D. chlorous acid   E. binary acid
   6._____

7. CH4 : CH_3OH :: C_4H_{10} : _____
   A. C_4H_9OH B. C_4H_8 C. C_4H_9O
   D. $C_4H_{10}OH$ E. C_3H_7COOH
   7._____

8. H^+ + OH → : NEUTRALIZATION :: H_3O^+ + OH^- : _____ : _____
   A. hydrolysis   B. hydrogentation   C. esterification
   D. neutralization   E. fermentation
   8._____

9. FLUORINE : NONMETALLIC ACTIVITY :: _____ : METALLIC
   A. lithium   B. sodium   C. potassium
   D. rubidium   E. cesium
   9._____

10. MATTER : MOLECULES :: _____ : ATOMS
    A. neutrons   B. protons   C. electrons
    D. energy   E. molecules
    10._____

11. SOLID : DEFINITE SHAPE AND DEFINITE VOLUME :: _____ :
    INDEFINITE SHAPE AND INDEFINITE VOLUME
    A. crystal   B. gas   C. liquid   D. fluid   E. weight
    11._____

12. CGS SYSTEM : MKS SYSTEM :: GRAM : _____
    A. meter   B. second   C. kilogram
    D. pound   E. centimeter
    12._____

13. FORCE : PRESSURE :: POUNDS : _____   13.____
    A. pounds/square inch   B. pounds/cubic foot
    C. grams/cubic centimeter D. square feet
    E. square feet/pound

14. (TWO FORCES, A (40 LBS) AND B (60 LBS), ACT ON THE SAME POINT   14.____
    IN THE SAME DIRECTION) RESULTANT : FORCE :: _____LBS. :
    40 LBS.
    A. 20   B. 40   C. 60   D. 80   E. 100

15. THE WEIGHT OF AN OBJECT ON AN INCLINED PLANE : FORCE   15.____
    TENDING TO PULL THE OBJECT DOWN THE PLANE :: _____ :
    HEIGHT OF PLANE
    A. base of plane
    B. height of plane
    C. length of plane
    D. coefficient of friction of plane
    E. material of which plane is composed

16. 540   CAL/G : BOILING :: _____ : MELTING   16.____
    A. 20 cal/g   B. 80 cal/g   C. 100 cal/g
    D. 720 cal/g   E. 1 cal/g

17. ISOCLINIC LINE : EQUAL DIP :: ISOGONIC LINE : _____   17.____
    A. zero dip   B. equal magnetic declination
    C. equal magnetic inclination   D. maximum dip
    E. aclinic line

18. SLIP RINGS : AC GENERATOR :: _____ : DC GENERATOR   18.____
    A. armature   B. motor   C. magneto
    D. commutator   E. brushes

19. FARAD : CAPACITANCE :: _____ : MUTUAL INDUCTANCE   19.____
    A. ampere   B. volt   C henry   D. ohm   E. watt

20. CANDLE : UNIT OF LIGHT INTENSITY :: UNIT OF SOUND : INTENSITY   20.____
    A. candlepower   B. lumen   C. foot-candle
    D. decibel   E. mach

21. $1,000,000 : 1 \times 10^6 :: 0.0001 :$ _____   21.____
    A. 1×10^4 B. 1×10^3 C. 1×10^{-4} D. 1×10^{-3} E. 1/1000

22. SPEED : RATE OF MOTION :: _____ : RATE OF DISPLACEMENT   22.____
    A. acceleration   B. velocity   C. average speed
    D. momentum   E. distance traveled
                               elapsed time

23. (FOR A FREELY FALLING BODY) 16 FT. : 1 SECONDE :: _____ : 3 SECONDS   23.____
    A. 16 ft.   B. 32 ft.   C. 48 ft.   D. 64 ft.   E. 144 ft.

253

24. MA : MG :: FORCE : _____   24.____
    A. acceleration   B. momentum   C. weight
    D. velocity   E. impulse

25. IMPULSE : FORCE × TIME :: MOMENTUM : _____   25.____
    A. acceleration × time   B. velocity × time   C. velocity × distance
    D. distance × time   E. velocity × mass

KEY (CORRECT ANSWERS)

1	A	6.	D	11.	B	16.	B	21.	C
2.	C	7.	A	12.	C	17.	B	22.	B
3.	C	8.	D	13.	A	18.	D	23.	E
4.	E	9.	E	14.	E	19.	C	24.	C
5.	C	10.	E	15.	C	20.	D	25.	E

TEST 3

1. WEIGHT OF 144 LB. : EARTH'S SURFACE :: _____ LB. : 4000 MILES   1.____
   ABOVE EARTH'S SURFACE
      A. 144   B. 108   C. 72   D. 36   E. 0

2. CENTRIPETAL FORCE : MASS OF A BODY :: _____ : RADIUS OF PATH   2.____
   OF BODY
      A. weight   B. velocity   C. velocity^2
      D. time   E. momentum

3. (A SHORT PENDULUM IS 25 CENTIMETERS LONG AND A LONGER   3.____
   PENDULUM IS 100 CENTIMETERS LONG.) THE PERIOD OF THE SHORT
   PENDULUM : THE PERIOD OF THE LONG PENDULUM :: 1 :_____
      A. 1   B. 2   C. 3   D. 4   4. 5

4. POWER : FORCE :: DISTANCE : _____   4.____
      A. efficiency   B. time
      C. ideal mechanical advantage   D. actual mechanical advantage
      E. friction

5. KINETIC ENERGY : MASS :: _____ : 2   5.____
      A. height   B. acceleration of gravity
      C. velocity   D. velocity^2
      E. weight

6. ACTUAL MECHANICAL ADVANTAGE : IDEAL MECHANICL ADVANTAGE ::   6.____
   WORK OUTPUT : _____
      A. efficiency   B. work input
      C. work used in overcoming friction   D. ideal effort
      E. actual effort

7. (FOR A SINGLE FIXED PULLEY) THE IDEAL MECHANICAL ADVANTAGE :   7.____
   1 :: ACTUAL MECHANICAL ADVANTAGE : _____
      A. 0   B. 1
      C. less than 1 but not zero   D. 1.5
      E. 2

8. (A SAFE IS PULLED UP AN INCLINED PLANE WHICH IS 20 FT. LONG   8.____
   AND 4 FT. HIGH BY MEANS OF A PULLEY SYSTEM HAVING AN IDEAL
   MECHANICAL ADVANTAGE OF 5.) THE IDEAL MECHANICAL ADVANTAGE OF
   THE COMBINATION OF MACHINES : IDEAL MECHANICAL ADVANTAGE OF
   THE PULLEY SYSTEM :: _____ : 5
      A. 100   B. 50   C. 25   D. 20   E. 10

9. ELEMENT : NUMBER OF ELECTRONS :: ISOTOPE OF THE ELEMENT : _____   9.____
    A. a different number of electrons   B. a different number of protons
    C. a different number of neutrons   D. the same number of neutrons
    E. a different atomic number

10. ATOMIC NUMBER OF AN ATOM : NUMBER OF PROTONS :: MASS NUMBER   10.____
    OF THE ATOM : _____
    A. sum of number of protons and number of neutrons
    B. difference between number of protons and number of neutrons
    C. sum of number of protons and number of electrons
    D. difference between number of protons and number of electrons
    D. difference between number of neutrons and number of electrons

11. COHESION : LIKE MOLECULES :: _____ : UNLIKE MOLECULES   11.____
    A. cohesion   B. adhesion   C. diffusion
    D. porosity   E. regelation

12. THE ELASTIC MODULES OF A MATERIAL : APPLIED STRESS :: THE   12.____
    ORIGINAL LENGTH OF THE MATERIAL : _____
    A. the original length of the material
    B. the strain
    C. the strain × the original length of material
    D. the weight of the material
    E. the strain × the cross-sectional area of the material

13. (IDEALLY FOR A HYDRAULIC PRESS) THE DISTANCE THE EFFORT   13.____
    PISTON MOVES : THE DISTANCE THE RESISTANCE PISTON MOVES ::
    _____ : AREA OF THE EFFORT PISTON
    A. the square of the radius of the effort piston
    B. the square of the diameter of the effort piston
    C. the square of the radius of the resistance piston
    D. the square of the diameter of the resistance piston
    E. the area of the resistance piston

14. THE DENSITY OF A SUBSTANCE : DENSITY OF WATER :: WEIGHT OF THE   14.____
    SUBSTANCE : _____
    A. the weight of an equal volume of water
    B. the specific gravity of water
    C. the weight of an equal volume of air
    D. the volume of the substance
    E. the amount of water present

15. OLD VOLUME OF A MASS OF GAS : NEW VOLUME OF THE GAS : OLD   15.____
    PRESSURE ON THE GAS : _____
    A. new pressure on the gas
    B. old temperature of the gas
    C. the reciprocal of the new pressure on the gas
    D. new temperature of the gas
    E. old density of the gas

16. (DENSITY OF A GAS) 1.50 G/LITER : 760 MM$_{HG}$ :: 1.4 G/LITER : _____ MM$_{HG}$

    A. 760   B. 730   C. 700   D. 150   E. 144

16.____

17. ONE CENTIGRADE DEGREE : ONE KELVIN DEGREE :: _____ : 1

    A. 1   B. 1.8   C. 273   D. 1/273   E. 32

17.____

18. 20°C : 68°F :: _____°C :; 77°F

    A. 21.8   B. 25   C. 36   D. 29   E. 88

18.____

19. 778 FT-LB : BTU :: _____ ERGS : CAL.

    A. 252   B. 4.19   C. 4.19×10^{-7}D. 0.024   E. 540

19.____

20. (FOR MAXIMUM RESONANCE WITH A GIVEN TUNING FORK) THE LENGTH OF AN OPEN TUBE : THE LENGTH OF A CLOSED TUBE :: _____ : 1

    A. 5   B. 4   C. 3   D. 23   E. 1

20.____

21. SPEED OF SOUND AT 0°C : 1090 FT/SEC :: SPEED OF SOUND AT _____°C : 1140 FT/SEC

    A. 5   B. 10   C. 20   D. 25   E. 50

21.____

22. (THE FREQUENCY OF A VIOLIN STRING, 30 CM. LONG, IS 288 CYCLES PER SECOND) 288 CYCLES PER SECOND : 30 CM :: 320 CYCLES PER SECOND : _____ CM.

    A. 27   B. 30   C. 33   D. 36   E. 39

22.____

23. (A LAMP OF UNKNOWN INTENSITY PROVIDES THE SAME ILLUMINATION OF A PHOTOMETER AT A DISTANCE OF 80 CENTIMETERS THAT THE STANDARD LAMP OF 20 CANDLES PROVIDES AT 20 CENTIMETERS.) INTENSITY OF UNKNOWN LAMP : INTENSITY OF KNOWN LAMP :: _____ : 1

    A. 2   B. 4   C. 8   D. 16   E. 32

23.____

24. (THE INDEX OF REFRACTION OF ORDINARY GLASS IS 1.5.) SINE OF THE ANGLE OF INCIDENCE : SINE OF THE ANGLE OF REFRACTION :: 186,000 MILES PER SECOND : _____ MILES PER SECOND.

    A. 186,000   B. 140,000   C. 279,000

    D. 124,000   E. 100,000

24.____

25. RESPIRATION : PHOTOSYNTHESIS :: CARBON DIOXIDE : _____

    A. water   B. starch   C. carbon dioxide

    D. oxygen   E. sugar

25.____

KEY (CORRECT ANSWERS)

1	D	6.	B	11.	B	16.	B	21.	D
2.	C	7.	C	12.	C	17.	A	22.	A
3.	B	8.	C	13.	E	18.	B	23.	D
4.	B	9.	C	14.	A	19.	C	24.	D
5.	D	10.	A	15.	C	20.	D	25.	D

TEST 4

1. ALBUMEN : EGG WHITE :: _____ : MILK   1.____
   A. glycogen   B. casein   C. gluten
   D. amine acids   E. myosin

2. VITAMIN A : NIGHT BLINDNESS :: VITAMIN D : _____   2.____
   A. pellagra   B. rickets   C. scurvy
   D. beri-beri   E. hemorrhages

3. PROTOPLASM : CELLS :: _____ : TISSUES   3.____
   A. cells   B. organs   C. systems
   D. organisms   E. species

4. TAPEWORM : PARASITE :: FUNGI : _____   4.____
   A. saprophyte   B. symbiosis   C. commensalism
   D. enzyme   E. catalyst

5. CARBOHYDRATES : GLUCOSE :: PROTEINS : _____   5.____
   A. fatty acids   B. glycerine   C. fructose
   D. amino acids   E. proteoses

6. PTYALIN : SALIVA :: _____ : GASTRIC JUICE   6.____
   A. secretin   B. amylopsin   C. trypsin
   D. steapsin   E. pepsin

7. NITROGEN-FIXING BACTERIA : NITRATES :: NITRIFYING BACTERIA :   7.____
   _____
   A. nitrogen   B. ammonia   C. nitrites
   D. proteins   E. starch

8. KATYDID : CAMOUFLAGE :: VICEROY BUTTERFLY : _____   8.____
   A. protective coloration B. countershading C. mimicry
   D. polyploidy   E. metamorphosis

9. ONE-CELLED ANIMALS : PROTOZOA :: FLATWORMS : _____   9.____
   A. porifera   B. coelenterata   C. platyhelminthes
   D. nemathelminthes   E. mollusca

10. SEED PLANTS : SPERMATOPHYTA :: ALGAE : _____   10.____
    A. spermatophyta   C. thallophyta   C. bryophyta
    D. pteridophyta   E. eumycophyta

11. PNEUMONIA : COCCUS :: TETANUS : _____   11.____
    A. diplococcus   B. bacillus   C. spirillum
    D. virus   E. spirochete

12. BREAD MOLD : FUNGI :: MUSHROOM : _____   12.____
    A. fungi   B. algae   C. bacteria
    D. bryophyta   E. pteridophyta

13. MAPLE : DICOT :: GINKGO : _____   13.____
    A. moncot   B. dicot   C. conifer
    D. angiosperm   E. gymnosperm

14. PHLOEM : DOWNWARD TRAVEL :: _____ UPWARD TRAVEL   14.____
    A. cambium   B. xylem   C. cortex
    D. periderm   E. pericycle

15. GEOTROPISM : RESPONSE TO GRAVITY :: _____ : RESPONSE TO TOUCH   15.____
    A. chemotropism   B. hydrotropism   C. phototropism
    D. thermotropism   E. thigmotropism

16. OSMOTIC PRESSURE : CELL TURGOR :: _____ : LOSS OF CELL TURGOR   16.____
    A. plasmolysis   B. imbibition   C. guttation
    D. selective absorption   E. translocation

17. STOMATA : LEAF :: _____ : STEM   17.____
    A. tendril   B. bud   C. lenticel
    D. rhizome   E. vein

18. POLLEN : STAMEN :: _____ : PISTIL   18.____
    A. stigma   B. anther   C. style   D. ovary   E. ovule

19. PLUMULE : LEAF :: _____ : STEM   19.____
    A. cotyledon   B. endosperm   C. hypocotyl
    D. testa   E. micropyle

20. PSEUDOPODIA : AMEBA :: _____ : PARAMECIUM   20.____
    A. celia   B. trichocyst   C. oral groove
    D. contractile vacuole   E. micronucleus

21. FLEA : BUBONIC PLAGUE :: ANOPHELES MOSQUITO : _____   21.____
    A. malaria   B. yellow fever   C. typhoid fever
    D. typhus fever   E. tuberculosis

22. TWO-CHAMBERED HEART : FISH :: THREE-CHAMBERED HEART : _____   22.____
    A. reptiles   B. birds   C. amphibia
    D. mammals   E. vertebrates

23. CEREBRUM : THOUGHT PROCESSES :: _____ : COORDINATION OF   23.____
    MUSCULAR ACTIVITIES
    A. medulla oblongata B. pons   C. gangion
    D. cerebellum   E. cortex

24. CRETINISM : THYROID :: ACROMEGALY : _____   24.____
    A. adrenal   B. thyroid
    C. parathyroid   D. Islands of Langerhans
    E. pituitary

25. MUTATION PRINCIPLES : MORGAN :: RADIATION GENETICS : _____   25.____
    A. Darwin   B. DeVries   C. Weismann
    D. Lamarck   E. Muller

KEY (CORRECT ANSWERS)

1	B	6.	E	11.	B	16.	A	21.	A
2.	B	7.	C	12.	A	17.	C	22.	C
3.	A	8.	C	13.	E	18.	E	23.	D
4.	A	9.	C	14.	B	19.	C	24.	E
5.	D	10.	B	15.	E	20.	A	25.	E

TEST 5

1. HEREDITY : EUGENICS :: ENVIRONMENT : _____   1.____
    A. eustachian   B. euthenics   C. Euglenas
    D. euthanasia   E. eutectoids

2. HAPLOID NUMBER : REDUCTION DIVISION :: DIPLOID NUMBER : _____   2.____
    A. mitosis   B. oogenesis   C. gametogénesis
    D. polar bodies   E. spermatogenesis

3. HEMOGLOBIN : RED BLOOD CELLS :: _____ : CHLOROPLASTS :   3.____
    A. lenticels   B. mcropyle   C. indophenol
    D. chlorophyll   E. chromosome

4. RETINA : EYE :: _____ : EAR   4.____
    A. tympanum   B. pinna   C. Eustachian tube
    D. cochlea   E. semi-circular canal

5. TUBULES : KIDNEY :: _____ : LUNG   5.____
    A. alveoli   B. auricle   C. glottis
    D. gall bladder   E. aorta

6. MAGGOT : FLY :: _____ : MOSQUITO   6.____
    A. pupa   B. chrysalis   C. wiggler
    D. egg   E. cocoon

7. SEPALS : CALYX :: _____ : COROLLA   7.____
    A. pistil   B. stamens   C. pollen grains
    D. petals   E. stigma

8. BRONCHI : LUNGS :: _____ : STOMACH   8.____
    A. trachea   B. epiglottis   C. duodenum
    D. larynx   E. esophagus

9. SEDIMENTARY : LIMESTONE :: _____ : MARBLLE   9.____
    A. igneous   B. strata   C. metamorphic
    D. weathering   E. fossil

10. WATT : POWER :: OHM : _____   10.____
    A. work   B. current   C. resistance
    D. potential   E. electricity

11. ELEMENT : COMPOUND :: ATOM : _____   11.____
    A. molecule   B. electron   C. isomer
    D. mixture   E. isotope

12. COTYLEDON : BEAN SEAD :: YOLK : _____   12.____
    A. endosperm   B. epicotyl   C. testa
    D. hypocotyl   E. egg

13. PTYALIN : SALIVA :: RENNIN : _____   13.____
    A. bile   B. gastric juice   C. intestinal juice
    D. pancreatic juice   E. substrates

14. CELLS : TISSUES :: ORGANS : _____   14.____
    A. ectoderm   B. endoderm   C. enzymes
    D. systems   E. carbohydrates

15. _____ : ANIMAL :: DIASTASE : PLANT   15.____
    A. adrenin   B. pepsin   C. ptyalin
    D. thyroxin   E. fats

16. STRIATED MUSCLE : THIGH :: UNSTRIATED MUSCLE : _____   16.____
    A. arm   B. finger   C. foot
    D. nose   E. stomach

17. RUNNERS : STRAWBERRY PLANT :: LAYERING : _____   17.____
    A. bryophyllum   B. onion   C. potato
    D. raspberry   E. tomato

18. MOLDS : SPORES :: GREEN PLANTS : _____   18.____
    A. flowers   B. leaves   C. roots   D. seeds   E. stems

19. GLENOID : HUMERUS :: ACETABULUM : _____   19.____
    A. coracoid   B. femur   C. radius
    D. tibia   E. medulla

20. SLATE : SHALE :: _____ : LIMESTONE   20.____
    A. feldspar   B. marble   C. gneiss
    D. mica schist   E. sandstone

21. AUXIN : PLANT :: _____ : ANIMAL   21.____
    A. pepsin   B. ptyalin   C. rennin
    D. thyroxin   E. stearin

22. CHLOROPHYLL : PHOTOSYNTHESIS :: ENZYME : _____   22.____
    A. digestion   B. respiration   C. fat digestion
    D. assimilation   E. ingestion

23. OPTIC NERVE : RETINA :: AUDITORY NERVE : _____   23.____
    A. cochlear window   B. Eustachian tube   C. organ of Corti
    D. stapes   E. semicircular canals

24. RESPIRATION : CARBON DIOXIDE :: PHOTOSYNTHESIS : _____   24.____
    A. carbon dioxide   B. chlorophyll   C. oxygen
    D. starch   E. sunlight

25. _____ : EYE :: DIAPHRAGM : CAMERA   25.____
    A. cornea   B iris   C. lens   D. pupil   E. retina

263

KEY (CORRECT ANSWERS)

1	B	6.	C	11.	A	16.	E	21.	D
2.	A	7.	D	12.	E	17.	D	22.	A
3.	D	8.	E	13.	B	18.	D	23.	C
4.	D	9.	C	14.	D	19.	B	24.	C
5.	A	10.	C	15.	C	20.	B	25.	B

TESTS IN VERBAL ANALOGIES – SOCIAL SCIENCE

DIRECTIONS: Each question contains two blank spaces. You are to select the words which will fill the blanks so that the sentence will be true and sensible. For the FIRST blank in each question, select a word or phrase preceded by letters A, B, C, D, or E. For the second blank in the question, select a word or phrase preceded by letters F, G, H, I, J. *PRINT THE LETTERS OF THE CORRECT ANSWERS IN THE SPACE AT THE RIGHT.*

TEST 1

1. _____ is to public assistance as citizenship is to _____.   1._____
   A. need   B. school attendance   C. worthiness
   D. child   E. welfare center
   F. passport   G. alien   H. immigration
   I. excise tax   J. indictment

2. _____ is to home relief as public institutional care is to _____.   2._____
   A. compensation   B. supplementation   C. direct relief
   D. survivor's insurance E. fiscal period
   F. removal of custody   G. adoption   H. day care
   I. voucher assistance

3. _____ is to "face sheet" as income is to _____.   3._____
   A. client   B. cash relief   C. relief standard
   D. case record   E. emergency assistance
   F. wages   G. home   H. debts
   I. taxes   J. bonus

4. _____ is to demography as man is to _____.   4._____
   A. politics   B. racial relations   C. stigmata
   D. social statistics E. democracy
   F. population   G. geography   H. woman
   I. marriage   J. anthropology

5. _____ is to tuberculosis as Terman is to _____.   5._____
   A. Wassermann   B. Mantoux   C. Schlick
   D. Ascheim-Zondek   E. Snellen
   F. litmus test   G. means test   H. lie detector test
   I. intelligence test J. CAVD test

6. _____ is to dementia as feeblemindedness is to _____.   6._____
   A. anger   B. luxation   C. insanity
   D. diagnosis   E. psychiatry
   F. myopia   G. amentia   H. tibia
   I. criminal   J. childhood

7. Frustration is to _____ as _____ is to relaxation.   7.____
   A. satisfaction   B. goal   C. need
   D. desire   E. motive
   F. tension   G. behavior   H. adjustment
   I. readjustment   J. reaction

8. _____ is to embezzlement as parole is to _____.   8.____
   A. intent   B. larceny   C. desertion
   D. guilt   E. conviction
   F. bail   G. plea   H. probation
   I. innocence   J. reformatory

9. Abandonment is to _____ as coercion is to _____.   9.____
   A. abduction   B. discovery   C. guardian
   D. adultery   E. desertion
   F. desertion   G. impotence   H. crime
   I. coition   J. constraint

10. _____ is to homicide as felony is to _____.   10.____
    A. courthouse   B. mayhem   C. negligence
    D. witness   E. manslaughter
    F. judge   G. crime   H. autopsy
    I. civil suit   J. prosecutor

KEY (CORRECT ANSWERS)

1.	A, G	6.	C, G
2.	C, H	7.	A, F
3.	D, F	8.	B, H
4.	D, J	9.	E, J
5.	B, I	10.	D, G

TEST 2

DIRECTIONS: Each question in this part consists of two capitalized words which have a certain relationship to each other, and a third capitalized word which is followed by five lettered words in small letters. Choose the letter of the word which is related in the SAME way to the third capitalized word as the first two capitalized words are related to each other. *PRINT THE LETTER OF THE CORRECT ANSWER IN THE SPACE AT THE RIGHT.*

1. CIVILIZATION : CEREMONY :: ATAVISM : _____   1.____
   A. tradition   B. religion   C. law
   D. ritual   E. taboo

2. CONFORMITY : IMITATION :: INDIVIDUALISM : _____   2.____
   A. emulation   B. uniformity   C. independence
   D. impulse   E. innovation

3. GENETIC TRANSMISSION : HEREDITY :: RECURRENT BEHAVIOR : _____   3.____
   A. environment   B. habit   C. adjustment
   D. ancestry   E. biological mechanism

4. GROUP : MOB :: SPEECH : _____   4.____
   A. herd   B. communication   C. discussion
   D. argot   E. gang

5. ACCLIMATIZATION : ADAPTATION :: ACCOMMODATION : _____   5.____
   A. organism   B. lethal selection   C. reconciliation
   D. relation   E. climatic area

6. PRIMARY GROUPS : MUTUAL IDENTIFICATION :: SECONDARY GROUPS :   6.____
   _____
   A. segmental relations   B. informal relations
   C. face-to-face groupings   D. intimate groups
   E. neighborhood groups

7. FERAL MAN : WILD :: MARGINAL MAN : _____   7.____
   A. participating   B. economically undeveloped
   C. divergent   D. ascetic
   E. structurally undeveloped

8. ACCOMMODATION GROUPS : CLUBS :: CONFLICT GROUPS : _____   8.____
   A. associations   B. aggregations   C. vocational groups
   D. sects   E. primary groups

9. SOCIAL DISSARANGING : SOCIAL COLLAPSE :: DISORGANIZATION :   9.____
   _____
   A. diffusion   B. unrest   C. disintegration
   D dissociation   E. revolution

10. CATEGORY : KIND :: AGGREGATION : _____
   A. interest   B. habit   C. space
   D. species   E. type

   10.____

11. DEFENDANT : PLEA :: PROSECUTION : _____
   A. judge   B. jury   C. verdict
   D argument   E. court

   11.____

12. U.S. : CONGRESS :: BRITAIN : _____
   A. House of Lords   B. legislature   C. republic
   D. Parliament   E. monarchy

   12.____

13. ELECTION : PRESIDENT :: APPOINTMENT : _____
   A. Prince Consort   B. U.S. Representative
   C. U.S. Senator   D. ambassador
   E. Mayor of the City of New York

   13.____

14. POLITICAL : EXILE :: SOCIAL : _____
   A. banishment   B. deportation   C. ostracism
   D. governmental E. religious

   14.____

15. IMPUTATION : ACCUSATION :: IMPUNITY : _____
   A. immunity   B. punishment   C. charge
   D. ascription   E. insinuation

   15.____

16. GUILT : PROOF :: INNOCENCE : _____
   A. assumption   B. presumption   C. conviction
   D. release   E. acquittal

   16.____

17. COUP D'ÉTAT : ;SEIZURE :: ELECTION : _____
   A. power   B. poll   C. population
   D. office   E. vote

   17.____

18. C.H. COOLEY : EMILE DURKHEIM :: CHARLES DARWIN : _____
   A. evolution   B. Karl Manheim   C. Louis Pasteur
   D. sociologist   E. Gregor Mendel

   18.____

19. CAPITALISM : U.S.S.R. :: MARXISM : _____
   A. Czechoslovakia   B. China   C. U.S.A.
   D. Yugoslavia   E. Albania

   19.____

20. "BY THE NATURE OF THE CASE" : IPSO FACTO :: "THAT YOU HAVE THE BODY : _____
   A. quid pro quo   B. habeas corpus   C. sine qua non
   D. writ of mandamus E. corpus striatum

   20.____

21. BUREAUCRACY : REPRESENTATION :: TRADITIONALISM : _____
   A. establishment   B. adaptation   C. formalism
   D. conventionalism E. institutionalism

   21.____

268

22. DENATURALIZATION : LOSS OF CITIZENSHIP :: DEMONETIZATION :   22.____
    ____
    A. national debt   B. loss of monies   C. revoking an illegal coin
    D. counterfeiting   C. removal of a coin

23. MACARTHYISM : "UN-AMERICAN ACTIVITIES" :: BILBOISM : ____   23.____
    A. blacklist   B. Black Muslims   C. "white supremacy"
    D. "boring from within"   E. "blue-sky" laws

24. EMINENT DOMAIN : 5TH AMENDMENT :: PRIOR TO INTRODUCTION : ____   24.____
    A. fair employment   B. Panama Canal decision
    C. right to vote   D. "gateway amendment"
    E. double jeopardy

25. SELLING IN VIOLATION OF RATIONING : BLACK MARKET ::   25.____
    VIOLATING THE SPIRIT OF CERTAIN RESTRAINS : ____
    A. shoddy goods
    B. selling rationed goods
    C. gray market
    D. underpriced goods
    E. the cessation of rationing goods

_____

KEY (CORRECT ANSWERS)

1	D	6.	A	11.	D	16.	A	21.	B
2.	C	7.	C	12.	D	17.	E	22.	E
3.	B	8.	D	13.	D	18.	E	23.	C
4.	D	9.	C	14.	C	19.	C	24.	D
5.	C	10.	C	15.	A	20.	B	25.	C

_____

TEST 3

Questions 1-8.

DIRECTIONS: Each question in this part consists of two capitalized words which have a certain relationship to each other, and a third capitalized word which is followed by five lettered words in small letters. Choose the letter of the word which is related in the SAME way to the third capitalized word as the first two capitalized words are related to each other. *PRINT THE LETTER OF THE CORRECT ANSWER IN THE SPACE AT THE RIGHT.*

1. "THIS GENERATION HAS A RENDEZVOUS WITH DESTINY" : F.D. ROOSEVELT :: "YOU CANNOT CRUCIFY MANKING UPON A CROSS OF GOLD : _____
   - A. Woodrow Wilson
   - B. William Jennings Bryan
   - C. Martin Van Buren
   - D. John F. Kennedy
   - E. Theodore Roosevelt

   1._____

2. INCUMBENT : OFFICE HOLDER :: INSURGENT : _____
   - A. opponent
   - B. bolter
   - C. extremist
   - D. iconoclast
   - E. revolutionist

   2._____

3. "NATURAL PERSON" : INDIVIDUAL :: "ARTIFICIAL PERSON" : _____
   - A. alien
   - B. denaturalized citizen
   - C. one who is deported
   - D. computer
   - E. corporation

   3._____

4. FUNDAMENTAL PRINCIPLES : CONSTITUTION :: POLITICAL PROGRAM : _____
   - A. principles of democratic government
   - B. regime
   - C. demarche
   - D. political philosophy
   - E. manifesto

   4._____

5. EXECUTIVE : EXPENSE ACCOUNT :: CONGRESSMAN : _____
   - A. patronage
   - B. perquisites
   - C. diplomatic immunity
   - C. graft
   - E. bonus

   5._____

6. ELECTION : OFFICE :: PRIMARY : _____
   - A. ward
   - B. precinct
   - C. election
   - D. nomination
   - E. succession

   6._____

7. IMPEACHMENT : LEGISLATURE :: RECALL : _____
   - A. House of Representatives
   - B. Senate
   - C. people
   - D. initiative
   - E. referendum

   7._____

8. ENGEL'S LAW : INCOME :: ENOCH ARDEN LAW : _____   8.____
    A. political expenditures   B. marriage
    C. tariff   D. lobbying
    E. Hatch Act

Questions 9-25.

DIRECTIONS: Each question in this part consists of two capitalized words which have a
             certain relationship to each other, followed by five lettered pairs in small letters.
             Choose the letter of the pair of words which is related in the SAME way as the
             words of the capitalized pair are related to each other. *PRINT THE LETTER
             OF THE CORRECT ANSWER IN THE SPACE AT THE RIGHT.*

9. ISOLATION : SOLIDARITY :: _____ : _____   9.____
    A. separation : unity   B. strength : weakness
    C. disjunction : partition   D. consolidation : insulation
    E. segregation : disintegration

10. WAR : NATION :: _____ : _____   10.____
    A. competition : struggle   B. power : politics
    C. competition : industry   D. soldiers : battles
    E. government : masses

11. ALIENATION : ASSIMILATION :: _____ : _____   11.____
    A. acclimatization : accommodation
    B. blending : merging
    C. isolation : fusion
    D. alien : emigrant
    E. foreigner : immigrant

12. MALTHIUS : DARWIN :: _____ : _____   12.____
    A. poverty : numbers   B. ape : man
    C. plant life : animal life   D. population : natural selection
    E. evolution : mathematics

13. MONOGAMY : POLYANDRY :: _____ : _____   13.____
    A. virtue : vice
    B. polygamy : miscegenation
    C. United States : Saudi Arabia
    D. social pathology : social organization
    E. primitive : civilized

14. NORM : GROUP :: _____ : _____   14.____
    A. pattern : statistic
    B. performance : individual
    C. natural : neurotic
    D. learned behavior : conditioned reflex
    E. law : government

15. PROVINCIAL : URBANE :: _____ : _____   15.____
    A. automated : antiquated   B. privacy : anonymity
    C. rural : bucolic   D. homogeneous : heterogeneous
    E. merchant : agrarian

16. ASCETICISM : ESPRIT DE CORPS :: _____ : _____   16.____
    A. individual : nation   B. monk : layman
    C. anchorite : spirit   D. solitude : fellowship
    E. community : country

17. PRIMITIVE : CIVILIZED :: _____ : _____   17.____
    A. literate : cultured   B. primate : anthropoid
    C. atavistic : Cro-Magnon   D. simple : complex
    E. aboriginal : indigenous

18. HONEST BALLOT ASSOCIATION : BOARD OF ELECTIONS :: _____ : _____   18.____
    A. election district : community B. counselor : litigant
    C. police : citizen   D. arbitration panel : jury
    E. citizen : authority

19. MONARCHY : PEERAGE :: _____ : _____   19.____
    A. anarchy : rebellion   B. democracy : government
    C. oligarchy : clique   D. dictatorship : the military
    E. republic : dictator

20. OPTIONAL : CHOICE :: _____ : _____   20.____
    A. voluntary : individual   B. orthodox : blind allegiance
    C. mandatory : election   D. faith : doctrine
    E. obligatory : volition

21. EX OFFICIO : "DUE TO THE NATURE OF THE POSITION" :: _____ : _____   21.____
    A. habeas corpus : "possession of the corpse"
    B. ex post facto : "before the fact"
    C. ad valorem : "without value"
    D. ipso facto : "this certain fact"
    E. amicus curiae : "friend of the court"

22. SQUARE DEAL : THEODORE ROOSEVELT :: _____ : _____   22.____
    A. Fair Deal : Franklin D. Roosevelt
    B. Good Neighbor Policy : Harry Truman
    C. New Deal : Franklin D. Roosevelt
    D. Great Society : John F. Kennedy
    E. New Frontiers : Lyndon B. Johnson

23. WARD : PRECINCT :: _____ : _____   23.____
    A. country : nation   B. state : city   C. parish : community
    D. state : country   E. city : state

24. FILIBUSTER : OBSTRUCTION :: _____ : _____   24.____
    A. bloc : party affiliation
    B. gerrymandering : defeat in election
    C. moratorium : suspension
    D. cession : concession
    E. secession : accession

25. TRESPASSING : INFRINGEMENT :: _____ : _____   25.____
    A. exemption : retraction
    B. franking : privilege
    C. extortion : persuasion
    D. "taking the Fifth Amendment" : immunity
    E. indictment : imprisonment

_____

KEY (CORRECT ANSWERS)

1	B	6.	D	11.	C	16.	D	21.	E
2.	B	7.	C	12.	D	17.	D	22.	C
3.	E	8.	B	13.	C	18.	D	23.	B
4.	E	9.	A	14.	B	19.	C	24.	C
5.	B	10.	C	15.	D	20.	B	25.	B

_____

NOTES

GENERAL INFORMATION
GENERAL VOCABULARY

ABRAHAM'S BOSOM: The rest of the blessed dead.

ACADEMICS: Plato's disciples were so called from the Academy.

ACADEMY: Plato founded his school in a gymnasium of this name near Athens. 368 B.C.

ACADEMY, THE FRENCH: A French scientific body limited to forty members.

ACADIA: Formerly the name of Nova Scotia.

ADAM'S APPLE: A part of the throat where, it is said, a piece of the forbidden fruit lodged.

ADMIRABLE CRICHTON, THE: James Crichton, an accomplished Scotchman of the sixteenth century.

AGES: The five ages of the world, according to Hesiod, are the Golden, the Silver, the Brazen, the Heroic, and the Iron

ALADDIN'S WINDOW, TO FINISH: Trying to complete another's work. Aladdin's palace was perfect except one window left for the Sultan to finish, but his treasure failed him.

ALBANY REGENCY: Name applied many years ago to some Democrats at Albany, N.Y.

ALBINO: A person with white skin and hair and red eyes.

ALBION: England, so called from the chalky white cliffs.

ALDINE PRESS: Founded by Aldus Manutius at Venice in 1496. Editions of the classics issued from this press were called the Aldine editions. This term is now applied to some elegant editions of English works.

ALEXANDRIAN LIBRARY: Was founded by Ptolemy Philadelphus. It contained 700,000 volumes, and was burnt 47 B.C.

ALEXANDRINE AGE: 323-640, when Alexandria was the seat of the highest culture.

ALHAMBRA: A magnificent palace and a fortress built by the Moors at Granada, in Spain.

ALL-HALLOWS: All Saints' Day, November 1st.

ALLAH: Arabic name of God.

AMBROSIA: Food of the Gods.

ANACHRONISM: An error in computing time.

ANACREONTICS: Poems composed in the manner of Anacreon, a great poet noted for his exact imitation of nature.

ANCIENT RÉGIME: The French Government previous to the revolution of 1789.

ANGLING, THE FATHER OF: Izaak Walton.

ANNUS MIRABILIS: (Wonderful year) A.D. 1666. Noted for the great fire in London, the Plague, and an English victory over the Dutch.

APOLLO BELVEDERE: One of the most beautiful and perfect representations of the human form is the statue of Apollo in the Belvedere Gallery of the Vatican Palace at Rome.

APPIAN WAY: The road from Rome to Capua. The oldest Roma road.

APPLES OF SODOM: Beautiful fruit, but full of ashes. Applied figuratively to the disappointment of sin.

APPLE, GOLDEN: Prize for beauty disputed before Paris, between Juno, Pallas and Venus; awarded by him to Venus.

ARGO: The ship in which Jason and his fifty-four companions sailed when going to Colchis for the Golden Fleece.

ARGONAUTS: The adventurers on the Argo.

ARGUS-EYED: Crafty, watchful. Argus had a hundred eyes; the jealous Juno put him on detective duty over Io.

ARMADA, THE SPANISH: A fleet of 130 ships gathered by Philip of Spain for the invasion of England in 1588. Queen Elizabeth was busy preparing for resistance when the news came that a storm had completely wrecked the Armada.

ARYANS: The stem of the Indo-European peoples.

ASTOR LIBRARY: Founded by John Jacob Astor in New York City.

AVALON: King Arthur's burial place, Glastonbury.

AYRESHIRE POET, THE: Burns. His birthplace was near Ayr in Scotland.

BARNBURNERS: A name given some years ago to radical Democrats.

BABYLONIAN CAPTIVITY: The seventy years' captivity of the Jews at Babylon, 608-538 B.C.

BACONIAN PHILOSOPHY: The inductive philosophy of Lord Bacon.

BARD OF AVON: Shakespeare, so called from his home being Stratford-on-Avon.

BARMECIDE'S FEAST: A mockery, a delusion and a sham. Barmecide asked a starving beggar to dinner, and seated him at a table of empty dishes.

BASILISK: A mythical serpent with power to fill by merely looking at its victim.

BASTILLE: French prison and fortress. People were incarcerated here by letter de cachet, without notice or trial. Destroyed by a mob, 1789.

BATTLE OF THE BOOKS: Satire by Dean Swift comparing ancient and modern literature.

BATTLE OF THE KEGS: A practical joke on the British General Loring. Detailed in a ballad of the Revolutionary War.

BATTERY, THE: A park in New York City adjoining the river.

BEACON ST.: The aristocratic residence street of Boston.

BEAUTY AND THE BEAST: A fairy tale. Beauty lives with the Beast to save her father's life. By her love she disenchants the Beast, who proves to be a great Prince.

BEDLAM: A mad-house.

BEELZEBUB: A Philistine deity.

BEGGING THE QUESTION: Assuming as true what you are to prove.

BELL THE CAT: In a convention of mice it was proposed to hang a bell on the cat's neck, to give warning of her coming. No one would serve on the committee.

BELL, THE PASSING: Rung formerly when persons were dying.

BESS, GOOD QUEEN: Queen Elizabeth.

BILLINGSGATE: Coarse language. Such as is used at the fish market of Billingsgate in London; a fishwife's tongue being said to be remarkably expressive.

BLACK DEATH: A plague which desolated Europe, Asia, and Africa in the fourteenth century.

BLACK FRIDAY: Gold panic September 26th, 1869. Immense fortunes lost and won same day. Investigation could never discover the true history of it.

BLACK HOLE OF CALCUTTA: Dark prison cell wherein Surajah Dowlah shut up 146 British soldiers; only 23 lived till morning.

BLACK PRINCE, THE: Edward, Prince of Wales, son of Edward III.

BLACK REPUBLICANS: The Republican party of U.S. so called when opposing the extension of slavery.

BLARNEY STONE: Its supposed virtue when kissed is to impart a smooth and oily tongue. Profusion of compliments is called blarney. This stone is in Blarney Castle, near Cork, Ireland.

BLUEBEARD: A wife-killing tyrant in a nursery story.

BLUE LAWS: Some severe New England statues were so called.

BLUE STOCKING: A literary society at Venice in 1400, whose members wore blue stockings, is the origin of this name for a female pedant.

BOHEMIAN: As opposed to Philistine, an artist or literary man living loosely by his wits.

BOIS DE BOULOGNE: A Parisian park, drive, and promenade.

BORDER MINSTREL, THE: Sir Walter Scott.
BORDER STATES: Maryland, Delaware, Virginia, Kentucky, Missouri.
BOURGEOISIE: A class of the people of France mostly composed of traders and
          manufacturers; the middle class.
BOURSE: Parisian stock exchange.
BOWERY, THE: A New York thoroughfare.
BOYCOTT: To refuse to have anything to do with a person. To let him severely alone. A trying
          ordeal passed through by Captain Boycott in Ireland in 1881. No one would sell to him,
          buy from him, work for him, or speak to him.
BRIDE OF THE SEA: Venice.
BRIDGE OF SIGHS: In Venice. Connects the Doge's Palace and State Prison. Over this
          bridge the condemned passes when on their way to be executed.
BRITISH MUSEUM: Library and museum in London.
BROADWAY: The principal street of New York.
BROOK FARM: A socialistic community to carry out the idea of Fourierism; was founded at
          West Roxbury, Mass., 1841.
BUNCOMBE: Clap-trap speeches, to cajole constituents, more than for immediate effect.
          Buncombe is in North Carolina. A North Carolina member said a fiery speech was not
          delivered to the House, but to Buncombe.

CACHET, LETTRES DE: (Sealed letters) Blank warrants with the seal of the French King
          already affixed for imprisoning or releasing any person in the Bastille.
CALEDONIA: Scotland.
CALUMET: An Indian pipe. In old times a treaty of peace with the red men would be ratified by
          smoking the calumet.
CAMPAGNA: The plains around the city of Rome.
CARBONARI: A secret political society organized in Italy, 1820.
CARMAGNOLE: Song and dance in the French Revolution.
CARTESIAN PHILOSOPHY: From Descartes, "*I think, therefore I exist."
CATACOMBS: Subterranean sepulchers. About three miles from Rome in the Appian Way, a
          vast number of long underground passages about three feet wide and ten feet high. On
          each side in niches were deposited the bodies of the martyrs and early Christians. These
          niches were closed with tiles or slabs of marble having proper inscriptions on them.
          During the persecutions the Christians concealed themselves in these caves.
CELESTIAL EMPIRE: China, whose first Emperors were all divinities.
CENTRAL PARK: The great park of New York City; contains 863 acres.
CHAMPS ELYSEES: A promenade in Paris.
CHAUVINISM: Patriotism of the blatant kind, from Chauvin, one of Scribe's characters.
CHEAPSIDE: A thoroughfare in London.
CHILTERM HUNDREDS, TO ACCEPT THE: A member of the English Parliament cannot
          resign, and cannot hold office during membership. If he wishes to leave, he can vacate
          his seat by accepting the office of Steward of the Chiltern Hundreds.
CHILTERN HUNDREDS: A tract in Buckinghamshire and Oxfordshire, England, to which is
          attached the nominal office of steward under the crown.
CHRIST CHURCH: The name of the largest college in the University of Oxford.
CID, THE: The Spanish hero, Don Roderigo Laynez, Count of Bivar.
CINCINNATI, THE: Society of American Revolutionary officers.
CITIZEN KING, THE: Louis Philippe of France.
COLOSSUS OF RHODES: A brass statue, one of the wonders of the world, which stood
          astride the entrance to the port of Rhodes.

CONFEDERATE STATES: The eleven states which seceded in 1861: Alabama, Arkansas, Florida, Georgia, Louisiana, Mississippi, North Carolina, South Carolina, Tennessee, Texas, and Virginia.

CONGRESSIONAL LIBRARY: At Washington, it is the largest in the United States.

CONSOLS: English public securities.

COPPERHEADS: Northern sympathizers with the South in the Civil War.

CORNCRACKERS, THE: Kentuckians.

CRAPAUD, JOHNNY: A Frenchman.

CREDIT MOBILIER: An authorized stock company. The American Credit Mobilier formed for raising money for the Pacific Railroad was involved in scandal in 1873.

CROCODILE TEARS: Counterfeit sorrow. A fable says the crocodile weeps as it eats its victim.

DAMOCLES' SWORD: Damocles, having commented upon the happiness which the tyrant Dionysius must enjoy, was invited by him to a feast where, whilst discussing the good things, he looked up and discovered a sword hanging by a single hair immediately over his head.

DARBY AND JOAN: The loving couple.

DARWINIAN THEORY: An explanation of the origin of species in animals, that they come from one or a few original forms, the present differences resulting from development and natural selection.

DE PROFUNDIS: The 130th Psalm; part of the burial service.

DEFENDER OF THE FAITH: Henry VIII received this title from Pope Leo X, and his successors have borne it ever since.

DIRECTORY, THE FRENCH: By the Constitution of 1795, the executive power was vested in five Directors; it lasted only four years.

DIXIE, THE LAND OF: The Southern States.

DIZZY: The nickname of Benjamin Disraeli, Earl of Beaconsfield.

DOE, JOHN: The fictitious plaintiff in ejectment suits, the defendant being Richard Roe.

DOOMSDAY BOOK: Compiled by order of William the Conqueror. It contained a survey and an estimate of value of all the lands in England.

DONNYBROOK FAIR: A once celebrated annual fair near Dublin.

DOUAY BIBLE, THE: The English Bible authorized by the Roman Catholic Church; first published at Douay, France.

DOWNING STREET: The official residence of the English Prime Minister since the time of Sir Robert Walpole is in Downing Street, London

DRURY LANE THEATER: In London; was opened in 1688.

DYING GLADIATOR: An ancient statue in the Capitol at Rome.

EASTERN STATES, THE: Maine, New Hampshire, Vermont, Massachusetts, Rhode Island, and Connecticut.

ECCE HOMO: A painting by Correggio representing the Savior crowned with thorns.

EL DORADO: A fabulous region in South America, surpassing all other countries in the production of gems and precious metals. A name for any wealthy country.

ELEPHANT, SEEING THE: Seeing the world.

ESCORIAL, THE: A royal residence built by Philip II; it is the largest structure in Spain, and one of the most splendid buildings in Europe. It is 22 miles from Madrid and contains a palace, a church, a monastery, free schools, and a mausoleum.

ETERNAL CITY, THE: Rome.

EUREKA: (I have found it.) Exclamation of Archimedes when he discovered the method of proving that the sum of the squares of the sides of a right-angled triangle equaled the square of the hypotenuse.

FABIAN POLICY: Delaying; dilatory. From Quintus Fabius Maximus, the Roman General, who successfully opposed Hannibal, the Carthaginian, by avoiding a battle and continually harassing him.

FAINEANTS, LES ROIS: (Do-nothing Kings) The last twelve Kings of the Merovingian Dynasty were so called. For about 100 years previous to 720, when Pepin dethroned Childeric III, they were mere puppets, and the supreme authority was exercised by the mayors of the palace.

FALERNIAN: A celebrated ancient Italian wine grown at Falernum.

FANEUIL HALL: In Boston, built 1742; called the "Cradle of Liberty." for there the Revolutionary patriots were wont to assemble.

FATHER OF HIS COUNTRY: George Washington.

FATHERS OF THE LATIN CHURCH: St. Ambrose of Milan, St. Augustine, St. Bernard, St. Hilary, St. Jerome, Lactantius.

FAUBOURG ST. ANTOINE: The part of Paris where the workingmen live.

FAUBOURG ST. GERMAIN: Aristocratic part of Paris.

FENIANS: A society of Irishmen formed in the United States in 1865 to free Ireland.

FIFTH AVENUE: A celebrated business street in New York.

FIGHTING JOE: The American General Joseph Hooker.

FLYING DUTCHMAN: A spectre ship cruising about the Cape of Good Hope. Forebodes trouble to whoever sees it.

FORTE: Strong point.

FORT SUMTER: In the harbor of Charleston, S.C. Here were heard the first sounds of the cannons' thunder in the late Civil War.

FOURIERISM: Charles Fourier, a French visionary, proposed a system of communism in which the world should be divided into "phalansteries" of four hundred families who were to live and work in common.

FRESHMAN: A student in his first year at college.

GADSHILL: Near Rochester, in Kent, England. Place where Falstaff met so many men in buckram. Charles Dickens' residence was at Gadshill.

GENRE PAINTING: Represents ordinary domestic and rural scenes.

GEORGE, ST., AND THE DRAGON: St. George, the patron saint of England, is said to have slain in Libya a hideous dragon whose daily food was a virgin.

GERRYMANDER: The geographical apportionment of districts to give preponderance to one political party. Started in Massachusetts, and named for its Governor, Elbridge Gerry.

GHETTO: The quarter in Rome to which the Jews were formerly restricted. Now, any restricted or segregated area.

GHIBELLINE: One of a faction in Italy in the thirteenth century, which favored the German Emperors, in opposition to the Guelphs, adherents of the Pope.

GIRONDISTS; THE GIRONDE: Moderate "Constitutional" Republican party in the French Revolution in 1789

GOBELINS: A tapestry and carpet manufactory at Paris, founded by Gobelin, a dyer, in the 16h century.

GODIVA, LADY: Wife of Leofric, Earl of Mercia, who offered to remit certain exactions to his tenants if she would ride naked through the streets of Coventry. She did so, all the people closing their doors and keeping within except one, "Peeping Tom," who was struck blind for peeping at her.

GOLDEN GATE: The entrance to the harbor of San Francisco.

GOLDEN HORN: The estuary of the Bosphorus, upon whose banks Constantinople is built.

GORDIAN KNOT: A difficulty; an obstacle. Gordius, King of Phrygia, consecrated to Jupiter a wagon, the beam and yoke of which were tied together by such an intricate knot that no one could unravel it. An oracle having foretold that he who could untie this knot would be master of Asia. Alexander cut it asunder with his sword.

GOTHAM: A name sometimes applied to New York City.

GREAT COMMONER, THE: William Pitt.

GREAT DUKE, THE: Wellington.

GREAT PYRAMID, THE: Is at Gheezeh, Egypt. It is 484 feet high.

GREENBACKS: United States Treasury notes. So named from their color.

GREEN ISLE, THE: Ireland. Sometimes also called the Emerald Isle.

GREGORIAN YEAR: 1582; it being proved that the years were eleven minutes shorter than what they were counted at. Gregory XIII took ten days of October out of that year and advanced the date so as to correct the calendar. The reform has been accepted throughout Christendom, except in Russia.

GRETNA GREEN: A Scotch village famous for runaway matches.

GRUB STREET: In London; used to be not4ed for its literary denizens.

GUELPHS: The adherents in the thirteenth century of the Papacy against the German Emperors. They were the constant opponents of the Ghibellines, and between them Italy was kept in turmoil.

GUILDHALL: The London town hall.

GUNPOWDER PLOT, THE: A plot to blow up the English Parliament in its House, November 5, 1605. A cellar underneath was stored with gunpowder intended to be touched off during the session by Guy Fawkes. The discovery was made in time to prevent mischief. To use a modern but inelegant phrase, the plot was considered by some people to be "a put-up job."

HABEAS CORPUS ACT, THE: Was passed in the time of Charles II and provides that the body of any person restrained of his liberty must on proper application be brought before a judge and the reason of his confinement stated. The judge will then determine the amount of bail he shall furnish, or he will remand him to prison or allow him his freedom, as the case may require. (1629)

HALCYON DAYS: A period of happiness; days of peace and tranquility. The halcyon, as the kingfisher was anciently called, was said to lay her eggs in nests on rocks near the sea during the calm weather about the winter solstice.

HANDICAP: Apportionment of the weights that must be carried in a race by different horses, considering their age and strength, to equalize their chances.

HANSARD: Name of the firm which prints the debates of the British Parliament.

HANSE TOWNS: In the twelfth century some commercial cities in the north of Germany formed an association for the protection of commerce. To these other similar cities in Holland, England, France, Spain, and Italy acceded, and for centuries this confederacy commanded the respect and defied the power of Kings.

HANSEATIC LEAGUE: The name of the confederation of Hanse towns. There were seventy-two cities in the league, and they held triennial conventions called Hansa. It has long since fallen to pieces. Four of its members, Lubeck, Hamburg, Bremen, and Frankfort, are called free cities, but are really part of the German state.

HARE, MAD AS A MARCH: The hare is wilder than usual in March.

HARPIES: Three ravenous and filthy monsters, each having a woman's face and the body of a vulture. Their names were Aello, Ocypete, and Celeno. Juno sent them to plunder the table of Phineus.

HARI-KARI: (Happy dispatch) Japanese official suicide.

HEGIRA: The date of Mohammed's fight from Mecca, July 16, 622. The epoch from which the Mohammedans compute their time.

HIGH CHURCH: The more conservative portion of the Episcopal Church.

HIGH SEAS, THE: The sea beyond three miles from the coast.

HISTORY, THE FATHER OF: Herodotus, the Greek historian.

HOBSON'S CHOICE: Take what is offered or go without. Tobias Hobson, an English stable-keeper, made whatever customer came to hire a horse to take the one nearest the door.

HOLY ALLIANCE: Formed in 1816 by Austria, Prussia, and Russia.

HOLY FAMILY, THE: The name of pictures representing in group the infant Jesus, St. Joseph, the Blessed Virgin, John the Baptist, Anna, and St. Elizabeth. The most celebrated area by Michelangelo at Florence, by Raphael in London, and by Leonardo da Vinci in the Louvre.

HOLY LAND, THE: Israel.

HONI SOIT QUI MAL Y PENSE: (Shame to him who evil thinks) Motto of the highest order of knighthood in Great Britain, that of the Garter, instituted by Edward III. At a ball, a garter of the Countess of Salisbury, having fallen off, was picked up by the King, who expressed himself in the above phrase and fastened it around his own knee. This incident led to the formation of the order.

HOTEL DE VILLE: The city hall in French and Belgian cities.

HOURIS: Beautiful virgins of Paradise; promised by the Koran for the delight of the true believers.

HUNDRED DAYS, THE: From March 20, 1815, when Napoleon escaped from Elba, to June 22, 1815, when he abdicated.

ICONOCLAST: (Image-breaker) A radical reformer.

ILIAD: A Green epic poem by Homer, relating the story of the siege of Troy by the Greeks.

INDEPENDENCE, DECLARATION OF: Issued July 4, 1776.

INDEPENDENCE HALL: In Philadelphia, Pa., where Congress met and adopted the Declaration of Independence.

INDEX EXPURGATORIUS: A list of books forbidden to be read by the Roman Catholic Church.

INNS OF COURT: The four London Law societies which have the sole right of admitting candidates to the Bar. They are Gray's Inn, Lincoln's Inn, the Inner Temple, and the Middle Temple.

INQUISITION: A tribunal established in some countries to try heretics.

IRISH AGITATOR, THE: Daniel O'Connell.

IRON CITY, THE: Pittsburgh, Pa.

IRON DUKE, THE: The Duke of Wellington.

IRON MASK, THE MAN IN THE: A mysterious French state prisoner.

JACK KETCH: The hangman. The name of an English hangman.

JACK ROBINSON: Before you can say Jack Robinson; at once. Jack Robinson was noted for the shortness of his visits; the servant had scarcely time to repeat his name before he would leave.

JACK, THE GIANT KILLER: A nursery hero.

JACK, THE AMERICAN, OR UNION: The blue ground of the American flag with the stars but without the stripes.

JACOBINS: A revolutionary club, 1789, in Paris, held its meetings in what had been the Jacobin Monastery. They were violent and extreme in the measures they proposed. Their name spread to all similar organizations and to individuals acting with them throughout France.

JACOBITES: Adherents of James II of England, and of the Stuarts, his descendants.

JERICHO, GONE TO: Disappeared; ruined.

JERUSALEM DELIVERED: An Italian epic poem by Torquato Tasso.

JOHN BULL: England. Nickname for an Englishman.

JUGGERNAUT: A Hindu god who has a famous temple in India. There is an immense car in the service of this god, which, when moved about the country, causes the greatest excitement. The car resembles a large building and its weight is very heavy. It is dragged along by the multitude and their fanaticism is so great that crowds of devotees cast themselves under the wheels and are crushed to death, a fate which they believe ensures paradise.

JULIAN ERA, THE: A method of reckoning time from 46 B.C., when Caesar reformed the calendar.

JUNIUS, LETTERS OF: Some remarkable political letters written during the reign of George II. Their authorship is unknown.

KANSAS BLEEDING: So called by Horace Greeley during the Free Soil controversy.

KING CAN DO NO WRONG, THE: Meaning that the Ministers and not the King are responsible for mistakes of government.

KING COTTON: A name given to the great Southern industry before the war.

KNICKERBOCKER: A member of any old Dutch family in New York. Derived from Irving's immortal history.

KNOW-NOTHINGS: A political party in the United States, whose cardinal principle was opposition to foreign office-holders.

KOH-I-NOOR: A Golconda diamond, the largest in the world, now one of the crown diamonds of England. Value, in the millions.

KORAN, THE: The Mohammedan Bible.

KREMLIN, THE: The royal Russian residence in Moscow, formerly; now the official seat of government.

LABYRINTH, THE: A celebrated structure built by Minos, King of Crete, which consisted of a maze out of which no one who entered could find the way back.

LACONIC: Curt. So called from the brief speech in fashion in old Laconia, afterwards called Sparta.

LAKE SCHOOL, THE: A society of English poets consisting of Coleridge, Wordsworth, and Southey.

LAND OF BONDAGE, THE: Egypt.

LAND O'CAKES, THE: Scotland.

LAND OF NOD, THE: Sleep, dreamland.

LAND OF PROMISE, THE: Canaan, the goal of the Jewish wanderings in the wilderness.

LANG SYNE: Long ago.

LANGUE D'OC: Provence, a part of France so called from the dialect in use.

LANGUE D'OEIL: All of France except Provence.

LAOCOON, THE: A celebrated statue in the Vatican representing Laocoon strangled by serpents.

LAODICEAN: A person luke-warm in religion.

LARES AND PENATES: The household gods.

LAST JUDGMENT, THE: The theme of a number of frescoes of the Renaissance period in Italy.

LAST SUPPER, THE: Similar to the above. Leonardo da Vinci's best canvas is on this subject.

LATERAN PALACE, THE: One of the Papal residences at Rome.

LAUGHING PHILOSOPHER: Democritus of Abdera, who believed that life was only to be laughed at.

LEANING TOWER, THE: A celebrated structure at Pisa, Italy, which leans thirteen feet out of the perpendicular; 178 feet high.

LILLIPUT: The pigmy land in Gulliver's travels.

LINGUA FRANCA: A dialect of French, Italian, and Arabic spoken on the Mediterranean Sea.

LION AND UNICORN: The supporters of the British royal arms.

LION'S SHARE: The bigger portion in a division. so called from one of Aesop's fables.

LITTLE CORPORAL, THE: Napoleon Bonaparte.

LITTLE GIANT, THE: Stephen A. Douglass.

LLOYDS: The originators of marine insurance.

LOMBARD STREET: The financial street of London.

LONE STAR STATE, THE: Texas.

LONG PARLIAMENT: The Parliament which sat for thirteen years at the beginning of the civil war in England. It sat from 1640 to 1653.

LORELEI: A malignant but beautiful watersprite of the Rhine.

LOTUS-EATERS, THE: Homer in the Odyssey describes the effect of eating the lotus as making the eater forget his home.

LOUVRE, THE: The art palace of Paris.

LOW CHURCH, THE: A part of the Episcopal Church which is opposed to ceremonies.

LUSIAD, THE: The Portuguese epic poem, written by Camoens, describing Vasco da Gama's adventures.

LYNCH LAW: Mob law. The name comes from a Virginia farmer who instituted the first vigilance committee in America.

MAB, QUEEN: The queen of the fairies. So called from an Irish fairy princess named Medh, who flourished in the night of time.

MACADAMIZE: Paving with broken stones. So called from the inventor, Sir John MacAdam.

MACARONIC VERSE: A verse made by mixing different languages.

MACHIAVELLISM: Political trickery.

MADAM TUSSAUD'S EXHIBITION: A famous London wax-works show.

MADONNA: The Blessed Virgin.

MAECENAS: A noted patron of poets during the reign of Augustus of Rome.

MAGNA CHARTA: The charter making the cornerstone of English liberty, extorted from King John Lack-Land.

MAID OF ORLEANS: Joan of Arc.

MAIDEN QUEEN, THE: Elizabeth of England.

MALTHUSIAN DOCTRINE, THE: The theory that the population of the world is growing faster than the food supply.

MAN OF DESTINY: Napoleon Bonaparte.

MAN OF IRON, THE: Bismarck.

MAN OF STRAW: An irresponsible person.

MARE'S NEST: A matter which seems of importance but turns out to be nothing.

MARRIAGE A LA MODE: The title of six satirical pictures by Hogarth.

MARSEILLAISE: The French national air, composed by Rouget de Lisle.

MARTINENT: A strict disciplinarian. So called from a French officer of the seventeenth century.

MASON AND DIXON'S LINE: The north boundary of the Slave States, dividing Virginia and Maryland from Pennsylvania.

MAUSOLEUM: The tomb of Mausolus, built by Queen Artemisia, one of the seven wonders of the world.

MAYFAIR: The west end of London.

MERCATOR'S PROJECTION: (Or Mercator's Chart), is so called after Gerard Mercator, a Flemish geographer of the sixteenth century, the first to give an unbroken view of the whole surface of the earth. In it all the meridians are straight lines perpendicular to the equator, and all the parallels parallel to the equator, the effect being to greatly exaggerate the polar regions.

MIDDLE AGES, THE: The period between the destruction of the Roman Empire and the revival of learning in Italy – c. 476 to 1500.

MIDDLE STATES, THE: New York, Pennsylvania, New Jersey, and Delaware.

MINNESINGERS: (Love singers) The German lyric poets of the twelfth and thirteenth centuries.

MISERERE: The fifty-first psalm.

MISSISSIPPI BUBBLE, THE: A hollow financial scheme in the last quarter of the 19th century.

MISSOURI COMPROMISE, THE: A measure that prohibited slavery north of 36°30' north latitude.

MISTRESS OF THE SEAS: England.

MOLLY MAGUIRES: A secret society in the United States. Many crimes were attributed to it, especially in Pennsylvania.

MONARCH, LE GRAND: Louis XIV, of France.

MONROE DOCTRINE: The United States is not to meddle in European affairs, nor to allow European Governments to meddle in the affairs of the American Continent.

MORGANATIC MARRIAGE: A marriage between a man of high rank and a woman of a lower one. She does not take her husband's title.

MOTHER OF PRESIDENTS: Virginia; having produced seven Presidents of the United States.

MOTHER CAREY'S CHICKENS: Stormy petrels.

MOUNT VERNON: The home of Washington, in Virginia.

MUSIC OF THE SPHERES: Order, harmony. Plato taught that each planet had a siren whose song harmonized with the motion of our sphere and with that of the others.

NAMBY-PAMBY: Childish. A term used for poor literacy productions.

NANTES, EDICT OF: A decree issued at Nantes, France, in 1508, by Henry IV, granting toleration to the Protestant religion. Revoked by Louis XIV, October 22, 1685.

NATION OF SHOP-KEEPERS: The name given to the English by Napoleon.

NEWGATE: A London prison.

NEW WORLD: The Americas.

NIBELUNGEN LIED: A German epic poem of the thirteenth century.

NOEL: Christmas Day.

NON-CONFORMISTS: Dissenters from the Church of England.

NORTHERN GIANT, THE: Russia.
NOTRE DAME: The Cathedral of Paris.

ODYSSEY: A narrative poem of the adventures of Ulysses on his voyage from Troy to Ithaca; by Homer.
OGRES: Giants who feed on human flesh.
OI POLLOI: The multitude.
OLD ABE: Abraham Lincoln.
OLD BAILEY: A London criminal court.
OLD DOMINION, THE: Virginia.
OLD GUARD, THE: A favorite regiment of Napoleon Bonaparte. In the Chicago Convention, 1880, the friends of Gen. Grant received this name. Any conservative group of standpatters.
OLD HICKORY: Gen. Andrew Jackson.
ORDINANCE OF 1787: An act fixing the government of the Northwest Territory of the United States.
ORLANDO FURIOSO: An Italian poem by Ariosto.
OSSIAN: The son of Fingal, a Scotch bard. Ossian's poems, published in 1760, were the work of James McPherson, a gifted Caledonian.
OSTEND MANIFESTO: Was issued by the United States Ministers to England, France, and Spain during Pierce's administration, declaring that Cuba must belong to the United States.
OSTRACISM: The Athenians expelled every public man against whom a sufficient number of votes were cast. The votes were written on oyster shells.

PALIMPSEST: A parchment having the original writing erased and new writing substituted.
PALL MALL: A street in London.
PALLADIUM: Is something that affords defense, protection, and safety. A statue of Pallas was the palladium of Troy.
PANTHEON: A circular building in Rome erected in the time of Augustus. It is now a church, the Rotonda.
PARADISE LOST: A poem by John Milton treating of the fall of man.
PARADISE REGAINED: Poem by Milton on the temptation and triumph of Jesus.
PARTHENON: A temple of Minerva in Athens.
PASQUINADE: A lampoon or satirical writing. Political squibs used to be posted on an old statue that stood in Rome near the house of a sneering old cobbler named Pasquin.
PHILIPPIC: An invective. The orations of Demosthenes against Philip of Macedon originated this word.
PHILOSOPHER'S STONE, THE: A substance supposed to have the property of turning anything else into gold.
PLUMED KNIGHT, THE: J.G. Blaine, American statesman.
PLYMOUTH ROCK: The rock at Plymouth, Mass., where the Pilgrims landed in 1620.
POOR RICHARD: Benjamin Franklin.
PHOENIX: A mythical bird, without a mate, renews itself every five hundred years by being consumed in a fire of spices, whence it rises from the ashes and starts for a new flight.
PIED PIPER OF HAMLIN, THE: Not being paid for having drawn, by the sound of his pipe, the rats and mice out of Hamelin into the river, he piped the children of the town into Koppelberg Hill, where 130 of them died.
PIGEON ENGLISH: A mixture of English, Chinese, and Portuguese.
PYRAMIDS: A number of remarkable old structures in Egypt.

QUAKER CITY, THE: Philadelphia, Pa.
QUEEN OF THE ANTILLES: The island of Cuba.

RED LETTER DAY: A fortunate day. In old calendars a red letter was used to mark the saints'
        days.
RED TAPE: Official routine.
REIGN OF TERROR: The time during the French Revolution between the overthrow of the
        Girondists, May 31, 1793, and the fall of Robespierre, July 27, 1794.
REYNARD THE FOX: A romance of the fourteenth century.
ROOST, TO RULE THE: To take the leading part.
ROLAND FOR AN OLIVER, A: Tit for tat. Roland and Oliver, two peers of Charlemagne. So
        many romances were related of these knights that, whenever one told an improbable story
        to match one that had been told before, it was called a Roland for an Oliver.
ROUGH AND READY: Gen. Zachary Taylor.
ROUND ROBIN: A petition or remonstrance signed by the names in a circle, so as to conceal
        who signed it first.
ROUND TABLE, THE: King Arthur's knights sat at a round table so that any distinction of rank
        was avoided.
ROUNDHEADS: The Puritans, who wore short hair.
ROZINANTE: The horse of Don Quixote.
RUBICON, TO PASS THE: To take an irretrievable step. When Caesar crossed the Rubicon,
        he became an enemy of the Republic.
RULE BRITANNIA: An English song.
RUMP PARLIAMENT, THE: A remnant of the Long Parliament broken up by Cromwell.

SABBATH DAY'S JOURNEY: About one mile.
SACK, TO GET THE: To be discharged. The Sultan, when he wanted to be rid of one of his
        harem, had her put into a sack and thrown into the Bosphorus.
SADDUCEES: A sect of the ancient Jews who denied the resurrection of the dead and the
        expectation of a future state.
SAGAS: Scandinavian books containing the Northern legends.
SAINT BARTHOLOMEW, MASSACRE OF: Massacre of the French Huguenots in the reign of
        Charles IX on St. Bartholomew's Day, 1572.
SAINT JAMES, THE COURT OF: The English court, so called from the Palace of St. James in
        London, formerly a royal residence.
SAINT MARK'S: Cathedral of Venice, Italy.
SAINT PAUL'S: The cathedral of London; designed by Sir Christopher Wren.
SAINT PETER'S: At Rome; is the most splendid church building in the world.
SAINT SOPHIA: A mosque in Constantinople, Turkey.
SAINT STEPHENS: A Gothic cathedral in Vienna, Austria.
SALT RIVER: Oblivion. Gone up Salt River is generally taken to mean political defeat.
SANCTUM: One's private office.
SANHEDRIM: The Jewish court of seventy elders.
SANS CULOTTES: (Without trousers) The French revolutionists.
SANS SOUCI: Palace of Frederick the Great, at Potsdam, near Berlin.
SANTA CROCE: A church in Florence, Italy, the burial-place of Michelangelo, Galileo,
        Machiavelli, and others.
SATURNALIA: A festival in honor of Saturn observed annually by the Romans by giving way to
        the wildest disorders. Unrestrained license for all classes, even to the slaves, ruled the
        city for three days, December 17, 18, and 19.

SCHOOLMEN: The medieval theologians.

SCOTLAND YARD: The headquarters of the London police.

SCOURGE OF GOD, THE: Atilla, King of the Huns.

SCYLLA: (Avoiding Scylla he fell into Charybdis) In trying to avoid one danger he fell into another. Scylla and Charybdis were the two dangers in the Strait of Messina, Italy.

SEPTUAGINT: A Greek version of the Old Testament prepared by seventy doctors.

SEVEN-HILLED CITY, THE: Rome.

SEVEN WONDERS OF THE WORLD: The pyramids of Egypt; the Temple of Diana at Ephesus; the hanging gardens of Babylon; the Colossus at Rhodes; the Mausoleum at Halicarnassus; the statue of Zeus by Phidias at Olympus; and the Pharos (or light-house) of Alexandria in Egypt.

SEVEN YEARS' WAR: The war of Frederick the Great against France, Austria, and Russia, 1756 to 1763.

SHAMROCK: The emblem of Ireland. St. Patrick made use of it to prove the doctrine of the Trinity.

SPANISH MAIN: The southwestern part of the Gulf of Mexico.

SPHINX: An emblem of silence and mystery. A monument near Cairo, Egypt; half woman, half lion.

STABAT MATER: A Latin hymn on the Crucifixion.

SIX HUNDRED, CHARGE OF THE: At the battle of Balaklava, October 25, 1854, by a mistaken order, the British light cavalry, 670 strong, made a most gallant charge on the Russians.

SLEEPING BEAUTY, THE: A fairy tale.

SMELL OF THE LAMP: A phrase first applied to the orations of Demosthenes, showing their careful and labored preparation. Demosthenes studied in a cave by lamplight.

SONG OF ROLAN: An old French poem recounting the deaths of Oliver and Roland at Roncesvalles.

SHIBBOLETH: A countersign. The password of a secret society. When the Emphraimites, after being routed by Jepthah, tried to pass the Jordan, they were detected by not being able to pronounce properly the word Shibboleth.

STAR CHAMBER: A court of criminal jurisdiction in England having extensive powers. It existed from the time of Henry VIII until that of Charles I.

"STONEWALL" JACKSON: Gen. Thomas J. Jackson, Confederate General.

SWEDISH NIGHTINGALE: Jenny Lind.

SORBONNE, THE: A university in Paris founded by Robert de Sorbonne in the thirteenth century.

TABOOED: Prohibited. A Polynesian word meaning consecrated; used for what is out of date or in bad taste.

TAMMANY HALL: A section of the Democratic party in New York City, named from their place of meeting.

TAMMANY RING: Or the "Tweed Ring," or "the Ring." A set of New York City officials which absorbed large sums of the city money. Exposed in 1871.

TERMAGANT: A shrew. Termagant was, according to the Crusaders, the wife of Mahomet.

TERRA FIRMA: Dry land.

THIRTY YEARS' WAR, THE: Between the Catholics and Protestants in Germany, 1618 – 1648.

THOR: Is the god of war, son of Odin, the Scandinavian Myth.

THREADNEEDLE STREET, THE OLD LADY OF: The Bank of England.

THREE ESTATES OF THE REALM: The nobility, the clergy, and the commonalty; represented in the two houses of Parliament.

TORY: The name of an English political party; opposite of Whig.

TOWER, THE: The citadel of London.

TROUBADOURS: Provencal poets from the eleventh to the fourth century.

TROUVÈRES: Northern French poets 1100 to 1400.

TRUMPET, TO SOUND ONE'S OWN: To boast. The entrance of knights into a list was announced by the heralds with a flourish of trumpets.

UFFIZI: A building in Florence in which is a magnificent art collection.

UNDERGROUND RAILROAD, THE: Organization for the escape of runaway slaves, about the middle of the 19th century.

UNDER THE ROSE: Confidentially. (Sub rosa)

UNTER DEN LINDEN: A street in Berlin having four rows of lime trees.

UNWASHED, THE GREAT: The mob.

UTOPIA: An ideal commonwealth. The imaginary island, scene of Sir Thomas More's romance of Utopia.

VALHALLA: The palace of immortality, where the heroes slain in battle dwell. (From the Saga legends)

VENI, VIDI, VICI: (I came, I saw, I conquered) Phrase used by Julius Caesar, announcing his victory at Zela.

VENUS DE MEDICI: A Greek statue at Florence.

VENUS OF MILO: A Greek statue found in the Island of Melos, 1820; it is now in the Louvre.

VERSAILLES: A palace at Versailles, ten miles from Paris.

WALL STREET: The great financial district of New York.

WALTON, AN IZAAK: An angler.

WATERS, THE FATHER OF: The Mississippi.

WAYS AND MEANS: An important committee of the House of Representatives; is charged with the duty of devising ways and means for the raising of government expenses.

WEDDING: The first anniversary of a wedding is the paper wedding, the gifts being paper articles; the fifth, wooden; the tenth, tin; the fifteenth, glass; twenty-fifth, silver; fiftieth, golden; seventy-fifth, diamond.

WESTMINSTER ABBEY: A church in London where many of the illustrious dead of England are buried.

WHITE FEATHER, TO SHOW THE: A display of cowardice.

WILD HUNTSMAN, THE: A spectral huntsman in the Black Forest. German legend.

WINDSOR CASTLE: .A royal residence near London.

WOODEN HORSE: A ruse at the siege of Troy.

XANTHOS: The prophetic horse of Achilles.

XANTIPPE: The scolding wife of Socrates,

YAHOO: A ruffian. The Yahoos in Gulliver's Travels are brutes shaped like men.\

YELLOW JACK: The yellow fever.

ZEND-AVESTA, THE: Persian Scriptures written in the Zend language.

ZOLLVEREIN: An association between German States for the maintenance of uniform tariff rates. (19th century)

————————

CLASSICAL MYTHOLOGY

ACHATES: The trusty friend of Aeneas.

ACHERON: The son of Sol and Terra, changed by Jupiter into a river of hell. Used also for hell itself.

ACHILLES: A Greek who distinguished himself in the war against Troy. Having been dipp4ed by his mother in the river Styx, he was invulnerable in every part except his right heel, but was at length killed by Paris with an arrow.

ACIS: A Sicilian shepherd, killed by Polyphemus because he rivaled the latter in the affections of Galatea.

ACTAEON: A famous hunter, who, having surprised Diana as she was bathing, was turned by her into a stag, and killed by his own dogs.

ADONIS: A beautiful youth beloved by Venus and Proserpine. He was killed by a wild boar. When wounded, Venus sprinkled nectar into his blood, from which flowers sprang up.

AEGEUS: A king of Athens, giving name to the AEgean sea by drowning himself in it.

AEGIS: A shield given by Jupiter to Minerva. Also the name of a Gorgon whom Pallas slew.

AENEAS: A Trojan prince, son of Anchises and Venus; the hero of Virgil's poem, the Aeneid.

AEOLUS: The god of the winds.

AEOUS: One of the four horses of the sun.

AESCULAPIUS: The god of medicine, and the son of Apollo. Killed by Jupiter with a thunderbolt for having restored Hippolytus to life.

AETHON: One of the four horses of the sun.

AGAMEMNON: King of Mycenae and Argos, brother to Menelaus, and chosen captain-general of the Greeks at the siege of Troy.

AGANIPPE: A fountain at the foot of Mount Helicon, daughter of the river Permessus.

AGLAIA: One of the three Graces.

AJAX: Next to Achilles, the bravest of all the Greeks in the Trojan War.

ALBION: The son of Neptune; went into Britain and established a kingdom.

ALCESTE, or ALLCESTIS: The daughter of Pelias and wife of Admetus, brought back from hell by Hercules.

ALCIDES: A title of Hercules.

ALECTO: One of the three Furies.

ALOA: A festival of Bacchus and Ceres.

AMMON: A title of Jupiter.

AMPHION: A famous musician, the son of Jupiter and Antiope, who built the city of Thebes by the music of his harp. He and his brother Zethus are said to have invented music.

AMPHITRITE: Goddess of the sea, and wife of Neptune.

ANDROMACHE: Wife of Hector.

ANDROMEDA: The daughter of Cepheus and Cassiopeia, who, contesting with Juno and the Nereides for the prize of beauty, was bound to a rock by them and exposed to a sea monster, but was rescued and married by Perseus.

ANGERONA: The goddess of silence.

ANTAEUS: The giant son of Neptune and Terra; squeezed to death by Hercules.

ANTEVERTA: Goddess of women in labor.

ANTIGONE: The daughter of OEdipus an Jocasta, famous for her filial piety.

ANUBIS: An Egyptian god with a dog's head.

APIS: Son of Jupiter and Niobe; called also Serapis and Osiris. Taught the Egyptians to sow corn and plant vines, and worshipped by them in the form of an ox.

APOLLO: The son of Jupiter and Latona, and the god of music, poetry, eloquence, medicine, and the fine arts.

ARACHNE: A Lydian princess, turned into a spider for contending with Minerva at spinning.

ARETHUSA: One of Diana's nymphs, who was changed into a fountain.

ARGUS: The son of Aristor; said to have had a hundred eyes; but being killed by Mercury when appointed by Juno to guard IO, she put his eyes on the tail of a peacock. Also an architect who built the ship Argo.

ARIADNE: The daughter of Minos, who, from love to Theseus, gave him a clew of thread, to guide him out of the Cretan labyrinth; being afterward deserted by him, she was married to Bacchus, and made his priestess.

ARION: A lyric poet of Methymna, who, in his voyage to Italy, saved his life from the cruelty of the mariners by means of dolphins, which the sweetness of his music brought together.

ARISTAEUS: A son of Apollo and Cyrene.

ASTRAEA: The goddess of justice; changed into the constellation Virgo.

ATALANTA: A princess of Scyros, who consented to marry that one of her suitors who should outrun her, Hippomenes being the successful competitor.

ATLAS: One of the Titans, and king of Mauretania; said to have supported the world on his shoulders; he was turned into a mountain by Perseus.

AURORA: The goddess of morning.

AUTUMNUS: The god of fruits.

BACCHANTES: Priests of Bacchus.

BACCHUS: The son of Jupiter and Semele, and the god of wine.

BAPTA: The goddess of shame.

BELLEROPHON: The son of Glaucus, king of Ephyra. He underwent numerous hardships for refusing an intimacy with Sthenoboea, wife of Proetus, the king of Argos. With the aid of the horse Pegasus, he destroyed the Chimera.

BELLONA: Goddess of war; sister of Mars.

BERENICE: A Grecian lady; the only person of her sex permitted to see the Olympic games.

BOLINA: A nymph rendered immortal for her modesty and resistance to Apollo.

BOREAS: The son of Astraeus and Aurora; the name of the north wind.

BRIAREUS: A giant who warred against heaven, and was feigned to have had fifty heads and one hundred arms.

BUSIRIS: The son of Neptune; a tyrant of Egypt, and a monstrous giant, who fed his horses with human flesh; was killed by Hercules.

BYBLIS: The daughter of Miletus; she wept herself into a fountain through love of her brother Camus.

CACUS: A son of Vulcan and a most notorious robber; slain by Hercules for stealing his oxen.

CADMUS: The son of Agenor, king of Phoenicia; founder of Thebes, and the reputed inventor of sixteen letters of the Greek alphabet.

CADUCEUS: Mercury's golden rod or want.

CALLIOPE: One of the Muses, presiding over eloquence and epic poetry.

CALYPSO: One of the Oceanides, who reigned in the island Ogygia, and entertained and became enamored of Ulysses.

CAMAENA, or CARNA: Goddess of infants.

CASSANDRA: A daughter of Priam and Hecuba, endowed with the gift of prophecy by Apollo.

CASTALIDES: The Muses, so called from the fountain Castalius, at the foot of Parnassus.

CASTOR: A son of Jupiter and Leda. He and his twin brother Pollux shared immortality alternately, and were formed into the constellation Gemini.

CECROPS: The first king of Athens; who instituted marriage, altars, and sacrifices.

CENTAURS: Children of Ixion, half men and half horses, inhabiting Thessaly, and vanquished by Theseus.

CERBERUS: The three-headed dog of Pluto, guarding the gates of hell.

CERES: The daughter of Saturn and Cybele, and goddess of agriculture.

CHARON: The son of Erebus and Nox, and ferryman of hell who conducted the souls of the dead over the rivers Styx and Acheron.

CHARYBDIS: A ravenous woman, turned by Jupiter into a very dangerous gulf or whirlpool on the coast of Sicily.

CHIMERA: A strange monster of Lycia, killed by Bellerophon.

CHIRON: A Centaur, who was preceptor to Achilles, taught Aesculapius physics, and Hercules astronomy, and who became the constellation Sagittarius.

CHRYSEIS: The daughter of Chryses, priest of Apollo, famed for beauty and for her skill in embroidery.

CIRCE: A noted enchantress.

CLIO: One of the Muses, presiding over history.

CLOTHO: One of the three fates.

CLYTEMNESTRA: The faithless wife of Agamemnon, killed by her son Orestes.

COMUS: The god of merriment.

CROCUS: A young man enamored of the nymph Smilax, and changed into a flower.

CROESUS: King of Lydia; the richest man of his time.

CUPID: Son of Mars and Venus; the god of love.

CYBELE: The daughter of Coelus and Terra; wife of Saturn, and mother of the gods.

CYCLOPS: Vulcan's workmen, giants who had only one eye, in the middle of their foreheads; slain by Apollo in a pique against Jupiter.

DAEDALUS: A most ingenious artificer of Athens, who formed the Cretan labyrinth, and invented the auger, axe, glue, plumb-line, saw, and masts and sails for ships.

DAMON: The friend of Pythias.

DANAIDES, or BELIDES: The fifty daughters of Danaus, king of Argos, all of whom, except Hypermnestra, killed their husbands on the first night of their marriage, and were therefore doomed to draw water out of a deep well, and eternally pour it into a cask full of holes.

DAPHNE: A nymph beloved by Apollo; the daughter of the river Peneus; changed into a laurel tree.

DAPHNIS: A shepherd of Sicily and son of Mercury; educated by the nymphs, and inspired by the Muses with the love of poetry.

DARDANUS: A son of Jupiter and founder of Troy.

DEIDAMIA: The daughter of Lycomedes, king of Scyros; wife of Achilles, and mother of Pyrrhus.

DEIPHOBUS: A son of Priam and Hecuba; married Helena after the death of Paris, but betrayed by her to the Greeks.

DEJANIRA: Wife of Hercules, who killed herself in despair, because her husband burnt himself to avoid the torment occasioned by the poisoned shirt she had given him to regain his love.

DELPHI: A city of Phocis, famous for a temple and an oracle of Apollo.

DEUCALION: The son of Prometheus, and king of Thessaly, who, with his wife Pyrrha, was preserved from the general deluge, and repeopled the world by throwing stones behind them; as directed by the oracle.

DIANA: Daughter of Jupiter and Latona, and goddess of hunting, chastity, and marriage.

DIDO: Founder and queen of Carthage; daughter of Belus, and wife of Sicheus. According to Virgil, she entertained Aeneas on his voyage to Italy, and burnt herself through despair, because he left her.

DIOMEDES: Son of Tydeus, and king of Aetolia; gained great reputation at Troy, and, with Ulysses, carried off the Palladium.

DIROE: Wife of Lycus, king of Thebes; dragged to death by a mad bull.

DRYADES: Nymphs of the woods.

ECHO: The daughter of Aer, or Air, and Tellus, who pined away for love of Narcissus.

ELECTRA: Daughter of Agamemnon and Clytemnestra; instigated her brother Orestes to revenge their father's death upon their mother and Aegisthus.

ELYSIUM: The happy residence of the virtuous after death.

ENCELADUS: Son of Titan and Terra, and the strongest of the giants; conspired against Jupiter, and attempted to scale heaven.

ENDYMION: A shepherd and astronomer of Caria, condemned to a sleep of thirty years.

EPEUS: The artist who made the Trojan horse, inventor of the sword and buckler.

ERATO: The Muse of lyric and amorous poetry.

EREANE: A river whose waters inebriated.

EREBUS: The son of Chaos and Nox; an infernal deity. A river of hell, and often used by the poets for hell itself.

ERINYS: (pl. Erinves) The Greek name for the Furies, or Eumenides.

EROS: A name of Cupid.

EUMENIDES: A name of the Furies.

EUPHORBUS: The son of Panthous; slain by Menelaus in the Trojan War.

EUPHROSYNE: One of the three Graces.

EUROPA: The daughter of Agenor; carried by Jupiter, in the form of a white bull, into Crete.

EURYALE: A queen of the Amazons. Also one of the three Gorgons.

EURYALUS: A Peloponnesian chief in the Trojan War. Also, a Trojan and a friend of Nisus, for whose loss AEneas was inconsolable.

EURYDICE: Wife of Orpheus; killed by a serpent on her marriage day.

EURYLOCHUS: One of the companions of Ulysses; the only one who was not changed by Circe into a hog.

EUTERPE: One of the Muses, presiding over music.

EVADNE: Daughter of Mars and Thebe; threw herself on the funeral pyre of her husband, Cataneus.

FABULA: Goddess of lies.

FAMA: Goddess of report, etc.

FATES: Powerful goddesses, who presided over the birth and the life of mankind, were the three daughters of Nox and Erebus, named Clotho, Lachesis, and Atropos. Clotho was supposed to hold the distaff, Lachesis to draw the thread of human life, and Atropos to cut it off.

FAUNA, and FATUA: Names of Cybele.

FAUNI: Rural gods, described as having the legs, fet, and ears of goats.

FAUNUS: Son of Mercury and Nox, and father of the Fauni.

FLORA: The goddess of flowers.

FORTUNA: The goddess of fortune; said to be blind.

FURIES: The three daughters of Nox and Acheron, named Alecto, Tisiphone, and Megaera, with hair composed of snakes, and armed with whips, chains, etc.

GÁLATEA: A sea-nymph, daughter of Nereus and Doris, passionately loved by Polyphemus.

GANYMEDE: The son of Tros, King of Troy, whom Jupiter, in the form of an eagle, snatched up and made his cup-bearer.

GERYON: A monster, having three bodies and three heads, and who fed his oxen with human flesh, and was therefore killed by Hercules.

GORDIUS: A husbandman, but afterward king of Phrygia, remarkable for tying a knot of cords, on which the empire of Asia depended, in so intricate a manner, that Alexander, unable to unravel it, cut it asunder.

GORGONS: The three daughters of Phorcus and Ceta, named Stheno, Euryale, and Medusa. Their bodies were covered with impenetrable scales, their hair entwined with serpents; they had only one eye betwixt them, and they could change into stones those whom they looked on.

GRACES: Three goddesses, Aglaia, Thalia, and Euphrosyne, represented as beautiful, modest virgins, and constant attendants on Venus.

HADES: A title of Pluto.

HARPIES: Winged monsters, daughters of Neptune and Terra, named Aello, Celaeno, and Ocypete, with the faces of virgins, the bodies of vultures, and hands armed with claws.

HEBE: The daughter of Juno, goddess of youth, and Jupiter's cup-bearer; banished from heaven on account of an unlucky fall.

HECTOR: The son of Priam and Hecuba; the most valiant of the Trojans, and slain by Achilles.

HECUBA: The wife of Priam, who tore her eyes out for the loss of her children.

HELENA, or HELEN: The wife of Menelaus, and the most beautiful woman of her age, who, running away with Paris, occasioned the Trojan War.

HELENUS: A son of Priam and Hecuba, spared by the Greeks for his skill in divination.

HELLE: The daughter of Athamas, who, flying from her stepmother Ino, was drowned in the Pontic Sea, and gave it the name of Hellespont.

HERCULES: The son of Jupiter and Alcmena; the most famous hero of antiquity, remarkable for his great strength and numerous exploits.

HERMES: A name of Mercury.

HERMIONE: The daughter of Mars and Venus, and wife of Cadmus; was changed into a serpent. Also, a daughter of Menelaus and Helena, married to Pyrrhus.

HERO: A beautiful woman of Sestos, in Thrace, and priestess of Venus, whom Leander of Abydos loved so tenderly that he swam over the Hellespont every night to see her; but he, at length, being unfortunately drowned, she threw herself, in despair, into the sea.

HESPERIDES: Three nymphs, AEgle, Arethusa, and Hesperethusa, daughters of Hesperus. They had a garden bearing golden apples, watched by a dragon, which Hercules slew, and bore away the fruit.

HESPERUS: The son of Japetus, and brother to Atlas, changed into the evening star.

HIPPOLYTUS: The son of Theseus and Antiope, or Hippolyte, who was restored to life by AEsculapius, at the request of Diana.

HIPPOMENES: A Grecian prince, who, beating Atalanta in the race by throwing golden apples before her, married her. They were changed by Cybele into lions.

HYACINTHUS: A beautiful boy, beloved by Apollo and Zephyrus. The latter killed him; but Apollo changed the blood that was spilt into a flower called hyacinth.

HYADES: Seven daughters of Atlas and AEthra, changed by Jupiter into seven stars.

HYDRA: A celebrated monster, or serpent, with seven, or, according to some, fifty heads, which infested the Lake Lerna. It was killed by Hercules.

HYMEN: Son of Bacchus and Venus, and god of marriage.

HYPERION: Son of Coelus and Terra.

ICARIUS: Son of OEbalus; having received from Bacchus a bottle of wine, he went into Attica to show men the use of it, but was thrown into a well by some shepherds whom he had made drunk and who thought he had given them poison.

ICARUS: The son of Daedalus, who, flying with his father out of Crete into Sicily, and soaring too high, melted the wax of his wings, and fell into the sea, thence called the Icarian Sea.

IO: The daughter of Inachus, turned by Jupiter into a white heifer, but afterward resumed her former shape; was worshipped after her death by the Egyptians, under the name of Isis.

IPHIGENIA: The daughter of Agamemnon and Clytemnestra, who, standing ready as a victim to be sacrificed to appease the ire of Diana, was by that goddess transformed into a white hart and made a priestess.

IRIS: The daughter of Thaumas and Electra; one of the Oceanides, and messenger and companion of Juno, who turned her into a rainbow.

IXION: A king of Thessaly, and father of the Centaurs. He killed his own sister, and was punished by being fastened in hell to a wheel perpetually turning.

JANUS: The son of Apollo and Creusa, and first king of Italy, who, receiving the banished Saturn, was rewarded by him with the knowledge of husbandry, and of things past and future.

JASON: The leader of the Argonauts, who, with Medea's help, obtained the golden fleece from Colchis.

JOCASTA: The daughter of Creon. She unwittingly married her own son OEdipus.

JUNO: The daughter of Saturn and Ops; sister and wife of Jupiter, the great queen of heaven, and of all the gods, and goddess of marriages and births.

JUPITER: The son of Saturn and Ops; the supreme deity of the heathen world, the most powerful of the gods, and governor of all things.

LACHESIS: One of the three Fates.

LAOCOON: A son of Priam and Hecuba, and high priest of Apollo, who opposed the reception of the wooden horse into Troy, for which he and his two sons were killed by serpents.

LAOMEDON: A king of Troy, killed by Hercules for denying him his daughter Hesione after he had delivered her from the sea-monster.

LARES: Inferior gods at Rome, who presided over houses and families; sons of Mercury and Lara.

LAVERNA: A goddess of thieves.

LEANDER: See Hero.

LETHE: A river of hell whose waters caused a total forgetfulness of things past.

LUBENTIA: Goddess of pleasure.

LUCIFER: The name of the planet Venus, or morning star, said to be the son of Jupiter and Aurora.

LUCINA: A daughter of Jupiter and Juno, and a goddess who presided over childbirth.

LUNA: The moon; the daughter of Hyperion and Terra.

LUPERCALIA: Feasts in honor of Pan.

MARS: The god of war.

MEDEA: The daughter of AEtes, and a wonderful sorceress or magician; she assisted Jason to obtain the golden fleece.

MEDUSA: The chief of the three Gorgons; killed by Perseus.

MAGAERA: One of the Furies.

MEGARA: Wife of Hercules.

MELPOMENE: One of the Muses, presiding over tragedy.

MEMNON: The son of Tithonus and Aurora, and king of Abydon; killed by Achilles for assisting Priam, and changed into a bird at the request of his mother.

MENELAUS: The son of Atreus, king of Sparta; brother of Agamemnon, and husband of Helen.

MENTOR: The faithful friend of Ulysses, the governor of Telemachus, and the wisest man of his time.

MERCURY: The son of Jupiter and Maia; messenger of the gods, inventor of letters, and god of eloquence, commerce, and robbers.

MIDAS: A king of Phrygia, who had the power given him of turning whatever he touched into gold.

MINERVA: The goddess of wisdom, the arts, and war; produced from Jupiter's brain.

MINOTAUR: A celebrated monster, half man and half bull.

MNEMOSYNE: The goddess of memory, and mother of the nine Muses.

MOMUS: The son of Nox, and god of folly and pleasantry.

MORPHEUS: The minister of Nox and Somnus, and god of sleep and dreams.

MORS: (Thanatos) God of death.

MUSES: Nine daughters of Jupiter and Mnemosyne, named Calliope, Clio, Erato, Euterpe, Melpomene, Polyhymnia, Terpsichore, Thalia, and Urania. They were mistresses of all the sciences, and governesses of the feasts of the gods.

MUTA: Goddess of silence.

NAIADES: Nymphs of streams and fountains.

NARCISSUS: A beautiful youth, who, falling in love with his own reflection in the water, pined away into a daffodil.

NEMESIS: One of the infernal deities, and goddess of revenge.

NEPTUNE: The son of Saturn and Ops; god of the sea, and, next to Jupiter, the most powerful deity.

NEREIDS: Sea-nymphs.

NESTOR: The son of Neleus and Chloris, and king of Pylos and Messenia. He fought against the Centaurs, was distinguished in the Trojan War, and lived to a great age.

NIOBE: Daughter of Tantalus, and wife of Amphion, who, preferring herself to Latona, had her fourteen children killed by Diana and Apollo, and wept herself into a stone.

NOX: The most ancient of all the deities, and goddess of night.

OCEANIDES: Sea-nymphs, daughters of Oceanus; three thousand in number.

OCEANUS: An ancient sea-god.

OEDIPUS: King of Thebes, who solved the riddle of the Sphinx, unwittingly killed his father, married his mother, and at last ran mad and tore out his eyes.

OMPHALE: A queen of Lydia, with whom Hercules was so enamored that he submitted to spinning and other unbecoming offices.

OPS: A name of Cybele.

ORESTES: The son of Agamemnon.

ORPHEUS: A celebrated Argonaut, whose skill in music is said to have been so great that he could make rocks, trees, etc., follow him. He was the son of Jupiter and Calliope.

OSIRIS: See APIS.

PALLADIUM: A statue of Minerva, which the Trojans imagined fell from heaven, and with which their city was deemed unconquerable.

PALLAS AND PYLOTIS: Names of Minerva.

PAN: The son of Mercury, and the god of shepherds, huntsmen, and the inhabitants of the country.

PANDORA: The first woman, made by Vulcan, and endowed with gifts by all the deities. Jupiter gave her a box which contained all the evils and miseries of life, but with hope at the bottom.

PARIS, or ATEXANDER: Son of Priam and Hecuba; a most beautiful youth, who ran away with Helen, and thus occasioned the Trojan War.

PARNASSUS: A mountain of Phocis, famous for a temple of Apollo; the favorite residence of the Muses.

PEGASUS: A winged horse belonging to Apollo and the Muses, which sprung from the blood of Medusa when Perseus cut off her head.

PENATES: Small statues, or household gods.

PENELOPE: A celebrated princess of Greece, daughter of Icarus, and wife of Ulysses; celebrated for her chastity and constancy in the long absence of her husband.

PERSEUS: Son of Jupiter and Danae; performed many extraordinary exploits by means of Medusa's head.

PHAETHON: Son of Sol (Apollo) and Climene. He asked the guidance of his father's chariot for one day as a proof of his divine descent; but, unable to manage the horses, set the world on fire, and was therefore struck by Jupiter with a thunderbolt into the river Po.

PHILOMELA: The daughter of Pandion, king of Athens; changed into a nightingale.

PHINEAS: King of Paphlagonia; had his eyes torn out by Boreas, but was recompensed with the knowledge of futurity. Also, a king of Thrace turned into a stone by Perseus.

PHOEBUS: A title of Apollo.

PLEIADES: Seven daughters of Atlas and Pleione, changed into stars.

PLUTO: The son of Saturn and Ops, brother of Jupiter and Neptune, and the god of the infernal regions.

PLUTUS: The god of riches.

POMONA: The goddess of fruits and autumn.

POLYHYMNIA: The Muse of rhetoric.

PRIAM: The last king of Troy, the son of Laomedon, under whose reign Troy was taken by the Greeks.

PROMETHEUS: The son of Japetus; said to have stolen fire from heaven to animate two bodies which he had formed of clay, and was therefore chained by Jupiter to Mount Caucasus, with a vulture perpetually gnawing his liver.

PROSERPINE: Wife of Pluto.

PROTEUS: The son of Oceanus and Tethyr; a sea-god and prophet, who possessed the power of changing himself into any shape.

PSYCHE: A nymph beloved by Cupid, and made immortal by Jupiter.

PYGMIES: A nation of dwarfs only a span long, carried away by Hercules.

PYLADES: The constant friend of Orestes.

PYRAMUS and THISBE: Two lovers of Babylon, who killed themselves with the same sword, and thus caused the berries of the mulberry tree, under which they died, to change from white to red.

PYTHON: A huge serpent, produced from the mud of the deluge; killed by Apollo, who, in memory thereof, instituted the Pythian games.

REMUS: The elder brother of Romulus, killed by him for ridiculing the city walls.

RHADAMANTHUS: One of the three infernal judges.

ROMULUS: The son of Mars Ilia; thrown into the Tiber by his uncle, but saved, with his twin brother, Remus, by a shepherd; became the founder and first king of Rome.

SALII: The twelve frantic priests of Mars.

SALUS: Goddess of health.

SATURNALIA: Feasts of Saturn.

SATURN: A son of Coelus and Terra; god of time.

SATYRS: Attendants of Bacchus; horned monsters, half goats, half men.

SEMELE: The daughter of Cadmus and Thebe, and mother of Bacchus.

SEMIRAMIS: A celebrated queen of Assyria, who built the walls of Babylon; was slain by her own son, Ninyas, and turned into a pigeon.

SERAPIS: See APIS.

SILENUS: The foster-father, master, and companion of Bacchus. He lived in Arcadia, rode on an ass, and was drunk every day.

SIRENS: Sea-nymphs, or sea-monsters, the daughters of Oceanus and Amphitrite.

SISYPHUS: The son of AEolus; a most crafty prince, killed by Theseus, and condemned by Pluto to roll up hill a large stone, which constantly fell back again.

SOL: A name of Apollo.

SOMNUS: The son of Erebus and Nox, and the god of sleep.

SPHINX: A monster, who destroyed herself because OEdipus solved the enigma she proposed.

STENTOR: A Grecian whose voice is reported to have been as strong and as loud as the voices of fifty men together.

STHENO: One of the three Gorgons.

STYX: A river of hell.

SYLVANUS: A god of woods and forests.

TACITA: A goddess of silence.

TANTALUS: The son of Jupiter, and king of Lydia, who served up the limbs of his son, Pelops, to try the divinity of the gods, for which he was plunged to the chin in a lake of hell, and doomed to everlasting thirst and hunger.

TARTARUS: The part of the infernal regions in which the wicked were punished.

TAURUS: The bull under whose form Jupiter carried away Europa.

TELEMACHUS: The only son of Ulysses.

TERPSICHORE: The Muse presiding over dancing.

THEMIS: The daughter of Coelus and Terra, and goddess of justice.

TIPHYS: Pilot of the ship Argo.

TISIPHONE: One of the three Furies.

TITAN: The son of Coelus and Terra, elder brother of Saturn, and one of the giants who warred against heaven.

TITHONUS: The son of Laomedon, loved by Aurora, and turned by her, in his old age, into a grasshopper.

TRITON: The son of Neptune and Amphitrite, a powerful sea-god, and Neptune's trumpeter.

TROILUS: A son of Priam and Hecuba.

TROY: A city of Phrygia, famous for holding out a siege of ten years against the Greeks, but finally captured and destroyed.

ULYSSES: King of Ithaca, who, by his subtlety and eloquence, was eminently serviceable to the Greeks in the Trojan War.

URANIA: The Muse of astronomy.

VENUS: One of the most celebrated deities of the ancients, the wife of Vulcan, the goddess of beauty, the mother of love, and the mistress of the graces and of pleasures.

VERTUMNUS: A deity of the Romans, who presided over spring and orchards, and who was the lover of Pomona.

VESTA: The sister of Ceres and Juno, the goddess of fire, and patroness of vestal virgins.

VIRIPLACA: An inferior nuptial goddess, who reconciled husbands and wives. A temple at Rome was dedicated to her, whither the married couple repaired after a quarrel.

VULCAN: The god who presided over subterraneous fire, patron of workers in metal.

ZEPHYRUS: The west wind, son of AEolus and Aurora, and lover of the goddess Flora.

ZEUS: A title of Jupiter

―――――――

IMPORTANT CHARACTERS IN LITERATURE

ABDIEL: "Paradise Lost," Milton. The faithful angel who opposed Satan in his revolt.

ABIGAIL: "The Bible." A waiting-maid.

ABLEWHITE, GODFREY: "Moonstone," Wilkie Collins. A disreputable spy.

ABOU HASSAN: "Arabian Nights." An Arab who was made to believe himself Caliph.

ABSALOM: (1) "The Bible" The son of David, King of Israel. (2) "Absalom and Achitophel," Dryden. A pseudonym for the Duke of Monmouth, an illegitimate son of King Charles II.

ABSOLUTE, CAPTAIN: "The Rivals," Sheridan. The hero of the comedy, the gallant and fortunate lover.

ABSOLUTE, SIR ANTHONY: "The Rivals," Sheridan. Father of Captain Absolute, a very irascible and absolute old gentleman.

ACHITOPHEL: "Absalom and Achitophel," Dryden. The pseudonym for the Earl of Shaftesbury.

ACRES, BOB: "The Rivals," Sheridan. A cowardly boaster, the butt of the comedy.

ACRASIA: "The Faery Queen," Spenser. An old witch, the personification of Intemperance.

ADAM, BELL: "Reliques," Percy. A celebrated archer.

ADAMS, PARSON: "Joseph Andrews," Fielding. An eccentric, good-natured clergyman.

ADRIANA: "Comedy of Errors," Shakespeare. The wife of Antipholus.

AGUECHEEK, SIR ANDREW: "Twelfth Night," Shakespeare. A coward and a fool.

ALADDIN: "Arabian Nights." The owner of a magic lamp and ring, which gave the possessor every wish he made.

ALLWORTHY, SQUIRE: "Tom Jones," Fielding. A good-natured old country gentleman.

ALP: "The Siege of Corinth," Byron. A brave and devoted man.

AMADIS DE GAUL: "Amadis de Gaul." The hero of a Portuguese chivalric romance, the authorship of which is unknown. It was translated into every language in Europe.

AMELIA: "Amelia," Fielding. A lovely woman, supposed to be drawn from Fielding's own wife.

AMINE: "Arabian Nights." A wicked sorceress who changed her three sisters into hounds.

AMLET, RICHARD: "The Confederacy," Vanburgh. A gambler.

AMRI: "Absalom and Achitophel," Dryden. Pseudonym for H. Finch.

ANDREWS, JOSEPH: "Joseph Andrews," Fielding. A hero ridiculously upright and pure.

ANERLEY, MARY: "Mary Anerley," Blackmore. A lovely and beautiful girl.

APEMANTUS: "Timon of Athens," Shakespeare. A cynic.

ARDEN, ENOCH: "Enoch Arden," Tennyson. A sailor, supposed drowned, who returns home to find his wife married again.

ARGANTE: "The Faery Queen," Spenser. A giantess.

ARIEL: "The Tempest," Shakespeare. A spirit of the air, perhaps the daintiest creation of the myriad-minded poet.

ARTFUL DODGER: "Oliver Twist," Dickens. A young thief who understands his business.

ARTHUR, KING: "Idyls of the King," Tennyson. A legendary British King, who established an order of chivalry known as the Round Table, and about whom many popular legends are afloat in Wales and Western France.

ASHTON, LUCY: "The Bride of Lammermoor," Scott. A beautiful character, loved and lost by Ravenswood.

ATALANTA: "Atalanta in Calydon," Swinburne. One of Diana's maidens.

AUTOLYCUS: "Winter's Tale," Shakespeare. An intellectual sneak-thief.

BABA, ALI: "Arabian Nights." The hero of the tale of the forty thieves, who breaks into the robbers' cave by means of the magical password "Sesame."

BABA, CASSIM: "Arabian Nights." Brother of the above, who forgets the password, and is captured by the robbers.

BACKBITE, SIR BENJAMIN: "School for Scandal," Sheridan. A scandal-monger.

BAGSTOCK, JOE: "Dombey and Son," Dickens. A pompous fellow.

BAILEY, YOUNG: "Martin Chuzzlewit," Dickens. A precocious youth.

BALDERSTONE, CALEB: "Bride of Lammermoor," Scott. The butler of Ravenswood.

BALTHAZAR: (1) "Comedy of Errors," Shakespeare. A merchant. (2) "Much Ado About Nothing," Shakespeare. A servant.

BANQUO: "Macbeth," Shakespeare. A chieftain murdered by Macbeth; later in the same play, a ghost.

BARDELL, MRS.: "Pickwick Papers," Dickens. Mr. Pickwick's landlady, who sues him for breach of promise of marriage.

BARDOLPH: "Henry IV," Shakespeare. A follower of Sir John Falstaff.

BARKIS: "David Copperfield," Dickens. A marrying man who eventually marries.

BATH, MAJOR: "Amelia," Fielding. A pompous officer.

BAYES: "The Rehearsal," Duke of Buckingham. A pseudonym for Dryden.

BAYNES, CHARLOTTE: "Adventures of Philip," Thackeray. The hero's sweetheart.

BEDE, ADAM: "Adam Bede," George Eliot. An ideal workingman.

BELCH, SIR TOBY: "Twelfth Night," Shakespeare. Olivia's hard-drinking uncle.

BELFORD: "Clarissa Harlowe," Richardson. The friend of Lovelace.

BELINDA: "Rape of the Lock," Pope. The heroine, whose hair is cut.

BELL, LAURA: "Pendennis," Thackeray. One of the sweetest heroines in English literature.

BELL, PETER: "Peter Bell," Wordsworth. An extremely prosaic man.

BELLASTON, LADY: "Tom Jones," Fielding. One of Tom Jones' sweethearts.

BELLENDEN, LADY: "Old Mortality," Scott. A Tory gentlewoman.

BELPHOEBE: "The Faery Queen," Spenser. A pseudonym for Queen Elizabeth.

BELVIDERA: "Venice Preserved," Otway. The heroine of the poem.

BENEDICT: "Love's Labor Lost," Shakespeare. A confirmed bachelor who was converted to matrimony by the lovely Beatrice. From this gentleman comes the name Benedict applied to married men who were not going to marry.

BENNET, MRS.: "Amelia," Fielding. An improper character.

BENVOLIO: "Romeo and Juliet," Shakespeare. One of Romeo's friends.

BERTRAM: "All's Well That Ends Well," Shakespeare. The hero of the play, who marries Helen.

BIANCA: "Othello," Shakespeare. Cassio's sweetheart.

BIRCH, HARVEY: "The Spy," Cooper. The chief character of the novel.

BILFIL: "Tom Jones," Fielding. Allworthy's nephew, a tale-bearer.

BLEMBER, MISS CORNELIA: "Dombey and Son," Dickens. A blue-stocking governess.

BOABDIL, CAPTAIN: "Every Man in His Humor," Johnson. A boasting coward.

BOEUF, FRONT DE: "Ivanhoe," Scott. One of King John's followers. A ferocious scoundrel.

BOFFIN, NODDY: "Our Mutual Friend," Dickens. The good-natured occupant of Boffin's Bower.

BOIS GUILBERT, BRIAN DE: "Ivanhoe," Scott. The master of the Knights Templars.

BONIFACE: "The Beaux' Stratagem," Farquhar. A landlord. Hence applied to landlords generally.

BOOBY, LADY: "Joseph Andrews," Fielding. One of the minor characters.

BOOTH: "Amelia," Fielding. The hero of the story.

BOTTOM, NICK: "A Midsummer Night's Dream," Shakespeare. A ridiculous weaver with whom Titania, the queen of the fairies, is forced to fall in love by a charm.

BOUNDERBY, JOSIAH: "Hard Times," Dickens. A prosaic, matter-of-fact manufacturer.

BOWLE, TOM: "Kenelm Chillingly," Bulwer. A blacksmith.

BOWLINE, TOM: "Roderick Random," Smollett. A sailor whose name has been applied to marines ever since.

BOX AND COX: "Box and Cox," Morton. The heroes of the farce.

BRADWARDINE, BARON: "Waverly," Scott. The father of Rose Bradwardine.

BRAMBLE, MATTHEW: "Humphrey Clinker," Smollett. A walking epitome of dyspepsia.

BRANGTONS: "Evelina," Miss Burney. Very vulgar people.

BRASS, SALLY AND SAMPSON: "Old Curiosity Shop," Dickens. A shystering lawyer and his sister.

BRICK, JEFFERSON: "Martin Chuzzlewit," Dickens. A ridiculous American editor.

BRIDGENORTH, MAJOR RALPH: "Peveril of the Peak," Scott. A prominent officer in the Puritan Army.

BRIDGET, MRS.: "Tristram Shandy," Sterne. Tristram's nurse.

BROWN, TOM: "Tom Brown's School Days" and "Tom Brown at Oxford," Thos. Hughes. The hero of one of the best boys' books ever written in English.

BUCKET, INSPECTOR: "Bleak House," Dickens. A detective.

BUMBLE: "Oliver Twist," Dickens. A beadle.

CAIUS, DOCTOR: "Merry Wives of Windsor," Shakespeare. Anne Page's Welsh lover.

CALIBAN: "The Tempest," Shakespeare. Prospero's monstrous servant.

CANDOR, MRS.: "The Rivals," Sheridan. A scandal-monger.

CARKER: "Dombey and Son," Dickens. A scoundrelly clerk.

CASSIO: "Othello," Shakespeare. Othello's lieutenant.

CAUDLE, MRS.: "Curtain Lectures," Douglas Jerrold. An artistic scold.

CAUSTIC, COL.: "The Lounger," Mackenzie. A satiricl gentleman.

CELIA: "As You Like It," Shakespeare. Rosalind's cousin.

CHADBAND: "Bleak House," Dickens. A hypocrite.

CHAMONT: "The Orphans," Otway. The hero of the play.

CHILLINGLY, KENELM: "Kenelm Chillingly," Bulwer. The hero of the novel.

CHRISTABEL: "Christabel," Coleridge. The heroine of the poem.

CHRISTIANA: "Pilgrim's Progress," Bunyan. The wife of the hero, Christian.

CHUZZLEWIT, JONAS AND MARTIN: "Martin Chuzzlewit," Dickens. The first a miser and murderer, the second the hero of Dickens' story.

CLARE, ADA: "Bleak House," Dickens. The wife of Carstone, and one of the most important characters in the story.

CLIFFORD, PAUL: "Paul Clifford," Bulwer. A beatified highwayman hero.

CLINKER, HUMPHREY: "Humphrey Clinker," Smollett. A philosophical young man who meets very singular adventures.

COELEBS: "Coelebs in Search of a Wife," Hannah More. A gentleman who has very precise ideas on the subjects of matrimony and woman.

COLDSTREAM, SIR CHARLES: "Used Up," Matthews. A fatigued and weary man of the world.

CONSUELO: "Consuelo," Georg Sand. The heroine of the novel, a rather inflammable young lady.

COPPER CAPTAIN, THE: "Rule a Wife, Have a Wife," Beaumont and Fletcher. A nickname applied to Peres, the boastful coward of the play.

COPPERFIELD, DAVID: "David Copperfield," Dickens. The hero of the novel, supposed to be a picture of Dickens' own life and character.

CORDELIA: "King Lear," Shakespeare. The faithful daughter of the King in the play.

CORINNE: "Corinne," Mme. de Stael. The heroine of de Stael's greatest work.

COSTIGAN, CAPTAIN: "Pendennis," Thackeray. The father of Pendennis' first sweetheart, a hard-drinking but amusing old man.

COVERLY, SIR ROGER DE: "Spectator," Addison. A model country gentleman of the olden time.

CRANE, ICHABOD: "Sleepy Hollow," Irving. The schoolmaster in the sketch.

CRAWLEY, RAWDON: "Vanity Fair," Thackeray. The hero of "the novel without a hero." The husband of Becky Sharp.

CRESSIDA: "Troilus and Cressida," Shakespeare. The heroine of the play, in love with Troilus.

CRUMMLES, VINCENT: "Nicholas Nickleby," Dickens. A theatrical head of a theatrical family.

CRUSOE, ROBINSON: "Robinson Crusoe," DeFoe. The hero of the most remarkable novel ever written. It has been translated into every civilized language on the globe. The story relates Crusoe's adventures on a desert isle upon which he was cast by the sea, and is one of intense interest.

CUTTLE, CAPTAIN: "Dombey and Son," Dickens. A nautical character who indulges in a number of queer mannerisms.

CYMBELINE: "Cymbeline," Shakespeare. A heroic King of Britain.

DALGARNO, LORD: "The Fortunes of Nigel," Scott. A Scottish nobleman of bad character.

DALGETTY, DUGALD: "Waverly," Scott. A famous and well-drawn soldier of fortune, whose name has become proverbial.

DEANS, DAVIE, EFFIE, AND JEANIE: "Heart of Midlothian," Scott. Famous characters in the story. Jeanie is the heroine.

DEDLOCK, LADY, AND SIR LEICESTER: "Bleak House," Dickens. Husband and wife, proud and unfortunate, but noble people.

DELAMAINE, GEOFFREY: "Man and Wife," Collins. A man of muscle.

DELPHINE: "Delphine," Mme. de Stael. The heroine of the novel.

DERONDA, DANIEL: "Daniel Deronda," George Eliot. The hero of the novel, one of the best character sketches which George Eliot has made.

DESDEMONA: "Othello," Shakespeare. The unfortunate heroine of the play, wife of the Moor, Othello.

DIDDLER, JEREMY: "Raising the Wind," Kinny. The prototype of all modern deadbeats.

DIMSDALE, REV. ARTHUR: "The Scarlet Letter," Hawthorne. The seducer of Hester Prynne.

DODS, MEG: "St. Roman's Well," Scott. A landlady.

DODSON AND FOGG: "Pickwick Papers," Dickens. Mrs. Bardell's attorneys in her suit against Mr. Pickwick.

DOGBERRY: "Much Ado About Nothing," Shakespeare. An absurd character who travesties justice.

DOMBEY, FLORENCE, MR. AND PAUL: "Dombey and Son," Dickens. Characters in the novel.

DOMINIE, SAMPSON: "Guy Mannering," Scott. An eccentric clergyman.

DON QUIXOTE: "Don Quixote," Cervantes. The hero of the novel.

DORA: "David Copperfield," Dickens. Copperfield's child-wife.

DORIMANT: "The Man of Mode," Etherege. A dandy.

DOROTHEA: "Middlemarch," George Eliot. The heroine of the tale.

DORRIT, EDWARD AND "LITTLE": "Little Dorrit," Dickens. The father of the Marshalsea Prison and his interesting daughter.

DRAWCANSIR: "The Rehearsal," The Duke of Buckingham. A bully.
DULCINEA DEL TOBOSO: "Don Quixote," Cervantes. A country girl whom Don Quixote selects as his lady love.
DUNDREARY, LORD: "Our American Cousin," Taylor. A typical and absurd English lord. The character was really created by the actor, Sothern.
EDGAR: "King Lear," Shakespeare. The son of Gloucester.
EMILIA: "Othello," Shakespeare. Wife of Iago, the villain of the play.
ESMOND, BEATRIX AND HENRY: "Henry Esmond," Thackeray. Heroine and hero of the novel, which is of the time of the English Revolution.
EUGENIA: "The Return of the Native," Hardy. A beautiful and unfortunate girl.
EVANGELINE: "Evangeline," Longfellow. Heroine of the poem; her wanderings are told in verse that will never die.
EVANS, SIR HUGH: "The Merry Wives of Windsor," Shakespeare. A Welsh clergyman.
EVELINA: "Evelina," Miss Burney. Heroine of the novel.
EYRE, JANE: "Jane Eyre," Bronte. Heroine of the novel.

FAG: "The Rivals," Sheridan. A servant.
FAGIN: "Oliver Twist," Dickens. The preceptor in the thieves' academy, where Oliver Twist is held a prisoner.
FAITHFUL, JACOB: "Jacob Faithful," Marryatt. The hero of the novel.
FALKLAND: "The Rivals," Sheridan. A jealous lover of Julia's and friend to Captain Absolute.
FALSTAFF, SIR JOHN: "Henry IV" and "The Merry Wives of Windsor," Shakespeare. This is Shakespeare's most comic character; Queen Elizabeth was so pleased with Sir John in Henry IV that, at her request, Shakespeare composed "The Merry Wives of Windsor" in order to give the fat knight a wider field for fun.
FANNY: "Under the Greenwood Tree," Hardy. A pretty school mistress.
FAT BOY, THE: "Pickwick Papers," Dickens. One of the minor characters in the novel, given to sleep and pie.
FAUST: "Faust," Goethe. The hero of the great German tragedy, who sells his soul to the Devil, and gets in return youth, wealth, and an attendant devil, Mephistopheles. Goethe was to Germany what Shakespeare was to England.
FELTON, SEPTIMIUS: "Septimius Felton," Hawthorne. The mystical hero of the novel.
FERDINAND: "The Tempest," Shakespeare. Son of the King, falls in love with Prospero's daughter, Miranda.
FERRERS, ENDYMION: "Endymion," Benjamin Disraeli. Hero of the novel.
FIGARO: "The Marriage of Figaro," Baumarchais. An exceedingly comical land sharp-witted barber.
FIRMIN, PHILIP: "The Adventures of Philip," Thackeray. The hero of the novel.
FLORIZEL: "A Winter's Tale," Shakespeare. The prince of Bohemia.
FLUELLEN: "Henry V," Shakespeare. A pedantic but brave Welsh officer.
FOKER, HARRY: "Pendennis," Thackeray. One of the minor characters.
FOPPINGTON, LORD: "The Relapse," Van Brugh. An idiotic dandy.
FOSCO, COUNT: "Woman in White," Collins. A complicated scoundrel.
FRANKENSTEIN: "Frankenstein," Mrs. Southey. The dreadful result of the labors of a German student, who makes a man in the dissecting room out of corpses and brings him to life by galvanism. The hideous hero of the novel has a series of most blood-curdling adventures.
FRIAR TUCK: "Reliques," Percy. The jolly companion of Robin Hood, the outlaw of Sherwood Forest.
FRIDAY: "Robinson Crusoe," DeFoe. Crusoe's savage servant.

GADGRIND, JEREMIAH: "Hard Times," Dickens. A tyrannical "practical" man.
GAMP, SAIRY: "Martin Chuzzlewit," Dickens. A comical and hard-drinking monthly nurse.
GARGANTUA: "Gargantua," Rabelais. Hero of the tale.
GAUNT, GRIFFITH: "Griffith Gaunt," Reade. Hero of the novel.
GAY, WALTER: "Dombey and Son," Dickens. Marries Florence Dombey.
GIBBIE, GOOSE: "Old Mortality" Scott. A half-witted boy.
GIL BLAS: "Gil Blas," Le Sage. The hero of a very famous novel. His adventures are of the
    most surprising character, and are told in a most interesting manner.
GILPIN, JOHN: "John Gilpin's Ride," Cowper. The absurd hero of the poem.
GINERVA: "Ginerva," Rogers. The heroine of the poem, accidentally locked in a trunk on her
    wedding day, and not found for years and years.
GOBBO, LAUNCELOT: "The Merchant of Venice," Shakespeare. A merry servant.
GONERIL: "King Lear," Shakespeare. The eldest daughter of the King, a traitor and an ingrate.
GONZALO: "The Tempest," Shakespeare. An old councilor.
GOSLING, GILES: "Kenilworth," Scott. A landlord.
GRANDISON, SIR CHARLES: "Sir Charles Grandison," Richardson. Hero of the novel.
GRAY, VIVIAN: "Vivian Gray," Disraeli. Hero of the novel.
GRUNDY, MRS.: "Speed the Plough," Morton. An old lady who represents worldly propriety
    and tale-bearing.
GULLIVER, LEMUEL: "Gulliver's Travels," Swift. Hero of the romance.

HAMLET: "Hamlet," Shakespeare. The melancholy Dane, hero of the play.
HARLEY: "The Man of Feeling," Mackenzie. Hero of the novel.
HARLOWE, CLARISSA: "Clarissa Harlowe," Richardson. Heroine of the novel.
HARRIS, MRS.: "Martin Chuzzlewit," Dickens. A fictitious person invented by Sairy Gamp, for
    the purpose of enforcing her statements by quoting the opinions of Mrs. Harris upon the
    subject under discussion.
HEADSTONE, BRADLEY: "Our Mutual Friend," Dickens. A schoolmaster in love with Lizzie
    Hexam.
HEEP, URIAH: "David Copperfield," Dickens. A hypocrite and sneak.
HELENA: "All's Well That Ends Well," Shakespeare. Heroine of the play.
HERO: "Much Ado About Nothing," Shakespeare. Daughter of Leonato.
HEXAM, LIZZIE: "Our Mutual Friend," Dickens. Heroine of the novel.
HOLOFERNES: "As You Like It," Shakespeare. A schoolmaster and pedant.
HOLT, FELIX: "Felix Holt," George Eliot. Hero of the novel.
HONEYMAN, CHARLES: "The Newcomes," Thackeray. A fashionable preacher.
HONOR, MRS.: "Tom Jones," Fielding. Sophia Western's waiting-woman.
HOPEFUL: "Pilgrim's Progress," Bunyan. A pilgrim.
HORATIO: "Hamlet," Shakespeare. The friend of Hamlet.
HOWE, MISS: "Clarissa Harlowe," Richardson. Clarissa's friend.
HUDIBRAS: "Hudibras," Butler. Hero of the poem.
HUNTER, MR. AND MRS. LEO: "Pickwick Papers," Dickens. Minor characters in the novel.

IAGO: "Othello," Shakespeare. The villain of the tragedy.
IMOGEN: ""Cymbeline," Shakespeare. Heroine of the play.
ISABELLA: "Measure for Measure," Shakespeare. Heroine of the play.
IVANHOE: "Ivanhoe," Scott. Hero of the novel.

JACK, COL.: "Col. Jack," DeFoe. The criminal hero of the tale.
JAFFIER: "Venice Preserved," Otway. Hero of the poem.

JAQUES: "As You Like It," Shakespeare. The melancholy philosopher.
JARNDYCE: "Bleak House," Dickens. A benevolent old gentleman.
JAVERT: "Les Miserables," Hugo. A detective.
JESSICA: "Merchant of Venice," Shakespeare. Shylock's daughter.
JINGLE, ALFRED: "Pickwick Papers," Dickens. An amusing adventurer.

KILMAUSEGG, MISS: "The Golden Legend," Hood. The golden-legged heroine of the poem.
KITELY: "Every Man in His Humor," Jonson. A jealous husband.

LADY BOUNTIFUL: "The Beau's Stratagem," Farquhar. A generous lady.
LAERTES: "Hamlet," Shakespeare. The son of Polonius, killed by his own sword.
LALLA ROOKH: "Lalla Rookh," Moore. Heroine of the poem, to whom Feramorz relates the
     stories told in the romance.
LANGUISH, LYDIA: "The Rivals," Sheridan. Heroine of the play.
LEAR, KING: "King Lear," Shakespeare. Hero of the play.
LEATHERSTOCKING, NATTY: "Pathfinder" and "Deerslayer," and other novels, Cooper. A
     huntsman and Indian fighter.
LEGREE: "Uncle Tom's Cabin," Stowe. Slave master.
LEIGH, AURORA: "Aurora Leigh," Browning. Heroine of the romance.
LEILA: "Giaour," Byron. Heroine of the poem.
LIGHTWOOD, MORTIMER: "Our Mutual Friend," Dickens. Minor character in the novel.
LISMAHAGO, CAPT.: "Humphrey Clinker," Smollett. A retired officer.
LITTLE, HENRY: "Put Yourself in His Place," Reade. Hero of the novel.
LITTLE NELL: "Old Curiosity Shop," Dickens. Heroine of the novel.
LOCKSLEY: "Ivanhoe," Scott. One of Robin Hood's pseudonyms.
LONG TOM COFFIN: "Pilot," Cooper. A boatman.
LOTHAIR: "Lothair," Disraeli. Hero of the novel, supposed pseudonym for the Marquis of Bute.
LOTHARIO: "The Fair Penitent," Rowe. A rake.
LOVELACE: "Clarissa Harlowe," Richardson. A rake.
LUMPKIN, TONY: "She Stoops to Conquer," Goldsmith. A country squire.
MACBETH: "Macbeth," Shakespeare. Hero of the play.
MACDUFF: "Macbeth," Shakespeare. Rival of Macbeth.
MAC IVOR, FLORA: "Rob Roy," Scott. Heroine of the novel.
MACKENSIE, MRS.: "Newcomes," Thackeray. A termagant widow.
MALAGROTHER, SIR MINGO: "The Fortunes of Nigel," Scott. An ill-natured courtier.
MALAPROP, MRS.: "The Rivals," Sheridan. A character famed for verbal blunders.
MALVOLIO: "Twelfth Night," Shakespeare. Olivia's conceited steward.
MANFRED: "Manfred," Byron. Hero of the tragedy.
MANTALINI: "Nicholas Nickleby," Dickens. The absurd husband of the milliner in the story.
MARCHIONESS, THE: "Old Curiosity Shop," Dickens. Mr. Dick Swiveller's remarkable little
     nurse.
MARGARET: "Faust," Goethe. The heroine of the tragedy.
MARLOW, YOUNG: "She Stoops to Conquer," Goldsmith. Hero of the play.
MEDORA: "The Corsair," Byron. Heroine of the poem.
MERDLE, MR.: "Little Dorrit," Dickens. A speculator.
MEISTER, WILHELM: "Wilhelm Meister," Goethe. Hero of the novel.
MEPHISTOPHELES: "Faust," Goethe. The Devil.
MERCUTIO: "Romeo and Juliet," Shakespeare. A wonderfully witty friend of Romeo's.
MICAWBER, WILKINS: "David Copperfield," Dickens. A remarkable character, always waiting
     for something to turn up.

MILLER, DAISY: "Daisy Miller," Henry James. An alleged representative American girl.
MINNA: "The Pirate," Scott. One of the heroines of the novel.
MIRANDA: "The Tempest," Shakespeare. Daughter of Prospero, beloved of Ferdinand; heroine of the play.
MONIMIA: "The Orphan," Otway. Heroine of the poem.
MOULDY: Henry IV," Shakespeare. One of Falstaff's recruits.
MUCKLEWRATH, HABBAKUK: "Old Mortality," Scott. A fanatical preacher.
NEUCHATEL, ADRIANA: "Endymion," Disraeli. A wealthy young lady.
NEWCOME, CLIVE, COLONEL, ETHEL: "The Newcomes," Thackeray. Characters in the best novel Thackeray has written.
NICKLEBY, MRS.: "Nicholas Nickleby," Dickens. The exasperating mother of the hero, Nicholas.
NORNA: "The Pirate," Scott. An insane soothsayer.
NYDIA: "Last Days of Pompeii," Bulwer. A blind flower girl.

OBADIAH: "Tristram Shandy," Sterne. A servant.
OBERON: "Midsummer Night's Dream," Shakespeare. The King of Fairyland.
OCHILTREE, EDIE: "The Antiquary," Scott. A beggar of prominence.
OLDBUCK, JONATHAN: "The Antiquary," Scott. Hero of the novel.
OLD MORTALITY: "Old Mortality," Scott. A gravestone cleaner.
OLIFAUNT, NIGEL: "The Fortunes of Nigel," Scott. Hero of the novel.
OPHELIA: "Hamlet," Shakespeare. Heroine of the tragedy.
ORVILLE, LORD: "Evelina," Miss Burney. Evelina's lover.
OTHELLO: "Othello," Shakespeare. Hero of the play, a Moor, husband of Desdemona.
O'TRIGGER, SIR LUCIUS: "The Rivals," Sheridan. A fire-eating Irishman.
OVERREACH, SIR GILES: "A New Way to Pay Old Debts," Massinger. A usurer.

PAGE, ANNA AND MRS.: "The Merry Wives of Windsor," Shakespeare. Characters in the play.
PAMELA: "Pamela," Richardson. An intensely good young lady.
PANGLOSS: "The Heir-at-Law," Colman. A pedantic teacher.
PANTAGRUEL: "Pantagruel," Rabelais. Hero of the sketch.
PARTRIDGE: "Tom Jones," Fielding. The hero's trusty follower.
PECKSNIFF, CHARITY, MERCY, MR.: "Martin Chuzzlewit," Dickens. Characters in the story.
PENDENNIS, ARTHUR, HELEN, MAJOR: "Pendennis," Thackeray. Well drawn and forcible characters in the novel.
PERDITA: "Winter's Tale," Shakespeare. Florizet's sweetheart.
PETRUCHIO: "The Taming of the Shrew," Shakespeare. The hero, and husband of Katherine.
PICKLE PEREGRINE: "Peregrine Pickle," Smollett. The wandering and immoral hero of the novel.
PICKWICK, SAMUEL: "Pickwick Papers," Dickens, Hero of the novel.
PIERRE: "Venice Preserved," Otway. A conspirator.
PISTOL, ANCIENT: "Merry Wives of Windsor" and "Henry IV," Shakespeare. Falstaff's most characteristic follower.
PLEYDELL, PAULUS: "Guy Mannering," Scott. A lawyer.
POINS, NED: "Henry IV," Shakespeare. A friend of Prince Hal.
PORTIA: "The Merchant of Venice," Shakespeare. Heroine of the play.
POUNDLINT, PETER: "Old Mortality," Scott. A preacher.
PRIMROSE, DR.: "Vicar of Wakefield," Goldsmith. The Vicar of Wakefield.
PRIMROSE, MOSES: "Vicar of Wakefield," Goldsmith. His son.

PROLIUS: "Two Gentlemen of Verona," Shakespeare. One of the two Gentlemen.
PROUDFUTE: "Fair Maid of Perth," Scott. A bonnet-maker.
PRYNNE, HESTER: "Scarlet Letter," Hawthorne. Heroine of the novel.
PUMBLECHOOK, UNCLE: "Great Expectations," Dickens. A bully and fraud.
PYNCHEON, PHOEBE: "House of the Seven Gables," Hawthorne. Heroine of the novel.

QUASIMODO: "Our Lady of Notre Dame," Hugo. A monster.
QUICKLY, MRS.: "Henry IV," Shakespeare. The famed hostess of the Boar's Head Tavern in Eastcheap.
QUILP: "Old Curiosity Shop," Dickens. A vicious dwarf.
QUINCE, PETER: "Midsummer Night's Dream," Shakespeare. Character in the interlude.

RANDOM, RODERICK: "Roderick Random," Smollett. Hero of the novel.
RASHLEIGH: "Rob Roy," Scott. The villain of the novel.
RASSELAS: "Rasselas," Dr. Johnson. Prince of Abyssinia, hero of the tale.
RATTLER, JACK: "Roderick Random," Smollett. A nautical character.
RAVENSWOOD: "The Bride of Lammermoor," Scott. Hero of the novel, lover of Lucy Ashton.
REBECCA: "Ivanhoe," Scott. A lovely Jewess.
REDGAUNTLET: "Redgauntlet," Scott. Hero of the novel.
ROB ROY: "Rob Roy," Scott. A Scottish chief, hero of the novel.
RODERIGO: "Othello," Shakespeare. Iago's dupe.
ROMEO: "Romeo and Juliet," Shakespeare. The hero of the play, lover of Juliet.
SABRINA: "Comus," Milton. River nymph.
SACRIPANT: "Orlando Furioso," Ariosto. King of Circassia, in love with Angelica.
SADDLETREE, BARTOLINE: "Heart of Midlothian," Scott. A learned peddler.
SANCHO PANZA: "Don Quixote," Cervantes. Worthy squire of a worthy master; the right man in the right place.
SANDFORD, HARRY: "Sandford and Merton," Day. Hero of the story.
SANGRADO, DOCTOR: "Gil Blas," Le Sage. A confirmed phlebotomist.
SCHEHEREZADE, QUEEN: "Arabian Nights." The Sultaness who tells the tales.
SCRUB: "The Beau's Stratagem," Farquhar. A facetious valet.
SEDLEY, AMELIA: "Vanity Fair," Thackeray. An amiable woman, but of no great decision.
SEDLEY, JOSEPH: "Vanity Fair," Thackeray. A fat, bashful East Indian.
SELIM: "Bride of Abydos," Byron. The hero.
SHAFTON, SIR PIERCIE: "The Monastery," Scott. A pedantic courtier.
SHANDY, TRISTRAM: "Tristram Shandy," Sterne. Hero of the story.
SHARP, REBECCA: "Vanity Fair," Thackeray. The designing heroine.
SHYLOCK: "Merchant of Venice," Shakespeare. A vindictive Jew.
SILVIA: "Two Gentlemen of Verona," Shakespeare. In love with Valentine.
SKIMPOLE, HAROLD: "Bleak House," Dickens. Always out of money.
SLIPSLOP, MRS.: "Joseph Andrews," Fielding. A waiting woman of doubtful character.
SLOP, DOCTOR: "Tristram Shandy," Sterne. An irascible physician.
SLY, CHRISTOPHER: "Taming of the Shrew," Shakespeare. A drunken tinker.
SLYME, CHEVY: "Martin Chuzzlewit," Dickens. A "gent short of funds."
SAMYKE: "Nicholas Nickleby," Dickens. An ill-used, poor, half-witted pupil of Squeers.
SNEERWELL, LADY: "School for Scandal," Sheridan. A gossip and back-biter.
SNODGRASS, AUGUSTUS: "Pickwick Papers," Dickens. A poetical character.
SNOW, LUCY: "Villette," Charlotte Bronte. The heroine.
SPARKLER, EDMOND: "Little Dorrit," Dickens. Man of fashion.
SQUEERS, WACKFORD: "Nicholas Nickleby," Dickens. The brutal master of Dotheboy's Hall.

SQUEERS, MASTER WACKFORD: "Nicholas Nickleby," Dickens. A spoiled child, the image of his father.
ST. LEON: "St. Leon," William Godwin. Hero of the tale, has the secret of perpetual youth and the transmutation of metals.
STEERFORTH, JAMES: "David Copperfield," Dickens. Talented and profligate.
STEGGS, MISS CAROLINA WILHELMINA AMELIA: "Vicar of Wakefield," Goldsmith. A pretender to gentility.
STIGGINS, ELDER: "Pickwick Papers," Dickens. Affects pineapple rum and Mrs. Weller.
STRAP, HUGH: "Roderick Random," Smollett. Roderick's follower.
SURFACE, SIR CHARLES AND JOSEPH: "School for Scandal," Sheridan. The first a good-natured rake, the second a hypocrite.
SWIVELLER, DICK: "Old Curiosity Shop," Dickens. A gay rattllepate and a good fellow.

TAMORA: "Titus Andronicus," Shakespeare. A Gothic Queen.
TAPLEY, MARK: "Martin Chuzzlewit," Dickens. Happiest when most miserable; jolly when he ought to cry.
TAPPERTIT, SIMON: "Barnaby Rudge," Dickens. A ferocious little apprentice.
TARTUFFE: "Tartuffe," Moliere. A hypocritical character.
TEAZLE, LADY: "School for Scandal," Sheridan. The heroine.
TEAZLE, SIR PETER: "School for Scandal," Sheridan. The old husband of Lady Teazle.
THERSITES: "Iliad," "Homer" and "Troilus and Cressida," Shakespeare. A foul-mouthed Greek.
THWACKUM: "Tom Jones," Fielding. A philosophical pedagogue.
TILLEMINA: "The Critic," Sheridan. A maiden very much crossed in love.
TIMON: "Timon of Athens," Shakespeare. A misanthrope, hero of the play.
TINTO, DICK: "Bride of Lammermoor," and "St. Roman's Well," Scott. An artist.
TITANIA: "Midsummer Night's Dream," Shakespeare. The queen of fairies.
TITMOUSE, TITTLEBAT: "Ten Thousand a Year," Dr. Warren. Astonished Parliament by an imitation of Chanticleer.
TITO: "Romola," George Eliot. The handsome, but weak, hero.
TODGERS, MRS.: "Martin Chuzzlewit," Dickens. The keeper of a commercial boardinghouse.
TOOTS: "Dombey and Son," Dickens. A simple, eccentric fellow.
TOPSEY: "Uncle Tom's Cabin," Mrs. Stowe. An ignorant young slave girl.
TOUCHSTONE: "As You Like It," Shakespeare. A clown.
TOUCHWOOD, PEREGRINE: "St. Roman's Well," Scott. An irascible East Indian.
TOX, MISS: "Dombey and Son," Dickens. A spinster, slightly curious.
TRADDLES, TOM: "David Copperfield," Dickens. A barrister and friend of Copperfield.
TRAPBOIS: "The Fortunes of Nigel," Scott. A usurer.
TRIM, CORPORAL: "Tristram Shandy," Sterne. The follower of Uncle Toby.
TRINCULO: "Tempest," Shakespeare. A jester.
TRIOL, MARQUIS: "The Pirate," Scott. A wealthy Zealander.
TROTWOOD, BETSY: "David Copperfield," Dickens. The kindest of women, but with an aversion to trespassing donkeys.
TRULLIBER, PARSON: "Joseph Andrews," Fielding. An ignorant clergyman.
TRUNNION, COMMODORE HAWSER: "Peregrine Pickle," Smollett. An odd nautical character.
TULKINGHORN, MR.: "Bleak House," Dickens. A wily solicitor.
TULLIVER, MAGGIE: "Mill on the Floss," George Eliot. The heroine.
TULLIVER, TOM: "Mill on the Floss," George Eliot. Her selfish, conceited brother.
TUPMAN, TRACY: "Pickwick Papers," Dickens. An obese admirer of lovely women.

TURVEYDROP: "Bleak House," Dickens. Dancing master and professor of deportment.

TUSHER, THOMAS: "Henry Esmond," Thackeray. A sycophantic clergyman.

TWEMLOW, MR.: "Our Mutual Friend," Dickens. A diner-out and friend of the Veneerings.

TWIST, OLIVER: "Oliver Twist," Dickens. Hero of the novel.

TWYSDEN, TALBOTT: "Philip," Thackeray. A public officer.

TYBALT: "Romeo and Juliet," Shakespeare. Nephew of Lady Capulet, slain by Romeo.

ULRICA: "Ivanhoe," Scott. An old witch.

UNA: "The Faery Queen," Spenser. The personification of Truth.

UNCAS: "The Last of the Mohicans," Cooper. A Mohican chief.

UNCLE TOBY: "Tristram Shandy," Sterne. A noble veteran, the real hero of the story.

UNCLE TOM: "Uncle Tom's Cabin," Stowe. A pious and unfortunate slave, the hero of the novel. This book added more converts to the abolition party than any other factor. It is the most remarkable and effective American work printed.

VARDEN, DOLLY: "Barnaby Rudge," Dickens. The heroine of the story.

VATHEK: "Vathek," Beckford. The hero of Beckford's remarkable novel.

VERNON, DI: "Rob Roy," Scott. The heroine of the novel.

VHOLES: "Bleak House," Dickens. A crafty lawyer.

VIOLA: "Twelfth Night," Shakespeare. A sweet little lady in love with Orsino.

VIRGILIA: "Coriolanus," Shakespeare. Wife of Coriolanus.

VIRGINIA: "Paul and Virginia," St. Pierre. Heroine of the novel.

VIVIAN: "Idyls of the King," Tennyson. The mistress of Merlin, the Enchanter.

WADMAN, WIDOW: "Tristram Shandy," Sterne. The lady who seeks to decoy Uncle Toby into matrimony.

WAMBA: "Ivanhoe," Scott. A clown.

WARDLE, MR.: "Pickwick Papers," Dickens. A jolly country gentleman, friend of Mr. Pickwick.

WEGG, SILAS: "Our Mutual Friend," Dickens. The villain of the novel.

WELLER, TONY AND SAMIVEL: "Pickwick Papers," Dickens. Father and son; the latter, Mr. Pickwick's serving man, is undoubtedly the most original and most humorous creation of Dickens' exuberant fancy.

WERTHER: "Sorrows of Werther," Goethe. Hero of the tale.

WESTERN, SQUIRE AND SOPHIA: "Tom Jones," Fielding. Father and daughter, the latter the heroine of the novel.

WHISKERANDOS, DON FEROLO: "The Critic," Sheridan. The lover of Tilburina.

WICKFIELD, AGNES: "David Copperfield," Dickens. Heroine of the novel.

WILD, JONATHAN: "Jonathan Wild," Fielding. A famous highwayman, and afterwards a noted thieftaker of London.

WILDAIR, SIR HARRY: "The Constant Couple" and "Sir Harry Wildair," Farquhar. The hero of both plays.

WILFER, BELLA, LAVINIA, REGINALD AND MRS.: "Our Mutual Friend," Dickens. One of the most entertaining family groups in English fiction. The first is the charming heroine of the novel. Lavinia is her abominable sister; Reginald, her angelic papa; while the somber background is made by the gloomy mamma, whose other name in the family is The Tragic Muse.

WILFRID: "Rokeby," Scott. Hero of the poem.

WILLIAMS, CALEB: "Caleb Williams," Godwin. The hero of a very remarkable novel.

WIMBLE, WILL: "Spectator," Addison. Pseudonym for Thomas Morecraft.

WINKLE, RIP VAN: "Sketch Book," Irving. The immortal sleeper of the Catskills.

WISHFORT, LADY: "The Way of the World," Congreve. Heroine of the play.
WORLDLY WISEMAN, MR.: "Pilgrim's Progress," Bunyan. One of Christian's difficulties.
WRAY, ENOCH: "The Village," Crabbe. A noble old man.
WREN, JENNY: "Our Mutual Friend," Dickens. The dolls' dressmaker.
WRONGHEAD, SIR FRANCIS: "The Provoked Husband," Vanburgh. Hero of the play.

YORICK: "Tristram Shandy," Sterne. A jester descended from the Yorick whose history is told by Hamlet.
YSEULT: "Tristram and Yseult," Matthew Arnold. A Cornish heroine of the olden time.

ZADOC: "Absolom and Achitophel," Dryden. Pseudonym for Sancroft.
ZANONI: "Zanoni," Bulwer. The mystical hero of the novel.
ZELUCO: "Zeluco," Dr. J. Moore. The prodigal hero of the novel.
ZOBEIDE: "Arabian Nights." The wife of the great Haroun al Raschid.
ZODIG: "Zodig," Voltaire. The Babylonian hero of the novel.
ZOPHIEL: "Paradise Lost," Milton. A swiftwinged cherub.
ZULEIKA: "The Bride of Abydos," Byron. Heroine of the poem.

———————